FEMINISM
AND
ANCIENT PHILOSOPHY

FEMINISM

AND

ANCIENT PHILOSOPHY

Edited by Julie K. Ward

ROUTLEDGE • NEW YORK AND LONDON

Published in 1996 by

Routledge
29 West 35th Street
New York, New York 10001

Published in Great Britain by

Routledge
11 New Fetter Lane
London EC4P 4EE

Library of Congress Cataloging-in-Publication Data

Feminism and ancient philosophy / edited by Julie K. Ward.
    p.   cm.
Includes bibliographical references and indexes.

ISBN 0-415-91601-1 (cl) — ISBN 0-415-91602-X (pbk)
1. Feminist theory. 2. Philosophy, Ancient.
   I. Ward, Julie K.,
HQ1190.F4187 1996
305.42'01—dc20
                                    95-51647
                                       CIP

To the memory of my friend and brother,
Christopher Grove Ward.

CONTENTS

ACKNOWLEDGMENTS

I would like to thank the following people for their inspiration and practical sense in the production of this volume: Peg Simons and Julien Murphy for their wise advice; Carmela Epright for her unwavering support; Colin Anderson for his knowledgeable help and computer skills; departmental colleagues like J. D. Trout, Paul Moser, Mark Waymack, Arnie VanderNat, Femi Taiwo, and David Yandell, who, in one way or another, offered assistance or preserved my sense of humor; Ezio Vailati for his level-headed understanding; and finally, friends like Eve Browning Cole, Lisa De George, Marcie Moore, and Rita Manning for their generosity and affection.

I also wish to thank the relevant authors, editors, and publishers for permission to reprint the following papers: "Plato's *Republic* and Feminism," by Julia Annas, which appeared in *Philosophy* 51 (1976): 307–21, published by Cambridge University Press; "The Metaphysical Science of Aristotle's *Generation of Animals* and its Feminist Critics," by Daryl Tress, which appeared in *The Review of Metaphysics* 46 (1992): 307–41, published by The Catholic University of America; "Feminism and Aristotle's Rational Ideal," by Marcia Homiak, which appeared in *A Mind of One's Own*, edited by Louise Antony and Charlotte Witt, (1993) 1–17, published by Westview Press; "Aristotelian Visions of Moral Character in Virginia Woolf's *Mrs. Dalloway*" by Patricia Curd, which appeared in *English Language Notes* (forthcoming), published by The University of Colorado; "Therapeutic Arguments and the Structure of Desire," by Martha Nussbaum, which appeared in *Differences* 2,1 (1989): 46–66, published by the Pembroke Center for Teaching and Research on Women, Brown University.

ABBREVIATIONS

Plato

Ap.	*Apology*
Chrm.	*Charmides*
Crat.	*Cratylus*
Cri.	*Crito*
Epist.	*Epistles*
Euthyd.	*Euthydemus*
Euphr.	*Euthyphro*
Gorg.	*Gorgias*
Menex.	*Menexenus*
Phaed.	*Phaedo*
Phdr.	*Phaedrus*
Phil.	*Philebus*
Pol.	*Politicus*
Parm.	*Parmenides*
Prot.	*Protagoras*
Rep.	*Republic*
Symp.	*Symposium*
Thaet.	*Theaetetus*
Tim.	*Timaeus*

Aristotle

Abbreviation	Latin Title	English Title
Cat.	*Categoriae*	*Categories*
De Int.	*De Interpretatione*	*On Interpretation*
An. Pr.	*Analytica Priora*	*Prior Analytics*
An. Post.	*Analytica Posteriora*	*Posterior Analytics*
Top.	*Topica*	*Topics*
Soph. El.	*Sophistici Elenchi*	*Sophistical Refutations*
Phys.	*Physica*	*Physics*
GC	*De Generatione et Corruptione*	*On Generation and Corruption*
DA	*De Anima*	*On the Soul*
PA	*De Partibus Animalium*	*Parts of Animals*
MA	*De Motu Animalium*	*Movement of Animals*
GA	*De Generatione Animalium*	*Generation of Animals*
Meta.	*Metaphysica*	*Metaphysics*
EN	*Ethica Nicomachea*	*Nicomachean Ethics*
EE	*Ethica Eudemia*	*Eudemian Ethics*
Pol.	*Politica*	*Politics*
Rhet.	*Rhetorica*	*Rhetoric*
Poet.	*Poetica*	*Poetics*

Hellenistic Texts

DL	Diogenes Laertius, *Lives of the Philosophers*
SVF	*Stoicorum Veterum Fragmenta*

Transliterations of the Greek letter *upsilon* in this volume use either the English letter "u" or "y," according to the choice of the author. Both are standard usages.

plete in scope, as various schools in these periods are not considered (including the Sophists, Cyrenaics, Cynics, and Skeptics), it offers a representative selection of work on or relating to the major thinkers or schools of ancient philosophy: Socrates, Plato, Aristotle, Stoics, and Epicureans. Spanning such a long period of ancient philosophy, the papers reflect a variety of subjects from the Stoic conception of women's nature to Aristotle's theory of reproduction to an analysis of Plato's use of narrative. While the collection is not marked by a single issue or approach, certain themes surface repeatedly among these papers such as the nature and capacities of women, the shape of moral thinking, and the role of the emotions, to name a few. Consequently, I have chosen to group the essays together on the basis of certain focal topics, rather than to separate them by school or by chronological period. The topics of the various subject areas are: women's nature and capabilities; the relation between reason and emotion in the good human life; special applications of Aristotle's moral theory; and the affiliation between *logos,* or philosophical language, and desire.

II. DESCRIPTION OF THE PAPERS

The collection opens with a group of essays on women's nature: do (free) women have the same nature as (free) men, and if they do, how can this be reconciled with their conventionally subordinate position? On this topic, we find Julia Annas and Susan Levin writing to rather different conclusions in their papers considering Plato's views of women's nature. Julia Annas, in an early essay on the topic, argues that the limited scope of Plato's proposal in *Republic* V that women, suitably educated, should rule the city along with men demonstrates that he should not be considered an early feminist. For Annas, contemporary feminism (in part, anyway) is concerned with producing equality of opportunity, suffrage, and the emancipation of women from the restrictions of domestic labor. Yet she finds that Plato's proposal ignores all of these goals: it is confined to a select fraction of women, and it does not attempt to provide goods or equality for women as such. Although Plato does not hold that women as women are naturally inferior in capacities to men and in this respect appears to agree with the view of contemporary feminism, in fact, Annas thinks the similarity is rather deceptive. For Plato's underlying interest in proposing that (some) women should rule is purely Utilitarian: women should be trained and be able to rule the city so as to free up an intellectual resource heretofore unavailable.[8] Furthermore, the actual argument in *Republic* V showing that women are by nature capable of performing any task which men perform related to ruling the city is marred by a final caveat that men will execute these tasks better than women. Since the proposals for women's ruling are contingent upon producing the greatest concord within the state and not upon a concern for women's status as such, Annas concludes that the argument of the *Republic* cannot be considered a precursor of contemporary arguments for women's emancipation, nor Plato a proto-feminist.

Susan Levin's paper comes to a rather different conclusion. By focusing on the distinction between the terms for "women" and "feminine" as opposed to "nature" and "being by nature," she argues that Plato differentiates between women's conventional and ideal capabilities. This fact explains what has troubled many interpreters of Plato, namely, that while he proposes women as philosopher-rulers in *Republic* V, elsewhere—*Republic* VIII and IX, for example—he makes various derogatory remarks about women and feminine behavior. Levin argues that if we are to understand Plato correctly in *Republic* V, we must read him as arguing about women's nature within the conditions given by the education and socialization of the ideal city, not outside of it. Thus, the negative comments about women in *Republic* VIII and IX do not contradict his proposals in V since they concern women living under non-ideal conditions. In consideration of Plato's other critical remarks about women, Levin canvasses texts outside the *Republic,* as well, and finds no contravening passage concerning the inferiority of women's nature as such, only references to what women are "accustomed" to say or to do given conventional training. Platonic dualism plays a pivotal, though implicit, role in the proposal for women rulers in *Republic* V. For since the soul and its capacities are not physically determined, the sex of the body is not determinative of the embodied soul's powers. Thus, possessing a certain set of physical or physiological properties implies nothing about the set of psychological or mental properties one possesses. This shows that dualism itself, even substantial, cannot be counted as theoretically opposed to feminism, as some critics have maintained.[9]

Plato's proposal concerning "having women in common" from *Republic* V[10] appears to be echoed in Stoic recommendations by Zeno, the founder of Stoicism (334–262 B.C.E.), and Chrysippus (c. 280–c. 206 B.C.E.), one of its foremost thinkers. Yet whether or not this implied that the Stoics held that (free) women were equal to (free) men in moral and intellectual status remains difficult to ascertain given other evidence concerning the Stoic view regarding what is permissible, as Elizabeth Asmis points out in her paper. For both Zeno and Chrysippus maintained that nothing prohibits acts that are conventionally forbidden such as incest, pederasty, and cannibalism. In this light, the Stoic recommendation for having women in common might appear to be nothing more than a claim about their interchangeability as sexual partners. Yet Asmis argues that in fact the Stoic proposals do amount to more than mere ridicule of sexual conventions, as was characteristic of the Cynics. Including in her discussion a series of overlooked texts by Antipater, Musonius, and Hierocles, as well as the more familiar ones by Chrysippus and Cicero, Asmis explains that the proposal about women must be seen in its connection with the Stoic account of the genesis of the larger human society. According to various Stoics, human society begins with the couple, followed by the family, and then the household, which is described as the "seed" of the state. The state is, in turn, superseded by the association of all humanity: this is the universal city termed *cosmopolis* in some sources. Located at the periphery of the widest circle of association, the universal city, one source, Cicero, places a select community of good men (*boni viri*) who are alike in being morally excellent. While the explicit reference to "men" in Cicero's account makes it clear that women are excluded from this final association of the wise, Hierocles, Musonius, and Antipater find it otherwise. Musonius argues that women possess the same virtue as men, while Antipater and Hierocles appear to hold that women are equal partners to men in the household and that one aim of marriage is a harmony of minds. Yet the inclusion of women in the final association of the wise at first appears problematical since the Stoics appear to agree that free women, although part of the city, are not citizens; thus, their role in the *cosmopolis* appears nonexistent, or at best, incidental. But Asmis argues that since the early Greek Stoics define the true city, that of the wise, as consisting of "human beings" (*anthropos*, plural), they do not restrict it to men and so do not deny that women can be as virtuous as men. Finally, Zeno's claim initially cited concerning men "having women in common" is not to be interpreted as demeaning women. While sexual permissiveness is compatible with wisdom, the community of the wise includes women as partners in actual virtue (Asmis, 89). Consequently, we are to see that the place of women in the community of the wise is chiefly ethical, not sexual.

In contrast to the Platonic and Stoic proposals concerning the possibility for some women to attain the same degree of virtue and wisdom as that of men, Aristotle is distinguished by his claims in the *Politics* that (free) women and men do not share the same kind of virtue or excellence (1260a2–24), that the male is more of a leader than the female (1259b1–2), and that the deliberative faculty in (free) women is present but "without authority" (*akyron*, 1260a12–13). However, whether these claims about women's inferior moral and intellectual capacities can be traced to a foundation in his biological theories remains controversial. While various feminists have argued that Aristotle's biological and social views about women constitute a single piece of cloth, the two scholars included here disagree but come to rather different conclusions about the significance of Aristotle's theory of reproduction in *Generation of Animals*. Daryl Tress argues that feminist critics of Aristotle's theory of reproduction have erred in their estimation of the theory on two counts. First, most contemporary critics of his theory begin with materialist assumptions, having no use for the teleological kinds of explanation that Aristotle employs in his theory of generation. Thus, the modern scientific account of reproduction ignores much of the metaphysical side of the account that Aristotle provides and in so doing, distorts his theory. Second, she maintains that an examination of the actual theory of generation in *GA* Bks. I–II indicates that the female plays a crucial role in the generation of offspring. For the female contributes something analogous to the male's semen in generation, namely, menstrual blood. While it must be admitted that the contributions are not equal in kind since menstrual blood contributes only the material cause in constrast to semen which provides formal, moving, and final causes in generation, Tress emphasizes that the activity of generation is the actualization of two potentialities (Tress, 46). Furthermore, by comparing Aristotle's theory to that of "preformism" current in his time, Tress notes that his account actually elevates the role of the female in the process of reproduction.

In contrast, Kathleen Cook argues that the role of the female in supplying the material cause in reproduction cannot save it from being unequal to the role of the male in supplying the three other causes (the moving, formal, and final causes). One problem, as she sees it, concerns the alleged inconsistency between the account of reproduction in *GA* Bks. I–II and that of inheritance in Bk. IV. The inconsistency arises from those who hold to an "essentialist" notion of Aristotelian form, according to which the form captures all and only the essential features of the human, is common to all members of the same species, and is supplied by the male parent. Other scholars have argued for a distinct view of form so as to preserve the consistency between the two accounts in *GA*. According to this second view, form includes characteristics below the species level and so covers attributes belonging to the individual features as well as those belonging to the species. Professor Cook, however, argues that the charge of inconsistency is misplaced: the account of inheritance in *GA* IV. 3 does not warrant the conclusion that the female contributes form to the child simply because the child exhibits characteristics of the mother. Rather, Cook holds, if certain maternal characteristics manifest themselves in the offspring, it is because they are present in the *kuema* (the embryonic union of *katamenia* and semen) by virtue of what is, essentially, a deficiency or lack in the female material contribution. So, while there is no inconsistency in Cook's view between the accounts of reproduction and inheritance, it follows that the female contribution in generation cannot be equal to that of the male, a conclusion driven at least partly by sexist assumptions. However, Cook rejects the idea that such assumptions overdetermine Aristotle's theory, and in this sense, it remains intact.

In the second group of papers, the authors are generally concerned with explaining the relation of reason to the emotions as it relates to Aristotle's notion of the flourishing human life. In "Feminism and Aristotle's Rational Ideal," Marcia Homiak examines the ideal for living that Aristotle proposes in his ethics: the best human life is one consisting of rational activity. Professor Homiak argues that, instead of being oppressive, the Aristotelian ideal holds emancipatory potential for women. Part of her argument here depends upon the potential dangers that ideals of altruism and compassion, such as are mentioned in the work of Gilligan, Noddings, Ruddick, and others, can pose to women in their socially and economically subordinated positions. In contrast to norms for women that focus on their emotionality, sympathy, and altruism, Homiak suggests that women need to consider a moral ideal that attempts to balance the emotions with reason. For without a component of rational deliberation about the good, lives conducted according to altruistic standards can become destructive and unhealthy given women's general secondary status in relation to men.

That Aristotle's ideal should be applicable to women is surprising given that his city, or *polis*, depends upon a hierarchical organization of human beings according to what Homiak calls "psychological freedom." This kind of freedom consists in the degree to which people can make reasoned choices about their lives. A common classical Athenian opinion, and one that Aristotle shares, is that non-citizens, like slaves, manual laborers, and free women, do not possess an ability to deliberate well about the good.[11] Consequently, these groups, according to Aristotle, require that another group with full deliberative capacity have authority over them. Now, since this description of the social and political structure is undemocratic, we need to ask in what respect an ideal emerging from this perspective can hold promise for women.

Homiak answers that although Aristotle's notion of the good society places free citizen men at its top and identifies the best human life as following activities associated with men, it is, nevertheless, not "masculinist" in the sense in which feminists such as Lloyd (1984) have defined the term. For Aristotle's ideal of the good life does not ignore the role of the emotions in a well-lived life, nor does it lack a conception of the place of personal relationships in the moral sphere. On the contrary, his rational ideal preserves a close relationship between reason and the emotions such that the virtues of character depend equally upon feelings as upon calculation. Since an analysis of Aristotle's rational ideal shows reason to be both guided and limited by emotion and feelings, it cannot be reduced to some form of impartialism. Furthermore, since it is bound up with character states such as justice, courage, and friendship that require a social community for their exercise, this ideal supports personal relationships and concern for others.[12] Thus, Aristotle's ideal of the human good supports a notion of intellectual and emotional competence and independence that Homiak thinks necessary for women in a contemporary society in which they live and work in economic and emotional subordination to men.

Deborah Achtenberg's paper, "Aristotelian Resources for Feminist Thinking," takes up the theme developed by Homiak concerning the relation of reason and the emotions in the well-lived life and extends it in various directions. Achtenberg situates her analysis by reference to several contemporary thinkers on psychology and moral development, including Kohlberg and Gilligan, Noddings, Silverstein, and Chodorow. The separation between an ethics of principle and of care that has emerged in recent moral and psychological discussions, however, preserves a distinction between reason and emotion that she finds inadequate to the demands of psychology and the moral life. Achtenberg argues that rather than following either the ethics of care or principle, feminists should consider a neo-Aristotelian conception of ethics in which emotions function along with reason in the activity of human virtues. Furthermore, she argues that since for Aristotle the emotions themselves are forms of perception, they, too, require cognition—the cognition of value—which is presented to us through particulars.

To explain the way in which Aristotle's position concerns itself with the emotions as well as with the weight of moral particulars, Achtenberg discusses the role of perception of value as it relates to Aristotle's theory of the moral virtues, or excellences. For Aristotle, moral virtues consist in part upon emotions—which depend upon feelings of pleasure or pain—and in part upon reason, but require being in a state of activity for their fulfillment. And that which makes possible their fulfillment, in part, is a moral situation and more importantly, a perception of what is good, or morally required, at that very time by the moral subject. Since "good" for Aristotle is an analogical equivocal,[13] it is not something that can be specified fully in abstraction from a moral context, but only grasped in the context itself by a type of perception, according to Achtenberg. A full understanding of Aristotle's moral theory, one taking account of the various elements mentioned, finds that it accomplishes two goals central to feminist theorizing: first, a unified conception of moral intelligence that ignores neither the emotions nor moral particulars, and second, a view of human beings whose individual nature is such as to flourish only in the society of flourishing others. According to Achtenberg, part of our adequacy as moral persons depends upon the capacity to recognize the good, that is, to provide what is needed for myself and others to grow.

The third section presents two papers dealing with special cases of Aristotle's moral theory: his account of moral character, and that of *philia*, or friendship. In the first paper, Patricia Curd begins with Virginia Woolf's claim that fiction is about character, and by connecting this concern with Aristotle's analysis of character in the *Ethics*, shows that an Aristotelian framework of moral character illuminates the reading of Woolf's novel, *Mrs. Dalloway*. Virginia Woolf's connection to Aristotle is not superficial, as Woolf herself studied and greatly admired Aristotle's *Poetics* and most probably was familiar with his ethical views as well. What we find in the characters of Woolf's *Mrs. Dalloway* is a constant concern with the importance of moral discernment, the place of emotion in the moral life, and a proper estimation of ends in life. Professor Curd argues that the picture that Woolf's fiction provides concerning moral virtue and character, although not presented systematically, can be compared to the theoretical discussion Aristotle furnishes us in *Nicomachean Ethics*. There Aristotle focuses on the roles that practical reason, moral intuition, and the emotions play in his notion of the morally excellent life. As Curd points out, these components must be properly combined so as to produce the person of moral character, the one who is best able to judge character in others. Woolf's Mrs. Dalloway is herself such a person, according to Curd, or is, at least, in the process of becoming one. For Mrs. Dalloway has achieved a balance between her reason and her passions and made actions and emotions "a true part of herself" (Curd, 151). Furthermore, it is through Mrs. Dalloway's eyes that we as readers perceive and understand the others around her; in this respect, also, we find Mrs. Dalloway to be Aristotle's person of excellent moral character.

In the second paper in this section, I consider whether and to what extent a feminist theory of friendship, that is, a friendship between women whose aim is the good of women, can profit from a reevaluation of Aristotle's theory of *philia*. In spite of the fact that elsewhere Aristotle holds women to have differing moral virtues from men and to be less able to deliberate than men, in his *Ethics* he claims that women are able to have friendships of character, or "virtue friendships," as they are usually termed. Thus, although his focus centers on friendships between men, I argue that the theory allows that women are capable of mutual ties of affection that aim at promoting morally excellent lives. This conclusion is reached by considering various components of his theory of friendship in *Nicomachean* and *Eudemian Ethics*, including *eunoia*, or mutual well-wishing, *philêsis,* loving affection, and *prohairesis*, or choice. Further, Aristotle's general notion of friendship as a *hexis*, a state of character that implies a balance between practical reason and emotion and aims at good activity, should be reconsidered for application to a feminist ideal of friendship.

In the final section of the collection, two papers consider the relation between language and desire from different perspectives. In the first, Anne-Marie Bowery focuses her exposition on Diotima's narrative speech in Plato's *Symposium*, arguing that an analysis of the narrative structure of the speech reveals several characteristics of Diotima's way of philosophizing that distinguishes it from Socrates' own. The essay centers on three related issues arising from the narrative analysis. First, Diotima's narrative style is more aptly suited to foster the philosophical education of her audience (namely, Socrates) than is Socrates' own narrative style. Second, the feature of self-inclusion in Socrates' narrative style distinguishes it from that of Diotima: in referring to himself in his narratives, Socrates demonstrates that his philosophy aims at self-knowledge. Finally, Plato employs narrative differently than does Socrates, in that Plato does not tell narratives about himself but remains the absent narrator of the dialogues. After consideration of these points, Bowery comes to the surprising conclusion that Plato's use of narrative closely mirrors that of Diotima, rather than that of Socrates. The implications of Diotima's mode of narrative for contemporary feminism, particularly French feminism, are twofold. First, it serves to combat the criticisms voiced by some feminists that Continental philosophy, even French feminism, while promising to break with the "patriarchal hegemony" of traditional Western philosophy (Bowery, 175), actually continues it. For Bowery argues that in the *Symposium* Plato gives us an account of truth "tethered to the female" (Bowery, 182–3), in the sense that Diotima's narrative style is shown to be more adequate than Socrates.' Second, the participatory aspect of Diotima's narrative, distinct from Socrates' narratives, allows her to foster philosophical exchange through interaction with her audience, an achievement that recalls the contemporary feminist conception of truth as created through mutual agreement and interaction.[14]

In the final paper, Martha Nussbaum opens with a passage from Epicurus in which "women" and "boys" are listed in parallel fashion with "drinking bouts," "fish," and other "luxuries" of the table as things that do not conduce to the truly pleasant life. Standard translations of this passage, she notes, do not preserve the actual things named but substitute the words "sexual love" for the terms mentioned, "women" and "boys." The implications of this substitution are deeply suggestive showing that our conceptions of desire are not ahistorical and descriptive, but normative and historically determined. Whereas heterosexuality clothes the contemporary notion of what desire is and what its objects are, it obviously did not determine the ancient conception. Furthermore, as the passage makes clear, the problem of sexual desire is subsumed under that of self-control, which Professor Nussbaum finds generally characteristic of the language of desire in the ancient world. But Nussbaum's larger thesis is that much of the ancient philosophical discussion about desire presupposes that emotion and desire are largely formed by socially instilled beliefs which themselves can be changed. Consequently, the purpose of much of the ancient discourse, especially in the Hellenistic period, was to persuade the reader or listener of wrongfulness of beliefs supporting certain desires. The process by which these fundamental beliefs come to be changed—through philosophical analysis and argumentation—is regarded by Hellenistic schools, like the Epicureans, as a kind of "therapy" considered to constitute an entire mode of living. Nor is this discussion of purely historical interest, for first, Nussbaum proposes the ancient notion of therapy as a model for change for the individual in contemporary society, arguing that the ancient debate about emotion and desire strikes a balance between the contributions of personal history and social learning. Second, she suggests that the ancient debate illuminates the extent to which desire and emotion, although socially constructed and culturally bound, are to a great extent culturally and historically overlapping experiences.

The present collection does not and—given its limits of space—could not furnish a comprehensive account of the nexus of ancient philosophy and feminist theory. Its more modest aim is to provide the reader with an illustrative survey of some of the recent work in these areas.

PART I

WOMEN'S NATURE
AND CAPABILITIES

PLATO'S *REPUBLIC* AND FEMINISM

Julia Annas

Not many philosophers have dealt seriously with the problems of women's rights and status, and those that have, have unfortunately often been on the wrong side.[1] In fact Plato and Mill are the only great philosophers who can plausibly be called feminists. But there has been surprisingly little serious effort made to analyze their arguments, perhaps because it has seemed like going over ground already won.

This paper is concerned only with Plato. I shall maintain what may surprise some: It is quite wrong to think of Plato as "the first feminist."[2] His arguments are unacceptable to a feminist, and the proposals made in *Republic* V are irrelevant to the contemporary debate.

The idea that Plato is a forerunner of Women's Liberation has gained support from the fact that in *Republic* V Plato proposes not only that women should share men's tasks but also that the nuclear family should be abolished.[3] This idea is put forward by some radical feminists today as an essential part of any program for the liberation of women. But I shall argue that Plato's grounds for the proposal are so different from the modern ones that he is in no sense a forerunner of them. Furthermore, where they differ, empirical evidence suggests that it is Plato who is wrong.

Plato's proposals about women[4] come at the beginning of Book V, where Socrates is represented as having to surmount three waves of opposition. The first wave concerns the admission of women as Guardians; the second concerns the communal life of the Guardians; the third concerns the practicability of the ideal state, and this leads into the discussion which occupies the rest of Books V–VII. The figure of separate "waves" is constantly brought before us; for Plato the capacity of women to be Guardians is a separate question from the replacement of nuclear family life.[5]

Plato begins his treatment of the first problem (*Rep.* 451) by extending the metaphor he has used already. Female watchdogs do just what the male ones do, except that they are weaker, and their lives are interrupted by giving birth. By analogy, the same is true of women; though they are weaker than men and their lives are interrupted by childbirth, they are otherwise the same, and so should be given the same upbringing and tasks as men, however distasteful the sight of ugly old women exercising in the gymnasium may be.

Now this is only metaphor—and in fact it does not pretend to be serious argument. Plato wants to give us a picture first, perhaps so that we have a vivid idea of what the arguments are about before they are presented, perhaps also so that he can meet and deflect mere ridicule right at the start, before the serious discussion. Still, the initial metaphor is important, for it continues to influence Plato in the actual argument.

Plato now *(Rep.* 453b–c) puts forward what he regards as a serious objection to the idea of women being Guardians. The opponent is made to say that it contradicts the principle on which the ideal state is constructed— namely, that each person is to do his own work, according to his nature *(Rep.* 453b5). As women differ greatly in nature from men, they should surely have different functions in the city *(Rep.* 453b10–11).

Plato dismisses this objection as merely captious. Of course it is true that different natures should do different things, but it does not follow that men and women should do different things unless it can be shown that they have natures that are different in the important respect of affecting their capacity for the same pursuit. Otherwise it would be like letting bald men, but not hairy men, be cobblers. Plato now claims that men and women differ only in their sexual roles: men impregnate, women give birth *(Rep.* 454d–e). The objector fails to show that there is any capacity that is peculiar to women, and Plato claims to show that there are no civic pursuits which belong to a woman as such or to a man as such (this is the part of the argument we shall come back to). Since there are no specific male or female competencies, men and women should follow the same pursuits, and women who have natures suitable to be Guardians should therefore be appropriately trained.

This is how Plato deals with the first "wave." There are three important points to be made about his argument.

1. Firstly, there is something very odd about the actual course of the argument from 455a–d. Plato has established the undeniable point that while women are different from men in some ways and similar in others, discussion at that level is sterile; the interesting question is whether the undisputed differences matter when we decide whether women should be able to hold certain jobs. This is the crucial point not only for Plato but for any sensible discussion of the topic. But Plato's argument is seriously incomplete.

At 455a9–b2 he poses the question, "Are there any occupations which contribute towards the running of the state which only a woman can do?"

Very swiftly he claims to show that there are none. Men are better equipped both mentally and physically (455b4–c6). So in every pursuit men can do better than women, though it is not true that all men do better than all women (455d3–5). Women, he says, are ridiculed when men do such traditional feminine tasks as cooking and weaving better than they do; still, it follows from what has been said that if men bothered to turn their attention to these tasks they would do them better. "The one sex is, so to speak, far and away beaten in every field by the other" (455d2–3).

Now it is hardly a feminist argument to claim that women do not have a special sphere because men can outdo them at absolutely everything. What is more important in the present context, however, is that Plato sums up his argument at 455d6–e1 by saying that there is no civic pursuit which belongs to a woman as such or to a man as such. But while he has argued that there are no pursuits appropriate for a woman as such, because men could do them all better, where is the argument that there are no specifically male competencies? There is not a trace of any such argument in the text, nor of any materials which could be used for one.

This is a serious gap, both because it is the point that the objector, if he were not being shepherded by Socrates (cf. 455a5–b2), would in fact press and because what Plato says about male and female capacities actually provides material for such an objector.

Anyone acquainted with the modern literature will realize at once that someone objecting to the idea that men and women should share all roles is not very worried about whether there are some jobs that only women are suited for. The reason for this is obvious enough: jobs that women usually do are badly paid or unpaid and lack status, and men are generally not interested in doing them. What really interests the objector is the claim that there are some occupations in society which only men are suited for: being doctors, lawyers, judges, taking part in politics by voting or holding office, owning and managing property. In the Athens of Plato's day women were not allowed to do any of these things, and the average Athenian would no doubt have simply assumed that they could not do them (as we can see from Aristophanes' *Ecclesiazusae*). Any feminist must take this objection seriously and meet it, simply because it has been historically the main objection to attempts by women to enter hitherto male professions or obtain hitherto male rights like the vote.[6] Yet Plato not only does nothing to meet this overwhelmingly obvious objection, he even provides materials for the objector. At 455b4–c6 he distinguishes three ways in which a gifted nature differs from an ungifted one. The gifted learn quickly, the ungifted only with difficulty. The gifted do not have to be taught very long before they can go on to make discoveries of their own; the ungifted need long instruction and are hard put to it to retain what they have learn. The gifted can put their thoughts into action; the ungifted are clumsy. Plato then asks rhetorically, "Do you know of any human pursuit in which men do not greatly excel women in all these qualities?" Clearly the answer is "No." But if men always excel women in these very important respects, the objector has all he wants: surely there are some pursuits (e.g., generalship) where these qualities are needed in a high degree and which it is therefore not reasonable to open to women. It is no good saying, as Plato at once does, that, "many women are better than many men at many things" (455d3–4). The objector does not need to claim that all men are always better than all women in a specific respect. If only men excel in a quality, then if efficiency is our aim[7] surely that makes it reasonable to regard a pursuit that requires a high degree of that quality as suited specially to men. The fact that women will not invariably come out on bottom is neither here nor there. In Plato's fiercely specialized state, the aim will be the maximum number of alpha performances.

This is an important argument. Scientific research into sex differences is an area of great controversy precisely because its results do have important social consequences; if men and women did have different types of intelligence, for example, then different types of education would surely be appropriate. But why does Plato not even notice the gap in his argument or the ammunition he is handing to the opposition? Of course he does not want to make the opponent's case seem strong. But it is possible that he genuinely does not see the disastrous relevance of his claims about men's superior intellectual gifts to his point about distinct fields of activity. He may be doing here what Aristotle often criticizes him for—taking metaphor for argument.

The metaphor of male and female watchdogs with which the subject was introduced would naturally lead Plato to think predominantly of human tasks which are analogous. And this is what we find. At 455e1, after the argument just discussed, he mentions that women are weaker than men at all pursuits. This suits his use of the analogy with the dogs, for there the difference in strength between male and female was not succinct reason to give them different tasks. And in the whole discussion that follows he simply shelves the question of intellectual differences between men and women. He never seriously discusses activities where these differences would matter and which are nevertheless to be open to women in the ideal state. There is only one reference to women officials (460b9–10) and even then they have a traditionally "feminine" role (inspecting newborn children). There is possibly a reference to women doctors at 454d1–3 (but the text is very uncertain), and some women are said to be capable of being doctors at 455e6–7. Against these two (or possibly three) meager and off-hand references to women doing jobs requiring some intellectual capacity, there are at least nine references[8] to women fighting, serving in the army, and doing gymnastics. On this topic Plato's discussion is full and emphatic. He is taking seriously the idea that the life of the human female is like that of any other female animal, with reproduction making only short breaks in physical activity otherwise like the male's. No doubt this is because he is mainly interested in the eugenic possibilities for his "herd."[9] The picture of the female watchdog diverts him from the problems he faces given his beliefs about female intellectual capacities.

So Plato's argument here is not one which a feminist would find useful or even acceptable. In any case, it has a serious gap, and it is not clear that Plato could repair it except by abandoning his beliefs about the intellectual inferiority of women.[10]

2. Secondly, the argument is not based on, and makes no reference to, women's desires or needs. Nothing at all is said about whether women's present roles frustrate them or whether they will lead more satisfying lives as Guardians than as house-bound drudges.

This is rather striking, since women in fourth-century Athens led lives that compare rather closely to the lives of women in present-day Saudi Arabia. The place of women in Athenian life is summed up forcibly in the notorious statement, "We have courtesans for our pleasure, concubines for the requirements of the body, and wives to bear us lawful children and look after the home faithfully" (Pseudo-Demosthenes, *Against Neaera*, 122). The contrast between this and the life of the Guardians is so striking that one would have thought some comparison inevitable. Yet Plato shows no inter-est in this side of the picture. Later on in Book V (465b12–c7) he talks about the liberating effect of communal life in freeing people from the struggle to make ends meet and the need to hand one's money over to women and slaves to take care of it. Here the woman's position in the household is pre-sented as something that the *man* is to be liberated from. There is nothing about the effect on *her* of communal living.

Of course Plato is not bound to be interested in the psychology of women, but his complete lack of interest underlines the fact that his argu-ment does not recommend changing the present state of affairs on the ground that women suffer from being denied opportunities that are open to men.

His argument has quite different grounds, in fact. The state benefits from having the best possible citizens, and if half the citizens sit at home doing trivial jobs then usable talent is being wasted. Here Mrs. Huby gets the point exactly right: "There was nothing worth while for a woman to do at home; she should therefore share in man's work outside the home" (Huby, 1972, 23). Plato's sole ground for his proposals is their usefulness to the state; the point is repeated several times.[11]

Of course there is nothing non-feminist about this argument.[12] But Plato's argument gains rather different significance from the fact that this is his *only* ground. His argument is authoritarian in spirit rather than liberal; if a woman did not want to be a Guardian, Plato would surely be committed to compelling her to serve the state. Though this question never arises in the *Republic,* at *Laws* 780a–c the Athenian says openly that women are to be compelled to attend the communal meals (all that is left of the communal life of the *Republic*), because most women will be shy and used to seclusion and so will not want to take part. This is rather far from modern liberal arguments that women should have equal opportunities with men because otherwise they lead stunted and unhappy lives and lack the means for self-development.

This point may have been missed because at 456c1–2 Plato says that the present set-up of society is "contrary to nature" (*para phusin*). We are not, however, entitled to claim that for Plato confinement to the home thwarts the nature of women. What is "contrary to nature" surely has to be understood as the opposite of what has just been said to be "according to nature" (*kata phusin,* 456c1), and this is the principle that similar natures should follow similar pursuits. The present set-up is contrary to nature only in the sense that women do not in fact do jobs that they are capable of doing. There is no suggestion in the present passage that by "contrary to nature" Plato means anything stronger, such as for example that women's present roles are imposed on them in a way which deforms their lives. (This is not a point peculiar to the discussion of women. The arguments in Book II that each person should have one occupation make no appeal to people's happiness or satisfaction in doing only one thing. Cf. 370b–c, 374 b–d.)

In the *Laws* also (805a–b) Plato says that it is stupid not to train and bring up boys and girls in the same way to have the same pursuits and purposes, and adds that nearly every state is half a state as things are, whereas it could double its resources (cf. 806c). For Plato the reason why housewifery is not a real occupation is that it makes no irreplaceable contribution to the state, and absorbs time and energy that could be put to publicly beneficial use. He is completely unconcerned with the sort of objection which is nowadays familiar, namely that housewifery is incapable of providing an intelligent woman with a satisfying life, and leads to boredom, neurosis, and misery.[13]

3. The third point leads on naturally from the second, since it is also a consequence of the fact that Plato justifies his proposals solely in terms of benefit to the state. The proposals for women are not a matter of their rights. There is nothing in *Republic* V that one could apply to the question of women's rights; the matter is simply not raised.

Of course Plato nowhere discusses men's rights either, and notoriously has no word for "rights," any more than he has for "duty" or "obligation." But the point is not lost if we abandon talk of rights and merely notice instead that Plato nowhere says that his proposals for women are *just*. It is remarkable in a work which makes proposals about women as radical as the *Republic*'s, and which has as much to say about justice as the *Republic* has, that inequality of the sexes is not presented as an injustice, and that the proposals to treat the sexes equally are not presented as measures which will make the state more just than its rivals. Yet the ideal state is just for reasons, explained in Books II–IV, which have nothing to do with the position of women in it. Nothing is said about any connection between the decline to the various forms of unjust state and the position of women in them.[14]

In fact it is rather unclear how the proposals of Book V relate to justice at all, whether in the state or in the soul. If women are to be Guardians, they must have just souls. We know from Book IV that the just soul has rightly organized parts—the *logistikon* or rational element, *epithumetikon* or desiring element, and *thumoeides,* the part usually called "spirit" or the like. If the Guardian women are just, presumably they have these parts of soul. But do women's souls have a *thumoeidic* part? As it is introduced in Book IV, *thumoeides* appears to be a capacity for aggressive and violent behavior, visible even in animals, but, one would have thought, notably lacking in fourth-century Athenian women. It is true that *thumoeides* is not limited to unthinking aggression, but even the more developed forms of behaviors that Plato regards as typically thumoeidic display, what Gosling[15] calls "admiration for manliness," are what we might call *machismo.* Unless the account of the just soul is to be done all over again for women Guardians to take account of female psychology, Plato must assume that women have the same aggressive tendencies as men. And in Book V he does make this assumption, and says that some women at any rate will be of the predominantly thumoeidic type (456al–5). But this seems to conflict with his statements elsewhere which say or imply that women's psychology differs from men's precisely in that they lack the thumoeidic qualities of courage and "guts"; by contrast with men they are weak, devious, and cowardly.[16]

I have argued so far that for Plato his proposals about women are justified entirely by the resulting benefit to the state and not at all by women's needs or rights. It is important that the state in question is the ideal state. As far as I can see, there is nothing in *Republic* V which would commit Plato to the view that it was unjust for fourth-century Athenian women to be treated as they were. The proposals for women arise when the just constitution of the ideal state has been determined. There seems no reason why analogous proposals should be made in an unreformed state. Why should women be able to do men's jobs where this will merely have the result that instead of operating in a private sphere in the home, they will be operating in a private sphere at work? Plato would have no grounds for arguing that it would be best and useful for the state for this to happen.

Is this an ungenerous way to take the spirit of Plato's proposals? We should notice that even in the ideal state Plato limits his proposals for women to the Guardian class. There is nothing to suggest that the worker class do not live like fourth-century Greeks, with the women at home doing the cooking and weaving. This seems to show that whether women should do men's jobs depends, for Plato, on the nature of the jobs. The ideal state might contain many discontented potters' wives wanting to be potters; but presumably the Guardians (male and female) would only tell them to stay at home and learn *sôphrosunê* in carrying out their appointed tasks.

If Plato's argument applies only to the performance of tasks which contribute towards the public good in the direct way that the Guardians' tasks do, it is clearly irrelevant to modern arguments for equality of opportunity. No modern feminist would argue that women should be able to do men's jobs when this will result in greater direct benefit to the state, and otherwise stay at home. The moment it could be shown that the state did not need the extra women public servants, there would be no grounds for letting them have the jobs.

It would in fact be surprising if Plato's argument were relevant to women's rights, because it is a purely utilitarian argument. This is, however, precarious ground for a feminist, for once more efficient means to the desired end are found, women can at once be thrust back into the home. Mill begins *On the Subjection of Women* with the statement that "the legal subordination of one sex to the other is wrong in itself." Plato is not committed to this by the *Republic*, and I see no reason whatsoever to believe that he thought that it was true. He thinks only that the present situation is wasteful and inefficient, and, under ideal conditions, should be changed.

This makes it easier to understand what seemed puzzling earlier, namely that Plato should combine a belief that the jobs of (Guardian) men should be open to women with a belief that women are physically and mentally inferior to men. It has always been difficult for those who see Plato as a feminist to understand why he stresses so much the comparative feebleness of women's contribution, for it is not usual to combine proposals like Plato's with extreme contempt for women. But on a purely utilitarian argument, since women represent a huge pool of untapped resources, it does not matter in the least if their contribution is not as good as that of men; and that is just what Plato seems to think.

Throughout Plato's works there are scattered examples of conventional contempt for women. At *Cratylus* 392bl–dl0, for example, we are told that the Trojan men called Hector's son Astyanax and the Trojan women called him Scamandrius, and that this means that the former is the right name, as men are more intelligent than women. Of course nothing can be built on this kind of remark, and it would be unprofitable as well as depressing to comb Plato's works for such passages. Nevertheless they are significant in that taken together they build up a consistent tone which is hard to reconcile with an attitude that could be called feminist. Even in Book V itself Plato remarks that the practice of despoiling the dead shows a "small and womanish mind" (469d7)—this in a context where half of the army doing the killing and despoiling are women. This might be put down to carelessness were it not for the *Timaeus*, where Plato not only says (42e), "Human nature being twofold, the better sort was that which should thereafter be called man," but says twice (42b3–c4, 90e6–91a4) that evil and cowardly men are reborn as women, that being the first step downwards to rebirth as animals. There could hardly be a more open declaration that women are inferior to men. If the *Timaeus* was written at roughly the same time as the *Republic*, this embarrasses those who want to see Plato in the *Republic* as a feminist. But if what I have argued is right, then the *Timaeus* is quite compatible with the *Republic*. Even if women are inferior to men, it will still be of advantage to the state to have women do what men do if it is of public benefit. The argument in the *Republic* does not need, or claim, more than this.

There is one striking and revealing passage which shows that even in the *Republic* Plato holds the view of women's inferiority which has its uglier expression in the *Timaeus*. At 563b7–9, equality (*isonomia*) and freedom between men and women turns up as one of the deplorable corruptions of the democratic state. Now what is wrong with the democratic state, in Plato's view, is that unequals are treated equally—young and old, for example, and slave and free. The only possible inference is that Plato himself holds that women are naturally inferior to men,[17] and that any actual state where they are on terms of equality has corrupted the natural hierarchy. It is true that in his hostile portrait of the democratic state Plato carries over some details from contemporary Athens (for example, the fact that slaves cannot be distinguished at sight from free men by their clothes) and so not all features of his description embody serious theses. But even at his most careless Plato could hardly have thought of fourth-century Athens as an example of a place where men and women were on terms of freedom and equality. The passage must, then, be taken as a deliberate and important statement of what Plato believes, and it shows conclusively that the *Republic* does not differ on this point from the *Timaeus*. Even in the *Republic*, Plato never advocates the view that men and women are equal.

It comes as no surprise, then, that when Plato stops believing that the ideal state can be realized, he also stops thinking that women should do the same jobs as men, even in a greatly improved state. In the *Laws* he has abandoned the idea that men and women might be totally devoted to the state as the Guardians were. And the *Republic*'s radical proposals about women lapse. Although women are still educated and forced into public to some extent, this is merely so that they can be controlled, since their potential for virtue is less than man's and they would get up to mischief (780d9–781b6). They are still to learn how to fight, but only so as to defend their homes and children in the last resort (804–806, 813e–814c). The only office they hold seems to be that of organizing a kind of women's moral vigilante group. Otherwise they are left in the position of fourth-century Greek women. They take no part in any political process, they are unable to own or inherit property in their own right, and they are perpetual legal minors always under the authority of male relatives or guardians. Women are married off by their fathers or brothers, and an heiress passes with the property to the nearest male relative,[18] as was the normal Greek practice of the time.[19]

Plato's argument that women should be Guardians thus has three crucial defects: it is not valid against an anti-feminist, it is irrelevant to facts about women's desires, and it is irrelevant to the injustice of sexual inequality.

WOMEN'S NATURE AND ROLE IN THE IDEAL *POLIS*: *REPUBLIC* V REVISITED

Susan B. Levin

Few of Plato's claims have generated as much controversy as his proposal in *Republic* V that women may serve as Guardians, in particular as philosopher-rulers. This demand for equality has been dismissed as ludicrous. Many commentators have raised doubts about the genuineness and extent of the proposed reforms. Bloom, for example, asserts that "Book V is preposterous, and Socrates expects it to be ridiculed" (1968, 380).[1] Others have maintained, in my view correctly, that Plato is indeed an advocate of women's equality.[2] In this paper I will introduce fresh arguments in support of the view that Plato gives serious consideration to and in fact endorses *Republic* V's proposal regarding women.

Though much attention has been paid to the remarks themselves, and to Plato's comments about women elsewhere, more can be done to situate his proposal with reference to key areas of inquiry in the early and middle dialogues. In my view, Plato's discussion is fully intelligible only if placed in the context of his exploration of the concept of *technê* in numerous early and middle dialogues. Far from being merely transitional, the discussion of women in *Republic* V is part of the dialogue's philosophical core. I contend that it plays an important role in Plato's argument, above all in Books V–VII, that philosophy is the *technê par excellence*. Situating the discussion of women in the framework of *technê* shows, at the very least, that the proposal is one to which Plato gives serious attention.

Having located Plato's discussion of women in the context of his treatment of the *technê* issue, I turn to his reflections on women's nature. The foundation for this discussion is provided by a consideration of the misogynist tradition in Greek literature and of Plato's use of *phusis* ("nature") and its cognates in his own discussions of human nature.[3] Some have thought that Plato cannot actually be a proponent of women's equality because, notwithstanding his seemingly positive comments in *Republic* V, he criticizes women on numerous occasions. As Vlastos (1989) has shown, this view rests on a failure to distinguish adequately between Plato's assessments of women under less than optimal and ideal circumstances. If one evaluates Plato's derogatory comments about women with this distinction in mind, they do not count as evidence against the view that I am defending.[4] The literary tradition—to which Plato relates himself in crucial ways in his treatment of women—makes frequent use of *phusis* in its criticisms of women, and Plato himself uses this terminology in a host of positive and negative comments about human nature. However, in none of those passages in which Plato makes derogatory remarks about women does he use *phusis* to explain why they behave in the ways of which he is critical, as he "would have [done] if his point had been that those bad 'womanish' traits were inherent in femaleness as such."[5] Study of passages containing *gunê*, *gunaikeios*, and *thêlus* on the one hand, and *phusis* and its cognates on the other, in dialogues up to and including the *Republic* supports the view that Plato distinguishes clearly between talk of women as they are at present and talk of them as they might be if evaluated and educated based on the caliber of their souls. The foregoing line of inquiry yields new evidence for the claim that Plato not only entertains but also endorses *Republic* V's proposal regarding women.

Following brief comments on Plato's view of the soul, which makes possible his positive conclusion about women's potential role as philosopher-rulers, I close by suggesting that the view of women presented in *Republic* V is compatible with what Plato says in the Phaedo and may actually be implied by the *Symposium*. In some sense, then, *Republic* V is the culmination of what precedes—a position which can be only briefly sketched out here, but which buttresses the claim that Plato's proposal is seriously intended.

I. The Concept of *Technê* in the Early and Middle Dialogues

In the early and middle dialogues, Plato is consistently occupied with two closely related questions: what entities can properly be said to be real (i.e., have natures) and who may justifiably be called *eudaimôn* (i.e., said to flourish)? Since one must practice certain *technai* in order to determine what is unqualifiedly real, and knowing what has this status is necessary for flourishing, one can understand Plato's qualifications for being *eudaimôn* only if one examines his views about *technê*.[6]

Plato reflects extensively on the character and value of those *praxeis* ("activities") in which human beings engage. With a view toward defending philosophy's claim to establish values, Plato must criticize other activities, above all poetry and rhetoric, which promote conceptions of *eudaimonia* ("flourishing") that he finds untenable. Plato tries repeatedly to show that these activities do not merit the esteem in which they are presently held, and that, contrary to popular belief, philosophy is the most laudable *praxis* of all. The concept of *technê* provides a framework in terms of which Plato can criticize sophistry or rhetoric and poetry, and demonstrate the superiority of philosophy. His goal is to show that the former do not qualify as *technai*, while the latter, in contrast, is the *technê par excellence*. Plato situates his positive characterization of philosophy against the backdrop of his negative account of rival *praxeis*; in his view, the praise of philosophy and demonstration of its rivals' inadequacies are essential and complementary aspects of a single project.

Plato uses the term *technê* in broad and narrow, or nontechnical and technical, senses. In the former case he follows prevailing usage, according to which the term refers to activities involving skill in a general, unanalyzed sense (i.e., in this context, use of the term *technê* is not based on a systematic inquiry into the nature of its referent).[7] In the latter, Plato employs a distinction between *technai* and *empeiriai* (i.e., mere "knacks") in order to differentiate what he takes to be two quite disparate sets of activities. Plato grants that in some sense both types of activities involve skill, but central to his project is careful attention to the issue of what being a genuine expert entails. In this context the notion of *technê* becomes highly normative, and the appellation one that is properly applied only to a select group of *praxeis*. Although central *technê* requirements are introduced quite early,[8] it is in the Gorgias that Plato provides a systematic account of those criteria which distinguish genuine *technai* from pseudo-*technai*, or *empeiriai*. He presents there four major *technê* requirements:

1. *Peri ti*: the "subject matter" of a genuine *technê* includes both the Form(s) in question and a specification of that toward which activity is directed.

2. Understanding: practitioners must be in the proper cognitive state, that is, operate with *epistêmê* ("knowledge" or "understanding") rather than mere belief; presupposed here is the existence of a small class of expert practitioners. One with understanding of the subject matter in question will be able to provide a rational

account (*logon didonai*) of those procedures which comprise the activity and their relevance to the end in question.

3. Teachability (and, by implication, learnability).[9]

4. Goodness: the activity in question must be of genuine benefit to human beings, not simply cater to their whims and indiscriminate desires.

In the *Gorgias*, the *technê* status of rhetoric is first assumed, then undermined. In the course of several dialogues, and above all in the *Republic*, the *technê* status of poetry is challenged and that of philosophy defended. In all of these cases, affirmations and denials of *technê* status involve the narrow or philosophic sense of that term. For purposes of illustration, and in order to situate most clearly Plato's discussion of women in *Republic* V, I focus here on the *Republic*'s use of the framework of *technê* as a tool for the critique of poetry and praise of philosophy.[10]

II. THE CHALLENGE TO POETRY'S *TECHNÊ* STATUS

Long before the establishment of "primary" schools, the Greeks had turned to poets for instruction on religion and morality. Marrou (1982, 3, xiv) emphasizes the preeminent role played by Homer in classical education, and identifies the *Iliad* as "the central pivot around which the whole of Greek education was to be organized." Over time, Hesiod, Pindar, and the tragedians Aeschylus, Sophocles, and Euripides were also recognized as influential educators.[11]

In Book X of the *Republic*, Plato refers to "an ancient quarrel between philosophy and poetry" (607b).[12] While extant sources indicate that Presocratic philosophers were critical of poets from fairly early on, it is only with Plato that the rivalry between philosophy and poetry takes center stage. Ferrari (1989, 129) observes that "since the imitative scope of a Homer extends to nothing short of how the greatest communities are led by their princes, the user's skill he can appear to arrogate is the very highest: that which Socrates would reserve for the Philosopher-King. . . . Poetry is thus in direct competition with philosophy for the education of the ruling class." In Plato's view, only the philosopher can adequately perform this pedagogical function, and only a philosopher—one, moreover, who shares Plato's basic metaphysical commitments—has the proper vantage point from which to assess poetry's merits and shortcomings.

Plato's critique of poetry in the *Republic* focuses above all on the goodness, understanding, and subject-matter conditions.[13] With regard to the goodness requirement, Plato emphasizes repeatedly that poets aim to produce pleasure in the audience without a concern for what is beneficial. He states, for example, that if epic or lyric poetry is admitted into the city, pleasure (*hêdonê*) and pain (*lupê*) will govern it rather than a concern for what is best (607a).[14] If a poet of the familiar sort requested admission to the ideal state, he would be acknowledged as "sacred and marvelous and pleasant (*hêdun*)," but refused entrance for the sake of the city's well-being (*ôphelias heneka*) (398a–b).[15] Plato insists that any poet who is to gain admission would have to show that his poetry "is not only pleasant (*hêdeia*) but also beneficial (*ôphelimê*) to communities and to human life generally" (607d).[16] Moreover, in Books VI–VII—beginning with the figure of the Sun—Plato makes clear that the good is fundamentally different in kind from anything to which the formulations of poets apply. *If* poets could meet the goodness requirement, they would be admitted into the ideal state. Failing that, regardless of how much gratification they produce, they must be excluded in order to prevent them from having a negative impact on the city's well-being.

Plato bases poets' inability to meet the goodness requirement on their shortcomings with respect to the understanding and *peri ti* conditions. For example, in Book II (363e–364c) he states that, according to poets, licentiousness and injustice are only disgraceful in opinion (*doxêi*) and by convention (*nomôi*), implying that poets only promote this view because they lack understanding and the right conception of what is natural (*phusei*). Shortly thereafter, he attributes poets' promotion of a defective conception of flourishing to their preference for appearance (*to dokein*) over reality (365b–c). In Book III, Plato identifies as a precondition for *mousikê*'s having a beneficial effect that its practitioners have knowledge of the natures of virtues and vices—"in all the combinations that contain and convey them"—on the basis of which they may distinguish clearly and reliably between those natures and their images (*eikonas*) (402b–c; cf. 409d–e).[17] The conclusion reached in Books II and III is that only poets with a genuine understanding of the nature of virtue and vice, rather than merely opinions about appearances, would be able to promote the right conception of *eudaimonia*.

Republic V, which presents a systematic distinction between knowledge and belief, above all by differentiating their objects, develops that distinction articulated previously in the *Gorgias* (454). Books VI and X, which presuppose the careful analysis of Book V, comment most directly on how poets fare with regard to their level of cognition. In Book VI, where the populace is likened to a powerful beast (493), Plato links together poetry and sophistry with respect to their destructive impact. Apropos of the understanding condition, Plato stresses that practitioners of these activities operate with and beget opinions rather than insight (regarding the production of beliefs cf. 496a); as in the *Gorgias*, Plato supports this claim by emphasizing practitioners' inability to exhibit their alleged wisdom in a "rational account" (*logos*) of the procedures they employ and their relevance to the end in question (493b–c).[18] In terms of the subject-matter requirement, Plato's repeated contrasts earlier in Book VI between the activity of the few which is directed toward Forms, and that of the multitude which centers on participants (484b–e, 485a–b, 490a–b), provide the foundation for the beast analogy; to emphasize the centrality of that contrast, the analogy is followed immediately by its repetition (493e–494a).

In Book X Plato concentrates on poets and underscores repeatedly their lack of insight (598d–602b). While some say that poets know all *technai* (598d–e), Plato insists that they know none. One cannot reasonably hold them to account the way one would doctors and generals when they discuss medicine and generalship, respectively. One must, however, hold poets to account where the issue is virtue and vice, since it is on their handling of such issues that their claim to excellence rests. While they allege to have mastery of these subjects, in fact they lack knowledge of them altogether (600e–601b); instead, they create products three removes from reality (597e), and deceive the audience by manipulating *onomata* ("words") and *rhêmata* ("phrases") to create false impressions of expertise. The conclusion to draw is not that virtue and vice are not the province of a genuine *technê*. They *are* the objects of a *technê*, but that *technê* is philosophy *not* poetry.

III. PLATO'S DEFENSE OF PHILOSOPHY
AS THE *TECHNÊ PAR EXCELLENCE*

Plato's most concerted attempt to depict philosophy as being at the top of the hierarchy of *technai* comes in *Republic* V–VII. There he makes clear that it not only satisfies all those conditions set forth in the *Gorgias*, but meets them to the fullest possible extent.[19] Based on his exploration of the subject matter of philosophy, the cognitive state of its practitioners, and their superlative ability to meet the goodness requirement, Plato concludes that philosophy is the *technê par excellence*.

In the early and middle dialogues, Plato distinguishes repeatedly between seeking merely to produce pleasure in others via flattery, and aiming to promote the good of those toward whom one's activity is directed. In *Republic* VI it turns out that the good—the ultimate object of aspiration—occupies a position at the top of the hierarchy of Forms (see 505a–509b,

517b–c, and 518c–d). Training in dialectic is indispensable preparation for apprehending the Form of the Good, and it is this apprehension, possible only for philosophers, that enables one to maximize the presence of good in the spatio-temporal realm. Hence, it is philosophers who satisfy the goodness requirement to the fullest possible extent. Practitioners of other *technai* function under the supervision of the dialectician insofar as they require the latter's expertise in order to determine whether the goodness requirement is being met to the highest degree possible within their own "areas of specialization."[20]

The *peri ti* or subject-matter requirement is central to the *Gorgias*. While Plato does not there specify the ontological status of that subject matter, the *Phaedo*, *Symposium*, and *Republic* make clear that Forms play this role.[21] In the *Republic* Plato emphasizes that *technai* are situated hierarchically with reference to one another based on differences in the way in which the activity in question is related to Forms. The second tier is typified by mathematical activity, which involves the direction of one's attention toward Forms, with, however, those natures being explored indirectly (i.e., via particulars like diagrams) rather than firsthand. Plato's praise of it in Books VI and VII is qualified: insofar as mathematical activity is directed ultimately toward Forms, it is to be lauded, while it is rightly subject to criticism due to its reliance on particulars and unquestioning use of hypotheses. Above it is that activity which Plato views as constitutive of philosophy proper. Here one proceeds solely via Forms, and all movement from particulars to Forms is viewed as merely preparatory (for a description of this type of activity, see 511b–c; cf. 533b–d).

While the inquiries of mathematicians and philosophers both concern Forms, only the latter have immediate access to those entities, combined with a systematic understanding of how they are interrelated. This understanding is based ultimately on that knowledge of the Good which sets the philosopher apart from everyone else. Hence, philosophy differs most fundamentally from other *technai* with respect to its subject matter because only it has the Form of the Good as part of its domain. Since it is the apprehension of this Form that allows one to have the most direct and complete access possible to other *eidê*, along with full knowledge of their interconnections, its being an element of philosophy's domain ultimately explains why philosophy has Forms as its subject matter in the strictest possible sense.

Books V–VII center on those individuals whose presence and ruling in the state make its very existence possible. There Plato emphasizes that they are distinguished from all others by their possession and depth of knowledge. In the final section of Book V, which initiates this discussion, Plato argues that philosophers are distinguished from everyone else by the fact that they operate with knowledge which is directed toward Forms, while all others have only belief which has as its objects entities that are F (e.g., just or courageous) with some qualification.[22]

At first glance that portion of *Republic* V in which Plato makes his remarks about women's equality does not appear to be tied closely to what follows. According to Grube (1974, 111), the first two-thirds of the book "deal with subjects which have been omitted or but lightly touched upon in founding the city, while the last third begins the description of the Platonic philosopher, his wisdom and his methods, which continues through the next two books." In a similar vein, Cornford (1941, 144) states that the earlier sections "form an interlude . . . only formally connected by the metaphor of the three 'waves'" with the final section of the book.[23] If, however, one understands the discussion of women in terms of its role in Plato's defense of philosophy as the *technê par excellence,* the structure of *Republic* V ceases to be problematic. As previously noted, the understanding requirement on *technai*, which stipulates that practitioners must operate with insight rather than mere belief, presupposes the existence—and delineation—of a small class of expert practitioners. In Plato's assessments of activities' claims to the rank of *technê*, discussions of these aspects of the understanding condition go hand in hand, and are mutually reinforcing. For example, in the *Cratylus,* which denies *technê* status to the *praxis* of naming as undertaken by the literary tradition, Plato's handling of the understanding condition comprises his argument both that the activity lacks practitioners of the requisite caliber and that those who have undertaken naming to date have operated based solely on *doxa.*[24] *Republic* V also treats these two complementary aspects of the understanding condition: the last section, which presents a systematic distinction between knowledge and belief, addresses the issue of what cognitive state distinguishes the philosopher, while the earlier portion, which contains Plato's discussion of women, helps to specify the range of human beings who may count as expert practitioners of *philosophia* under ideal circumstances.[25] It is, thus, far from coincidental that Plato presents his insights about women, which pertain directly to the issue of who may possess this highest form of expertise, as a prelude to detailed remarks on the cognitive state in which that expertise is manifested.

On this interpretation, *Republic* V is a unity in a far stronger sense than is captured by interpretations which treat the book as merely transitional.[26] At the very least, locating Book V in the context of Plato's exploration of the *technê* issue supports the view that the proposal about women is one to which he gives serious attention. In my view, it also helps to buttress the conclusion that Plato endorses the proposal itself. For current purposes, however, in arguing that second point I rely most directly on Plato's discussion of women's nature.

IV. PLATO ON THE NATURE OF WOMEN

Remarking on Plato's relationship to Greek literary treatments of women, Vlastos asks: "Why should Plato have assumed that being female would decrease one's chances of turning out to be a super-person instead of a mass-person? The Greek poetic vision of humanity would give no quarter to that prejudice" (1989, 139). This formulation does not do full justice to the originality of Plato's views about women as presented in *Republic* V or to the complexity of "the Greek poetic vision." In Greek literature, there is a basic division between cases in which authors offer condemnations of women as a *genos* and those in which women are assessed positively or negatively based on their psychological or behavioral characteristics.[27] With respect to the former, Andromache notes (if only for the sake of argument) that the female *phusis* is prone to evil (Eur. *Andr.* 352–54). Sophocles emphasizes the fundamental difference between men's and women's *phuseis,* with women's *phusis* portrayed in unflattering terms, at Trach. 1062.[28] Another negative generalization about women which centers on *phusis* is made at Eur. *Med.* 407–9, where Medea says that although women are by nature "most helpless in doing good deeds," their nature also makes them "of every evil the cleverest of contrivers."[29] At Eur. fr. 1061N[2], in turn, a speaker, presumably male, laments that "we are exhausted from keeping watch over the race of women. Since women are not by nature just, why bother continuing to try to hold them in check when such attempts are bound to fail?" (*Mochthoumen allôs thêlu phrourountes genos; hêtis gar autê mê pephuken endikos, ti dei phulassein kaxamartanein pleon?*).[30] For still other passages falling in this category, one may consult Eur. *Med.* 928; *Phoen.* 198; and *Or.* 605–6.[31]

With regard to the latter type of case, already in Homer one finds recognition of a tendency to speak negatively of women as a *genos,* combined with at least an intimation of regret that such a tendency exists: Penelope, who is praised highly for her virtuous conduct in Odysseus' absence, is contrasted with Clytaemestra, and it is said that the song which conveys Clytaemestra's story "will be forever hateful. A bad name she gave to womankind, even the best" (*Od.* 24.193–202).[32] Hesiod generalizes on several occasions (*W.D.* 53–105, 373–75, and *Th.* 570–602); however, he also sets good (*agathai*) women apart from bad (*kakai*) (*W.D.* 699–705). In addition, Semonides' poem about women lists ten types, nine of which are characterized in negative terms; however, the tenth, who is likened to a bee, is praised.[33] While Semonides views most women in a negative light, the key point for present purposes is that he does not speak critically of the entire *genos* of women. At Eur. *Bacc.* 314–18, in turn, Teiresias distinguishes between types of women with respect to the quality of chastity by speaking of their different *phuseis,* and in the *Ion* (399–400) Creusa laments the fact that "[s]ince good and bad women are not distinguished, all of us are hated. To this misfortune we are born" (*kan tais kakaisin agathai memeigmenai misoumeth'; houtô dustucheis pephukamen*).[34] Moreover, in two crucial fragments, Euripides argues that good and bad women differ quite markedly in their natures (*diapherousi d' hai phuseis,* 494N[2]), and criticizes sharply those who make unqualified, and indeed untenable, negative generalizations about women (657N[2]).[35] One can explain the presence of such pointed remarks only if one assumes the existence of influential opponents holding the opposite view.

One finds in Plato both a reliance on the literary tradition and a qualitative leap beyond it.[36] On some level Plato aligns himself with both views articulated by the poets. On the one hand, he makes unreflective comments about women as a *genos.* On the other, he insists that women differ radically in type. How can he do both? Crucial to his account—and here he diverges fundamentally from the literary tradition—is a distinction between assessments that apply correctly under current circumstances, and those that are appropriate if one has ideal conditions in view. It is with respect to the former that he aligns himself with those offering negative generalizations, though, even here, his condemnations do not always apply to all women (i.e., he recognizes some distinctions between better and worse even under present conditions). With respect to ideal circumstances, he sides unquestionably with those comments which make crucial distinctions of type. In another key departure, while negative literary generalizations do make use of the term *phusis,* when Plato addresses directly the issue of women's *phusis* in dialogues up to and including the *Republic*, he does so in a positive light, with ideal conditions in view. Moreover, his treatment of this issue, like that of other topics, differs from literary approaches by virtue of its sustained and systematic character. In the present case, this feature of Plato's account may be explained with reference to his conduct of the debate within the framework of *technê*. In fact, when Plato specifies what is at stake with regard to women, he emphasizes that the point of contention is their qualification to practice *technai* (454d7–9). Having established the general principle that women's fitness to pursue any *technê* is based on the quality of their *psuchai* ("minds" or "souls") (454c–e), Plato narrows his focus to the issue of immediate concern, which is that subset of *technai* involved in the conduct of the ideal *polis* (455a). Above all, the central point of contention is women's capacity to engage in the *technê par excellence,* that is, whether or not any may possess a philosophical *phusis.*[37]

The *Republic*'s discussion of naturalness in connection with human beings is extensive, and makes abundant use of *phusis* and terms cognate with it.[38] In Book II Plato introduces the Principle of Specialization, according to which people are naturally suited for different types of jobs, and individuals should pursue those occupations for which they are qualified "by nature" (*kata phusin*) (370a–c).[39] There is a hierarchical relation between jobs; guardianship is far superior to any type of work involving production and manual labor, hence its practitioners must have superior natures. Having subdivided the Guardian class into two, and argued for the existence of a tripartite soul, in Book IV Plato speaks again of what is natural in connection with human beings. From the perspective of the ideal, only one type of relation between the soul's elements—reason's ruling in the soul and making decisions with a view toward the welfare of the individual as a whole—is *kata phusin* ("in accord with nature" or "natural"); all other types are *para phusin* ("contrary to nature" or "unnatural"). One might wonder how Plato is able to speak, at the same time, of different types of human nature and of only one type of relation between the soul's elements as "natural." The latter kind of remark is based on the idea that reason sets humans apart from animals and grants them access to reality. This view of reason is manifest, for example, in the *Phaedo*'s frequent identification of soul with intellect (see, e.g., 65b9, 76c6, and 11–13) and in the *Republic*'s use of a human being to stand for reason in a vivid representation of the three aspects of the *psuchê* as fused in the individual (588c–d).[40] To the extent that characteristics which humans share with animals dominate in minds of other types, one may conclude that those *psuchai* are structured in ways that do not give precedence to that which, in the strict sense, constitutes our nature as human beings; hence, Plato's comment in Book IV that other arrangements are *para phusin* (444d).

Based on what he has said in Books I–IV, Plato has essentially two options open to him when he considers in Book V how the male-female distinction meshes with his earlier remarks on what is natural and unnatural. First, he could argue that the reason of women, unlike that of men, cannot but be subservient to the lower two elements of the soul, and hence that women's souls will always be structured in ways that are *para phusin*. Second, Plato might insist that women, like men, may achieve that relation of mutual dominance and subordination of the soul's elements which sets the philosopher apart from all others and which Book IV depicts as *kata phusin* (444d). In what follows, I introduce considerations in support of the view that Plato embraces this second option.

It has been claimed that Plato cannot seriously embrace Book V's proposal regarding women because, despite what appear to be positive comments there (see 449a–457c and 466c–d), he criticizes them on numerous other occasions. Hence, what Plato bestows with one hand, he takes away with the other. If, however, one evaluates Plato's derogatory comments with the distinction between current (or less than optimal) and ideal circumstances in mind, those remarks need not, and in fact cannot, count as evidence against the view that he seriously intends the proposal concerning women's equality.[41] In this regard, it is worth emphasizing that a large number of Plato's disparaging comments are found in *Republic* VIII and IX, where he discusses degenerate types of constitution and human being, that is, those departing to varying extents from the ideal (see 549c–550b, 550d, 557c, 563b–d, and 579b–c).

In such passages, Plato derides females because the spirited and appetitive elements of their *psuchai* dominate at reason's expense (see most notably 387e–388a, 395d–e, 431b–c, 469d, 549c–550b, and 550d). However, Plato is also typically critical of males for their shortcomings in this very same respect. In describing the origin of the timocratic man, for example, Plato says that his mother exhorts him in his youth to prize honor and money, the quest for which falls within the scope of the spirited and appetitive elements, respectively, but adds that when he consorts with males outside the home he hears the very same things praised (549c–550b).[42] In addition, as Plato emphasizes in Book X, even the best man is vulnerable to feelings and emotions (e.g., grief) if his education has not strengthened his reason such that they may be experienced in a moderate fashion. Moreover, at key junctures Plato refuses to offer blanket condemnations of women even under present conditions. So, for example, at 387e–388a he qualifies his criticism by noting that lamentations must not be attributed to women who are *spoudaiai* ("good"). In this regard one may also consult 398e, where Plato rejects the use of certain modes because they are useless to women who are to be good (*epieikeis*). In fact, Plato shows himself, both in the *Republic* and in other dialogues, to be negatively inclined toward most people under present conditions. Ultimately Plato's worry is that currently almost everyone—male and female—is prone to be governed by emotions and base desires. As Senter (1977, 9–11) argues, Plato views the traits he derides as undesirable in themselves, not because they are "feminine," and the traits in question are equally undesirable for both sexes.

As discussed above, in Greek literature the terms *phusis* and *phuein* are used to convey wholesale condemnations of women. Moreover, Plato himself uses *phusis* and its cognates in multiple contexts, prominent among them his reflections on human nature and subdivisions thereof. Yet in none of the passages cited above does Plato employ this terminology to explain why women behave in the ways of which he is critical, as he surely would have if he had wished to depict the traits in question as ineradicable.[43]

Based on the cross-referencing of passages featuring *gunê, gunaikeios*, and *thêlus* on the one hand, and *phusis* and its cognates on the other, one may venture the following observations.[44] Instances in which members of these two classes of terms are found in a close relation to one another break down into three basic types.[45] In the first group of passages, Plato's tone toward women is neutral. He does not single them out for a positive or negative assessment, and, in all but one instance, *phusis* and its cognates are not used in direct or explicit references to women. At *Symposium* 189d5–e4, for example, Aristophanes says that the present human *phusis* differs from the original one since human beings came initially in three types, one of which was an androgynous form composed of male and female (*thêlu*) elements. He notes later that his speech is not aimed specifically at Pausanias and Agathon: while they likely "belong to the group that are wholly masculine in nature (*tên phusin*) . . . I am speaking about everyone, men and women (*gunaikôn*) alike" (193c1–3).[46] For other passages falling in this category, one may consult *Prot.* 325a6–b2; *Menex.* 237d4–238a5; *Symp.* 191a5–b4, 191c4–d3, 206c4–5; *Rep.* 423e7–424a8, 451c2–6, and 620c2.[47]

The second group consists of passages in which Plato makes negative assessments of women either directly or by implication. The terminology of *phusis* is typically not found in close proximity to such remarks (see, e.g., *Apol.* 35b, *Phdo.* 60a, *Rep.* 387e–388a, 550d, 557c, and 605e). Even where it is, however, as at 579b4–8, Plato does not frame his criticisms in terms of what is natural or unnatural for women.[48] Plato's failure to use such terminology is noteworthy since, as previously noted, this is precisely the language one would expect him to use if he thought the deficiencies in question were irremediable.[49] Notably, far from using *phusis* to convey his critical assessments, in the *Phaedo* Socrates attributes Xanthippe's conduct to habit, noting that she says "just the sorts of things which women are *accustomed* (*eiôthasin*) to say" (60a4–5). This passage should be read in conjunction with 81b–c, where Plato notes that a soul which is in the habit (*eithismenê*) of preferring the visible to the invisible world will be unable to recover that insight into Forms which all souls gain prior to embodiment.

With the exception of 620c, no passages falling in these first two groups speak directly or explicitly of women's *phusis*. In contrast, in the third set of cases in which terms from the two groups appear in close proximity to one another, Plato does address that issue explicitly; in fact, at the start of the discussion in *Republic* V, Plato emphasizes that precisely this will be the focus of inquiry, stating that he must now consider "whether female human nature (*phusis hê anthrôpinê hê thêleia*) is capable of sharing with the male all tasks or none at all, or some but not others" (452e6–453a3). When Plato does treat the issue directly, all of the pertinent comments, without exception, involve or presuppose significant departures from prevailing *ethos*[50]—which is itself criticized as *para phusin* (456c1–2)—and pertain to women under optimal conditions (i.e., those in which assessments of human beings are made based on the quality of their *psuchai,* and people receive that education and nurture to which those *psuchai* entitle them). All but one of these passages are found in Book V, where Plato maintains that women are capable of becoming philosopher-rulers (for numerous related combinations of terms from the two groups, see 453a1–458c8 and 466d3). The sole remaining passage occurs at the end of Book VII, where, at the close of his discussion of the philosopher-rulers and their *paideia,* he reiterates for the sake of emphasis that "you must not suppose that my words apply to the men more than to all women who arise among them endowed with the requisite natures (*phuseis*)" (540c).

Clearly there is a marked distinction for Plato between talk of women as they are presently and talk of them as they might be if assessed and educated based on the caliber of their souls. When he makes pronouncements about their *phusis*, he nowhere criticizes them for what they are, but speaks only of what they might become. In his evaluation of women and men alike, Plato's ultimate point of reference is the ability to use one's reason to apprehend Forms or natures proper. Men and women with this capacity have a philosophical *phusis*. All others are assessed negatively to varying extents, depending on the distance between the caliber of their souls and that of the highest type of human being.

V. CONCLUSION

When Plato contrasts those who may and those who may not properly be called *philosophoi* prior to *Republic* V, both within and outside the *Republic*, he concentrates on differences in the quality of people's minds. When Plato discusses the body, as in the *Phaedo,* he does so not as a basis for distinguishing between the natures of human beings due to their physical or biological characteristics, but because differences in the quality of people's minds are reflected in differences in the sort of relation that obtains between mind or soul and body.[51] More generally, in treating the issue of who may be considered a *technê* practitioner, Plato separates those whose cognitive abilities and achievements qualify them for this role from those whose capacities and accomplishments do not equip them for it. Prior to *Republic* V, he does not combine discussion of this issue with consideration of possible correlations between physical or biological and mental characteristics, and he never says that women are precluded from being *technê* practitioners. Had Plato's interests not prompted him to sketch a proposal for an ideal state, he might never have needed to treat directly the question of whether women are capable of practicing *technai*. However, since the *Republic*, which contains that proposal, discusses the roles of *all* citizens who combine to form that state, Plato must address the issue explicitly. Moreover, once the question arises, Plato must answer it in a particular way based on his theory of the soul, in particular its nature and independence.

In *Republic* V, Plato states that one's entitlement to practice a given *technê* is based on the quality of one's *psuchê* (454d). Moreover, he poses the question of whether women observable physical or biological differences between human beings correlate reliably with differences in the quality of their *psuchai*. For purposes of illustration, Plato appeals to the distinction between baldness and hairiness (454c), which would be readily acknowledged as constituting an incidental type of physical difference between people in the present context.[52] His focus then shifts to differences in reproductive roles, which were generally thought to correlate quite predictably—and with restrictive implications for women—with differences in the quality of people's minds and hence with their fitness to engage in a wide range of activities.[53] Rejecting the prevailing view, Plato denies that one can infer people's fitness to perform a certain type of job in society based simply on whether they are biologically male or female.[54] The reason for this denial was his recognition of a philosophical commitment, based on his conception of the soul, to the view that men and women could in principle reach the same level of psychic activity.

Oddly enough it is Plato's dualism, for which he has been criticized by feminist theorists, that helps make possible his revised account of women's roles.[55] This dualism ensures that the soul's powers are not determined by the sex of the body in which it is encased. In the persuasive formulation of N. Smith (1983, 473), "the reason it is unnatural to discriminate on the basis of sex in such cases is that the nature involved (the soul) is sexless."[56] Smith's argument focuses on Plato's discussion of metempsychosis. In the myth at the end of the *Phaedo,* and in the Myth of Er at the close of the *Republic*, Plato makes clear that souls are not attached to bodies of one particular sex, or even to human bodies; with regard to the former, souls currently encased in bodies of one sex may enter bodies of the other sex in a subsequent incarnation. Plato presents the case of Epeius as involving a shift from male to female (*Rep.* 620c). Epeius is identified by Homer as the winner of the boxing match in the funeral games for Patroclus (*Il.* 23.664–99), and as the builder of the Trojan horse (*Od.* 8.492–93). As Smith (1983, 473) notes, Plato's example of a man becoming a woman involves an "awe-inspiring boxer" whose description by Homer "hardly distinguishes him as unjust and cowardly." While it would be speculative to contend that any stronger conclusion follows from the fact that Epeius' soul shifts from a male to a female body, there is certainly no suggestion that this change constitutes a demotion. Plato lays further stress on the irrelevance of reproductive roles from the perspective of *phusis* by noting that all types of human lives—which may be lived by both men and women—are available for selection, and that the caliber of individual psuchai determines the choices made (618a–b).

Interestingly, although negative comments about women serve as stage-setting in the *Phaedo,* one finds no disparaging remarks in that dialogue when Plato discusses Forms and the soul's immortality. Plato's dualism is in the foreground there as in no other dialogue. In his consideration of immortality generally, and recollection specifically, Plato discusses the nature of the soul and its relation to the body. In the account of recollection, he maintains that all *psuchai,* "before taking on human form . . . had knowledge" (76c). A soul that is in the habit (*eithismenê*) of preferring the visible to the invisible world will be unable to recover that insight which makes possible the soul's separate existence at death (81b–c). As Plato emphasizes in the Affinity Argument (78b–84b), soul becomes entangled with body to the extent that the former is subject to the wrong influences. Only if its nurture orients it toward Forms will the soul be detached from the body as far as possible both during life and in death (84a–b). Plato stresses repeatedly (e.g., at 81d, 83d, 84a–b, and 107d) that the education and upbringing one receives determine what becomes of one's soul in life and following death. Philosophy is the only activity that releases the soul, often identified in this dialogue with the intellect, from its restrictive connection to the body, thereby making possible its contact with Forms (82b10–83b4). *All* souls originally had some glimpse of the Forms. While under current circumstances women's upbringing would seem to have as its result that they do not progress as far in the process of recollection as do men, this is compatible, at any rate, with its having better and more equitable results once both males and females are subject to the correct curricula and other pivotal influences.[57]

A final point might be raised concerning the issue of precisely what can and cannot be inferred about Plato's view of women based on what he says in the *Phaedo*. Socrates' treatment of his wife Xanthippe has been cited as documenting Plato's belief in women's inherent inferiority (see Saxonhouse 1976, 203). In my view, the evidence does not provide a clear justification for that conclusion. The difference between Xanthippe and Socrates' male friends is certainly not that she is emotional while they are not, since, as Plato makes clear at the dialogue's beginning and end, the men are all strongly affected as well (59a–b and 117c–d); in fact, at the latter juncture, Socrates observes that it was mainly to avoid this type of scene that he dismissed the women (117d–e). Since women and men are not distinguished in the *Phaedo* by the fact that the former give way to displays of emotion while the latter do not, one may conjecture that the difference is that for women being governed by emotion is, at least currently, a more prevalent state of affairs. As previously emphasized, rather than speaking of a natural deficiency, Socrates criticizes Xanthippe for saying the sorts of things which women are accustomed (*eiôthasin*) to say (60a4–5). Moreover, given certain characterizations of Xanthippe as idiosyncratic in crucial respects, nothing can be concluded about the nature of women based simply on references to her.[58]

I turn finally to the *Symposium*, which combines with the *Phaedo* and *Republic* to form the core group of dialogues in which the middle-period theory of Forms is presented and defended. The *Symposium* plays an intermediate role by exploring in more detail than the Phaedo the various stages through which recollection moves, and setting the stage for *Republic* VII's detailed account of the advanced curriculum. The *Symposium* undertakes a revision of traditional *paideia* insofar as it emphasizes that the ultimate objects of human aspiration are Forms and sketches that process of abstraction through which genuine learning moves. Plato emphasizes that the only erotic relationship between human beings truly worthy of that name must have this type of *paideia* as its core. Although Plato takes one aspect of the prevailing *ethos* as his point of departure, namely, the educative dimension of male homosexual relationships, he has Socrates' teacher—i.e., the one who describes the content and objects of the new "curriculum"—be a woman. If he had wished, Plato could easily have avoided giving a woman this pivotal role in the dialogue, and I agree with Halperin (1990) that answers to the question "Why is Diotima a woman?" cannot be solely negative in form. On the positive front, Plato may intend to signal by his choice that women are not in principle excluded from undergoing that process of recovery in which recollection consists. Indeed, on the assumption that Diotima *as Plato describes her* is not an historical being, his selection of her for this crucial role in the dialogue may be indicative of his view that while no existing woman is in a position to occupy the position of philosopher, certain women are capable by nature of developing and ultimately performing in the ways required by that job.[59] It is also worth noting Plato's strong emphasis in the *Symposium*, as in the *Republic*, on the distinction between current and ideal circumstances, with the speeches of Phaedrus and Pausanias as the most definitive representatives of the former, and that of Socrates—who insists that he is guided by Diotima—as the sole representative of the latter.

With regard to the possibility that women could be philosopher-rulers, it is important to stress that the attraction to beautiful bodies is only the point of departure for the ascent. Most importantly, as Moravcsik (1971) has argued, the causal relation between its steps is not such that each is a necessary condition for its successor. Each step's constituting such a condition would entail the claim, which Moravcsik (1971, 289) rightly rejects, that "nobody can appreciate the beauty of mathematics without having appreciated bodily beauty." If one accepts Moravcsik's view of the causal relation between the steps of the ascent, then the physical attraction between males which serves, on level one, as an impetus to the creation of fine discourses is not an essential precondition for reaching those stages where the objects of *erôs* become increasingly abstract. On the foregoing interpretation of the ascent and of why Plato makes Diotima Socrates' mentor, what is stated explicitly in *Republic* V is not only compatible with what Plato says in the Phaedo, but perhaps also implied by the *Symposium*.[60]

In a noteworthy fragment, Euripides states that anyone who stops maligning women will be on the receiving end of abuse (*gunaika d' hostis pausetai legôn kakôs, dustênos ara kou sophos keklêsetai,* 36N[2]). Remarks such as this indicate just how strong the social pressure must have been to continue being misogynistic. While it is certainly true that Plato does not support equality of training, education, or opportunity for all women, and in that sense cannot be considered an advocate of feminism, he does argue against the common and simplistic equation of the capacity to bear children, or relative physical weakness, with the inferiority of women by nature. Given the weight of that social pressure referred to by Euripides, Plato's serious consideration and endorsement of *Republic* V's proposal are remarkable indeed.

THE METAPHYSICAL SCIENCE OF ARISTOTLE'S *GENERATION OF ANIMALS* AND ITS FEMINIST CRITICS

Daryl McGowan Tress

I

How does life begin? How is it and why is it that a child comes into being? To answer these questions about life and its origins requires a system of presuppositions about a great many metaphysical matters, such as causation and its modes of operation, relations of identity and difference, and, perhaps above all, the transition from not-being to actualized existence. In his treatise, *Generation of Animals* (*GA*), Aristotle takes up the theme of the origins of animal and human life. His treatment of the subject is both empirical, offering descriptions of how the process occurs in nature, and metaphysical, pursuing the deeper how and answering questions about why it is that offspring are generated and how this phenomenon is meaningfully connected to the cosmos as a whole.

In recent years, feminist critics of the history of philosophy have been severe in their condemnation of Aristotle as a chief spokesman, if not founder, of sexism in the philosophical tradition: "We have become accustomed to regarding Aristotle as the fountainhead of one long tradition of Western misogyny."[1] The theory proposed in *GA*, which in outline reads that in generation the male parent contributes the form and the female parent contributes the matter, is adduced by some of Aristotle's critics to show that he regards females as inferior to males in the process of reproduction and that this view of female inferiority can be seen to be carried into other, if not all, areas of his philosophizing.[2]

Despite Aristotle's current status as *defective* from a feminist point of view, his treatise is worthy of renewed exposition for several reasons. First, his path to understanding how and why life begins—his very ability to ask how and why together—is richer and more fruitful than our modern view of reproduction, which is constructed for the most part on materialistic presuppositions. It is largely a modern materialist view of reproduction that feminism has inherited. From the start, the phenomenon Aristotle is studying is generation rather than reproduction, and the method he adopts for apprehending this expanded phenomenon is empirical-metaphysical rather than strictly mechanical or medical. Aristotle's ability to integrate metaphysical considerations with scientific ones offers modern readers a model for a rationally enlarged conception of generation.[3] In anticipation, we may say at this point that the results of his analysis show generation to be entwined with multiple dimensions of the natural world, not merely the sexual partners who are the parents of the offspring.[4]

Second, one reason that the feminist critics fail to appreciate the virtues of Aristotle's metaphysical science of generation has to do with the differing aims of classical metaphysics and modern feminism. Aristotle's intentions in taking up generation are metaphysical; he asks, What is generation? and looks to see how the phenomenon accords with the principles he has laid down in the *Metaphysics* and the *Physics*. The feminist, on the other hand, asks about reproduction, Who controls it? That is, the question is one of power and the aim is political: the altering of perceived unfair power relations. Because feminism is centrally concerned with power and politics, it tends to have little use for metaphysics and little patience with it. This impatience is apparent in the methodology of some feminist criticism of Aristotle, in the quoting of offensive sentences out of their context as evidence in the sexism case against him. This practice neglects the overall form and much of the content of Aristotle's treatises, and inevitably leads to misreadings of these complex and difficult texts, in particular to misconstruals of the very gender issues to which Aristotle's feminist critics wish to draw attention.

Third, when reading Aristotle's offensive comments without the benefit of a knowledge of his historical context, his feminist critics generally have failed to notice the ways in which Aristotle's theory of generation has the effect of elevating the female role in generation, when compared to another view that prevailed in his day. "Preformation," according to which the mother does not significantly contribute to generation, had wide currency in Aristotle's time (and was still holding its own into the nineteenth century). Aristotle argues against this approach on metaphysical grounds and states emphatically from the beginning of *GA* that male and female together are the principles of generation. In this respect, his treatise is worthy of our attention because it represents an advance in biology and, contrary to the usual feminist interpretation, an advance also in the appreciation of the maternal contribution to generation. As this exposition of *GA* proceeds, the three foregoing points will be shown in greater detail.

This is not to say, however, that the feminist criticism is simply to be dismissed. To begin with, there appears to be a long history of the use of Aristotle's treatise against women.[5] The text is complex and is liable to be misunderstood and misused. In *GA*, Aristotle devotes greater attention to the male contribution to generation, and it may appear to modern readers that the female contribution is less active and important than that of the male. The association of the male contribution with the superior "form" and the female contribution with "matter," along with the appearance of a preponderance of causal power in the male, is what feminists have noticed and is what has led, in part, to their objections against Aristotle's unfairness. A feminist critic, whose aim is to avoid any devaluation of the maternal contribution to reproduction, might insist that Aristotle be judged by a standard which at the very least makes the female and male equally active, and which guarantees that their contributions are of equal value by seeing them as the same in kind.[6] This implicit or explicit demand is, however, another instance of feminism's inattention to Aristotle's metaphysical aims. In fact, what imbalance there is in his treatment arises not from misogyny or sexism, but from particular philosophical problems Aristotle is addressing in the treatise.[7]

Examination of the philosophical problems involved in the subject of generation is what is required to move beyond accusation toward understanding the extent and the source of the perceived sexual imbalance that develops in this work. Let us now consider what those philosophical problems are and how they emerge within the original thinking that Aristotle brings to bear on the phenomenon of generation.

II

The work whose title is translated *Generation of Animals* is in the Greek *peri zoion genêseos,* "on the coming into being of living creatures." *Genêseos,* from the verb *gignomai,* is used primarily to refer to the "origin" or "source" or "beginning" of a natural entity. The root *gen-* concerns family, offspring, creation, birth, descent. What should be noted from the outset is the contrast between modern concepts of "reproduction," leaning on metaphors of production and manufacture of artifacts, and the ancient focus on procreation and begetting of living things as a process which occurs in a larger natural nexus.[8]

The expanded meaning available in the Greek title serves as a reminder that Aristotle raises his scientific questions regarding generation in a philosophical context; that is, his scientific questions are metaphysically informed and they are raised within a long lineage of attempts at understanding *genêsis,* the transition from not being to being.

It is worth paying particular attention to the opening of *GA* to determine what Aristotle's own aims are in this treatise. The subject, announced in the title, is the generation of animals. But how does this subject itself arise? The very first lines of the treatise answer this question. Aristotle explains that with one exception, he has already spoken of all the parts of animals, and of the various causes of these parts. Thus, in respect to generation of animals, a part remains to be described and a cause explained. He does not make it plain why this subject was saved for a separate work. It is, however, the final, culminating treatise of his zoological works. This is a series of books which, according to traditional dating, begins with *History of Animals*— Aristotle's general observations and descriptions of animal life—and proceeds thence to consider, first, the material parts and functions (*Parts of Animals*), and then those parts and functions which involve both matter and psyche (*Movement of Animals*, *Progression of Animals*, and ultimately *Generation of Animals*).[9] The progression of this series of investigations follows Aristotle's general principle of learning: we first study that which is closest or most available in our actual experience (thus, in this case, the initial record of observations of nature and inquiries into the material parts) and work from there toward that which is first in the order of being. So, at the start of *GA* we have with Aristotle, as it were, already gone through virtually every other part and principle of these creatures as preparation for the investigation of generation. Those studies lead to the present one, that is, back to the source of the "coming to be" of animal life.

From the first lines of the treatise Aristotle speaks of causes, indicating that generation, governed by causes, is an ordered, intelligible process. By contrast, generation is not to be viewed as mere effluence, nor as a mere rearrangement of parts, nor as a divine dispensation. That is, generation is not to be understood poetically, or artistically, or religiously. He delineates the four basic causes: (1) the final cause, "'that for the sake of which' a thing exists, considered as its 'end'"; (2) the formal cause, "the logos of the thing's essence" (715a4–5). Together, the final and formal causes determine a distinctively metaphysical trajectory for the discussion of generation, involving universal characterization of nature's mode of operation and a vision of nature working not only in accord with the forces of necessity but also for the good.[10] (3) The material cause is "the matter for the thing"

(715a6). As Aristotle says in the *Physics*, it is "material for the generating process to start from" (194b24). In *GA*, the female parent provides the material cause. (4) The moving cause is "that from which comes the principle of the thing's movement" (715a6). In speaking of the moving cause in the *Physics* he says, "There must be something to initiate the process of the change or its cessation" (194b30). In *GA* Aristotle singles out the moving cause as most germane to the phenomenon of generation; he is particularly interested in determining how life or the principle of motion arises.

The inclusion of formal and final causes in a scheme explaining the origination of an organism presents a chief point of difference between classical and modern scientific outlooks. Eliminating formal and final causes from scientific explanation proper was an explicit goal of some early modern empiricist philosophers, such as Francis Bacon and John Locke.[11] In their battle with the Aristotelian outlook, they insisted that only the material and moving causes be used as instruments of scientific investigation. They intended, ultimately, to eliminate Aristotle's concept of substance altogether from scientific analysis and thereby, from their point of view, eliminate subjective elements from scientific study.

For different reasons, but with some similar results, contemporary feminists have targeted essentialism—in the relevant sense the position that human beings possess an original nature which determines or structures development in significant ways prior to social conditions—as a concept which must be eradicated. Feminist theorists oppose above all essentialism's deterministic consequences. For example, feminist critics might point to some passages in *GA* itself as evidence of the way in which Aristotle conceives of a woman's nature as biologically determined and hence unchangeable, inescapable. It is true that in *GA* Aristotle defines female and male biologically, in terms of their differing generative roles. He says, "By a 'male' animal we mean one which generates in another, by 'female' one which generates in itself" (716a14–15). Beyond this simple statement of fact, however, Aristotle presently does not venture. His essentialism has no necessary consequences here for differing valuations of the female and male roles in generation. Indeed, Aristotle makes the important declaration that "the male and the female are the principles of generation" (716a5–7).[12] Aristotle's statement at the opening of the treatise that male and female are the *archai* of generation functions as the principal thesis in his theory of generation. The remainder of his discussion is intended to display both how male and female function as *archai* and the physical and metaphysical considerations that derive from this basic thesis. Aristotle not only does not depart from this basic commitment, but the entirety of *GA* should be regarded as the working out, scientifically and philosophically, of the basic observation that male and female together are the principles of generation.[13]

As evidence that female and male are both principles of generation, Aristotle mentions that they both secrete *sperma*, generative fluid.[14] Even when, several lines later, he asserts that female and male differ with respect to their *logos*, "in that the power or faculty possessed by the one differs from that possessed by the other" (716a18), Aristotle's explanation of the differing powers concerns, once again, the differing generative functions of the female and male and only those: the power to give rise to offspring either within oneself or within another. Clarifying further his understanding of the two sexes he states, "Male and female are indeed used as epithets of the whole of the animal, [but] it is not male or female in respect of the whole of itself, but only in respect of a particular faculty and a particular part" (716a28–31). That is, male and female do not differ substantially, but differ only with respect to their separate capacities to give rise to young, and with respect to the parts of their bodies which serve this function.[15]

Essentialism need not be a source of gender problems, as many feminist critics contend. Rather, conceived along Aristotle's lines it can provide the outline of a solution to a variety of practical and theoretical difficulties relating to the two sexes. As we will see in detail, Aristotle's understanding of the four causes permits the distinctions in female and male anatomy and physiology to be acknowledged as far as they go, and allows for him to retain a way of indicating the dimensions, both physical and metaphysical, in which female and male are the same.

In *GA* I, male and female are co-principles of generation and therefore stand as the principles of the orderly unfolding of nature. Aristotle supports this initial thesis first with descriptions of the generative anatomical parts of the two sexes in a variety of species, followed by a discussion of the more controversial subject, the generative fluids. So in *GA* I. 3–16 Aristotle examines the arrangement of the testicles or seminal ducts in fishes and serpents, lizards and tortoises, birds and dolphins and man; as well as the placement of the uterus or uterus-like organs in crustacea and cephalopods, insects and octopuses. He develops ideas, regarding the variations in generative anatomy of different species of animals, which rest on nature's operating principles: what happens does so because it is necessary or because it is better. The anatomical forms serve the functions of copulation and of gestation, either because copulation and gestation must take place in a particular way for a class of animals, or because it is better that it occur that way.[16] Then, having described those anatomical parts that serve generation (that is, having shown that female and male are both principles of generation in this respect), in *GA* I. 17 Aristotle leaves behind the anatomy (or the "instru-mental parts") and begins his discussion of the generative fluids, the *spermata.* The discussion of *sperma* bears crucially on the correct under-standing of Aristotle's view of the role of female and male in generation.

III

Somewhat surprisingly, the question that first occupies Aristotle regard-ing *sperma* is, Is *sperma* drawn from the whole body? Two different theo-ries had currency in his time: Hippocratic *pangenesis,* the notion that *sperma* comes from all parts of the body and thereby provides the parts of the body for the offspring, and the "preformationist" or "homunculus" theo-ry that the *sperma* contains an animalcule or a little human already formed and waiting simply to grow.[17] Aristotle is trying to contend with these on his way to establishing his own claims about the nature of the generative fluids. He presents a variety of reasons for objecting to *pangenesis* and preforma-tion.[18] All of his reasons argue against what he regards as the real problem: the materialistic reduction and oversimplification that those two theories represent. Both theories fail to explain what principle organizes the many parts of the body. Generation, after all, produces a substantial entity, a uni-fied and coherent creature. In the case of *pangenesis* it would be absurd, of course, to suppose that the many parts of the body come together in their ordered, regular way merely by chance; nor can it be imagined that the parts actively arrange themselves. Something above and beyond the parts alone must be operative in order to explain the regular generation of animals. For Aristotle, this something is *psyche,* soul, "the first actuality of a natural body which potentially has life" (*DA* 412a27). In his view, body is aimed at soul from the very beginning. This is a principle which the materialisms, *pange-nesis* and preformationism, do not comprehend. His conclusion to the prob-lem at hand, then, is that *pangenesis* must be rejected; *sperma* is not drawn from all parts of the body but rather goes to all parts of the body. In this way, he emphasizes final causality over what he regards as ultimately unworkable mechanical explanations (725a23).[19]

Aristotle will have more arguments to offer in Book II against preforma-tionism, the view that an animalcule or homunculus is transferred from the father and planted in the mother's body, with her functions being strictly incubation and feeding.[20] His mention of it at this point (722b5), however, permits us to note that preformationism had been employed in Greek cultur-al life to deny women any role in generation, and consequently to deny them any significant connection with their children and any connection of their children with them. A stunning example of this can be found in Aeschylus's *Eumenides,* when Apollo defends Orestes' murder of his mother in this way:

> The mother of what is called her child is no parent of it, but nurse only of the young life that is sown in her. The parent is the male, and she but a stranger, a friend, who, if fate spares his plant, preserves it till it puts fourth.[21]

Aristotle's opposition to preformationism is not founded on the grounds that it demeans women's part in generation. Rather, it fails to make sense on its own terms because it cannot explain how female offspring could be produced: how could the female generative parts arise from a male body? (cf. 734a1–12). Against this historical background, Aristotle's alternative theory, by establishing the female as a principle of generation, represents an important elevation of the woman's role in generation. Furthermore, political assumptions and considerations are notably absent in Aristotle's treatment of this subject. That is, his aims at this point, in distinction from the feminist critique which itself is already directed toward the politicization of sexuality, do not include the demotion or the elevation of women and their role in the process of generation. Instead, arguments are assessed by him one by one, on theoretical grounds or on observational grounds or on both, and conclusions are drawn about the phenomenon itself.

Some of Aristotle's feminist critics have misread him on this fundamental issue, mistaking Aristotle's theory for a version of preformationism, and hence they have assigned to him the sexist consequences of that theory. The claim frequently made is that Aristotle reproduces and enlarges a model in which the female body serves only passively in generation as a source of warmth and nourishment for the growing embryo whose source is strictly the male parent.[22] But his effort in Book I of *GA*, as we have begun to see, is to reject preformationism, which these critics confuse with Aristotle's own view, and to establish the validity of his own initial thesis that male and female are both *archai* of generation.[23]

Other feminists criticize Aristotle's theory as inferior to the other of his rival theories, *pangenesis.*[24] *Pangenesis,* in Empedocles' version, holds that male and female both make contributions of the same sort,[25] and so this theory appears more acceptable by general feminist criteria. But proponents of *pangenesis* fail to take seriously Aristotle's stated objections to Empedocles' theory, namely, that the parts torn apart from each other (in the female and male parents, prior to being fitted together) would be in such an incomplete and imperfect state that they could not stay alive and healthy. On the other hand, if each separate part of the body had a vital principle of its own to maintain its life and health, then it would remain to be shown what organizes or coordinates all these separate vital principles and how they merge to form one unified organism. Aristotle's objections to Empedocles here (and explicitly later in *GA* 764al–765a4) are in keeping with the other arguments he has made against excessively materialistic theories of generation: these theories, Empedocles' included, which rely for their explanations exclusively on a thing's material constituents, simply cannot account fully for the regularity and ordered nature of generation. Thus, Aristotle's rejection of Empedocles' approach is not motivated by an unwillingness to allow the female a fuller share in generation, as these feminist critics believe. His end here is to establish a metaphysical point: the necessary inclusion of non-material explanatory principles (in this case, the soul or form of the body as organized, and the whole, unified, mature animal as the *telos* or final cause of the process, along with the action of the eternal and divine).

Returning to the progress of the discussion in *GA*, we can, in fact, make some sense of why Aristotle's discussion of the generative fluids should begin as it does, with what sounds like a subordinate and somewhat technical question about whether or not *sperma* derives from the body as a whole. This question allows him at the outset to display the current rival theories of generation and to critique them in terms of their reliance on limited materialist presuppositions. Having explained the insufficiency of these approaches and stated in a preliminary way his own alternative—that is, a generative theory which fully includes physical causal components as well as nonmaterial organizing and directing principles whose aims and mode of operation differ from material causal principles—Aristotle can pursue his examination of the working of both physical (material and moving) causes and the metaphysical (formal and final) ones, along with the ways in which these causes cohere.

We might note, then, the way in which Aristotle's discussion is shaped by rival theories against which he defines his own. His determination to establish the metaphysical dimension of generation against both the Presocratic materialists and the Hippocratic medical establishment leads to special highlighting of form over matter in Books I and II, perhaps in part to make form more readily evident to his opponents. In the treatise, the special attention to form, later to be identified as the male's contribution to generation, may seem to some modern readers to be one more instance of Aristotle's concentration on the male at the expense of the female. Read in its historical context, however, we see that the chief point of difference between Aristotle's theory and other theories concerned the concept of form, and so it naturally required fuller explication. On the other hand, another rival theory which remains within Aristotle's range of vision is Plato's, in which eternal Forms remain at some removal from material things. Aristotle wants to be sure that no mistake is made in this direction either. In his own theory, form is united with matter fundamentally to produce substantial entities. It is this very union which Aristotle is challenged to demonstrate in *GA*.

Next Aristotle examines the general nature of *sperma* and says, "Now the aim of *sperma* is to be, in its nature, the sort of stuff from which the things that take their rise in the realm of Nature are originally formed" (724a17). Analyzing the meaning of the "from which" in his definition of *sperma*, he shows that the two senses of "from which" that are relevant for generation are the matter from which and the movement from which a living creature derives. The question whether *sperma* is one or the other, or perhaps both material and moving cause, is raised and then temporarily set aside while a more precise determination of *sperma* and its derivation is pursued. Aristotle concludes that *sperma* is derived from a healthy residue, what remains from the body's useful nourishment (725a11). He then raises a crucial question:

> Does the female discharge *sperma* as the male does, which would mean that the object formed is a single mixture produced from two *spermations*; or is there no discharge of *sperma* from the female? And if there is none, then does the female contribute nothing whatever to generation, merely providing a place where generation may happen; or does it contribute something else, and if so, how and in what manner does it do so? (726a31–32)

The question reveals why Aristotle is concerned about the claim that the female discharges *sperma* as the male does. If the female's *sperma* is the same as the male's, the fetation resulting from copulation might appear to be (merely) a mixture; that is, each of the two parents would contribute the very same thing, and then somehow when they are added together a living creature comes into being. On such a view, the appearance of a new substance would depend entirely on the accumulation of a sufficient quantity of material being. According to Aristotle, however, such a "mixture" view leads to impossible results. Primarily, if the contribution to generation by the male and the female were identical, there would be nothing to prevent each from generating on its own, without the other, or for that matter for females to generate together by mixing menstrual blood, or for males to mix their fluids to produce offspring.[26] But this is manifestly not the way nature operates. Male and female, together, constitute the *archai* of generation, as Aristotle has already established. Their separate insufficiency indicates, for him, that their contributions must be of different kinds. Furthermore, Aristotle's dissatisfaction with a strictly materialist reading of generation reveals why he would be unwilling to accept a "mixture" theory of the phenomenon, a view to which he would be committed if the female fluid were the same *sperma* as the male's. Either (a) there is no organizing principle, which is inadequate; or (b) there are two organizing principles, which is one principle too many. If (a), the material mixture has no organizing principle, then there is no possible explanation for how a unified, coherent, highly complex and directed creature is formed or forms itself from the body's residual food. But if (b), the male and female *sperma* are identical and so both contain organizing principles, one is then left with the daunting task of explaining how these independent principles could unite, as they must, to create a single principle to direct the unified development of the particular creature.

Here is what Aristotle decides on the question: menstrual fluid is a residue of healthy nourishment and it is "the analogous thing" in females to the male fluid. (The generative fluids of both male and female are blood or are derived from blood.) He demonstrates the status of menstrual blood as healthy (it is not a colliquescence, he explains), as a residue (which has been distilled from the body's nourishment, as has semen), and above all as generative or *sperma*tic, that is, as playing a causative role in generation. In Aristotle's scheme, menstrual blood is not a waste product, nor is a woman's body regarded as simply a warm environment for the growth of the fetation. Despite the feminist claim that for Aristotle the female makes little, if any, genuine contribution and functions only as a container for the developing embryo, his determination that the menstrual fluid is *spermatic* is exactly what we would expect, since it is perfectly consistent with the initial thesis that male and female are both *archai* of generation.

Aristotle must now, for the reasons mentioned above, find a way of differentiating menstrual fluid from semen. Thus to his original question, Does the female discharge *sperma* as the male does? the answer must be yes and no. The female contributes *sperma* but not as the male does; she does not contribute semen. Her contribution is less fully heated or concocted than the male's semen. Misogyny does not direct Aristotle's analysis and lead to his yes and no conclusion. On the contrary, Aristotle here is rejecting the identification of generative fluid with the male semen, and establishing instead a fuller conception of *sperma* that includes both male and female contributions, contributions that do differ in kind. Each is unique; both are necessary.[27]

From the opening of the treatise this scheme is being prepared, as Aristotle reminds his readers of the basic four causes. Two of these causes, the material and the moving, are components of causality physically understood; and the other two, the formal and the final, are components of causality metaphysically understood. Having established in *GA* I, both by way of empirical scrutiny and theoretical considerations, that male and female are co-principles of generation and that they differ with respect to their contributions to generation, Aristotle begins to assign causal efficacy to the male and female parents according to his scheme of the four causes.

Aristotle makes his first assignment seem easy. The menstrual blood, the *katamenia,* being heavier and bulkier, looks like a material contribution. Aristotle could also draw upon the evidence that during gestation the developing fetus must be nourished; the female parent can generally be said to be the source of nourishment for growth, so the association with material might seem obvious on these grounds as well. So Aristotle declares that "the contribution which the female makes to generation is the matter used therein" (727b30); the *katamenia,* then, is the material cause of the offspring. There is, of course, nothing commonplace about the material the female parent provides; rather, it is specialized and highly refined for generation. Unlike ordinary material, it contains all the parts of a body, potentially (737a23). Furthermore, it is specialized for generating just the kind of animal the female parent is. Aristotle soon takes an opportunity to make his second and third assignments on his list of philosophical causes: "The male provides the 'form' as well as the 'principle of movement,'" that is, the male provides the moving and formal causes (729a10). The analogy he offers to justify associating both the moving and the formal principles with the male is the coagulation of milk when rennet is added to it. Just as the rennet initiates a reaction in the milk such that the fluid is set in motion and begins to coalesce, so the semen imparts a motion to the generative material of the female which causes it to set.

However unsatisfactory this analogy is, since animals and human beings decidedly do not begin simply by being "set" like cheese or custard—and Aristotle himself would reject any materialistic explanation of substantial generation by means of chemical or other strictly physical reaction—the analogy is illuminating in at least one way. After having assigned the first sort of physical principle, the matter, to the female, Aristotle looks to assign the second kind of physical principle, the moving cause, to the male. This he will do (with a good deal of the explanation of how still to come in Book II), thereby providing full *physical* accountability, via female and male, for the generation of the offspring. But the physical dimension, while distinguishable, is not separable from the metaphysical one, as Aristotle's example about the rennet setting the milk shows. When the rennet and milk react, setting up a motion in the milk, the motion is not arbitrary, but is already ordered; it is motion toward the form. It might better be said that the motion *is* the forming. (Additionally, we can observe that the fully actualized form functions as that for the sake of which, that is, as the final cause.) With this analogy of rennet and milk which he calls upon several times in *GA* (739b21–34, and at 772a22–25, where he notes the disanalogy), Aristotle indicates the linkage between physical and metaphysical levels of explanation, and why it is in his system that the moving and material causes of the physical level are especially bound to the metaphysical. Living motion is always directed, always ordered, and its order and direction can be properly understood only in terms of form and *telos*.[28]

In elaborating his ideas about semen and its causal powers, Aristotle moves as far as possible away from the materialisms of *pangenesis* and preformation. His idea is that the semen does not contribute in any way to generation by its material (729b1–22), but rather produces a specific effect by way of "some disposition, and some principle of movement" (726b21). Aristotle is emphatic that the male's contribution is nonmaterial; instead, he says, the semen is a tool which Nature uses to impart motion (730b19).

Aristotle certainly makes his point against the materialist philosophers and physicians by regarding semen in this way. He also furthers his own philosophical mapping of generation by way of the four causes; in terms of physical causality, he now has the two necessary components, matter and motion, which together in his scheme are adequate to provide a physical explanation of the phenomenon of generation. But he has yet to explain how the semen, a material fluid, could convey form or soul.[29] This is a philosophical problem, to which Aristotle develops a startling answer in Book II. But in Book II, the linkage of moving cause with the male, and material cause with the female, as it is developed in terms of act and potency, has furnished further evidence in the sexism case, and this also needs to be examined.

IV

Aristotle's move from the level of physical causality to that of metaphysical causality is apparent immediately at the start of *GA* II. If we were to express the central question of Book I as, How does generation occur? and see Aristotle's answer to be that generation occurs through the archai, male and female, then his metaphysical deepening of that initial question is presented at the beginning of Book II: How are these *archai* themselves generated? Aristotle takes note of the route of physical explanation available for answering the question about the source of the sources, but he postpones that exploration (until Book IV) and instead offers a commentary on how the two *archai* arise: not out of the forces of necessity but because of "what is better (*to beltion*)," that is, on account of the final cause (the cause 'for the sake of which,' 731b23). Aristotle declares that, viewed in this metaphysical way, the determining principle of generation has its source in the upper cosmos. He seems to realize that his readers might wonder about such a statement, and he explains that there are some things which are eternal and divine, other things that admit both of being and non-being. The things that are eternal and divine reside in the upper cosmos and they act "as a cause which produces that which is better in the things that admit of it" (731b26–27). As he explains in the *Metaphysics*, the final cause "causes motion as being an object of love" (1072b4). Living creatures like ourselves, who come into being and pass away, are acted upon by the divine and the beautiful to the extent that we are capable of being affected. The divine and beautiful give rise in us (by means of final causality) to that which it is better to have or be: it is better to be ensouled than to be only a body; it is better to be than not to be; it is better to be alive than dead. This is the metaphysical "why" of the generation of animals: generation occurs for the sake of actualizing a good. The good is not actualized absolutely in this way, since it is impossible for individual creatures to exist eternally; but it is accomplished specifically, Aristotle says, that is, by way of the eternal perpetuation of the species.[30] Thus, male and female as such serve generation, and generation serves the end of actualizing the good (eternal, beautiful, divine being).

In his thoroughness Aristotle wishes to give not only the metaphysical explanation for the existence of male and female but to explain as well the fact that these two principles for the most part are separate in the animal world. He states that because that which possesses the form is better and more divine than that which possesses the matter, "it is better also that the superior one should be separate from the inferior one" (732a5). In this instance, as in some other in *GA*, we have evidence of the infusion of Aristotle's commonplace views into his more careful philosophical thinking. There is, after all, no reason he has given to hold that those whose generative fluid transmits form are superior as a kind or class to those whose generative fluid transmits matter. It is true, of course, that within Aristotle's metaphysics form has pre-eminence over matter, but neither Aristotle nor his reader is entitled, on the basis of what has been established so far in *GA*, to conclude that this pre-eminence accrues to male creatures *qua* male.

Recall from Book I that organisms are male or female not as a whole but only with respect to their generative roles; he establishes further that both male and female are fully members of the same species, one implication of which is that both male and female individuals possess the same "substantial formula" of matter and form (see 730b34–5, for example; and *Metaphysics* X. 9). There is no philosophical justification, then, for his remark about the superiority of the male.

Aristotle's attention returns to *sperma*. It is "no small puzzle," he states, to determine how any animal is formed out of the *sperma*. He analyzes the process of forming into three components: (a) out of something, (b) by something, and (c) into something. The "out of something" is the "material out of which," supplied by the mother.[31] But the question Aristotle says he is interested in pursuing at this point is not, Out of what? but, By what? This "by what" is analyzed as something either external or internal to the fetation. He acknowledges that he is confronted with a problem: it is hard to see how something external could be in a position to act to form the fetation, for what is in close enough contact with it to form it? On the other hand, if there is something in the fetation from the start that forms it, Aristotle is then dangerously close to the *pangenesis* and preformation theories which hold that the miniaturized creature or the parts of the creature are already in the generative fluid. Aristotle opts for a more subtle dichotomy than internal-external, and switches to the concepts of "actual" and "potential" to solve the dilemma.[32] The "something" by which the fetation is formed is declared to be soul; this must be so since the fetus is living and growing, and all living things possess soul, the first actualization (or perfection, *entelechia*) of a living body (*DA* II.1). Aristotle takes the opportunity to repeat that none of the physical properties alone can explain the *logos* or the highly organized nature of the organism (734b32–33).[33] The *logos* derives from the parent who imparts movement. This parent is in actuality (that is, a living animal of a specific kind) what the offspring is potentially.[34] With the conjunction of material and moving causes, the newly formed organism has separate identity, and one part develops which can direct the rest of the new animal's growth. As Aristotle puts it, "Nothing generates itself, though as soon as it has been formed a thing makes itself grow" (735a14).

What are we to understand happens here? The generation of a new creature is, within Aristotle's conceptual scheme, the actualizing of a potential. The two specialized potentialities contributed by the female and male *archai* actualize in conjunction with one another. The offspring is the actualization of the union of the two potentials. His theory has been read by feminist critics and other commentators as maintaining that in the act of generation the passive, potential female matter is bestowed with life by the actualized and soul-bearing form of the male. This, however, is not Aristotle's view. Rather, the dynamic of generation which he develops in *GA* is subtle and at the same time is perfectly consistent with principles he lays down in both the *Physics* and *Metaphysics* regarding potency and act. Instead of associating the female and her contribution with passive potentiality and the male and his contribution with activating actuality, Aristotle sees both adult parents as actualities, both female and male fluids as potentialities, and the offspring resulting from their conjunction as an actuality.[35] Even though the male parent's *sperma* bears the form which, in Aristotle's system, has preeminence over matter, that pre-eminence is minimized by virtue of the potential status of both the female and male *sperma* and the actual status of the female and male parents. Thus male and female continue to be regarded by him as co-principles of generation.

Aristotle's discussion of act and potency in connection with movement in *Physics* III. 3 is illuminating in this regard. There he explains that the two potentialities, mover and moved, actualize together, and that the result is singular: "The actualizing of the two potentialities coincides" (*Physics* 202a19). In the passage in the *Physics* mover and moved together give rise to motion.[36] Correspondingly, in *GA* the conjunction of mover (male fluid) and moved (female fluid) gives rise to generation. Moreover, because in the generation of animals the moving cause is also bearing the formal and final causes (that is, the structure for and aim of the animal's development), once the conjunction of the material and moving causes occurs all four causes are really at work, and the necessary and sufficient conditions have been met for (the beginning of) the realization of the new offspring. Everything it needs is available. So, Aristotle states, "Nothing generates itself, though as soon as it has been formed it makes itself grow" (735a14); and he repeats and develops this conclusion (735a16–17) that once a creature is formed—in the coactualization of the female and male principles—it must grow. The parallel case of motion is again pertinent since, for Aristotle, nothing moves itself, just as nothing generates itself. But having been generated, being a natural creature now possessing its own internal principle of motion, it must move, or, biologically speaking, it must grow.

At the start of *GA* II.2, Aristotle returns to the topic of *sperma* and of semen in particular. One of his questions is, what becomes of the stuff of the semen after it has done its job? An explanation is required here to meet the suspicions of the partisans of *pangenesis* and preformation. That the semen cannot all be recovered after copulation is taken by them as evidence that the substance of the semen has been used up materially in the creation of the fetation. Now Aristotle can make short work of this question. He states as a general rule that the soul principle for which the semen is a vehicle is partly separable from physical matter (especially in those animals which possess a divine element) and partly inseparable from it. Here, once again, Aristotle stakes out his own position, distinct from the materialists and from Plato. The physical part of the semen, as fluid, "dissolves and evaporates." Semen has conveyed something indispensable to the fetation, but this something is the soul principle, neither an animalcule nor unassembled anatomical parts, as Aristotle's rival theorists contend. He closes these questions by reiterating his position that spermata and fetations have soul potentially but not in actuality (737a17–18). The semen is a residue, and, Aristotle says,

> The female's contribution, of course, is a residue too, just as the male's is, and contains all the parts of the body potentially, though none in actuality; and "all" includes those parts which distinguish the two sexes. Just as it sometimes happens that deformed (peperomenon) offspring are produced by deformed parents, and sometimes not, so the offspring produced by a female are sometimes female, sometimes not, but male. The reason is that the female is as it were a deformed male; and the menstrual blood is sperma, though in an impure condition; i.e. it lacks one constituent, and one only, the principle of soul. (737a22–30)

Aristotle's comment that the female is "as it were a deformed male" is no doubt the one most frequently quoted by his feminist opponents. It is on the face of it a disturbing remark. We find, however, in the immediate context of the comment, confirmation that Aristotle regards both semen and menstrual fluid as *spermatic* residues. We also have seen through the course of this discussion that in order to maintain that both are truly generative and to avoid simultaneously a materialistic theory of generation, Aristotle has had to differentiate the two fluids, and the differentiation turns on the conveyance of sentient soul by the semen. His unfortunate comment about the female as a deformed male is prompted in this passage by a specific difficulty encountered earlier: to the extent that Aristotle's theory of generation includes a material component, and to the extent that is associated exclusively with the female, he must explain how it is that the material for the formation of a male body is available in a physical female body which does not possess male anatomical parts. Recall that he rejected preformationism on just such grounds: How could the father's body supply the sex-specific body parts for female offspring? His comment here about deformity is intended to anticipate and counter an objection to his theory; his crude-sounding analogy is meant to show that females can and do produce male offspring because they do possess (potentially) the "extra" male organs. But they themselves, as females, do not manifest them and so might be said, in this way only, to be like those who are deformed or underdeveloped in that they possess parts which are of no use to them.[37] Aristotle is not in this passage offering a philosophy of woman as a deformity of nature or as an underdeveloped human but rather he is trying to solve some technical difficulties facing his theory. He overcomes them by positing an extended potentiality to this generative material of the female, potential to generate what the female herself does not exhibit.

Returning for a moment to Book I, we find that in attributing the material cause to the female, Aristotle makes the following remark: "The natural substance of the menstrual fluid is to be classed as prime matter" (730a32). Prime matter comes up for discussion in the *Metaphysics* and in the *Physics*. He explains there that "prime" means "primary in general," that is, that out of which the four elements arise, the most fundamental stuff of the cosmos, and also "primary in relation to the thing," the very first material of a particular entity (*Meta.* 1015a8–9). It has been suggested that the remark about menstrual fluid as prime matter should be interpreted as "primary in relation to the thing."[38] But considering Aristotle's comment now in connection with his celestial move in Book II where he tells of the tie between semen and the element of the stars, aether, there is reason to suppose that Aristotle has in mind both the particular and the cosmic meaning of "primary." What he posits in his remark that the menstrual fluid is prime matter, therefore, is that it serves as a highly specialized basic material out of which the new entity will arise, and also that there exists a tie between the generated creature and the most primordial stratum of the natural world. What is produced, then, in the first two books of *GA* is an "axis" that stretches from the bottom to the top edges of the universe, along which the appearance of the new creature must be understood. The primordial, pre-elemental power that inheres in prime matter expresses itself (as potentiality) in the adult female's generative material. The active, moving power that is unique to the heavens expresses itself (as potentiality) in the male generative material. Viewed on a cosmic scale, then, the generated offspring is the outcome of the meeting of a vast scale of forces as these are embodied in the *archai* of generation, the female and male.[39]

Aristotle turns his attention next to the different patterns of embryological development found among the creatures in his classificatory scale (the scale of *GA* II. 1 based on the creatures' perfection). Consideration of this topic and the others he studies later in the treatise is beyond the scope of this paper. In assessing the course of the discussion in Book II up to this point, however, it is evident that Aristotle has provided a deepened and more thorough meta-physical analysis of generation and its sources in the female and male. This is precisely what he indicates he will do in the first lines of Book II:

> I have already said that the female and male are *archai* of generation and I have also said what is their *dynamis* and the *logos* of their essence. As for the reason why one comes to be formed and is female and another male ... insofar as this occurs on account of what is better, i.e. on account of the final cause (the cause "for the sake of which"), the principle is derived from the upper cosmos (*anothen echei tên archên*). (73lb18–24)[40]

In these lines Aristotle offers the thesis developed in the discussion that follows: the principles of generation, the female and male *archai,* are them-selves generated according to the direction of the better, that is, final causal-ity as it affects nature as a whole. This direction has its ties to the upper cosmos, he says, the system of concentric spheres whose movement is con-tinuous and eternal.[41] After explaining the working of this causality, that things are affected by the noble and eternal to the extent that they are able to be, Aristotle moves immediately to the classification of animals in the nat-ural world. Having supplied the details of the distinctions among the animal kinds in his hierarchy, he observes, "We should notice how well nature brings generation about in its several forms: they are arranged in a regular series" (733a35–bl). We are now in a position to see that Aristotle regards the female and male as the means for this orderly unfolding of nature's series according to the direction of the better. This is what it means in his system to be a principle of generation, rather than a tool or machine. The principles of generation are themselves tied to all four aspects of causality as it operates from the particular individual case to the universal. The female and male *archai* generate particular offspring, and they stand at the head of the ordering of the animal species. At the same time they themselves stand on an extended axis of cosmic causal influence, actualizing more remote potentialities.

It is evident now why Aristotle's discussion turns to potency and act in Book II (734b). It is not, as sometimes supposed, that he turns to these con-cepts because there is no other solution available to the aporia about the for-mation of the fetation by an internal or external agent. A solution is needed for this technical problem, to be sure; but by introducing potency and act Aristotle shows, first, that the process of generating offspring requires the application of the same physical and metaphysical concepts as other phe-nomena require in order to be understood. The action involved in giving rise to offspring is consistent with the way nature moves and changes always and in all respects (the potency of the *spermata* becoming actualized), and thus generation is an intelligible process. He also shows, second, that generation, understood on the full natural scale, beyond the capacities and activities of the individual parents, is itself the actualization, insofar as it is possible, of nature's ultimate aims.[42]

V

In Book I, Aristotle accomplishes his aim of demonstrating that male and female are both principles of generation. He shows there that they are both, clearly, anatomically fitted for the work of generating offspring, and he also establishes the more controversial point that both contribute generative fluids so that male and female must both be regarded as causally efficacious in generation. He studies their coeffectiveness, however, primarily at the level on which material and motive causality operates, that is, the physical level where necessity is the dominant factor. In Book II Aristotle deepens his reflections on metaphysical causality in generation in his effort to give a full reckoning of generation in terms of all four causes stated at the outset of the treatise. He does this, as we have seen, both with respect to generation of individual offspring and to generation understood as the coming into being of nature itself as an ordered whole directed by final causality.

In our examination of these sections of Books I and II we have seen Aristotle's complex philosophical elaboration of his initial thesis that female and male are both *archai* of generation. Contrary to the feminist claim, then, that in his system only the male parent effects generation, it is now clear that for Aristotle both are causally effective. In establishing his thesis, Aristotle critiques rival theories, demonstrating that among their shortcomings, they become unworkable because of the sexual imbalance upon which they are premised. Indeed, it is Aristotle's theory in which the female and her distinctive contribution is recognized and integrated. Methodologically, the necessity for a full and detailed reading of Aristotle's text has become evident; excerpted sentences or passages can neither convey the intellectual context within and against which he worked nor represent accurately the intricacies of his thinking on this subject. Above all, a close reading of the text provides us with a glimpse of a theory quite unlike the reproduction theory bequeathed by modern science: Aristotle's metaphysical science of generation ties the offspring meaningfully to the parents, and the parents and offspring together to the whole of nature.

SEXUAL INEQUALITY IN ARISTOTLE'S THEORIES OF REPRODUCTION AND INHERITANCE

Kathleen C. Cook

Much feminist criticism of Aristotle has focused primarily on two areas: (1) his views about the biological inferiority and even deformity of female animals and human beings and the relative insignificance of the role he seems to assign them in reproduction and inheritance; and (2) his claim in the *Politics* that women should be ruled by their husbands and the further claim he offers by way of justification—that while women are rational beings, their reason is *akouron* (not authoritative).[1] Moreover, these views and claims are seen to be made more pernicious because Aristotle himself is seen as the first to intellectually rationalize popular beliefs concerning the biological, moral, and intellectual inferiority of women, and his claims and arguments are seen as having had a pervasive and longlasting effect in and on the Western cultural tradition.

The accusation of intellectual rationalization is clearly articulated by DuBois: ". . . [A]lthough women had long been subordinated to men in Greek culture, Aristotle rationalizes and explains their status in terms of abstract principles" (DuBois, 1988, 184). Many writers have attributed widespread influence to Aristotle and implied blame:

> It is impossible to exaggerate the influence of Aristotle's claims that women are physically, mentally, and socially, although not sexually, inferior by nature to men. These ideas were to pervade the theological, philosophical, medical, and political writings of later ages. (Peradotto and Sullivan, 1984, 3)

Others have blamed him more straightforwardly.[2] Not only a recognition of this influence but in some cases even a willingness to call it a kind of sexism can be found in authors whose main project is in some way to "defend" Aristotle against feminist charges of sexism.[3]

Extensive feminist criticism has provoked some writers to mount a defense of Aristotle or his ideas. Johannes Morsink, for example (1979), and more recently, Daryl M. Tress (1992) have sought to deflect some of the criticism directed by feminists towards Aristotle's biology. Morsink is motivated by a desire to preserve Aristotle's honor as a scientist by defending against claims that his science is infected by "prejudice." Similarly, Tress (Tress, 1992, and this volume) seeks to view Aristotle's claims about the role of females in generation in the fuller context of his theorizing and in comparison to the competing accounts of his contemporaries and predecessors. Moreover, a debate is ongoing concerning the presence and location of sexism and sexist assumptions and motivation within Aristotle's biological writings. Parties to this debate include both feminist critics and defenders of Aristotle. The feminist critics disagree about the level(s) at which sexist assumptions come into play and whether or not such assumptions or claims render Aristotle's views or theories inconsistent.

In this paper I shall consider Aristotle's theories of reproduction and inheritance as found in his *Generation of Animals* with two goals in mind: clarifying to what extent Aristotle's premises, conclusions, and theories commit him to claims that females are inferior and defective and attempting to understand to what extent Aristole should be seen as the sources of such ideas or should be blamed for their influence on later philosophical and scientific thought. I shall also consider some methodological issues that arise in the practice of feminist historians of philosophy, and more generally, I shall consider the usefulness to the history of philosophy of praising and blaming the philosophers of the past.

I. THE THEORY OF REPRODUCTION

I shall here present various points that, loosely conceived, constitute a long argument.[4] First, Aristotle assigns unequal roles to male and female parents in the theory of reproduction found in *GA* I–II. Second, it seems difficult to sustain a reading of this material that suggests there is some way in which the contributions are equal, even in spirit. Third, there seems to be reason to think that the primary determinant of Aristotle's position concerning the unequal parental contributions to reproduction are his views about explanation—that it must be based on an account in terms of four *aitiai* or causes[5]—and his understanding of sensible substances in terms of his form–matter analysis.[6] However, while that unequal assignment is constrained in major ways by certain features of his metaphysics and his account of explanation, it would not seem to be fully *determined* by them. Fourth and moreover, beliefs about female inferiority and a tendency to link females and matter seem to be operating as further assumptions of some sort, enabling Aristotle to conclude that the male and female contributions are what he claims them to be. Fifth, the assumptions mentioned in my third point above are not simply based on popular "sexist" prejudice, but seem to have roots in an intellectual tradition formulated in the Pythagorean "Table of Opposites," evidenced in, for example, Plato's *Timaeus,* and paralleled in literary sources.[7] Sixth, although there is strong evidence for a linkage in and before Aristotle between matter and females and form and males, there would not seem to be reason to claim that Aristotle was employing "gendered" metaphysical principles if by that is meant something stronger than association or analogy. Consequently, if this analysis is correct, it will be incorrect to identify Aristotle as either the originator of these views or their initial intellectual validator. It will be true, however, that he is seen to be relying in some way on views of the inferiority of females in deriving certain of his theoretical conclusions, and it will not be possible to maintain that he arrived at these conclusions solely on the basis of philosophical or scientific considerations and "value free" premises.[8] It will, however, be equally incorrect to say that he simply appropriated common prejudices or biased opinions about female inferiority.[9]

Aristotle's theory of reproduction as found in *GA* I–II has been a common focus of feminist criticism in that it seems to assign to female parents a far less significant role in sexual animal reproduction than that assigned to male parents. In addition, some scholars have tried to defend Aristotle's account on the grounds that both male and female parents play significant and necessary roles in his theory and by stressing the ways in which that theory actually assigns a more significant role to female parents than does at least one competing theory. Furthermore, there has been some controversy concerning to what extent "sexist" claims or claims about female inferiority are being relied upon as premises in Aristotle's arguments in support of various aspects of his theory. It seems worth sorting out on precisely what grounds, if any, Aristotle's theory of reproduction is an appropriate target for feminist criticism.

There seems to be clear and relatively abundant textual support here for (1) and (2) :

(1) The form which Aristotle says is contributed to the developing animal offspring by the father, the male parent, is in his view

more important and superior to the matter which, in his theory, is contributed by the mother, the female parent (729a10–12, 730a26–27, 732a4–10, 738b20–28).

(2) The male parent is said to be the source of three of the four causes that contribute to the coming to be of the offspring: the formal, efficient or moving, and final cause or end. The female contributes only the matter (cf. above passages and 641a 21–43).

Tress has argued that Aristotle demonstrates ". . . that male and female are both principles of generation. . . . [and] he also establishes the more controversial point that both contribute generative fluids so that the male and female must both be regarded as causally efficacious in generation" (1992, 30). She further speaks of their "coeffectiveness" and on the final page states: "Contrary to the feminist claim, then, that in his system only the male parent effects generation, it is now clear that for Aristotle both are causally effective" (1994, 340–41).

I do not think that talk about "causal efficaciousness" and "coeffectiveness" and even "distinctive contribution" can in the end mean anything more than the clearly correct claim (disputed only perhaps by those writers who conflate Aristotle's view with those of people who think females are mere flowerpots or furrows in the earth) that the female parent's contribution to the offspring is necessary and unique—that is, the male does not contribute anything material and that she and only she contributes one of the four causes, the material cause. It would seem, however, that what is most striking to feminist critics of Aristotle's account of reproduction (and what is surely the case) is that Aristotle assigns to females here a role which by the lights of his own metaphysics is inferior and less significant, albeit necessary. It seems difficult to sustain the claim that the roles of the two parents are equally important or to avoid the fact that female parents are given a less significant and inferior position by the theory,[10] but we can now ask to what extent views about female inferiority are used to arrive at these conclusions.

Morsink is particularly interested in responding to Horowitz and to those parts of her paper in which he sees her suggesting that the form-matter hypothesis might be an already value-ridden premise or that it had a "sexist origin." He declares, "In the case of the form-matter hypothesis it is very important that we discover the non-sexist reasons Aristotle may have had for adopting this view" (1979, 86). It is the honor of Aristotle as a great man of science that is to be protected. "If the form-matter hypothesis which runs throughout Aristotle's biology is a value laden and a priori premise, then we must reassess our estimate of Aristotle's contribution to the life sciences" (1979, 86). An important difference between the attempts of Morsink and Tress to defend Aristotle is that Tress seeks (though I think unsuccessfully) to defend Aristotle's *conclusions*; she believes that the inequality of the assigned roles is required unless one wishes to be a materialist, which Aristotle does not. Morsink is more concerned with preserving the integrity of the argument and the theory formation through insuring that the premises that are used are not adopted for sexist or value-laden reasons. He develops a rather convincing account of how Aristotle arrives at his conclusions in a dialectical context in which the theory of *pangenesis* is seen as the other alternative.[11] This account involves explaining the importance to Aristotle of the difference in sex-organs of the two sexes and his view that different organs must indicate different jobs, as well as a discussion of Aristotle's assignment of relative temperatures to males and females and the reasons why Aristotle thought the female *katamenia,* or menstrual blood, must be the material contribution. But towards the end of this discussion Morsink notes:

> In addition to these empirical considerations, it is important to note that Aristotle, from the very beginning of the treatise, has the theory of the four causes in mind .... So he is prejudiced, but it is a scientific rather than a sexist prejudice. Given the success his theory of the four causes and the concomitant form-matter distinction has given him in other areas, his attempt to extend the application of the theory to the problem of the generation of animals is by no means misplaced. Against this background and the need to identify a material and a formal cause, the menstrual blood is more likely than not to be identified with the material cause. (1979, 99)

Like Morsink, I, too, think that Aristotle's commitment to matter-form analyses and to explanations by the four causes are important here. I believe his commitment to them puts constraints on his theory of reproduction. I differ from Morsink here in that I believe these are settled commitments on Aristotle's part that it is most unlikely that he would abandon. Since he thinks that all cases of genuine or "unqualified" coming to be or generation proceed in accordance with a certain account in which matter and form play a role (see *Phys.* 190b1–5, 10–16, and 319b4–21, 320a2–8), I do not think he should be seen as attempting "to extend the application of his theory to the problem of the generation of animals." Moreover, I suppose I am less convinced that these decisions to associate males with heat or menstrual blood with the matter are being made simply on empirical grounds. It is not so much that I am inclined to attribute sexist motivations to Aristotle here as that I am struck by the truth of the claim that the female contribution, menstrual blood in this case, "is more likely than not to be identified with the material cause." This is so, I would argue, not merely because that is an inferior contribution and sexism assigns it to the female parent, but because there was already in Aristotle's time a strong pattern of associating females with the unlimited or indefinite (through the Pythagorean Table of Opposites) and, indeed, with something like matter (in Plato's *Timaeus* 50d–51a). So, while I think that it would be unlikely that Aristotle would assign to female parents a *superior* reproductive role (equal roles not being available given the hylomorphic analysis), I also think it unlikely, given his intellectual context, that he would attribute to the female the causal factor responsible for giving structure, definition, or boundary.

The grouping together of the three causes—formal, moving, and final—on the one hand and matter alone on the other (see *PA* 415b8–12), and the relative valuations of form and matter are positions already found in Aristotle's other metaphysical and scientific writings, and so a view in which both parents were assigned equal contributions would seem to be ruled out. We need, then, to look at the assignment of matter to the female and form to the male parent. Concerning inequality in the male and female contributions to reproduction, there is inequality of significance and value between matter and form ontologically. Furthermore, the grouping together of form, moving cause, and final cause is present both in living things and, in a looser way, even in artificial production. So these two ways in which females are clearly accorded inferior positions—the form contributed by the male parent being more important than the matter contributed by the female, and the fact that the male parent is the source of three of the four causes to the female parent's one—is all in place once the female is assigned to the matter and male to the form.

However, the following may help us to see why one might think that Aristotle's views on explanation and form and matter are not totally determinative of his parental division of labor: Aristotle could have said the male semen was like matter that was poured or injected into a mold. But he did not, and if we were to ask why he did not, I think it might be fair to say that his not doing so was overdetermined. A possible answer might be that he held the "prejudice" that the male parent played a more important role, but not only popular opinion, but also some scientific theories, the material conditions of women's lives, and the intellectual background I just spoke of all point towards assigning matter to the female parent.

Sabina Lovibond has pointed out the extent to which the paired oppositions of the Pythagorean Table of Opposites reflect both binary thinking
and a grouping together of "female" with not only "bad" but also with the
unlimited or indefinite and odd (1994). While much of her discussion focuses on the apparent influence of these Pythagorean ideas on Plato, I would
like to suggest that it seems to have significant implications for how we
should view the sources of some of Aristotle's apparent assumptions about
female inferiority and the "naturalness" (in our sense, not his) of his assigning matter (which is more indefinite than the defining form) as the contribution of the female rather than the male parent. There can be, of course, no
question about the extent to which Aristotle was aware of these ideas since
he himself is the source of our information about the table (*Meta.* 986a22ff).

It would seem both that Aristotle's theory of reproduction is not simply
premised upon popular prejudice about the inferiority of females, and that
there is reason not to attribute these ideas to Aristotle as their source or initial intellectual legitimator, although these ideas are used by him. While his
metaphysical theory puts constraints on the sort of theory of reproduction
that he is able to formulate in that it precludes equal parental roles, he also
fails to associate the better position with females as opposed to males,
though perhaps it was overdetermined that Aristotle did not choose that
option. Without suggesting that we should blame Aristotle for not formulating a theory which gave females the more important role, it seems unnec-
essary to me to insist for the sake of maintaining his scientific reputation
that extra-scientific claims (whether from common opinion or earlier philosophical ideas) never entered into his theorizing.[12]

At this point someone might object that what I have said about the influence of Pythagoreanism and Plato, for example, shows that there is no neat
line in Aristotle's thought between metaphysical concepts and gender categories and that what has been said is compatible with Aristotle's working
within a gendered metaphysics. This seems to me true perhaps in some
weak sense but not in the sense that matter and female are identified, for
example. Aristotle himself stresses the mere coincidence of the two in a
passage from *Phys.* I.9 (192 a20–24).

II. The Theory of Inheritance

Here we are interested in understanding Aristotle's views concerning
the male and female contributions to inheritance and again asking the question of what role, if any, is played by views about female inferiority in the
formulation and argument for this theory. Before setting out, however, we

must note that both for some feminist critics of Aristotle and for his inter-preters more generally, the central question here is often seen to be that of the relation between this account of inheritance and the discussion of repro-duction. An inconsistency or change of position is often alleged for two rea-sons. First, the accounts of form are sometimes seen as incompatible. It is thought that the theory of inheritance in *GA* IV requires or implies that sub-stantial form is not shared by all the members of a species. Form is thus able to incorporate the inherited traits from the male parent that are not the species-common ones. It is also often thought that the conception of form operative in the theory of reproduction is just that of a species-wide essence that is either common or individual in number only. And therein is sometimes thought to lie an inconsistency.[13] Second, the views of the nature of the female contribution to the offspring are sometimes thought to be inconsistent. In the account of reproduction, the female parent is said to contribute matter only, whereas some have thought the account of inheri-tance commits Aristotle (willingly or not) to some female parental contri-bution of form or some quasi-formal component.

Gareth Matthews in his extremely suggestive paper, "Gender and Essence in Aristotle," argues for the claim that gender cannot be for Aristotle included in the essence (1986). He also points out Aristotle's embrace of what he has called the "norm-defect" theory of gender, which sees the male animal as the norm and the female as defective by contrast. I shall contend that the norm-defect theory plays an important role in enabling Aristotle to continue to maintain that the female parent contributes only matter to the offspring and that only the male parent is a moving cause and contributes form, even after he has acknowledged in *GA* IV that ani-mal offspring are able to inherit traits such as being snub-nosed from their female parents and maternal ancestors as well as from male parents and paternal ancestors.[14]

That is, if we were to set aside Aristotle's belief in the norm-defect the-ory for a moment and try to understand how he can both believe that (1) the female contributes only matter and not form or moving cause to the off-spring and (2) the offspring can inherit inessential traits from the female as well as the male parent, we run into the following problem. Let us suppose that Aristotle thinks that there is a species-common essence that is con-tributed by the male parent, that the male semen is the moving cause of the offspring, and that a number of different features of the offspring (including those associated with the genus, those associated with the species [these both included in the essence], its sexual identity [not in the essence] and such other inherited traits as shape of nose, chin, and so on) are determined through movements which it sets up in the material contributed by the female parent. Let us suppose, further, that in the material contributed by the female parent to the offspring are included a set of powers or capacities (*dunameis*) which may be activated by incorporation in cases in which the movements of the semen fail to master the matter as a result of insufficient heat (766b26–34, 767b22–24 and 768a2–15). These *dunameis* find their way into the female generative material, or *katamenia,* through there being present in the blood of all blooded animals (including male and female parents) a set of potential movements which can be actualized by the soul as nature (which is the internal principle of movement) or the moving cause. This set of potential movements is for the transmission of inherited characteristics to the various parts of the body. This happens not only as those parts are initially formed in the embryonic stage, but as they grow in the embryo and in the complete animal after birth, and are maintained, nourished, and sometimes even replaced throughout the life of the organism.

It is the soul of the organism working through its heart that makes this transference possible, but it is by virtue of these *dunameis* in the blood that it is able to resemble its parents to the extent that it does. Both the male semen and the female *katamenia* are concocted residues of blood with such powers, but the more concocted male semen also contains, according to Aristotle, *dunameis* which will convey the genus-common and species-common essential features.[15] So there are present in the *katamenia* potentially or in potentiality (*dunamei*) a set of movements for conveying to the offspring a variety of inessential traits including sexual identity, nose shape, etc. But just as in adults of either sex such capacities in the blood need a source of motion coming from the heart to activate them,[16] so, also, in the developing embryo such powers must be activated by being incorporated into the motion of the semen contributed by the male parent.

However, in the embryo, this activation of the *dunameis* from the female parent's contribution occurs only in those cases in which the parallel set of motions actually present in the male semen does not prevail or fails to master the matter. (This can happen in a variety of partial ways: I can as a female have my mother's nose and my father's chin, for example.) So it turns out that what seem to be similar traits or, in fact, the very same trait (a snub-nose, say) can be conveyed to the offspring by two rather different mechanisms and, moreover, that the cases in which the movements in the male semen fail to prevail over or master the matter contributed by the female are described by Aristotle as cases in which they change into their opposite. It is here that the notion of the female as not only the opposite of the male, but also as defective or lacking becomes important (cf. 765b8–9,

766a30–36, 766b8–18, and 775a14–15). I think that all the traits that are inherited from the female on this model are seen by Aristotle from a metaphysical standpoint as the absence, or privation, of the male traits—including not only the trait of being female itself, but also, e.g., the mother's nose shape (cf. 767b22–24, 768a2–15). Now, this may seem easier to make sense of in the case of being female (however outraged we may be by Aristotle's embrace of this doctrine), but how are we to make sense of the fact that the shape of my (alas!) snub-nose inherited from my mother is to be described as the absence of the shape of my father's Jimmy Stewart nose? My suggestion is this: that Aristotle thinks that this is all analogous to what we (playing Aristotle) might say in the case of a sculptor who has in mind to form the arms of his statue in a certain way. Insofar as he starts out with a particular shape of arm in his mind but fails to impose it because he, as moving cause, is not able to fully or in this way fully prevail over the matter, the product with regard to this feature—the arm—is characterized by the absence of his idea: his idea fails to be imposed, but it does have an arm, and an arm of a certain sort. But which sort it is is a result of the features (in this case *dunameis*) already present in the matter—features which would have never come to the fore in a case of fully successful mastering.[17]

In addition to criticizing Aristotle for sexist inconsistency, feminists have also criticized Aristotle here for his account of the female animal as defective, for what Matthews has called the norm-defect view. While this view is often somewhat neglected in scholarly interpretations of the theory of inheritance (Matthews being, of course, an obvious exception), I believe that without it Aristotle's account would be at best plagued by unresolved tensions. It is the fact that Aristotle sees not just being female but considers the hereditary contribution of the female parent to the offspring as being not just the opposite of the male contribution, but defective (and characterizable as the absence or lack of it) that enables him to avoid a kind of equality of contribution that his form-matter account makes it difficult to consistently sustain. So rather than sexism driving Aristotle's inconsistency here, a view about females as defective seems to be playing a role in helping him avoid inconsistency.[18]

In what way(s), if any, is Aristotle's biological theory sexist?[19] We begin by noting that among feminist criticisms of Aristotle's biology we find a number of different complaints, including: (1) that the conclusions incorporated into his theories of reproduction and inheritance, for example, claim that females are inferior and defective, (2) that Aristotle is alleged to be responsible for originating or rationalizing such claims, (3) that his philosophical or scientific method is undermined by his reliance on assumptions about the inferiority and defectiveness of the female, and (4) that his theories of reproduction and inheritance are inconsistent and that this inconsistency is a product of Aristotle's ingrained sexism.

A number of these issues have been considered in my discussion so far. Roughly, I have found (1) to be true, and while being unsympathetic to the spirit of (3), I nevertheless have identified two places in which Aristotle's argument seems best understood as partially explained by assumptions that females are inferior, defective, or both. I have argued against the claims made by (2) and (4). However, as I noted at the start of our discussion, Aristotle is also frequently blamed as a central and powerful influence on the biological, intellectual, and moral conceptions of women and female animals more generally. I shall momentarily turn to the issue of Aristotle's influence and to the justifiabilty and value of praising or blaming philosophers of the past for such historical influence. First, however, I need to explore further some methodological issues raised by criticisms (3) and (4) and my responses to them.

III. CONSISTENCY, CHARITY, AND METHOD IN THE HISTORY OF PHILOSOPHY

Claims that the theories or arguments of past philosophers are flawed or even totally undermined by their incorporation of views about female inferiority have been somewhat common in feminist philosophical criticism of canonical figures.[20] Inspired by writers such as Skinner and Macpherson,[21] I would like to suggest that it may make more sense to assume that there is not a simple or, at any rate, obvious inconsistency. I believe there is some way of understanding what they intend to be saying by which their claims do not appear inconsistent, some way in which, for example, one or more of their claims (written or spoken) mean something different from what they are being read by us as saying. They may mean something different from what they would mean if we wrote or spoke them, but they could, nevertheless, be understood as consistent by their contemporary audiences.

If we return to Aristotle with these sorts of suggestions in mind, we notice that both some feminist critics and a number of other interpreters have tended to find a surface inconsistency—even if they struggle to interpret it away—in Aristotle's views concerning the equality or inequality of the male and female contributions. Aristotle clearly says that the offspring can inherit traits from both male and female parents as well as more distant relatives, but I think we may be too ready to assume that these contributions must be equal or similar. It is clear if we take Aristotle at his word that he sees the contributions to inheritance as being unequal and dissimilar, but taking him at his word in this instance involves, in turn, taking seriously his view that the production of offspring resembling the male parent is most natural and perfect and that females are defective. Aristotle would presumably take it as a given that the contributions are different and he does not seem to regard the chances for hereditary success of male and female parents to be equal so it is unclear why we should think that *from his perspective* (as opposed to ours) there would be a presumption of either equality of contributions or similarity of the mechanisms of transmission of inherited traits by male and female parents.[22]

These questions about consistency and interpretation are closely related to another question that we need to consider; namely, how should we decide which premises or assumptions we take to be operative in the arguments of philosophers like Aristotle in cases in which the premises are not explicitly stated or the conclusion cannot be derived from those assumptions that are stated or known to be accepted on the basis of independent evidence? Some distinctions drawn by Michael Frede in the methodological introduction to his collected papers (1987) may help to highlight some important issues at this point.

Frede distinguishes between studying ancient philosophy as part of the history of philosophy or as part of some other history. He describes a methodological procedure for studying the history of philosophy in which we first try to construct an interpretation of the past philosophers' views which we ourselves would consider reasonable, not just in its reasoning, but also in its premises. Only when we cannot do that do we retreat to trying to find an interpretation that the past thinker would himself find reasonable but that we would not—one based, for example, on reasoning or premises which we would reject but which given the historical context would seem true to the philosopher of the past. Only if and when that fails would we rely on nonphilosophical reasons (e.g., he was afraid of women, or he wanted to please the king). Frede himself is very sensitive to the fact that the procedure just described will not on its own yield a true understanding of the thought of past philosophers. He thinks this is true partly because even in cases in which these philosophers have what they take to be good reasons for their views, there may also be nonphilosophical reasons (e.g., moral concerns, social conditions, facts about the history of religion) affecting the formation of their views:

> To consider the philosophical thoughts of ancient philosophers only as such, will provide one with a very partial understanding of ancient

philosophy. The history of philosophy goes further than this. But it, too, does not provide us with more than an abstract, general understanding of ancient philosophy. To understand it as much as possible, in its concrete, complex detail, one has also to look at all the other histories to which it is tied by an intricate web of causal connections which run both ways. (xix)

I am in agreement with almost all of what Frede says about the different histories that we need to attend to in order to study ancient philosophy well and the sort of philosophical–reason–respecting methods we need to put at the center of our practice as historians of philosophy.[23] However, leaving aside whether we would want to fully embrace the methodology for approaching the history of philosophy that Frede describes, I think we could agree that something like this order of business would seem right to many who are practitioners of the history of philosophy, and it is there that I would like to suggest an important tension arises concerning feminism and the practice of the history of philosophy. While feminist historians of philosophy seeking to interpret the work of a figure like Aristotle might be willing to attempt to restrict the use of nonphilosophical reasons in their interpretations, and in that way differ from feminists who are not trying to construct a history of philosophy, they may sometimes be uncomfortable in giving priority to interpretations that would either produce an argument reasonable to us or one that we think might be reasonable to Aristotle, for example. By doing that, we might eliminate that part of the philosophy of the past figure that as feminists studying the history of philosophy we feel a particular duty to reveal—for example, his views about female inferiority. We are interested in whether Aristotle held such views and in trying to understand their role in his theorizing. Therefore, when there are interpretive decisions to be made, it will not be enough to say we should follow some generally agreed upon principles of philosophical charity, historical or otherwise. This is because it is just such a principle (the one according to which the most charitable interpretation is one we would find reasonable ourselves), that will leave the feminist historian of philosophy uneasy in a range of cases in which questions of female inferiority and sexual inequality are at issue. Cynthia Freeland has observed that ". . . feminist readings of historical texts should attend to paradox, contradiction, and what has been repressed."[24] While not all feminist historians of philosophy will see their practice in exactly this way, they surely see it as part of their project to refuse to read away contradictions and inconsistencies or to repress sexist assumptions, and they will not be able to fully embrace a methodology that requires these things in the service of an ideal of philosophical charity.[25]

Interestingly, Frede's own ideas about the other sorts of histories we need to attend to in order to understand ancient philosophy (e.g., social history) provide us with the tools we may need to be able to think about how to approach the history of philosophy as feminists. Different feminists who are historians of philosophy will make different decisions about just how to proceed—at which point, for example, to bring in one of the other histories. Moreover, even those who choose not to use this model will, I think, be able to identify their own methodological commitments (and those of others) more clearly by attending to the distinctions Frede draws.

In the end, Frede's position is that to gain a full and robust understanding of ancient philosophy, one cannot simply approach the subject as a philosopher or even as a historian of philosophy. How does this bear on the issues we have been considering here? First, I think it may help put into perspective the various interpretations of feminist writers who are not philosophers, feminist philosophers, feminist historians of philosophy, historians of philosophy, and others. It may be that some who have written about Aristotle's theories of reproduction and inheritance are happy to explain Aristotle's views about female inferiority and defectiveness or his "inconsistency" and the motivation for it by appealing to explanations that are not philosophical or even drawn from the history of philosophy. Others trying to follow the general sort of history-of-philosophy methodology described by Frede (or some close approximation of it) produce philosophical explanations or explanations from the history of philosophy which, as a result of their charitable principles of interpretation, minimize or even ignore what look to some feminist readers like sexist aspects of the philosopher's thought. Such historians of philosophy may then be accused, often unjustifiably, of being sexist apologists for the philosopher of the past. Frede's distinctions help us to see clearly that it is the methodology being employed in such cases which we might want to question, rather than the motives of its practioners.

On a more personal note, when I began this project I thought a good interpretation of these theories in *GA* would end up acknowledging that Aristotle's conclusions and, in some cases, some of the assumptions in the theories, judged females as inferior and defective. While I had no desire to defend Aristotle, it seemed we should try to figure out what Monty Furth called in one of his section headings "the underlying and interesting source of the sexism" (1988, 132). My hunch was that it should be possible to locate discrete sections of the argument in which assumptions about inferiority and deficiency were playing a role. I thought I had given a correct diagnosis of where the assumptions came into play, and then I began to worry. What did I mean by saying that Aristotle was relying on those assumptions? Did I want to say they were functioning as premises for him? Was I sure he had no other philosophical or scientific reason to hold them? Why not say he believed females were inferior because they had less heat? This did not seem adequate. It was so clear he had additional reasons for thinking this. I found myself focusing on overdetermination. Why should I try so hard to locate the place where the views about inferiority entered if so much of this was to be seen as socially determined? In the work of Frede just discussed and in an exemplary paper of Gareth Matthews' (1986), I see a methodological framework in which to attempt to answer some of these questions.

Matthews' paper is distinguished by the ways in which he reminds his readers that there are distinctions to be drawn between philosophical and nonphilosophical reasons and explanatory factors and his measured willingness to attempt to locate the places in which the nonphilosophical factors may be coming into play. These features of his methodology can be seen in his discussion of the norm-defect theory.

> That Aristotle should have been inclined to accept the norm-defect theory is, no doubt, overdetermined. He lived in a male chauvinist society in which a popular version of the norm-defect theory was widely accepted. He was not, by temperament, a radical or revisionistic thinker. Thus one is not at all surprised to find him giving expression to the norm-defect theory. . . . In any case it is not the sociological or psychological reasons for expecting Aristotle to opt for the norm-defect theory that I shall be interested in, but rather the philosophical and especially the metaphysical reasons (1986, 19).

Matthews believes that Aristotle's other commitments, in particular his view that animals reproduce by the transmission of *eidos,* or form, and his view that it is by paternal agency only that *eidos* is transmitted,[26] make it impossible for him to say that each feature-cluster constitutes an *eidos,* and so he turns to the notion of a natural failure to help explain "stable gender-related feature clusters" (1986, 23):

> As I have constructed Aristotle, then, his main philosophical reason for accepting the norm-defect theory of gender difference is that he needs to account for the stability of these two [male and female] feature clusters. It is not open to him to suppose these clusters are anchored in distinct *eide,*[forms, species] given his views on generation. His only option

seems to be to understand the feature cluster of one of the two sexes as a natural failure. That, as it turns out, males are supposed to be successes and females failures is, I think, better explained by psychological and physiological factors than by philosophical ones. (Matthews, 1986, 23)

IV. SEARCHING FOR SEXISM AND BLAMING THE DEAD FOR THEIR INFLUENCE

In addition to blaming Aristotle as a source or intellectual legitimizer of a variety of ideas about the inferiority of females and women, feminist critics often point to the strength, pervasiveness, and long-lasting effects of his intellectual authority in a number of areas of Western thought. I would like to suggest, first, that such claims may not be completely accurate and are at least somewhat exaggerated. More importantly, however, despite willingness among commentators to see this as a legitimate sort of criticism, it seems to me to be quite strange and morally puzzling. We might think that whatever problematic features attach to such criticisms would attach equally to praise given to past thinkers for being "feminists" ahead of their time. However, although I would argue that such claims are often peculiarly inappropriate and anachronistic and can have a distorting effect on historical work, at least we may be able to make moral sense of praising someone for the ability to transcend her social and historical context to see the truth about some matter of morality or political theory that now seems rather obvious to us but would have been totally missed by most of the praised philosopher's contemporaries (e.g., J. S. Mill's understanding of various aspects of the oppression of women). But from a moral perspective, such praise would seem to fall under the general heading of praising someone for heroic moral sensibility and, in some cases, moral activity. To blame people for failing to demonstrate such sensibility would seem to fall under the general heading of blaming them for not being a kind of moral hero or saint—something many of us think to be a mistake. It also seems that Aristotle is being blamed for consequences he had no reason to foresee, even assuming he was hoping to convert readers and listeners to his ideas. His ideas about the inferiority of females and women were hardly likely to change how women were treated or thought of in his society. Those ideas had strong intellectual antecedents and were not at odds with common opinion or the societal treatment of women. How could he foresee, for example, the use that Christianity would make of his ideas about women or the use that Spanish conquerors and colonists in the New World would make of his arguments concerning slavery?[27]

In addition to questioning the moral justification for and coherence of blaming philosophers for their historical influence, I would suggest that searches for either villains or heroes and heroines are very often a distortion of the history of philosophy, just as approaching the work of a particular past philosopher with a critical or defensive stance can cause distortion in our interpretation of his ideas, arguments, and theories.[27] As feminists, we need to understand the origins and historical development of ideas and arguments about, for example, women's nature. As historians of philosophy, we are also attempting to understand the role(s) played by these ideas and arguments in the philosophical work of earlier philosophers. I would suggest that searching too hard for villains (or heroes and heroines) among the philosophers of the past has the potential to interfere with both of these projects.

THE STOICS ON WOMEN

Elizabeth Asmis

Zeno (334–262 B.C.E.), the founder of Stoicism, wrote in his *Republic* (*Politeia*) that "women should be common to wise [men] so that any [man] has any [woman] he comes upon by chance." The Stoic Chrysippus (c. 280–c. 206 B.C.E.) agreed in his "On the Politeia."[1] This arrangement was said to result in a paternal love for all children equally and the elimination of the jealousy associated with adultery. The details point to an underlying agreement with Plato's proposal in the *Republic* that men and women are equally fit to be philosopher rulers in a state that forms a single, sexually permissive family. Zeno also demanded that men and women "wear the same clothing and that no part [of the body] be hidden" (DL VII. 33–*SVF* 1.257). Yet more shocking provisions follow. Both Zeno and Chrysippus argued that there is nothing wrong with incest, pederasty, sodomy, or eating human flesh. There is nothing wrong with a son having intercourse with his mother, or a father with his daughter, or anyone having sex with anyone at all. Sexual promiscuity is as permissible as cannibalism (*SVF* 1.249–56, 3.743–53).

Did the early Stoics, then, advocate the equality of women? The usual answer is: it appears so, but the evidence is insufficient.[2] An additional bit of evidence is the title of a work by the Stoic Cleanthes, "On [the claim] that the virtue of a man and a woman is the same," which suggests an affirmative answer (DL VII. 175). Late in antiquity, the Christian Lactantius attributes to the Stoics the view that men and women have an equal capacity for virtue, so that both men and women should philosophize.[3] This view was argued explicitly by the Roman Stoic Musonius in the first century C.E.[4]

But the apparent equality of women, along with sexual promiscuity and other affronts to convention, is usually regarded as a Cynicizing aberration of the early Stoics. Indeed, there is a remarkable overlap in the evidence. The Cynic Diogenes wrote a *Republic* in which he said that "women should be [held] in common." Diogenes did not recognize the convention of marriage, but proposed that a man should mate with any woman he has persuaded.[5]

Diogenes also assigned the same dress and occupations to men and women.[6] Another early Cynic, Antisthenes, held that "the virtue of a man and a woman is the same" (DL VI. 12.). Hipparchia joined the Cynic Crates in marriage as his equal as a Cynic philosopher (DL VI. 96–98). Notoriously, the Cynics flouted all conventions, especially sexual conventions.

There are important differences, however, between the Stoics and Cynics. Whereas the Cynics shunned theory, the Stoics constructed an elaborated ethical system as justification for their precepts. How do women fit into this system? Further, the Stoics were known from the beginning as upholders of law and order, in contrast with the anti-social Cynics and the apolitical Epicureans. According to numerous reports, Zeno and his followers were agreed that the wise man should marry, have children and engage in politics. How does Stoic political conservatism agree with Cynical challenges to tradition? It is not surprising that the most shocking of their remarks are segregated in Von Arnim's collection of Stoic fragments (Von Arnim, 1964) under the separate title "Cynica," as though they cannot be integrated with the rest of Stoic philosophy.

If the Stoics did advocate the equality of women, we may well ask, what sort of equality is this? The sources for the early Stoa focus on their equality as sex objects. Any woman is equal to any other woman or man as a sexual partner. How is this type of equality related to moral and intellectual equality between women and men? How do women figure in the very elaborate ethical trajectory mapped out by the Stoics? The usual answer is that in the Hellenistic period, only the Cynics and Epicureans admitted women to the ranks of the wise. This paper aims to obtain a clearer picture by placing the bits of evidence into the wider context of Stoic social and ethical theory. It will have a wide sweep, both in its survey of Stoic theory and in chronological range. Even though the Stoics kept revising their doctrines and shifting their emphases, there is a strong continuity in the overall structure of Stoic thought. Among the writings that will be highlighted is a rather neglected series of texts on marriage by Antipater (second or first century B.C.E.), Musonius, and Hierocles (second century C.E.).[7]

I. SOCIAL CIRCLES

The Stoics embedded the family in a social order which ultimately encompassed the entire human race. We have two sources: one is well known; the other has been overlooked. Frequently cited, Hierocles sketches an elaborate pattern of concentric circles. Cicero does so before him in his book *On Duties*, and we will start with him.

Following the Stoic Panaetius, Cicero distinguishes three main circles in his set of concentric circles: the family, political society, and the community of all humans. He subdivides the family into numerous smaller circles:

> Since it is common to the nature of animals that they have a desire (*libido*) for procreation, the first community consists of the conjugal couple (*coniugium*); the next consists of children; then there is a single household (*domus*) [in which] everything is in common. This is the starting-point of the city (*urbis*) and the seed, as it were, of the state (*rei publicae*). There follow associations of brothers, then of first and second cousins, who depart to other households, like colonies, because they can no longer be contained in the same household. There follow marriages and connections by marriage, from whom come still more relatives. This propagation and progeny is the origin of states (*civitatum*). Blood connection and benevolence binds humans in friendship. For it is important to have the same ancestral monuments, to celebrate the same rites, to have common graves. (*On Duties* I. 54)

Society begins with the couple. Humans share with other animals the desire for procreation; and this accounts for the first association, the couple (*coniugium*). Next is the association that encompasses children. Next is a single household, described as the "seed" of the state. After the single household, there are communities of siblings, then cousins. These associations consist of several households. Next, the communities widen to include links by marriage, from which arise further family connections. The extended family, held together by the sharing of ancestral rites and graves, is "the origin of states."

Cicero mentions only two stages of political development: states (*civitates*, Greek *poleis*); and nations (*gentes*, *nationes*). The former lie "within" the latter. A state is bound by common laws, contracts, roads, temples, and so on; a nation may be bound by a common language (*On Duties* I. 53 and III. 69). Finally, there is the association of all humans, united by their common humanity:

> The widest association among humans, uniting all among all, is that in which it is necessary to hold in common whatever nature has created for the common use of humans. Whatever is prescribed by laws and civic statutes must be observed in the way determined by the laws themselves, but other things must observed in such a way that, as the Greek proverb says, friends have all things in common. (*On Duties* I.51, cf. III. 69)

This widest of all communities is the universal city that includes all humans. It is called cosmopolis in our other sources. It is governed by natural law, which determines everything that has not been regulated by civil law. Cicero lists fire, water, and advice as examples of what all humans should share with each other.

Against these concentrically expanding communities, Cicero places the union of "good men" (*boni viri*). This is the most unified and "firmest" of all social unions. At this stage, men are joined in friendship by the similarity of their moral dispositions. This similarity consists in the perfection of reason, that is, the attainment of virtue. Members of this community resemble each other perfectly in their virtue. In consequence, one man is so attracted by the virtue of another as to love another as much as himself, so that in the words of Pythagoras there is a union of "one out of several."[8] This community is the crowning development of the community of all humans. Restricted to a very few individuals, it may be regarded as a kind of periphery of the entire circle.

Cicero's reference to "good men" immediately raises the question: is this a community of males only? In the Greek sources, it is called the community of the "wise" (*sophoi*). Although the grammatical gender of the adjective *sophoi* is masculine, this usage need not refer only to males; it may refer also to a group consisting of both males and females. Cicero's addition of the term *viri* ("men" as opposed to "women") to the adjective *boni* ("good") restricts the community of the good to males. Are the "wise", then, only men? Or does Cicero unnecessarily, or even unwittingly, use language that refers only to men because he personally favors men as candidates for wisdom? Does Stoic theory accommodate women among the wise?

The key to the answer lies, I suggest, in the notion of "common." This is the underlying theme that unites all communities. Each stage is a "community," (Latin *communitas*, *societas*, Greek *koinônia*), in which certain things are held in "common" (*communia*, *koina*). First, couples unite for the common goal of having children. In the second community, parents hold children in common. Next is the common household. As families extend over ever more households, family members are united by common ancestral rites and graves. In the city, laws and public spaces are in common; nations are joined by a common ethnicity or language. In the widest circle, all humans have their humanity in common. In the special community of the good, what is common is virtue. If women are capable of virtue, then both men and women will have each other's virtue in common.

We need to consider, then, whether women can grow equally with men in moral and intellectual development as they pass from one community to another. The first step is to supply an element that is missing from Cicero's circles: the center. Hierocles fills in this gap. He sets out a similar pattern of concentrically expanding communities from the family to political organizations to the community of all humankind.[9] In addition, he places the individual at the center as the first circle. Cicero omits this focal point because he deals only with communities, consisting in the successive growth of what is "common." Hierocles' theme is "appropriation" or "conciliation," *oikeiôsis*, making something "one's own," *oikeion*. This process begins with the individual human being: the mind is at the very center of the circle, and the body is the innermost circle around the mind. Hierocles' second circle is the family composed of parents, siblings, wife and children. Third is a wider family circle encompassing uncles, aunts, grandparents, cousins. Next is the circle of all family members. Then comes the local organization (*deme*), the tribe, the city, a confederation with neighbors, the nation. The largest circle, which comprizes all others, is humankind.

Hierocles' circles are demarcated somewhat differently from Cicero's, but they map the same progress. Although Hierocles jumps immediately from the individual to an already extended family, elsewhere he also recognizes the couple as the first social union. He calls the couple the "first and most elementary community (*koinônia*)." Neither can a city exist without households, he argues, nor is a household complete without marriage— it is only "half-complete". The couple is "syndyadic," to be succeeded by ever larger forms of "synagelastic" ("herding") associations, in which one person needs another. Hierocles mentions common meals and the theater as public events that foster friendship among members of the city.[10]

By placing the individual at the center, Hierocles shows that the growth of society is a continuation of the process of *oikeiôsis* that begins with the individual. Appropriation begins with an individual's affection for himself or herself. As soon as an animal is born, it so loves itself as to have an impulse to preserve itself. But "appropriation" is directed not only at oneself, but also at others. Hierocles distinguishes between two kinds of affection: "good will" (*eunoêtikê*), directed at oneself, and "cherishing" (*sterktikê*), directed at kin (*syggenikê*).[11] We are not here concerned with self-appropriation, which consists in the development of one's reasoning capacity. Self-appropriation, however, goes hand in hand with social appropriation. In social development, we not only make things our "own," but also make them "common." Hierocles' term *syggenikê* suggests that there is a recognition of ever wider groups of "kin" or family, extending as far as kinship with the whole human race (*genos*).[12] Finally, the closest type of kin is the family of the wise.

Chrysippus shows how the two types of appropriation are connected. "As soon as we are born," he states, "we are conciliated to ourselves and our parts and our own offspring."[13] We are born as reproductive creatures, even though we cannot exercise this function until later. According to Stoic psychology, the human soul has eight parts: reason, the five senses, voice, and the reproductive capacity (*SVF* 1.143). In being conciliated to our "parts," we are also conciliated to having children. Self-love, therefore, is followed by the love of offspring and then by an ever-expanding love of others. Each successive stage enfolds the previous stage. At its greatest expansion, human love extends to all human beings. At its perfection, it unites the wise in a meeting of minds.[14]

Beginning with "appropriation" of oneself, the second step is appropriation of a partner for the sake of having children. Third is the appropriation of one's children. The second and third stages are closely linked. The conjugal bond is not simply a sexual, but rather a reproductive bond. Couples unite for the sake of having children. Moreover, as Cicero argues, nature would not have bestowed this reproductive urge if it did not also instill in parents a love for their children. This love, which can be seen in other animals besides humans, makes parents tend and care for the young. From this parental love arises the love for all of humanity. Cicero explains the connection as follows:

> Just as it is manifest that we shun pain by nature, so it is clear that we are impelled by nature itself to love those to whom we have given birth. From this arises the natural, communal "appropriation" (*commendatio*) of humans among themselves, so that it is necessary that a human does not appear "alien" from another for the very reason that he (she) is human. (Cicero, *On Ends* III. 62–63)

The avoidance of pain belongs to the type of appropriation that is directed at oneself, or self-love. Altruism begins with a desire for children and the consequent love of children. By filling in successive stages of social appropriation, we move from the love of children to the love of all humankind. After appropriating a reproductive partner and children, we appropriate an ever larger circle of family members, then neighbors, fellow citizens, and finally the whole of humankind. With each succeeding stage, an individual strives to help and protect an ever larger domain of "his own" (*oikeion*). At every stage, the "other" becomes something "of one's own"; it is no longer "alien." Finally, in the community of all humans, no human is "alien" to another.

This is the most detailed genealogy of human society that we have from antiquity. It is also highly original. Although the Stoics are clearly indebted to Aristotle's construction of the city from households, their analysis is both more comprehensive and more cohesive.[15] The Stoics start the social process by joining a reproductive partner to an individual, then extend it all the way to the cosmopolis, and pack the entire progression with a dense array of intervening stages. As the ultimate state of perfection, they add the community of wise persons. This entire growth is teleological. From the beginning, the individual aims at an ever-closer as well as more extensive union with other human beings. This union has two stages. First, the individual aims at preserving an ever-larger group of humans, from the birth of children to the community of all humans. Second, as a member of the human community, an individual strives to achieve the most intimate union of all, union with another fully rational being. At this final goal, individuality is transcended by a perfect union with another.

The Stoics transformed the ordinary contrast between nature and convention by asserting that all stages of socialization are "in accordance with nature." By nature, humans are animals that differ from the rest by being rational. Among the things humans have in common with other animals is a strong impulse for procreation, together with a love for their offspring. Our common animal nature accounts for the first two stages of socialization, the married couple and the community of parents and children. There is, nonetheless, something that is unique to humans at these stages. As rational beings, humans have the impulse to reproduce rational creatures. This impulse grows naturally into a bond with all rational creatures in the cosmopolis. Ultimately, nature achieves the union of one perfectly rational being with another as another "self."

This complete progress has two main stages. First is a progression from self-love to love of all human beings. Humans are imperfectly rational in this progression. Second, there is an instantaneous change to a perfectly rational being who is "conciliated" only to other perfectly rational beings. From pure egotism we proceed to the purest altruism. In Stoic terminology, the first type of progress consists of "first things according to nature." Examples are health, physical beauty, good memory, marriage, having children, political office. The second stage is the attainment of what is "perfectly" natural, that is, perfect rationality. It includes altruistic love of others (*SVF* 3.178, 186, 188, etc.). An individual learns successively to subordinate self-interest to the interests of family, fatherland, humankind, and the rational order of the universe (Cicero, *On Ends* III. 64). The interest of the individual is not thereby abandoned. For by benefiting the whole, a person also benefits the part.[16]

We proceed from one stage to the other by performing "duties," *kathêkon-ta*. Duties are either intermediate or perfect. Intermediate duties all belong to the first stage of development. They include obligations to take care of one's health, marry, have children, honor parents, participate in politics, honor one's fatherland, help other humans. Perfect duty consists in performing all these activities "well," that is, on the basis of a virtuous disposition. A person begins by performing a duty, then learns to perform it well (*SVF* 3.494, 495, 498, 516, 517). A further distinction is that duties are with or without "special circumstances." So far, duties have been stated without qualification: they are duties "without special circumstances." "Under special circumstances" (*kata peristasin*), it may be a duty to do the opposite, such as maim oneself, not marry, and so on (*SVF* 3.496; see Inwood 1985, 202–205).

The progression of social circles forms in this way an ethical progression. A person ascends to virtue or wisdom by making it an aim to marry, have children, participate in politics, and so on. A person need not attain these aims, for circumstances may prevent their attainment. But in order to attain virtue, a human being must endeavor to attain marriage, parenthood, participation in politics, and so on, except in special circumstances. These initial aims are distinguished from the final goal, virtue, by being called "first things according to nature." They are all "indifferent," that is, neither good nor bad. Only virtue is good, and only vice is bad. "Indifferent" things, however, are not wholly without distinction. Zeno, followed by almost all Stoics, divided them into "preferred," "dispreferred," and neither. "First things in accordance with nature" are "preferred" indifferents. Whereas marriage and having children of one's own are "preferred," adultery and destroying another household are said to be "dispreferred." The latter are "contrary to nature;" yet they too are "indifferent." Adultery is not bad unless it arises from a morally bad disposition. The ultimate goal is virtue. It is reached when the intention to marry, have children, and so on, arises from a good moral disposition.[17]

Women clearly have an important role in this progression. First, they are joined in partnership with men in a series of family relationships. As human beings, they have a role in the cosmic city that consists of all humans. What is not clear is their status in particular cities or in the community of the wise. We need to ask also what is their function in the family. In general, are women viewed as morally or intellectually equal to men, or not? We do not have Stoic texts by women. Therefore, we cannot look directly at their self-image. We have many texts by men, on the other hand, that reveal a great diversity of attitudes to women. They also reveal, I think, a common theoretical structure underlying the different perspectives.

II. WOMEN

This section will focus, first, on the couple together with the family and household, then on the city, including the cosmic city. The final section will treat the ideal city, the community of the wise.

(A) THE COUPLE

The Stoics wrote on the topic of marriage throughout their history. Persaeus, a student of Zeno, wrote a book, *On Marriage,* which is not extant (*SVF* 1.435). The first extended text that we have is an excerpt from Antipater's book *On Marriage.* It is not clear whether this is Antipater of Tarsus, student of Diogenes of Babylon and head of the Stoic school after him (c. 150–130 B.C.E.), who engaged in philosophical debate with the Academic Carneades, or Antipater of Tyre in the first century B.C.E., who wrote a work *On the Cosmos* and is said to have introduced the Roman Cato to Stoicism. In any case, the document is clearly Stoic and belongs to the second or first century B.C.E. In addition, we have excerpts on marriage by Musonius (first century C.E.) and Hierocles (second century C.E.). Seneca (first century C.E.) also wrote a treatise on marriage, but only a few anecdotes are preserved.

These writings form part of a huge literary tradition. Although they are infused with Stoic doctrine, it is often difficult to disentangle commonplace sentiments from Stoic theory. It is a major aim of this section to determine how the Stoics reformulated traditional ideas on marriage. As we have seen, it is a key element of Stoic ethics that altruism begins with the desire for children. The desire for children is the foundation of marriage, and the consequent love of children is the foundation of the family and subsequently of all friendships. This view had an enormous influence on Hellenistic, Roman, and Christian ethics.

In the first union, the couple, each partner is drawn to the other for the sake of having children, not for the sake of each other. "Conciliation" is directed at the production of children; the spouses are "conciliated" to each other only insofar as they help each other reproduce. The process of conciliation continues when children are born: father and mother are now joined in the effort to raise their children. Each successive stage aims at the propagation of an ever larger circle of family members. Members are joined to each other as helpmates for the particular purpose of the association.

In the initial "dyadic" association, the spouses do not love each other as their "own." Loving a person as another self belongs to the final stage of development, the community of wise people. At the stage of the couple, what the spouses have as their "own" and in common with each other is a joint reproductive effort. Their love for each other consists in the "passion to reproduce" (*libido procreandi*) in Cicero's words. This desire for off-spring is *erôs*, but it is not just that: it is an *erôs* for procreation. The Stoics defined *erôs* in a number of ways. Understood simply as sexual passion, the Stoics held, it is indifferent—neither good nor bad.[18] The *erôs* for pro-creation is also indifferent, but it is natural and "preferred." Zeus himself experienced it when he mated with Hera to create the world (*SVF* 2.622). Lust is something else again, though it has the same name, *erôs*. When it is defined as a "desire for bodily intercourse," *erôs* is an irrational emotion, contrary to nature, and bad.[19] What makes sexual passion between man and wife natural is that it is an impulse to propagate the human race.

The young man begins his effort to raise a family by choosing a bride. Antipater's advice to the bridegroom is highly pragmatic (*SVF* 3.62, Antipater). It contains nothing about the feelings of the bride and groom for each other. Instead, Antipater urges the young man to investigate her circle of acquaintances, first the father, then the mother, then a wider circle consisting of slaves and free servants, neighbors, and any other persons who have had occasion to enter the house. Wealth, good, birth, and beauty do not matter. What matters is the moral character of both parents and whether the parents have been able to transmit it to their daughter or have failed because of "too great a love." All this is general good advice. But it also fits Stoicism, as exemplified by the narrower and larger circle of acquaintances, parental love, and the exclusive concern with moral char-acter. There is more emphasis on the father, who comes first in the list, than on the mother. Antipater describes the father as "political," judicious, just, and so on, whereas about the mother he says only that the daughter usually takes after her. This emphasis does not imply that the mother (or wife) is inferior to the male partner. But the perspective is certainly male: the hus-band-to-be scrutinizes the father in detail as a kind of model for himself.

It is a duty, Antipater contends, for a well-born, "political" young man to marry (*SVF* 3.63, Antipater). Just as a city is incomplete without women, Antipater argues, so a household is incomplete without a wife. As a citi-zen, a man has the duty to preserve the city by leaving behind offspring. As we have seen, people marry in order to reproduce. Antipater does not present this, however, as the only reason for marrying. Without marriage and children, Antipater adds, a man will miss out on the "truest and gen-uine good will."

It happens that the man who does not have experience of a married wife and children has not tasted the truest and genuine good will. For other friendships and loves resemble mixtures composed of juxtaposed items, like beans, but the [love] of husband and wife resembles homogeneous mixtures, just as wine mixes completely with water. For they alone share not only property, children who are dearest to all humans, and soul, but also bodies. In another way, too, it is reasonable to regard it as the greatest [love]. For other associations have other recourses as well. "But [a wife] must look toward one soul" [Euripides, *Medea* 247], that of the husband (for a wife who comes from a sensible mother and father agrees to this), and [she] must make this one person the goal of life and make it [her] aim to please him. Both sets of parents willingly grant that the first [shares] of good will should be bestowed by the wife to the husband, and by the husband to the wife.

Antipater offers two arguments. First, he uses the Stoic distinction between mixtures by juxtaposition, as exemplified by seeds, and through-and-through mixtures, as exemplified by wine and water.[20] Marriage belongs to the second kind; husband and wife share completely their property, children, souls, and bodies. The mingling of souls appears to be their common good will. The emphasis on the mingling of bodies is somewhat puzzling. For one might expect a mingling of souls, but only a juxtaposition of bodies. A possible explanation is that couples mingle their bodies by mingling their seed. A more radical interpretation is that each partner acquires the other's body as a part of oneself. As we shall see, Musonius also highlights the body when he says that spouses have everything in common, "even the body" (fr. 13a). By marrying, a man can overcome even the isolation of the body which, as Hierocles shows, is the initial condition of human existence.

Antipater's first argument on good will treats husband and wife as equals. The second begins with a shift of emphasis to the husband. Quoting Euripides, Antipater says that a wife must make it her aim to please her husband alone. But he concludes by assigning equal affection to the husband for the wife and to the wife for the husband. Before they are married, children love their parents above all. In marriage, as the parents consent, this affection is transferred from parents to the spouse: husband and wife must love each other first of all. In both of his arguments, therefore, Antipater shows that as far as love and good will are concerned, the spouses are equal.

In the first sentence of the quoted passage, Antipater joins conjugal love to love of children as exemplifying the "truest good will." This may seem surprising in view of the well-attested primacy of parental love in Stoic theory. There is no conflict, however, if we assume that spouses love each other in the first place as helpmates in the production of children. From this starting-point, spouses learn to care for each other. Conjugal good will grows as each partner subordinates his or her own interest to the household as a whole. Antipater shows this progression in the remainder of his passage on marriage. The husband, he says, must teach the wife to administer the household, to be pious, self-restrained, and foresighted, and in general to consider along with him "whence and how, and whether [something] will be beneficial and preserve the whole." By learning to assume these tasks, the wife makes it possible for the husband to have the leisure time to engage in discussion and politics. Husband and wife are bound to each other in good will as he helps her run the household and she helps him participate in civic affairs.

This system of mutual help sounds remarkably conventional. Aristotle proposed that the wife should serve the husband by taking care of the household while he participates in the leisure of political life. In Aristotle's view, the "male is by nature more of a leader than the female," whereas the deliberative faculty of a woman is *akyron,* "without authority" (*Pol.* 1259b1–2 and 1260a123–13). The virtues of men and women, such as temperance, courage, and justice, are not the same. Instead, those of the male are "ruling," those of the woman "serving" (*Pol.* 1260a21–24). The husband rules the household, while the wife is ruled. Before Aristotle, Xenophon expressed a similar position; he, too, assigned different virtues to husband and wife (*Oeconomicus* 7).

Just like Xenophon, Antipater would have the experienced husband train the young wife. Like Aristotle, he has the wife serve the husband so he can have time to spend outside the house. But there is a difference. Although Antipater assigns a directive role to the husband, he regards husband and wife as partners that have an equal role in supporting the household. Against those who contend that a wife is a burden, Antipater argues,

> a married wife would seem to be one of the most pleasant of burdens, and the lightest. For it is just like acquiring another hand from somewhere if one has a single hand, or obtaining another foot from elsewhere if one has a single foot. For just as he would walk much more easily where he wanted, and bring things and carry them away, so the person who brought in a wife would more easily acquire the amenities that preserve life and are useful. Instead of two eyes they use four, and instead of two hands they use a second pair, so that by using all together a person can more easily do

the work of the hands. Therefore if one pair should tire, it could be tended by the other. In general, having become two instead of one, a person would be more likely to succeed in life. (*SVF* 3.63, Antipater)

Antipater stresses the egalitarian role of the husband in the household by comparing him to one of two hands or feet. Instead of showing him rule the household, he shows him collaborating on an equal basis with the wife. Further, this partnership of equals is more than the sum of the parts. It is "much easier" to walk with two feet than with one. One foot or one hand, used by itself, can accomplish much less than a foot or hand used in a pair. By collaborating with each other, the two partners achieve a whole that procures greater benefits than two persons could achieve by working separately. By contributing to the whole, moreover, a spouse does not neglect his or her own advantage, but secures a greater advantage for himself or herself.

The Stoics used the metaphor of parts of a body all along the social ascent. Hierocles compares the individual citizen to one finger in a hand composed of five fingers.[21] The five-fingered hand stands for the city (which could hypothetically have just five citizens), just as the two-handed or two-footed body stands for the household. Likewise, each member of the cosmic city is viewed as a part, such as a hand or foot, of the whole cosmic body.[22] In all cases, the community is viewed as an organic whole. The individual subordinates private interest to the whole and thereby promotes his or her own interest.

This emphasis on cooperation does not imply intellectual equality, but neither does the directive role of the husband imply inferior intellectual capacity on the part of the wife. Did Antipater and other Stoics go on to add moral equality to the equality of helpfulness and good will? We have seen that Cleanthes at least discussed the topic of moral equality. In the preserved texts, Seneca is the first Stoic to state explicitly that men and women have an equal capacity for virtue.[23] Seneca did not elaborate, and it is easy to miss this observation among the many misogynist remarks that he makes. A little later, his compatriot Musonius defended the equality of women in detail. Using Stoic terminology, he claimed that "the conciliation for virtue naturally belongs not only to men, but also to women." Women, he argued, have precisely the same virtues as men. In consequence, both men and women must seek to be philosophers, and boys and girls must be educated in the same way.[24] This is how Plato argued in the *Republic*. Both Seneca and Musonius were practical ethical philosophers, not theorists, and they were open to influence by other philosophical schools. We must ask, therefore, whether they grafted a Platonic view on Stoic ethics or whether the earlier Stoics, too, held that women have the same capacity for virtue as men.

Musonius argued that, as human beings, women have the same virtue as men. He added this premise (fr. 4):

> If both [men and women] must become good in the virtue that befits a human being (*anthrôpos*), and be alike capable of wisdom and temperance, and share in courage and justice, the one no less than the other, will we not educate each alike and teach both equally the skill from which each would come to be a good human being?

Since women and men have the same capacity for virtue, it follows that both must be taught equally the skill of being good. There is, indeed, a difference in physical strength; and this makes a difference to the jobs they hold:

> Since in the human race, the nature of males is stronger and that of women weaker, the most suitable jobs must be assigned to each nature and heavier jobs must be given to the stronger and lighter to the weaker.

Thus, wool-working and housekeeping are more suitable to women, and gymnastics and outdoor camping to men. Nonetheless, women can do any job that men can do:

> All human jobs are equally in common and are common to men and women, and none must be assigned by necessity to one [sex]. Rather, some are more suitable to one nature, others to the other.

Because men and women differ in physical strength, some jobs are more suitable to one sex than the other. But all jobs can be done by either sex. When "strength, or need, or opportunity dictate," a job usually done by one sex will be done by the other. All jobs are "common" to all humans.

Although Musonius' position has much in common with Plato's, there is a striking difference. Although he assigns equal moral capacity to women, Musonius does not draw the consequence that women must share all jobs equally. In Plato's *Republic*, women are soldiers and rulers equally with men. Musonius thinks that the household is more suitable to women—not, of course, that they must stay in the household: women can assume the jobs usually done by men, but that is the exception. What makes some jobs more suitable than others is physical strength. Plato, too, pointed out the difference in strength. But he argued that women must share all jobs equally with men, and he added that they are on the average not as good as men. Musonius does not hint at any inferiority except in physical strength. The unequal distribution of jobs does not prevent women from attaining the virtue of a human being, which is the same for men and women.

The main difference in jobs, according to Musonius, is that a woman is usually a householder, whereas a man is usually active as a citizen. This makes no difference, however, to the virtue of each. Musonius argues that a woman needs to be just in order to be a good householder, whereas a man needs to be just in order to be a good citizen. The jobs tend to be different, but the virtue is the same. In pointed opposition to Plato, as well as Aristotle, Musonius asserts that the job of being a householder "belongs most of all to a philosopher" (fr. 3). A person does not need to be a soldier or ruler in order to be a philosopher. Musonius assigns to men the job of "fighting on behalf of women and children" (fr. 7). It is part of a citizen's duty to be a soldier, and this demands gymnastic training and outdoor camping, which are more suitable to men than to women. But a woman's courage is the same as a man's (fr. 3). Even though a woman may not have a role as a citizen, she can still be a philosopher.[25]

Musonius defended marriage vigorously. His arguments contain numerous reminiscences of Antipater. He points out that "a household or a city" does not consist of men alone (fr. 14). His claim that the wife "serves her husband with her hands" (fr. 3) recalls Antipater's hands argument, even though it also hints at a directive role on the part of the husband. Like Antipater, Musonius demands equality of service from husband and wife:

> Husband and wife must . . . consider all things in common and nothing private, not even the body itself. For great is the creation of a human being, which this bond achieves. But this is not yet sufficient for the person who marries; for this can come about also when people join without marriage, just as animals join with each other. But in marriage there must be a completely joint life and care of husband and wife for each other, in health and in sickness and at all times. Each partner goes into marriage desiring this, just as each desires to have children. (fr. 13a)

In language that has been taken over into Christian marriage vows, Musonius assigns two aims to marriage: reproduction, and the care of husband and wife for each other. Musonius agrees on this with Antipater, but he goes further. He depicts a perfect union. When the spouses have "perfect" care and concern for each other, then the association is "beautiful" (*kalê*).

Using Stoic terminology, Musonius presents the perfect state of caring as morally good. Reproduction is indeed the purpose for which man and wife marry, but the conjugal relationship is not complete until the partners, each of whom must be good (fr. 13b), are joined in a perfect sharing of concern for each other. This conforms to the Stoic distinction between "primary things of nature" and the ultimate goal of nature. In Musonius' view of marriage, the first natural aim is to have children and the ultimate goal is conjugal altruism.[26] In keeping with his recognition of a woman's capacity for virtue, he places her in the community of the good.

Hierocles charts a similar progress. He assigns two advantages to the husband: the assistance of children, and the "sympathetic good will" of the wife.[27] Procreation redounds ultimately to the benefit of the parents, for while parents help their children at first, the children reciprocate later. Hierocles illustrates the good will of the wife with many commonplace arguments. The wife cheers up the husband, for example, when he comes home weary from work. She inquires solicitously how he fared outside and imparts to him her concerns about the household inside. Hierocles crowns these commonplaces by ascending to the stage of moral perfection. Apart from the practical benefits, he points out, married life is intrinsically "beautiful" (*kalon*). The partnership of husband and wife is the ultimate "adornment" of a household, sanctified by the "gods of marriage and birth." The spouses have everything in common "as far even as their bodies and, even more, their souls." Like Antipater and Musonius, Hierocles singles out the union of bodies. At the same time, he gives preference (as indeed all the Stoics did) to the union of souls. This consists in concord. Hierocles appears to agree that while the primary purpose of marriage is procreation, the ultimate goal is a harmony of minds.

Hierocles clearly places the wife in the traditional position inside the household and the husband outside. More than that, he reiterates the Aristotelian view that a wife is ruled by her husband. A household without marriage is incomplete, he argues, for the reason that "a ruler is inconceivable without the ruled, nor is the ruled conceivable without a ruler."[28] In Hierocles' view, perfect sharing goes hand in hand with the subordination of the wife. This looks like a subversion of the view that a woman has the same capacity for virtue as a man. But it need not be. As we saw, Musonius combined a household role for the wife with a capacity for virtue and wisdom. Aristotle held that a woman is morally inferior in her role as housewife. But is this necessary? The Stoics maintained that a slave can be just as morally good as a free man. Why not, then, a woman?

We have come around in our discussion from the first union, the couple, to the final union, the community of the wise. It remains to give separate attention to the role of marriage among the wise. But before this, we need to move quickly through the family to the city. As the family expands, both husband and wife take on new duties. Joining their household to other households, they participate in a wide array of family activities, including religious rites. The city brings a whole new set of duties.

(B) THE CITY

We have already noted that both the household and the city are incomplete without women. The woman is a part of the city, just as much as she is a part of the household. What is her role in the city? If she is not a citizen, can she yet ascend to virtue?

Let us return, for a moment, to Aristotle. Like the Stoics, Aristotle began society with the pairing of man and wife, which he valued as a natural form of friendship (*philia*, see *EN* 1162a16–17). But Aristotle admitted only men to the rank of citizen and to the highest stage of human rationality. Defining a "citizen" as a person capable of holding political office and making judicial decisions (*Pol.* 1275a22–23), he excluded women from this function and confined them within the household. The friendship among citizens, he held, transcends the natural friendship between husband and wife as the more worthy choice.

A "city" was defined by the Stoics as "a multitude of human beings living in the same place, governed by law" (*SVF* 3.329). We also have a set of three definitions: "a place in which to live," "an arrangement of human beings," and the combination of these definitions (*SVF* 3.328). A variant is that it is an "arrangement of humans who live in a place together with citizens" (*SVF* 2.528). The last definition implies a distinction between inhabitants and citizens. This agrees with the conventional distinction between citizens and other inhabitants, such as slaves and foreigners, although it does not tell us anything specifically about women.

The largest city is the cosmic city that comprises all humans. In this community, humans are joined by gods, who rule over them as subordinates. The gods are perfectly rational, whereas humans are imperfectly rational. Humans are included in the cosmic city in the same way as children are included along with men in a particular city: children are "citizens by nature," even though they are without understanding and do not perform the duties of a citizen (*SVF* 3.334). This distinction suggests that, as members of the cosmic city, all humans are citizens "by nature," capable of attaining the status of citizen in the cosmic city whether or not they qualify as citizens in any particular city.

The cosmic city is governed in accordance with the universal law that applies to all rational beings (*SVF* 2.528, 3.333–33). This law is "natural": for it is the command of nature and has not been devised by humans. The particular laws devised by humans for their communities are additions to this natural law (*SVF* 3.323). While particular laws vary from one community to another, they must be in harmony with universal law. It is our duty to obey both kinds of law, while giving priority to the universal law. When there is a conflict, the proviso "except in special circumstances" sanctions disobedience to particular laws. Humans have rights as humans—that is, as rational beings, and these must be respected by particular laws. As a general rule, we must obey established laws as far as they apply, and natural universal law for the rest.

Just as each member of a city must subordinate self-interest to the interests of the whole city, so all humans must subordinate their personal interests to the those of the whole human community. This leaves much uncertainty on how to balance the interests of successive communities and, in general, how to secure the welfare of a part within the whole at each stage. The Stoics adopted widely differing solutions to this problem. It is illustrated vividly by a debate in the second century B.C.E. between Diogenes of Babylon and his pupil Antipater of Tarsus. The question was: should a seller reveal everything about his wares, including deficiencies, to the buyer? Diogenes said no: a person has the obligation to disclose only what is demanded by the laws of his country. Antipater responded that the seller must share all knowledge since he must care above all else for a fellow human being (Cicero *On Duties* III. 51–55, III. 91).

A well-known example of the relationship of positive to natural law is Seneca's injunction to treat slaves humanely (Seneca *Epistle* 47). Although there is no private property in the cosmic community, states may allocate private property (Cicero, *On Duties* I.21). Slaves are a form of private property and the Stoics did not propose to abolish it. Legal slavery, they held, is something "indifferent," neither good nor bad. At the same time, the Stoics demanded that slaves be treated as human beings in accordance with the natural law of the community of humans. Another example concerns sex. Sexual relations are categorized by the Stoics as "indifferent," Zeno shocked his audience by saying that it makes no difference what part of the body one rubs: masturbation is not good or bad. Nor does it matter whom one rubs: incest is indifferent (*SVF* 1.256). All that matter is that one perform the act with the right attitude. Yet cities have regulations concerning sex and these must be obeyed except in special circumstances. Where the laws do not specify behavior, one is free to act in accordance with

natural human law. This law would presumably permit homosexual relationships, so long as they do not inhibit procreation or any other natural
aims. It would also prohibit rape, on the ground that this is an act of vio-
lence against another person and so infringes the universal natural law to
help other humans.

Where does this leave women? In the Hellenistic period, women made
some progress in acquiring citizen rights, and there are conspicuous examples of women rulers in the royal families of Egypt and elsewhere.[29] For
the most part, though, women did not have a part in ruling cities. The Stoics
accepted the existing range of political institutions as stages on the ascent to
virtue. Although there is only one good system of government, the city of
the wise, many kinds of government serve as training grounds for virtue.
Just as the Stoics accepted slavery, they accepted the conventionally inferi-
or political status of women. Yet this does not imply that women are inferi-
or by nature. By adding the cosmopolis as a stage that enfolds all political
institutions, the Stoics indicate that women are citizens "by nature," having the potential to attain perfect rationality in the same way as men.
Despite their conventional status as political subordinates, women have the
capacity to be rulers, just as slaves—or free men—do.

From the natural status of women as citizens, the Stoics did not draw
the consequence that women must have the same political privileges as
men, any more than they were willing to manumit all slaves. Although
women and slaves are naturally citizens, their non-citizen status in any particular city is not an infringement of a natural right. The two seemingly
contradictory roles are entirely compatible, for non-citizens have the use
of reason no less than citizens in any particular city. Human beings may
exercise their reason to the full in menial tasks no less than in the job of
ruling a city. The type of task is indifferent: what matters is the moral disposition, and this does not require participation in politics for its full development.

The Stoics thought it a duty for men to be politically active, except for
special circumstances. They excused men from politics for reasons of
health, study, or simply a distaste for political affairs (Cicero *On Duties,* I.
71). Political inactivity does not prevent a man from attaining virtue.
Conversely, it is a duty for women to administer the household, but they
may participate in politics under special circumstances. They, too, are not
prevented by political inactivity from attaining virtue. We may suppose that
just as men may be excused from politics by ill health, study, or personal
distaste, so women may be excused from a household role for the same reasons. Under normal circumstances, men are naturally suited to be active

outside the household and women within the household. But there is no indication in our sources that women contribute any less to the welfare of the city by administering the household than men do by administering the city, or that women exercise their rational faculty any less.

Just as men and women are partners that contribute equally to the household, so, it appears, they have an equal role in the city. Their civic contribution is simply different. As members of the city, whose lives are regulated by the laws of the city, women perform many kinds of civic duties. Their family obligations are part of these duties. In addition, they participate in civic religious rites, in retail trade, and so on. Like men, they must obey the laws of the city. Even if they do not enact or enforce the laws, women further the welfare of the city just as much as men do by their observance of them. What matters to intellectual growth is not the making of civic laws, but obedience to the cosmic law and, secondarily, to the particular laws that are in agreement with it. This is, in a sense, a devaluation of political life as we know it from Aristotle. People who participate in politics appear as government officials, or bureaucrats, more than as leaders; they are looked upon as civil servants rather than as rulers. This fits, very roughly, the political circumstances of the Hellenistic period.

We have not yet reached the true city—the only real city. This is the good city, composed of good humans and the gods. The next section examines this city.

(C) THE WISE

We asked earlier why Cicero refers to wise humans as "good men" (*boni viri*). The question demands, first of all, a closer look at the terminology. The sources on Stoicism always speak of the wise person, *sophos* (*sapiens* in Latin) by using the masculine gender. This usage is partly a matter of grammatical convention. In Greek and Latin, the masculine gender is regularly used to refer not only to males, but also to males and females jointly. At the same time, it should be noted that the Stoics, who were not averse to linguistic innovation, did not go out of their way to make grammar fit an egalitarian view of women.[30] Cicero could have spoken simply of "the good" (*boni*) without adding the noun "men," so leaving it open whether women are included. More explicitly, he could have said "good men and good women," just as the Greek sources, too, could have referred to "wise men and wise women." The language used in our sources certainly focuses on men as candidates for wisdom.

The question is: does their candidacy exclude women? If the theory does not exclude women from wisdom, what accounts for the bias in favor of men? We may note that in the very section in the *Republic* in which Plato proposes his community of men and women philosophers, he makes a jarring reference to "womanly" pettiness (469d) and in general considers events, including the distribution of sexual rewards (468c), from the point of view of the man. Theoretical openmindedness is not safe against entrenched attitudes. Stoic ethical theory is no less radical than Plato's. But, unlike Plato, the Stoics accommodated convention within their philosophical ascent. It is not at all surprising that their conventionalism should express itself in the adoption of a male perspective. As we might expect, the perspective varies greatly among the Stoics. Antipater, Musonius, and Hierocles take into account the opportunities available to women, whereas Panaetius, Cicero, and Seneca tend to shut women out.

In favor of women, we may start by counterbalancing the use of the male gender with the Stoic definition of the city. The true city, the Stoics held, is a city of the wise (*SVF* 3.327). All other cities are not really cities. This type of distinction pervades Stoic philosophy: true virtue, true beauty, true love are not found except in wise persons. In defining a city as a "multitude of human beings (*anthrôpôn*) governed by law," the Stoics define the true city, the city of the wise, as a gathering of "human beings," regardless of gender. They are not restricting the city of the wise to men. By using the term "human beings" instead of "men," they implicitly include women. In the same way, they define the "state" (*politeia*) as "the good upbringing of human beings (*anthrôpôn*) in society" (*SVF* 3.332). Women are not excluded from being trained well—that is, from being trained to be virtuous.

It is a fundamental principle of Stoic ethics that the first natural aims of the ethical ascent, such as marriage and parenthood, remain as aims in the final stage, the attainment of virtue. What has changed suddenly (for the change to the state of virtue is instantaneous) is that it is now the goal to pursue these aims well. The goal is no longer the attainment of the "first things according to nature," but instead the manner of pursuing these aims, that is, virtue.[31] The initial aims, however, remain. Thus, the wise person has the duty to care for his health, marry, have children, and so on, in a virtuous manner, provided (as always) that there are no special circumstances that would make it preferable to have different aims, such as ill health or celibacy. Although the primary aims of nature are indifferent with respect to virtue, they remain as things that are, on the whole, preferred.

There are numerous testimonies showing that, upon becoming wise, a person does indeed have the same aims as before, even though they are now subordinated to the final goal, virtue. Among the many texts demanding marriage of the wise man, Zeno reportedly said in his *Republic* that "the wise man will marry and have children." Zeno also said that the wise man "will participate in politics unless there is an obstacle." Chrysippus concurred (DL VII.121; *SVF* 1.271). According to the Christian Jerome, Chrysippus held that the wise man must marry "in order not to offend Jupiter Gamelius and Genethlius," "Jupiter of Marriage and Birth" (*SVF* 3.727). Jerome thinks this reason ridiculous. But it agrees with the Stoic view that marriage is a natural duty, sanctioned by the divine natural law. Hierocles repeats the orthodox doctrine when he says that just as the wise man must marry except in special circumstances, so we all must do so.[32] Neither the family nor obedience to civic laws is abandoned at the stage of wisdom.[33]

What, then, do we make of Zeno's claim in the *Republic*, cited at the beginning of this paper, that wise men have "women" (or "wives," *gynaikas*) "in common"? We have seen an ascending scale of things held "in common": children, other family relations, civic institutions. The wise, too, have something in common—their virtue, or wisdom. This is what makes them love each other like themselves. As wise persons, what they share is precisely their wisdom—nothing else. In the community of the wise, therefore, men have women (wives) in common insofar as they love them for their virtue.[34]

If this is right, it is a misinterpretation to understand the sharing of women in Stoicism as sexual promiscuity. Rather, the sharing consists in altruistic love. Is there, nonetheless, sexual promiscuity? And is this the reason for this misinterpretation in our sources? To answer this question, we need to consider: are there private marriages among the wise? Here we must distinguish between Stoics and Cynics. Whereas the Cynic, reject the convention of marriage, the Stoics are firmly committed to it from the time of Zeno. Sexual relations, as we have seen, are "indifferent," while marriage is a preferred "indifferent" and adultery is "dispreferred." The wise person will observe the duties of marriage and obey the laws of his or her particular state. He or she will not commit adultery except in special circumstances. Nor will the wise person normally practice incest, or masturbate in public, or engage in the other types of anti-social behavior flaunted by the Cynics. In special circumstances, indeed, this kind of behavior may be reasonable. Take as a hypothesis, the Stoics proposed, that a wise man and his daughter are the only two persons left on earth (*SVF* 3.743). The only way in which the human race can be preserved is for the father to have sex with the daughter. Will the wise man consent? Yes, the Stoics said, he will consider it his duty to propagate the human race. This is a natural duty and the circumstances override any conventional prohibition against incest.

The distinction between "indifferent" and "good" allows the Stoics to condone as well as oppose Cynic behavior. There is nothing inherently wrong with Cynic behavior, the Stoics said; neither is it good. Cynic anti-conventionalism is "indifferent," even though it is in general "dispreferred." Neither the ordinary person nor the wise man will practice a Cynic way of life except under special circumstances. As we have seen, there is much overlap between Cynicism and Zeno's proposals in the *Republic*, but the guiding principles are entirely different. The Stoics agree with the Cynics in shifting ethical predicates away from acts to mental states, but they do not thereby recommend anti-conventional acts.[35]

Zeno, then, held both that wise men have women (*gynaikas*) in common as partners in virtue and that sexual relations make no difference with respect to virtue. It is not surprising that these two claims were conflated in our sources into the composite claim "women should be common to wise [men] so that any [man] has intercourse with any woman he comes upon by chance." The community of women among the wise is ethical, not sexual and sexual promiscuity is permitted, within limits, in such a community. As partners in virtue, the women are wise just like the men. Both men and women have each other in common insofar as they share in virtue, regardless of whether they are married to each other. A wise man will have all wise women in common, even though he also aims to be married to a woman who may or may not be wise. It is misleading, therefore, to translate *gynaikas* as "wives": wise men have wives or women in common only insofar as all are wise. Nor does it follow from the community of women among the wise that men and women have sex freely with each other. Rather, wisdom is compatible with sexual permissiveness. Instead of showing that wise men are exempt from the institution of marriage, Zeno's claim that "wise men have women in common" shows that women rank among the wise.

Epictetus provides some additional support. He asks: what will wives be like in a community of the wise? They will themselves be wise (*Diatribes* 3.22.68). At the same time, Epictetus takes issue with the claim that marriage is not a hindrance to doing philosophy. Leaving aside the Stoic wise person, he argues that the Cynic philosopher will not take a wife in this imperfect world, for it is too much of a distraction from the divinely-appointed job of being messenger of God (*Diatribes* 3.22.67–82). This does not undermine Stoic doctrine: the Cynic philosopher occupies a special position as a delegate of god in this world. Confronted by the example of Crates' marriage with Hipparchia, Epictetus allows that the Cynic philosopher may marry "under special circumstances." This is a reversal of what the Stoic wise person must do. Presumably, the Cynic philosopher will marry in the event that the wife will be a help rather than a distraction in his duty as god's delegate. The Stoic wise person will marry to fulfill the duty of propagating the human race.

It has often been suggested that the Stoic wise person has different obligations as a member of existing society and as a member of the utopia that consists of wise persons only. This distinction has led to the view that the wise man engages in two different kinds of behavior: in existing circumstances, he does marry, have children, and so on; in the ideal society, he does not. This bifurcation contradicts, it seems to me, the Stoic's unitary mapping of the ascent to virtue. No matter how far humans have progressed on the road to virtue, the wise person will always live as a member of the larger human community, which necessarily includes the wicked. The community of the wise is necessarily a part of the cosmopolis that includes all humans. Wise persons may be distinguished from others as forming a special community; but they live necessarily in an imperfect society, for no human being is born virtuous. There cannot be two standards of behavior: the wise person must adjust his or her behavior to both kinds of society. There is no incompatibility. Thus, the wise person will normally have a married partner, who may be wise or not. He or she will exercise wisdom by having children with the spouse and joining in perfect friendship with other wise persons, whether this includes the spouse or not.[36]

The social ascent starts with the *erôs* for procreation. How does *erôs* fit into the community of the wise? As we saw earlier, there is an irrational type of *erôs*, defined as the desire for bodily intercourse and this certainly does not fit in. But this is not true *erôs*. True *erôs*, the Stoics held, is "an attempt at making friends because of the beauty that appears [in the beloved]" (DL VII. 130). This beauty is moral beauty for it is the only real kind of beauty. The Stoics similarly redefined *hôra,* normally understood as youthful good looks, as "the flower of virtue" (DL VII. 130). A person shows an aptitude for moral beauty through the outward appearance and the wise person is attracted by this beauty. A wise person has all the virtues, including "erotic virtue." This virtue, which is joined, among others, by "sympotic" virtue (that of "drinking with" others or having a party), was a matter of mirth to some of the Stoics' opponents (*SVF* 3.79–80, Diogenes). The Stoics were entirely serious about it. They defined it as "knowledge of hunting after young [persons] of natural aptitude, turning [them] to virtue" or, in general "the knowledge of loving (*eran*) well" (*SVF* 3.717, 721–22). The wise person is necessarily "erotic"; for he or she loves the capacity of the young for virtue. This *erôs* is a "holy" love (Cicero *On Ends* III.68).

The ordinary person is "erotic" only in the sense of being an "erotomaniac," someone who is "mad" with sexual desire (*SVF* 3.717).

Along with saying that the wise person will marry, Zeno said in his *Republic*, "the wise [person] (*sophon*) will fall in love (*erasthêseshai*) with young [people] who show through their appearance (*eidous*) a natural aptitude for virtue."[37] Zeno called *erôs* "the God of friendship and freedom" and said it produces only concord. In his *Republic*, he said that it helps save the city (*SVF* 1.263). Zeno's statement about the wise person raises two questions: do the "young" include both males and females and can the "wise person" be female? We have by now answered the second question in the affirmative. This implies that the answer to the first question is also "yes." One of our sources says indeed that *erôs* is the hunt after a "young boy" (*meirakiou*) (*SVF* 3.719). But this wording simply reflects the usual preoccupation with males.

As an educational zeal for the moral education of the young, *erôs* corresponds to the reproductive zeal for young offspring. True *erôs* transcends this reproductive impulse in the community of the wise. The wise still have reproductive *erôs*, but what matters is that they pursue reproduction in a good way. As truly erotic persons, they intend to reproduce not just humans, but human rationality. Whether they have sex with the young people that they educate does not matter. They may, so long as civic laws, together with natural law, do not prohibit it. Strictly speaking, the community of the wise excludes the young who are still being trained to be wise. Wise persons replenish their own community by going outside it to educate those who show promise, whether male or female. *Erôs* saves cities by educating the young persons who live in them, but above all it saves the wise city—the true city—by perpetuating the wisdom of its members.

PART II

REASON AND EMOTION: ARISTOTELIAN SYNTHESIS

ARISTOTELIAN RESOURCES
FOR FEMINIST THINKING

Deborah Achtenberg

INTRODUCTION

Around the early 1980s, two women wrote important books on how psychological theory privileges typical male developmental patterns over typical female ones thus making normal male patterns the model for health and, as a result, seeing normal female patterns as examples of developmental lag. In *The Reproduction of Mothering*, Nancy Chodorow takes on Freud and his discussion of oedipal-stage development (1978). In *In a Different Voice*, Carol Gilligan discusses the stages of healthy development outlined by Lawrence Kohlberg (1982). The books are similar in certain ways, yet vastly different in others. They are similar in noting that both Freud, in Vienna, and Kohlberg, in Cambridge, take as central to psychological health dispassionateness and separateness from others. In the case of Kohlberg, as Gilligan points out, concern to maintain relationships and to help and please others places one at a low level of development in comparison to those who subordinate relationships to rules or to universal principles. In the case of Freud, Chodorow shows the difference between the experience of the boy, who according to Freud must separate from his mother and suppress his desire for her in order to develop, and the experience of the girl, whose development requires neither of these. Both point out that it is problematic to make dispassionateness and separateness a model for psychological health when society asks of women that they be passionate and connected to others.

The accounts differ in a dramatic way, however, and a way that has become paradigmatic for differences in feminist thought since that time: Gilligan accepts the distinction made between male and female and privileges the female over the male; Chodorow, on the other hand, discusses the social and familial construction of these gender patterns and questions whether they have been valuable either for males or for females. Gilligan's work has been followed by works such as Nel Noddings's *Caring: A Feminine Approach to Ethics and Moral Education* in which Noddings argues for an ethic of care and against an ethics of principle based on valuing and calling female emotional expressiveness, interpersonal connectedness, and concern for particulars over concern for universals (1984). Chodorow's work has been followed by works such as Olga Silverstein's *The Courage to Raise Good Men* in which she argues, from her clinical experience with men in her psychological practice, that our Freud-inspired practices of separating boys from their mothers on the supposition that doing so will increase their autonomy has often instead resulted in a flatness of emotional tone and an inability to sustain relationships (1994).

The approach taken by Gilligan and Noddings is, in my view, a kind of neo-romanticist feminism, replete with all the difficulties of neo-romanticism itself. First, rationalists both dichotomize certain terms and privilege one set of dichotomized terms over the other: reason over passion, individual over community, universal concerns over concern regarding particulars. Then romantics respond by privileging the other set: passion, community, and care for particulars. The problem with this romantic reaction is that the original dichotomies are preserved rather than rejected in it: passion, though seen as superior to reason, is still seen as separate from it; our communal drive is seen as separate from our individual drive; our concern for people close to us and our concern for humankind as a whole are seen as mutually exclusive.

Because I do not see that any of these in fact are separate, I prefer the approach taken by Chodorow and Silverstein over the approach taken by Gilligan and Noddings. Of course, it would be illicit simply to assume that opposites that figure in important ways in human development are never dichotomized. To do so would, perhaps, be another offshoot of the neo-romantic stress on organic connectedness over individualist separation that I am criticizing. I think, however, that there are arguments for the view that the terms mentioned above are not dichotomized. Regarding the connection between reason and passion, we need only look to the arguments of those who have claimed that emotion is intentional or that emotions have cognitive content as a constitutive feature—in arguments going as far back as to Husserl in the continental European tradition and Searle in the Anglo-American. According to these arguments, emotions are not brute reactions but are in part caused and constituted by how we understand the world and by the experiences we have had of it.

Regarding separation and relatedness, there is an argument for the claim that both are necessary for emotion and development. The argument is pro-led by twentieth-century object relations theorists in their discussions of the development of a healthy sense of self. In these discussions, given by Margaret Mahler, Donald Rinsley and others, normal development is seen to result from experiencing oneself both as separate from others and as con-nected to them.[1] Studies both of normal child development and of adults suffering from the personality disorders common to our age show that development suffers both when a child is prevented in his or her attempts to move away from the nurturing parent in order to experience autonomous functioning and also when a child is thwarted in his or her attempts to express love for and dependence on the nurturing parent. The denial of either of these results in characteristic inabilities to fully function in the world both for men and for women.

For feminists who accept the arguments I have just mentioned—that emotion is not separate from reason and that the ability to connect with oth-ers is not separate from the ability to separate from them—it seems to me that a certain kind of feminism is required. It is a feminism for which both reason and emotion as well as both connectedness and separateness, are seen as crucial to human development, whether female or male. For this kind of feminism, I suggest that a crucial divide in the history of thought is not between those who privilege emotion and connectedness and those who privilege reason and separateness. Instead, it is between those who think that both reason and passion and both autonomy and connectedness are important and those who privilege either reason or passion or autonomy or connectedness. When we divide things up in this way, we find sources for feminist thought in surprising places, for many thinkers who in other respects are sexist nonetheless do not dichotomize reason and passion, or separateness and connectedness.

In this essay, I will argue that Aristotle is a philosopher to whose work we may look for such resources for feminist thinking. This is, of course, in a way odd, since Aristotle is a paradigmatically sexist thinker. According to him, women are naturally inferior in the ability that is most definitively human, namely, the capacity for rational activity. Women have reason, he maintains, but it is not sovereign in them—that is, it does not govern their action. Hence, women must be ruled by their husbands (*Pol.* I. 5 1254b13–14, I. 13 1260a12–13). Still, if we look to Aristotle's discussion of male development, we find him arguing for the centrality both of reason and passion for human development and for the importance both of relatedness and separation in human flourishing. Moreover, interestingly, the central intellectual component of emotional development for Aristotle is the very capacity to recognize and be motivated by our recognition of the types of relatedness and separation that enable us to flourish and not by the types that do not. I hope, with this last point, to contribute something new to recent discussions of Aristotle and of feminism, namely, the idea of the centrality to emotional development of our ability to recognize those types of relatedness in which one thing or person is not replaced or harmed by another, but is enabled to flourish, develop, or grow.

I

The distinction between an ethics of principle and an ethics of care is made after the long dispute between deontologists, or those who believe that some acts are absolutely prohibited, and consequentialists, those who believe that when we act we ought to maximize the good for all concerned, is seen to have reached an impasse. At that point, some philosophers, some feminists among them, note that each of these types of ethics is an ethics of universal rules or principles, and they suggest that neither type is adequate since what is crucial to human flourishing is not that we follow certain universal rules when we act but, instead, that in our acts, and in our lives as a whole, we have a rich awareness of particulars and are motivated by our care for them.[2]

One difficulty, however, with making a contrast between an ethics of principle and an ethics of care is that the terms are not parallel. The first suggests what it is we ought to know and act in accord with, namely, principles. The other suggests what it is we ought to feel, namely, care for particular persons. Ethics of principle and ethics of care are answers to different questions, one to the question about what is good in the world (it is never good to do certain types of things; it is always good to maximize good), the other to the question what is good in the soul or emotional dispositions (to care). The part of ethics that has to do with what is good in our souls—that is, what emotional dispositions are good for us to have—is not an alternative to the part of ethics that has to do with what is good in the world—that is, what states of affairs are good. Instead, the two topics are complementary, and both are necessary for a complete discussion of ethics.

Of course, a proponent of an ethics of care could respond by saying that I have oversimplified her or his view by leaving out the fact that the care in an ethics of care is care for particulars. In so responding, the proponent of an ethics of care would be pointing out to me that such an ethics does not focus wholly on the feeling and leave out the world since the feeling, care, is directed towards particulars in the world. In addition, she or he might agree that those who espouse an ethics of principle are directed to the world but claim that they are directed to the wrong part of it—to universals rather than to particulars. This response would be faulty, however, since both deontologists and consequentialists are generally talking about application of rules to particulars. The difference between an ethics of principle and an ethics of care is not that one deals with the question how to relate to universals and the other with how to relate to particulars. Instead, it is that one suggests we relate to particulars by applying certain universal rules to them and the other does not.

Then, one might ask, if, when following an ethics of care, we are not relating to particular people on the basis of universal rules, on what basis are we relating to them? The answer given to this question generally is one of two sorts. Sometimes it is said that we relate to particulars on the basis of a rich awareness of them. At other times, it is said that that on the basis of which we relate to particulars cannot be spelled out ahead of time.[3] Neither of these answers is, in my view, adequate. Though it is true and important that appropriate action requires a rich awareness of particulars (and true and important as well that some who have called themselves "deontologists" or "consequentialists" have not thought enough about this), still when we decide how to act in relation to particulars, it is not enough to have a rich awareness of them. We must, instead, have an awareness of something specific about them that appropriately motivates us to act. We can know a great deal about the particulars involved in a certain state of affairs without knowing how to act in that state of affairs. One answer sometimes given to this question is that we must be aware of salient particulars or of the salience of particulars.[4] Once again, though this is true and important (especially since it points out the importance of interpretation and not mere recording of facts for a good life), it is not sufficient, since surely it is a certain kind of salience that we must be aware of in deciding how to act and we need to know what kind of salience in particular it is. In addition, though it is true that states of affairs are often, perhaps even generally, so complexly different than other states of affairs that no rule can be given ahead of time for how to act, this does not preclude the idea that there is some type of guide for how to act, even if one that cannot fully be specified ahead of time, nor does it preclude the idea that the backward glance of the philosopher ought to be able to discern what the guide was.

Another problem with the distinction made between an ethics of principle and an ethics of care is that it suggests a problematic separation between reason and emotion since an ethics of principle is understood by those who make the contrast to be an ethics according to which a certain sort of knowledge is crucial to ethics, specifically, knowledge of universals and an ethics of care is one according to which a certain type of feeling, care, is central.[5] If emotions are not separate from reason, however, but are both in part conditioned by and in part constituted by certain types of cognition, it is inappropriate to make that distinction.

Once again, then, we are pointed towards the necessity for specifying what it is we are aware of when we are aware of something about particulars that appropriately motivates us to act. If we can specify what that is, we can save the important insight made by proponents of an ethics of care, as well as by many proponents of virtue ethics, that a rich awareness of and emotional response to particulars is crucial both to good action and to an overall developed and flourishing life. Aristotle, in my view, gives us a model for how we might do that. In saying this, I do not mean to suggest that we go "back to Aristotle" but that we look to Aristotle for guidance in thinking about directions we might want to take in the future. Let us begin by considering the relation between reason and emotion in Aristotle's ethics.

For Aristotle, emotion and reason are not separate. I do not mean by this that for him emotion and reason are identical. They are not. Nor do I mean that he thinks they cannot conflict. He knows that they can. Instead, I mean two things: first, that for a person whose character is well-developed, emotion and reason are in harmony, not in conflict; second, that for him emotions are types of cognition.

1. For a person whose character is well-developed, emotion and reason are in harmony. For Aristotle, though virtue requires knowledge, knowledge is not sufficient for virtue. In fact, one of Aristotle's principal differences with Socrates is on this very point. Socrates, according to Aristotle, believes that virtue is practical wisdom or right *logos* (since he thinks virtue is knowledge), while Aristotle thinks it is the state that is with practical wisdom or right *logos* (*EN* VI. 13 1144b24–30).

What is required in addition to knowledge according to Aristotle is suitable emotional development. The reason that suitable emotional development is required in addition is that Aristotle believes, once again in contradistinction to Socrates, that there is such a thing as incontinence. That is, he believes that one can know what is best for oneself but, as a result of one's emotions, not do it. "The incontinent person," he says, "knowing that what he does is base does it due to emotion while the continent person, knowing that his desires are base, does not follow them due to *logos*" (*EN* VII. 2 1145b12–14). The incontinent person is one in whom reason and emotion conflict and in whom emotion determines what is done counter to what is best; the continent person is one in whom reason and emotion conflict and in whom reason controls emotion to such an extent that it is reason that determines what is done and the person acts for what is best.

Virtue is not mere continence, according to Aristotle, however. The best state is not one of control by reason over emotion. Instead, the best state, the state of the virtuous person, is one in which desires and reason are in harmony. The virtuous person's emotion, according to Aristotle, " ... speaks with the same voice as reason on everything" (*EN* I.13 1102b28). The virtuous person does not act well because his emotions are under the control of his reason. Instead, the virtuous person does what he wants to do. The virtuous person's desire and reason have the same object.

Thus, it should not surprise us to find that when Aristotle defines virtue as a settled disposition to choose well, he goes on to define "choice" as "deliberate desire." For Aristotle, virtue is both a settled disposition to deliberate well and to desire what one has decided upon: "choice will be deliberate desire for things that are in our power. For when as a result of deliberation we have decided, we desire in accord with our deliberation" (*EN* III. 3 1113a10–12).

Nor is it surprising that, for him, virtue is a mean not just with respect to actions but also with respect to emotions. A courageous person, for example, is not just one who tends to act in a certain way, specifically, one who tends to do what is appropriate in fearful situations, rather than being one who tends always to rush ahead in them or one always to retreat; but one who also tends to feel a certain way, specifically, who tends to feel confidence and fear when appropriate, rather than feeling fear or confidence most of the time whether it is appropriate to the situation or not. The virtuous person's emotions are in harmony with his reason.

For Aristotle, then, virtue is not a type of control by reason of emotion. It is not a kind of force against emotion. It is not a kind of suppression or repression of emotion. It is not, even, a type of channeling of emotion. Instead, for him, virtue is a harmonious relation between reason and emotion in which reason and emotion have the same aim. An indication that this is the case for him is his claim that a sign that one has acquired a virtuous disposition is that one takes pleasure in virtuous acts (*EN* II 3 1104b5–13).

2. Emotions are types of cognition. What accounts for the fact that virtue is not, for Aristotle, mere control, suppression, or channeling of emotion? Many ethical and psychological theorists diverge from him on this. Some of those who diverge believe that emotions are brute or instinctual, not shaped by our perceptions or experiences of the world, but part of our original nature. Among those who hold this view, some maintain that virtue results from channeling those emotions in a certain way. Hobbes, for example, thinks that we become just when there is an all-powerful sovereign who is a center of fear. We cease to exploit others because we know that if we do, the sovereign will retaliate.[6] For others who hold this view, virtue results from suppressing our brute or given emotions in a certain way. Freud, for example, thinks sexual drives are basic to us and that all morality derives from the oedipal stage recognition that we cannot act on, but must repress, those drives.[7]

Aristotle, to the contrary, thinks that emotions are not brute drives, but are forms of perception. Emotions, as a result, are not mere givens but are shaped by our awareness of our world. Some textual exegesis is required to see this since Aristotle's definitions of emotion do not, by themselves, make his whole view of what an emotion is clear. He does not define emotions as species of perception but as species of pleasure or pain.

Perhaps he does so because the definitions of emotion occur in works of practical philosophy. For Aristotle, practical philosophy is necessarily imprecise and for two reasons. One reason is that the subject matter of practical philosophy is imprecise or indefinite in certain ways (*EN* I. 3 1094b14–25, II. 2 1103b34–1104a10). Another reason is that in some cases in which accounts could be made more precise, such greater precision gets in the way of the goal of practical philosophy, namely, action (*EN* I. 7 1098a26–1098b4). Arguably, it is the latter type of imprecision that is operative here. For the sake of good action, one need not know the precise definition of an emotion. A precise account is one that rests on first principles (*Meta.* I. 2 982a25–26). An imprecise account is not one that is inaccurate in some way, but is instead one that is "experience-near." A more precise account spells out that on which experience rests.

In the context of making it clear that virtues are not mere emotions but, instead, stable and evaluatively directed dispositions to experience emotion, Aristotle in the *Nicomachean Ethics* defines emotions as follows: "By emotions I mean desire, anger, fear, confidence, envy, joy, friendship, hatred, longing, emulation, pity, in general the [states of the soul] that are accompanied by pleasure and pain" (II. 6 1105b21–23). In the *Rhetoric*, where Aristotle needs to point out that the understanding of emotion is important for persuasion since emotions change our decisions, he defines them as follows: "Emotions are [states of soul] due to changes in which our decisions come to differ and which are accompanied by pleasure and pain, for example, anger, pity, fear and all other such [states] and their opposites" (II. 1

1378a19–22). In another part of the *Nicomachean Ethics*, Aristotle goes even further and indicates that it is not simply that emotions are accompanied by pleasure and pain but that pleasure and pain are the genus of which emotions are the species: "For example, both fear and confidence and desire and anger and pity and in general pleasure and pain can be felt too much or too little and in either case not well" (II. 6 1106b18–21).[8]

On the other hand, as Martha Nussbaum and Hilary Putnam point out, Aristotle indicates in *De Anima* that emotions are species of perception, by saying, "getting angry, being confident, desiring, in general perceiving" (I. 1 403a5ff).[9] They make a persuasive textual argument for their claim. When Aristotle uses phrases of the form "x, y, z, and in general (*holôs*) A," they argue, what he means is that A is a genus of which x, y, and z are species.[10] Thus, in the passage from *De Anima*, Aristotle means that emotions such as anger, confidence, and desire are species of perception.[11]

We are left with a puzzle, however, since on the same textual grounds cited by Nussbaum and Putnam we must argue, based on 1106b18–21 (cited above) that emotions are, for Aristotle, species of pleasure and pain.[12] Moreover, if emotions are species of perception for him, another puzzle arises, namely, perception of what? We need some way of resolving both of these puzzles. The second is particularly difficult to resolve, since we know what sorts of beings there are for Aristotle—the sorts denoted by the categories—and it does not seem that a perception of any one of them is the same as an emotion. Surely an emotion is not a perception of certain qualities, quantities, times, places, substances, and so forth. We do not want to say that an emotion is a perception of white, for example, or of fifty feet, or of five o'clock or of Athens or of a human being. A perception of something as white is just a perception of it as white. A perception of something as fifty feet long is just that, a perception of it as fifty feet long. Neither of these perceptions is even necessarily accompanied by an emotion, much less is it a species of one.

Aristotle does provide a resolution of these puzzles. For, he defines pleasure itself as a type of perception. Moreover, he tells us what it is a perception of. As he says in *De Anima*, "To be pleased or pained is to activate the perceptual mean towards what is good or bad as such" (III. 1 431a10–11). All perception is, according to Aristotle, an activity of what he calls "the perceptual mean." We need not here be concerned with a precise understanding of what Aristotle means by "the perceptual mean." What is important for our considerations is that activity of the perceptual mean is perception and thus to be pleased or pained is to perceive something good or bad as such.[13]

As a result, there is no problem for Aristotle with defining emotions as species of pleasure and pain and as species of perception, since pleasures and pains are themselves types of perception. Moreover, he tells us what pleasures and pains are perceptions of, namely, of what is good or bad as such. Perception, of course, has particulars as its object, since perception is reception of sensible form. Hence, by "good as such" or "bad as such," Aristotle cannot mean something like "the good" or "the bad." Instead, he means perception of something good as good or something bad as bad. In other words, to feel pleasure is to perceive particulars as good, to feel pain is to perceive them as bad.

For example, when we pity, we perceive someone to be experiencing undeserved suffering. Pity, Aristotle says, is ". . . a certain pain at an apparent destructive or painful evil happening to someone who does not deserve it and which one might expect oneself or one of one's own to suffer . . ." (*Rhet.* II. 8 1385b13–14). Moreover, the apparent or imagined evil must not be imagined in general but imagined as close at hand. So he continues his definition: "and this is when it appears to be near. For it is clear that one who is going to feel pity must believe that some evil of the sort that either oneself or one of one's own might suffer be present" (14–18). Pity, in other words, does not result simply from imagining undeserved suffering but from imagining it as actually being present in this particular situation. It results from imagining a particular person's current experience to be one of undeserved suffering. In this example, then, emotion is the perception (or, imagination or appearance) of particulars as bad. Other examples can easily be provided including examples of emotions that involve the perception of particulars as good, such as friendship (a friend wishes for and takes pleasure in good things received by the one befriended).

Given that pleasure is the perception of particulars as good and pain the perception of particulars as bad, it is no wonder that we could not find a category of being of which pleasure is the perception. For good and bad are not categories of being according to Aristotle, but are transcategorials, as he argues in *Nicomachean Ethics* I. 6.[14] Once again, then, we can conclude that emotions, for Aristotle, are perceptions of particulars as good or bad. Using contemporary terminology we can say that emotions, for Aristotle, are perceptions of the value of particulars.[15]

For Aristotle, then, emotion and reason are not separate. In the virtuous person, they have the same aim. In addition, the virtuous person's disposition is not one of control by reason over emotion but of a harmony between them. Moreover, emotions are themselves not separate from reason. Instead, emotions are types of awareness. Specifically, emotions are types of perception since emotions are types of pleasure and pain and pleasure and pain are perception of particulars as good and bad. Emotions are not brute, then, but are types of rational awareness, specifically, they are awareness of the value of particulars.

This is a tremendously important conclusion. For, with suitable specification of what we mean by value, we can meet the demand of rule-based ethicists and others that there be a type of rational guide for our decisions regarding action while at the same time preserving the sense of the proponents of an ethics of care, or of virtue theory in general, that what is important is emotional sensitivity and awareness of particulars. For, what we are aware of when we are aware of salient particulars is their value and this awareness provides us with both a guide and an appropriate motivation for action.

Moreover, again with a suitable specification of what we mean by value, we can preserve the intuition that states of affairs are so complexly different than other states of affairs that rules about how to act cannot be given ahead of time without giving up the idea that there is some kind of guide for how to act. The guide, I will argue, is a concept of value which, though universal, shows up quite differently from one state of affairs to another. That is to say, value is general or universal, thus meeting the demands of rule-based ethicists, while it shows up quite differently in different situations, thus meeting the demands of the proponents of an ethics of care, and of other types of virtue theory, that how to act cannot be specified fully ahead of time.

II

What, then, is that suitable specification of what we mean by value? This, of course, is a large question, one to which this essay can contribute only a small part. It can contribute an answer to the question what is Aristotle's specification of what he means by value, or, to be more accurate, of what he means by the good.[16] For Aristotle, good is universal in one respect but particular in another. One can, regarding good, grasp the universal without knowing how it will show up in particular cases. One can, that is, know the universal without knowing what its instances or applications will be like. The universal involved is such that its applications are quite different, one from another, and different in ways that are not predictable or deducible but in ways that can only be seen or perceived. Why? Because good is a certain sort of analogical equivocal.

Good is equivocal because a variety of persons, things, or states of affairs are appropriately called "good" though what it is for them to be good is not the same from case to case. According to Aristotle, when the name "X" is common to different things but the account of their being X (*logos tês ousias*) differs, X is equivocal.[18]

Though good is equivocal, it is not merely ambiguous. Some equivocals are merely ambiguous. Sharp is an example. It is equivocal since it is appropriate to call different types of things "sharp" though what it is for them to be sharp differs. A note is sharp because it is too high. A knife is sharp which is capable of efficient cutting. Sharp is merely ambiguous, however, because there is no connection between what it is to be sharp in one case ("too high") and in another ("capable of efficient cutting").[19]

Good is a non-ambiguous equivocal because there is a connection between what it is to be good in one case and in another. The two main types of non-ambiguous equivocals for Aristotle are focal equivocals and analogical equivocals. In each case, a certain type of relatedness is crucial. In the case of focal equivocals, different things are appropriately called "X" because they have perhaps different relations to some one thing.[20] In the case of analogical equivocals, different things are appropriately called "X" because they have the same relation to perhaps different things.[21]

For example, "healthy" is, according to Aristotle, a focal equivocal. What it is for a body to be healthy is not the same as what it is for medicine to be healthy or exercise to be healthy. A healthy body is one with an active and stable disposition to be effected in such a way that it both is perserved and flourishes. Healthy medicine and exercise, on the other hand, are medicine or exercise that result in healthy body. "Healthy" is a focal equivocal because one account of what it is to be healthy (healthy body) is included in all the other accounts of what it is to be healthy (healthy medicine, healthy exercise). Different things are appropriately called "healthy" because they have perhaps different relations to some one thing, namely, a healthy body.[22]

"Good," on the other hand, is an analogical equivocal. Different things are appropriately called "good" according to Aristotle because they have the same relation to perhaps different things. This view is important for our purposes because it implies that perception of value is perception of a certain sort of relatedness. Moreover, as I will show, it is a sort of relatedness which itself cannot be defined ahead of time but must be seen.

A passage in *Nicomachean Ethics* I. 6 shows us that "good" is a analogical eqivocal. In it, Aristotle can be interpreted to claim that good is not a focal or ambiguous equivocal but an analogical one:

> But, how is it said? For it does not seem at least to be like those which are
> equivocal by chance. But is it by all being from one or aiming towards

one? Or, rather, is it by analogy? For as sight is in the body, so mind is in the soul, and another in another. (*EN* I. 6 1096b26)

Aristotle prefers the third alternative, that good is an analogical equivocal, as we can see from the fact that he says "or, rather" and gives what appears to be a short argument by example for that alternative.[23]

"Analogy" or *analogia* in Greek, means "same *logos*" or "same relationship." To say that "good" is an analogical equivocal is to say that different things, persons, states of affairs, etc., are appropriately called "good" because they are relata of a specified relationship. What is the relationship? The examples Aristotle uses in the two passages quoted above are examples of the internal relationship he calls *entelecheia* or *energeia,* that is, of the relationship that obtains between a *telos* and the things of which it is the *telos.* As sight is the good or *entelecheia* of the eye, so health is the good or *entelecheia* of the body. The good of anything is its *telos.* The relationship by virtue of which things are good is *entelecheia* or *energeia.*

Corroborating passages are easy to find. In the immediately following chapter, I.7, Aristotle states very clearly that the good of each practice and craft is its end (*telos*):

> What, then, is the good of each [practise and craft]? Or is it that for the sake of which the rest is done? In medicine, this is health; in stategy, victory; in housebuilding, a house; in another, another; and in every practice and choice it is the end (*telos*). For all the rest is done for the sake of this. (*EN* I.7 1097a15)

More general support is available in the *Metaphysics* where Aristotle regularly identifies the good of a thing with its end (*telos*) or the for the sake of which (*hou heneka*): "The remainder are causes as the end, that is, the good (to *telos* kai t'agathon) of the others" (*Meta.* III. 2 996a23), and ". . . everything which is good by itself and due to its own nature is an end . . ." (*Meta,* V.2 1013b25.)[24]

A passage in *Metaphysics* IX.6 provides further corroboration. In it, Aristotle says that *telos* cannot be defined but must be seen by analogy. What we mean by it, he says, is clear in different cases by induction:

> What we mean is clear by induction from particular cases and one must not seek a definition of everything but also see (*synhoran*) the analogy— that as that which is building is to that which is capable of building, so that which is awake is to that which is asleep, and that which is seeing to that

which has its eyes shut but has the capacity to see, and that which is separate from matter to the matter, and that which is unwrought to that which is
wrought up. Let "energeia" be determined by the first part of each of these
differences and "'the potential" by the second. But all things are not said
in the same way to be in *energeia* but by analogy—as a first thing is in or
to a second so a third is in or to a fourth; for some are as movement is to
potentiality and others as substance to a certain matter. (*Meta.* IX. 6
1048a35–b9)[25]

Aristotle makes clear in the passage that *energeia* is an analogical term. He
also makes another important claim, namely, that *energeia* cannot be
defined but must be seen in different instances by analogy. His reason for
the second claim is that "all things are not said in the same way to be in
energeia but by analogy." In other words, *energeia* is not a relationship that
is the same in different cases but is a relationship that differs in different
cases. Some relationships are the same in different cases (for example, the
relationship that obtains between two and four and between five and ten).
Others are different in different cases.[26] *Energeia* is a relationship that is different in different cases.

As a result, *energeia* has both a universal and particular component. It is
universal because a variety of things, persons, and states of affairs can share
in it. It is particular because what it is to share in it is different in different
cases. The relevance of this for our discussion should be obvious. Good,
understood in this way, is a guide which shows up differently from one situation to another, one of which we can have a universal grasp, without pre-
cluding the idea that awareness of particulars is important as well.

The relationship that we can grasp universally without knowing ahead of
time what its instances or applications will be like is, as stated above, the
relationship that obtains between different *telê* and the things, persons, or
states of affairs whose *telê* they are. What is that relationship like? To put
the question differently, what is a *telos*? I have previously proposed that by
"*telos*" Aristotle means constitutive limit.[27] Limits are of two kinds. Some
are destructive or harmful. They destroy or harm what they limit. Others are
constitutive. They are constitutive of what they limit, being more fully or
securely, what it already is. They are constituents or components of its
flourishing.[28] As the edges of a table not only limit the table, but constitute
it, so a virtue such as courage not only limits our activity, but allows it to be,
fully, what it is. *Telê* are in contrast with limits that are not constitutive: split
the table with an ax and the new limits will not constitute, but destroy, the

table; engage the enemy recklessly and you will not engage the enemy at all, but be defeated by him or her. Limits differ; not all limits are destructive or harmful. Those which constitute an action or thing are beneficial; they are its *telê.*

Because *telos* means constitutive limit, we can translate it, and its variants, *entelecheia* and *energeia*, by a family of terms that themselves mean, or pertain to, constitutive limitation: "completion," "development," or "fulfillment," as well as the more usual translations, "end" and "goal."[29] That Aristotle thinks *telos* means constitutive limit is indicated by the contrast he draws between acquisition or realization of a *telos* and the acquisition of a new quality, that is, between *teleiôsis* (completion) and *alloiôsis* (alteration).

For example, it would be absurd, Aristotle says in the *Physics,* to suppose that the coping or tiling of a house is an alteration and not a completion, or that in receiving its coping or tiling, a house is altered and not completed. So also with virtues and vices and with the things that possess or acquire them: "for virtues are completions and vices departures," Aristotle says, "thus, they are not alterations" (VII.3 246a17–b3). Being tiled is to a house, we may say, as receiving virtue is to a human being. In being tiled, a house does not lose the characteristic of being a house, that is, cease being able to do what houses as such do, namely, provide shelter; instead, it becomes a more complete house, that is, one more fully or securely able to provide shelter. Similarly, in acquiring a virtue such as courage, a human being does not lose the characteristic of being a human being, that is, cease being able to do what human beings are peculiarly able to do, namely, to act; instead, courageous human beings are more fully or securely able to act, since they face their fear and, in the face of it, act anyway. In being tiled, a house is not altered but developed. Similarly, in acquiring virtue, a person is not altered but developed. By contrast, in fading from white to beige, a house loses the characteristic of being white; the house is altered since the white color is destroyed and replaced by a different color. Similarly, in becoming tan from exposure to the sun, a human being loses the characteristic of being pale; the human being is altered since the pale color has been destroyed and replaced by the dark one.[30]

For another example, according to Aristotle in *De Anima,* neither the change from the capacity for knowledge to the possession of it, nor from the possession of knowledge to the exercise of it, is alteration. Alteration is the destruction of one quality and its replacement by another, while both coming to know and exercising knowledge are examples of change into one's qualities, or, at least, into one's fulfillment, dispositions or nature (II. 5

417b2–16). Change into fulfillment, disposition or nature is not alteration—or, if we decide to call it that, then we must correct for having done so by making a strong distinction between two very different kinds of alteration.[31]

These examples show that there are two kinds of change for Aristotle—change in which the characteristic that changes is destroyed and replaced and change in which the characteristic that changes is preserved and enriched. A *telos* is a principle of preservation or enrichment. A being which achieves its *telos*, which achieves *entelecheia* or *energeia*, will be preserved or enriched. Of course, enrichment or fulfillment cannot be achieved in just any way. Some activities or relationships stand in the way of it. Too much water, for example, will destroy a plant, rather than enabling it to grow. It is in this sense that a *telos* is a limit. If the limit is observed, then a being will be preserved or enriched. Giving the plant the appropriate amount of water will allow it to grow and bloom. It is in this sense that the limit is a constitutive one: a *telos* does not destroy and replace what it limits but, instead, is constitutive of it.

The examples show, as well, two important kinds of relationships for Aristotle—relationships in which one thing or person is replaced, harmed or destroyed by another and relationships in which one thing or person is preserved, developed, enriched, or enabled to flourish. The latter type of relationship is what value is for Aristotle. Moreover, awareness of this relationship either obtaining or not obtaining among particulars (in part) constitutes our emotions and motivates our actions. Finally, adequate awareness of this relationship obtaining or not obtaining among particulars is the central cognitive component of ethical virtue according to Aristotle. Put differently, the central cognitive component of ethical virtue for Aristotle is, as feminists and other proponent, of particularity have pointed out, awareness of particulars; however, it is not just awareness of particulars, but awareness of something about particulars, namely, awareness of their value.

One way to show this would be to go through examples of various virtues and show that the central cognitive component in each case is awareness of the value or *energeia* of particulars. For example, in the case of moderation, the central awareness is whether the food, drink, sex before me will lead to health or fitness or away from them. Health and fitness are, of course, *energeia* of the body (*EN* III. 11 1119a16–17). In the case of magnificence, the central awareness would be whether particular large expenditures are fitting or not (*EN* IV. 2 1122a22–23). The fitting is, arguably, a case of *energeia*. In the case of pride, the central awareness would be of one's own virtue, since pride is believing oneself worthy of the greatest honors when one is worthy of them and the greatest honors belong to those who have the greatest virtue according to Aristotle (*EN* IV. 3 1123b1–2, 1123b17–20, 34–36). Virtue is, of course, *energeia* of the soul.

Carrying out the project of going through each virtue in detail is beyond the scope of this essay, however. Another way of showing that the central cognitive component of ethical virtue for Aristotle is awareness of the value of particulars would be to counter an objection to my view. Someone might object that the central cognitive component of ethical virtue for Aristotle is not awareness of the value of particulars, but awareness of the mean. Virtue is, after all, a stable disposition regarding choice that lies in a mean; choice involves both deliberation, or more generally, practical wisdom, and desire. Hence, the cognition that the ethically virtuous person needs more than any other is not awareness of the value of particulars but awareness of the mean.

For Aristotle, the view that virtue is a stable disposition having to do with choice and consisting in a mean regarding passions and actions ought not be understood on a "middling amount" interpretation (that is, the virtuous person is not one who tends to feel a middling amount of passion or carry out actions to a middling degree) nor on a "mixture of opposites" interpretation (that is, the mean emotion is a mixture of the two opposite or extreme emotions).[32] Regarding the former, consider two virtues for which it is obvious that the mean is not a middling amount, namely, pride or great-souledness and magnificence or befitting-greatness. In each case, the mean is not a middling but a great amount and what makes the emotion a mean is not that it is a middling amount but that it is fitting or appropriate (the proud person merits his self-esteem since he has all the virtues; the magnificent person's great expenditures are fitting). Regarding the latter, the mixture of opposites' interpretation, a longer textual analysis would show that though Aristotle specifically states in the case of some other types of mean that the mean is a mixture of opposites, he simply does not say that about the ethical mean. This consideration is compelling since, according to Aristotle, "the mean" is equivocal, and so what are features of the mean in one case may not be features of it in another.

I propose, instead, that by saying that the ethically virtuous person has a stable disposition that lies in a mean between extremes of deficiency and excess, Aristotle means that the ethically virtuous person has a stable disposition to feel a certain type of feeling or do a certain type of action when it is what is appropriate or needed and that this stable disposition has two opposites: the disposition not to feel a certain type of feeling or do a certain type of action even when it is appropriate or needed (deficiency) and the disposition to feel a certain type of feeling or do a certain type of action even when it is not what is appropriate or needed (excess).

For example, the courageous person is not a person who is disposed always to feel confident, nor, obviously, is the courageous person one who is disposed never to feel confident. Instead, the courageous person is the one who is disposed to feel confident when it is appropriate to do so and to lack confidence when lacking it is appropriate. The person who tends to be confident all the time is reckless. The one who tends to lack confidence all the time is timid. Moreover, the courageous person is not one who is disposed always to rush ahead, nor, obviously, one who is disposed never to rush ahead. Instead, the courageous person is one who is disposed to rush ahead when rushing ahead is appropriate and not to rush ahead when not to rush ahead is appropriate. The person who tends to rush ahead all the time is reckless. The one who tends never to rush ahead is timid. Courage, then, has two opposites, one of excess (recklessness) and one of deficiency (timidity).

If this interpretation is correct, then it would be crucial to show that by "appropriate" or "needed" Aristotle means "the good." In fact, he does. In the *Sophistical Refutations,* he defines the needed. "*To deon,*" he says there, is equivocal. It has two meanings. It denotes something which is inevitable (*t'anangkaion*) or, alternately, it denotes things which are good (*t'agatha*). (177a24, 165b35).[33] Since Aristotle of course cannot mean that the virtuous person chooses and does what is inevitable, he must instead mean that the virtuous person is one who chooses and does what is good.[34] Similarly, the appropriate (*ho kairos*) is the good in the category of quantity, specifically, in the subcategory of time. Aristotle confirms this understanding of "kairos" by defining it, in the *Prior Analytics,* as "needed time" ("*chronos deon*") and then associating the needed with the good, specifically, with the beneficial (*ophelimon*) (I. 36 48b35–37).[35] "*Ho kairos*" is, thus, a category of "the needed" or "the good." Moreover, it is a term used sometimes simply to stand for the appropriate or good in general.[36] To aim at the mean, then, is to feel certain types of emotion or engage in certain types of action when they are appropriate where by "the appropriate" Aristotle means "the good."

Again, this argument can only be put briefly here. Still, in its brief form it indicates that, for Aristotle, the central cognitive component of ethical virtue is awareness of the value of particulars, where value is a kind of relatedness in which one thing, person, or state of affairs is not replaced, destroyed, or harmed by another, but is enabled to flourish or grow. This then suggests a new way of conceiving the issue of relatedness and separation. It suggests that the important issue is not whether to stress relatedness over separateness but is, instead, the ability to recognize the types of relatedness that lead to or constitute development, growth, or flourishing and the types that lead away from it or are detrimental to it. The question, in other words, is not whether relatedness is better than separation, but in each case whether relatedness or separation is valuable. Let us see if Aristotle himself follows this suggestion in the case of human relatedness and separation.

III

The important question is, what does the presence of an other hold out for me? Will the other subsume me, overwhelm me, harm me, injure me, destroy me? If so, then it would be best for me to remain separate and independent. Or can I be together with an other so that I am not harmed or destroyed, so that I retain my own identity, am benefited, can develop, flourish, and even grow? If so, then connection would be desirable. It is because experience suggests to many of us that each is possible that relationships with others both are so frightening and, at the same time, hold out such great hopes. We seek relationships, hoping the ones we find will benefit us, while avoiding other relationships and looking for a sphere of separateness and independence as well.

Of course, there are some who believe that relationships are a form of constraint—perhaps necessary constraint, but constraint nonetheless. Rousseau, for example, thinks that my original, individual nature is good and that social interaction is always some kind of deformation or slavery. When we enter social life, we become slaves and lose our goodness: "As he [man] becomes social and a Slave, he becomes weak, timorous, groveling, and his soft and effeminate way of life completes the enervation of both his strength and his courage."[37] For another example, Hobbes thinks that in our original nature we are distrustful ("diffident") and, as a result, warlike, and that the first function of society is to establish an all-powerful sovereign to control and channel our natural impulses. Nature, Hobbes says, "dissociate[s], and render[s] men apt to invade, and destroy one another. . . ." Men need "a common power to keep them all in awe."[38]

Still, another view is that my original state is not my nature, but a state of neediness and potential which can be fulfilled or warped, depending on circumstances and, crucially, on the types of relationships into which I enter. My nature, on this account, is not a completed given, but a given project, the completion or ruin of which involves relationships with others. This developmental view is, of course, Aristotle's, and it is one worth considering. At birth we are a set of needs and potentials waiting to be fulfilled or warped, in need of relationships with others for either one. Those that enable us to meet our needs or fulfill our potential are valuable. Those that do not, or that stand in the way of our doing so, are not valuable, or are harmful. We ought to seek the former, and avoid the latter.

1. Politics and Friendship. The two types of relationship we most need to fulfill our potential are politics and friendship. One part of the meaning of Aristotle's well-known argument that because human beings have speech they are by nature political (*Pol.* I. 2 1253a2–3, 7–10) is that cities are necessary for the development of the capacities required for a flourishing life. Life, according to Aristotle, is activity. Human activity (*ergon*) is rational activity whereby "rational activity" Aristotle means something like rationally and evaluatively intentional activity.[39] Whenever we act, we activate one or both of our two capacities for rational activity, namely, intellect or emotion. In order to lead not just any life, but a flourishing life, we must develop those two capacities. Intellectual virtue comes from teaching and ethical virtue from habituation. Good cities make each of these possible. Hence, politics is necessary for human flourishing.

Friendship, too, is required for the fulfillment of our potential. Friendship, according to Aristotle, is necessary, natural, and beautiful. It is necessary because it is a means to human flourishing (for example, friends are our refuge in poverty and misfortune). It is natural because we have a natural impulse to it (for example, parents feel it by nature for offspring). It is beautiful because it completes us, that is, because it is a constituent feature of, not just a means to, a flourishing life (in the best friendships, one contemplates one's friend's good actions, is able to be more continously active, and shares in discussion and thought) (*EN* VIII. 1 1155a3–31).

2. Limits on the Value of Politics and Friendship. Of course, to say that, for Aristotle, political and friendship relationships are necessary for human development and flourishing does not mean that all of them are valuable no matter what they are like. Instead, only the good ones are. In each case, relationships are necessary only if the one relating aims at the good of the one being related to for his or her own sake. In the case of political community, Aristotle calls regimes of that sort "correct." They are regimes in which the ruler rules for the common advantage and are opposed to despotic regimes, called "errant," in which the rulers rule for their own advantage (*Pol.* III. 6 1279a17–21, III. 7 1279a25–31). In the case of the friendship relationship, there are two types (utility friendship and pleasure friendship) in which one loves the other due to some good one gets from him or her and only one in which one loves the other for his or her own sake (virtue friendship) (*EN* VIII. 3). Hence, not every type of political and friendship relationship is to be sought.

Moreover, there are other types of limitations on the value of relation-ships as well. The phrase "human being is by nature political" so rings in our ears that we may find it hard not to characterize Aristotle by that phrase and nicely contrast him with modern individualists such as Hobbes, Locke, and Rousseau. Still, we might better think of Aristotle as one who both recognizes our need for connection and our need for separation than as the simple proponent of the former. We can see this in comments he makes in his critique of communism of property and of communism of women and children.

For example, one reason Aristotle gives for opposing communism of property is that communal property results in more not fewer lawsuits since we are more at odds over what we have in common (*Pol.* II. 4 1263b15–25). The desired benefit—care for all—is spoiled by a problem—contention. For another example, according to Aristotle, love is diluted not increased by community of women and children. For there are two things that cause love and care—that something is one's own or that something is dear—and neither of the two would result if women and children were held in common (*Pol.* II. 4 1262b15–24). Hence, for Aristotle, separation from people, as well as connection to some of them, is required for human flour-ishing.

For Aristotle, then, human beings have need both of separateness and connection if they are to develop and flourish. Relationships are not mere constraints on us, since we are naturally incomplete and in need of others both to develop and flourish. Not all types of connection serve that goal, however, but only those in which the other aims at my good for my sake. Moreover, we cannot extend our relatedness indefinitely, or we risk weak-ening relationships or, even, increasing conflict.

CONCLUSION

What philosophy can learn from feminism is how many philosophic claims asserted to be universally applicable in fact are claims applicable to one group that are falsely asserted to be applicable to all. Chodorow and Gilligan have helped philosophers become aware of such false assertions of universality in discussions of psychological development. Feminism promises to work a major transformation in philosophy as, one by one, we discover that topics thought to be untouched by issues of gender—for exam-ple, justice, nature, contract—in fact have been shaped and distorted by them.

What feminism can learn from philosophy is how feminist issues sometimes are examples of broader philosophic issues that have their own
dynamic. Through understanding the dynamic, feminists can enrich and
guide their understanding of specifically feminist issues. One of the dynamics of recent philosophy is a swinging back and forth between rationalism in
one or another of its modern forms and romanticism as the reaction to the
narrowness of modern rationalism. The recurrence of the swings—whether
Pascal against Descartes, Rousseau against Hobbes, Nietzsche against all
rationalism, postmoderns against the positivists, Gilligan against Kohlberg,
or virtue theorists against rule-based ethicists—suggests that there is something fundamentally problematic in the two positions themselves.

In this essay, I have stated part of what I think is problematic about the
two positions, namely, that each is limited: one asserts that what is fundamental to human psychological development is dispassionateness, separateness, and universalism while the other asserts, in reaction, that what is
fundamental is emotion, connection, and care for particulars, when in fact
healthy human development requires development of both sets of characteristics. Though it is important to point out that denying the intrinsic value of
passion, connection, and care for particulars is harmful to women and to
feminism since such characteristics are often associated with women, it is
also important to point out that restricting women to these characteristics is
harmful as well—and can simply be another type of sexism—since both sets
of characteristics are necessary for full development for women as they are
for men. As a result of this fact, we can see that feminism is going to have
two moments, each necessary but, by itself, partial. One moment is claiming
general human characteristics that wrongly have been called only male as
one's own and instantiating them in one's own life; the other is elevating
human characteristics that have been devalued because they have been
called only female and instantiating those characteristics in one's life. Each
moment is necessary for a complete feminism since both sets of characteristics are necessary for each person's full development. Which moment is
more important will vary from period to period both in the life of a person
and in the life of a culture. Still, it is important not to fix feminism in either
of the two moments, since constraining women within such limitations may
seem all too appealing to larger cultural institutions that have a stake in
restricting the lives of women.

At some point, philosophers are going to have to look beyond the modern rationalism/romanticism split to a type of philosophy that accepts the
idea that reason and emotion, separation and connection, care for particulars, and for universals are correlative concepts, not dichotomized ones. In

this essay, I have used Aristotle as a resource for our thinking about how we might want to do this. Aristotle does it by arguing that emotions are not separate from reason, either in virtue, since it requires both of them, or in emotions themselves, since they are forms of perception; by arguing that the type of cognition crucial to the development of virtue is the cognition of value where cognition of value has both a universal and a particular component since we can know the general concept of value without knowing how it will show up in particular circumstances; and by arguing that the important issue in each case of human relationships is not simply whether to be connected or separate, but whether a particular connection or separation is valuable. With Aristotle's example in mind, perhaps philosophers and feminists can race one another to see who can be first to come up with a philosophy of human being that includes all these aspects, not just some of them.

FEMINISM AND ARISTOTLE'S RATIONAL IDEAL

Marcia Homiak

Several years ago, as part of a meeting of the Society for Women in Philosophy, I was asked, along with two other feminist philosophers working on canonical male figures in the history of philosophy, to participate in a panel entitled "What's a Nice Girl Like Me Doing in a Place Like This?" The title reflected the organizers' view that there was something politically suspect about feminists working on established male figures—and something particularly suspect in this case, where the three philosophers in question (Aristotle, Hobbes, and Kant) were well-known for their benighted views on women.[1] How could we reconcile our commitment to feminism with a scholarly life devoted to the study of philosophers who explicitly describe women as inferior to men, as unfit for the best life available to human beings, as incapable of being full moral agents?[2]

In addition to these long-acknowledged problems regarding women, there have recently come to be other difficulties associated with working on Aristotle, Hobbes, and Kant. With the growing interest in revising and reorganizing the "canon" of the humanities, so as to include works by and about not only women, but also non-Western and nonwhite peoples, devoting one's scholarly life to the study of Aristotle, Hobbes, and Kant seems to be an even more egregious departure from progressive values and ways of life. For the use and teaching of canonical works, which are predominantly white and male, has encouraged an ignorant and prejudiced view of works, writers, and subject matters outside the canon. Moreover, many of the values associated with canonical works have, historically, been used to denigrate and oppress women, nonwhite men, and the uneducated in general.[3] Thus, teaching the works of the traditional canon has encouraged not only ignorance and elitism but also sexism and racism.

I have said that the values associated with the traditional canon have historically been used to denigrate women, nonwhite men, and the uneducated.

One might think this historical fact renders these values themselves suspect. They may be thought skewed and incomplete or, worse yet, inherently Western, Eurocentric, or masculine. I want to explore one value in particular that is associated with most of Western philosophy and with much of the traditional humanistic canon. I am referring to the value of reason and to the value of exercising one's rational faculties. Aristotle, Kant, and Hobbes each recommends, as the best life available to human beings, a rational life, though each has a different view about what this life requires and includes. I shall discuss only Aristotle's views on these matters, and I shall argue that his picture of the rational life is neither inherently masculine nor inherently exploitive. Instead, I shall claim, his ideal is worthy of emulation by both women and men.

Ethical systems that promote rationality as an ideal have recently come under considerable criticism from feminist scholars. Much of this criticism has been influenced by Carol Gilligan's work comparing girls' and boys' ways of reasoning about ethical questions.[4] In her work *In a Different Voice*, for example, Gilligan suggests that males and females have, in general, different orientations or perspectives toward moral values and moral strategies. Women tend to adopt a "care" perspective, in which what matters to them is the preservation of relationships and connection with others; men tend to adopt a "justice" perspective, in which what matters is acting on impartial and universalizable principles. Since relationships are matters of intimacy and personal feeling, the care perspective is associated with a focus on emotion, especially on the altruistic emotions. Since impartial and universalizable principles are a result of reasoned reflection about what to do, where such reflection is carried out without the distractions of emotion and without a prejudiced concern for one's own interests or the interests of specific others, the justice perspective is associated with rationality and with the value of one's status as a rational being capable of such reflection.[5]

Thus, the basis of the feminist criticism of rational ideals is that such ideals, in their application to moral questions, ignore the role of emotion and of the nonuniversalizable particularity of human life.[6] But these domains, of emotion and of specific and particular relationships, are the domains historically associated with women. Hence, the rational ideal suggests that the concerns most typical of women's lives are irrelevant to the best human life and to reasoning about what to do. Lawrence Blum has described the type of philosopher whom Gilligan's work has been used to attack, the type Blum calls the "moral rationalist": "It is the male qualities whose highest expression he naturally takes as his model. In the same way it is natural for him to ignore or underplay the female qualities as they are found in his society—sympathy, compassion, emotional responsiveness. . . . The moral rationalist philosopher thus both reflects the sexual value hierarchy of his society and indirectly gives it a philosophic grounding and legitimation."[7] Not only are the concerns of women irrelevant to the rational ideal but they also may be thought to be incompatible with it. If that is so, then the rational ideal suggests that women are not capable of living moral lives.

In effect, the rational ideal suggests that the best human life and a moral life is available only to those who engage in the kind of rational reflection necessary to determine properly how to live. We have seen how such an ideal tends to exclude women's concerns from the moral life, or women themselves from the moral life, if women are thought incapable of the necessary rational reflection. As I have mentioned, the rational ideal can also be taken to exclude other persons whose lives tend not to be associated with the rational. In Aristotle's view, for example, menial laborers are not fit to be citizens of the best state, since Aristotle believes that menial labor is a deterrent to engaging in the rational activity characteristic of human beings. More broadly, the rational ideal can be taken to exclude persons who have been associated with the body and bodily functions rather than with rational activity, however rational activity is to be understood. Oppressive stereotypes of "inferior" peoples have tended to include images of their lives as determined by what is animal or bodily. This is a way in which the rational ideal can support prejudiced views of nonwhites and uneducated people.

But the fact that the rational ideal has been, or can be, used to exclude particular groups from that ideal does not show that the rational ideal is defective. Even assuming one could establish that particular groups actually possessed the characteristics on which their exclusion was based—for example, that they were more "physical" or more "compassionate"[8]—one would have to show that their having these characteristics is incompatible with the rational ideal. And even if it could be shown that having these characteristics is incompatible with living according to the rational ideal, that would not be sufficient to show that the rational ideal is suspect or even that it is incomplete. The problem might lie, instead, with the way these "non-rational" characteristics are being understood. It is possible that, upon examining them carefully, they may not be found worthy of emulation. The rational ideal may emerge as a more attractive model after all.

I want to examine Aristotle's picture of the rational ideal, and to explore its worthiness to serve as a model for a good human life, by looking at three groups that fail, in Aristotle's opinion, to embody the rational ideal. These groups are menial laborers, slaves, and women of varying political status.

Once we see how these people fail to embody the rational ideal, we can understand more clearly what we are committed to in living according to that ideal. Then we will be in a better position to determine whether Aristotle's rational ideal is incompatible with the traits of character typically associated with women (for example, with being more caring, more compassionate, more altruistic) and whether it is incompatible with a more "physical" or "bodily" life.

I shall argue that his ideal is not incompatible with being altruistic or with performing physical labor. But, I shall claim, if altruistic traits of character and physical work are not themselves to become oppressive, they must include precisely the activities Aristotle describes as rational. I shall treat the compatibility between the rational ideal and physical work relatively briefly, since the main focus of my concern is the relationship between caring for another and being rational, as Aristotle understands it. On the view I shall propose, being caring and compassionate must be expressed within a life lived according to the rational ideal, or else these traits become destructive and unhealthy. To explicate destructive care, I use examples of contemporary women's lives, since they are often structured so as to preclude women from exercising the rational activities Aristotle most valued. Thus, some of Aristotle's reservations about women's lives are sustained, though not, of course, for the reasons he offered. If my interpretation of the rational ideal is correct, and the activities Aristotle considers rational are critical components of a non-oppressive life, then we have good reason to embrace his ideal rather than to reject it.

PSYCHOLOGICAL FREEDOM IN ARISTOTLE'S IDEAL STATE

Aristotle recognizes different sociopolitical classes or categories of women and men. These classes are ordered along a spectrum that reflects the different degrees to which individuals have realized the capacities and traits characteristic of human beings, where these capacities and traits are understood to be rational. To the extent that one fails fully to realize these capacities and traits, one fails to be fully human. At the extreme end of this sociopolitical spectrum, some individuals—namely (natural) slaves—aren't really human beings at all and hence are not women and men, properly speaking.[9] Because they lack crucial rational characteristics, Aristotle thinks they can justifiably be treated differently from other individuals who more completely realize human capacities and traits. There is, in effect, a hierarchical ordering of different human natures, according to which those who completely realize their human nature rule all those who do not or cannot.

In Aristotle's ideal state there are three broad categories of men: citizens; free persons who are not citizens, including artisans, tradesmen, and day laborers[10] (for the sake of convenience, I shall refer to these persons simply as menial or manual laborers); and persons who are neither free nor citizens (slaves). Male citizens spend the major portion of their adult lives in democratic decision-making (after serving in the military when young and before becoming priests when too old) (*Pol.* 1329a2–34). They are members of the assembly, members of juries, city officials of various kinds, and so on. They take turns ruling and being ruled (*Pol.* 1332b26–27; 1295b14–27). Ruling is the activity that distinguishes these men from other groups of men in the political community. The suggestion is that through participatory democracy with other citizens like themselves, they alone fully realize their characteristic human rational capacities and traits. These rational powers, associated with the rational part of the soul (*EN* 1139a12), consists of deciding, classing, discriminating, judging, planning, and so forth (*EN* 1170b10ff.).[11]

Menial laborers should not, according to Aristotle, be citizens in the best state, presumably because menial labor, in Aristotle's view, impedes the full exercise of one's rational powers (cf. *Pol.* 1277b2–6, 1278a20–21). How is this so? (i) One answer might be that menial labor involves much routine and monotonous work, in which little use is made of choosing, judging, deciding, and discriminating. There is little room for the personal style and self-expression that characterize more interesting and challenging activity. But obviously this need not always be the case. Though the sculptor Pheidias counts as a menial laborer, his work involves highly sophisticated decision-making and discrimination. If his doing manual labor impedes the full expression of his rational powers, it must do so in some other way. (ii) We must consider not only the work Pheidias does but also the conditions under which he does it. Like other menial laborers, Pheidias's decision-making powers are constrained by his need to survive. He must travel to the cities where his skills are needed, and the building projects he oversees must fit the constraints imposed by city officials or private citizens. The exercise of his rational powers is limited by, and therefore dependent upon, other people's decisions and desires. In this way he does not have complete control over his own decisions and actions.

This lack of control is evidenced in at least two ways. First, the fact that Pheidias' decisions and actions are constrained by his need to earn a living may require him to compromise his moral principles. He may be "compelled" by his superiors (cf. *EN* 1110a25) to act in ways he would not ordinarily choose. His actions are then a combination of the voluntary and the involuntary (*EN* 1110a1 1–19). Second, even if Pheidias is not required to take "mixed" actions (*EN* 1110a11), the fact that his decisions and actions are constrained by the desires of others means that he cannot fully express his conception of what is worth sculpting, how it is to be done, and so on. He cannot design and direct the project according to his own ideas of what is interesting and important. He must accommodate his creations to the values of others.[12]

In Aristotle's view, then, the citizen and the menial laborer (in contrast to the citizen and the slave) have the same psychological capacities. What distinguishes them are the circumstances under which they choose and decide. The menial laborer does work that often does not require much decision-making. More important, however, is the fact that the laborer's concern for economic survival constrains his decision-making in that he does not have complete control over what work he is to do and how it is to be accomplished. On the other hand, a natural slave, in Aristotle's view, lacks the very capacity for deliberation and decision (*Pol.* 1260a12). So, presumably, if he were not a slave, he would not be able to control his own life even to the extent that a menial laborer can. A slave acts wholly in the interests of another person; this is why he is not free (*Pol.* 1278b32–37). To the extent that a manual laborer lacks control over his life and must act in accordance with what others desire and require of him, his life is slavish (*Rhet.* 1367a32–33).

Indeed, to the extent that any person's life is not the product of his own decisions and desires and is overly or improperly dependent on the desires, decisions, and opinions of other people, Aristotle deems that person's life slavish. In the *Nicomachean Ethics*, for example, Aristotle is able to say of various nonvirtuous male citizens in nonideal states that their lives are slavish. Of course, it is difficult to be precise about what constitutes "too much" or the "wrong kind" of dependence on others' decisions and desires. Surely every person who is not self-sufficient is dependent on others' actions and decisions. But many forms of dependence that arise from the absence of self-sufficiency are innocuous in that they do not undermine one's status as a rational being. I may not be able to fulfill my desire for hazelnut ice cream if there is no one to make it available to me; however, because I do not produce it myself and must rely on others to do so does not render me unable to make the sorts of decisions that serve to realize my specific rational abilities or the rational abilities I share with other rational beings. What Aristotle wants to avoid, and which he thinks only the virtuous person successfully avoids, is the kind of dependence on others that impedes, rather than encourages and extends, the full realization of one's rational abilities.

Let me illustrate with some examples from the *Nicomachean Ethics*. Aristotle tells us that the inirascible person is slavish in that he is willing to accept insults to himself and to overlook insults to his family and associates (*EN* 1126a7–8). He does not have enough self-esteem to allow himself to get angry at others' ill treatment of himself, his family, and his friends. He lacks confidence in his own judgments and perceptions and will have a tendency to accept the judgments and perceptions of others as correct. Hence, he is apt to allow others to make decisions for him. Flatterers are another example of servile persons (*EN* 1126a2). They want to improve their position by gaining the favor of more privileged people (*EN* 1127a7–9). To do this, they must accept the correctness of the privileged person's desires and decisions, and thus they must accept a situation in which many of their decisions are, in effect, made for them by others. Flatterers and inirascible people are in a psychological situation analogous to that of skilled menial laborers like Pheidias.

Aristotle describes intemperate people as slavish, too, but not because others make decisions for them. Indeed, intemperates may control their lives in just the ways that inirascible people and flatterers do not. They may make their own decisions, and they may be able to implement their decisions without having to accommodate others' preferences and interests. But they misuse their rational powers and undermine their development in that the activities they enjoy make too little use of these powers. Intemperate people enjoy physical sensations rather than the discriminating and choosing that surrounds tasting and touching (*EN* 1118a32–b1). Their psychological situation is like that of menial laborers whose work is routine and monotonous. There is so little decision-making going on that even natural slaves, who lack the powers of deliberation and decision, can experience the intemperate person's enjoyments (*EN* 1177a7).

In contrast to these various slavish types is the male citizen of Aristotle's ideal state. He is different even from a Pheidias who has full control over the specific sculptural projects he is engaged in. On Aristotle's view, not even such a Pheidias would have fully realized his powers of choosing and deciding. The male citizens of Aristotle's ideal state fully realize their characteristic human powers in the political activity of democratic decision-making. They realize their human powers fully in these circumstances because the deliberations involved in democratic decision-making are comprehensive and overarching. Here the exercise of the human powers is not restricted to specific decisions about what statues to sculpt, what materials to use, and so on. Rather, these are higher-level decisions about what is best for the community itself. So they would include decisions about other, more specific activities (cf. *EN* 1094a27). The exercise of the human powers is *generalized* and extended to cover virtually every aspect of human life, including, for example, questions of war and peace, finance, legislation, public works, cultural projects, and sexual matters.[13]

As far as men are concerned, then, we can determine a ranking from the complete human being who is able to actualize his powers fully because he is a politically active citizen of the ideal state, to a slave who cannot actualize the characteristic human powers because he is without them to begin with. In between are various types of incomplete, slavish persons, ranging from wealthy aristocrats (in nonideal states) to manual laborers.

What about the women who are the wives or companions of these different men, the wives of free citizens in the ideal state, the wives of free citizens in nonideal states, the wives of manual laborers, and the female companions of slaves? (I do not discuss unmarried daughters, since, for our purposes, their situations will not differ markedly from those of married women and married female slaves.)

Although Plato seems to have had moderately progressive views about some women (namely, those he thought capable of ruling the state),[14] Aristotle's views on women's nature are, without exception, objectionable. Aristotle claims that free women cannot be fully actualized human beings, no matter what their political status, since they are, like slaves, naturally defective. Although free women do not lack the capacity for deliberation and decision, as slaves do, their capacity for deliberation, Aristotle says, is not "authoritative" (*Pol.* 1260a13). Women are contrasted with (presumably male, free) children, whose deliberative capacities are merely "incomplete" (*atelês, Pol.* 1260a14). The deliberative capacity in women, then, we may assume, is permanently stunted. Unlike free, male children, no amount of education and practice in decision-making, and no change in their economic or social circumstances, will enable women to deliberate properly about what is best. They may give too much weight to what is pleasant or to what appears to be good. In effect, a woman may give over the rule of her soul to its non-rational part and thereby endanger the proper functioning of the household (cf. 125b4ff.).[15] Hence, decisions about what is best must be made for her by men. A free woman's life will always, then, be slavish, since her life is not controlled by her own decisions.

Because natural slaves lack one of the features characteristic of human beings, they cannot, strictly speaking, be human beings, and hence they cannot be women or men—that is, they cannot be adult members of the human species. (I say they cannot "strictly speaking" be human beings, because it seems clear that Aristotle cannot actually deny that slaves are human beings. This is suggested, for example, by *EN* 1161a34ff., where Aristotle admits that there can be friendship and justice between masters and slaves "to the extent that a slave is a human being."[16]) But despite this "species difference" between free persons and slaves, it is hard to see the extent to which the life of any free woman is relevantly different, in regard to her departure from the ideal of fully realized human being, from that of a slave (male or female). Although a free woman presumably can deliberate about how best to carry out the decisions of her husband, or father, her actions are ultimately determined by the decisions of free men, as are those of slaves. Perhaps this is why Aristotle does not bother to discuss female slaves in any detail. As far as their legal status is concerned, it is the same as that of male slaves. As far as their psychological status is concerned, it seems no different, relative to the ideal, from that of free women.

IS ARISTOTLE'S IDEAL EXPLOITATIVE OR MASCULINE?

I have sketched a view of psychological freedom in Aristotle, according to which a complete human being is one who fully realizes his characteristically human powers (the powers of judging, choosing, deciding, planning, discriminating, and so on) in the political activity of democratic decision-making. Democratic decision-making is characterized by a political structure that is egalitarian (each citizen participates equally in decision-making) and comprehensive (each citizen participates equally in the same, broad type of decision-making). Citizens participate in decisions about matters that fundamentally affect the course of their lives. These higher-level decisions influence the lower-level decisions individuals make about the specific lifeplans they pursue (cf. *EN* 1094a27).

Two questions arise about the life Aristotle admires and recommends. First, does the realization of this ideal life require that some segments of the political community exploit the labor of other segments so that they (the exploiters) have time for the decision-making involved in ruling? And, second, is this ideal life inherently masculine? If we answer either question affirmatively, we have good reason to reject Aristotle's recommendations. I think there is a fairly straightforward response to the first question. I shall indicate that briefly here.[17] Most of my attention will be directed to the second question.

Aristotle believes that the realization of the life he admires does require that rulers exploit menial laborers, since he believes that the conditions under which menial labor is performed will involve the laborer in relations of dependence that prevent the full actualization of the rational powers.

Hence, rulers cannot be menial laborers. As I have suggested, Aristotle is not crazy to believe this. But it is important to distinguish between a menial life (a life whose main activity is menial labor performed under conditions of dependence) and a life that may involve menial labor but is not restricted to it. Aristotle may be correct to think that a life restricted to menial labor (where such labor can be monotonous, routine, exhausting, and carried out for the sake of an end external to it—housework is a good modern example) will demand little use of the human rational powers and will impede the development of the type of character one needs to exhibit the moral virtues. But surely he would not be correct to think that engaging in some menial labor, as part of a life that is devoted to the full expression of the rational powers, will have a devastating effect upon character. Indeed, as he notes at *Pol.* 1333a9–11: "Actions do not differ as honorable or dishonorable in themselves so much as in the end and intention of them."[18] Just as citizens take turns ruling and being ruled, then, they could take their turns at menial labor, while preserving for themselves the type of life that Aristotle considers fully human. Thus, as far as I can tell, the best kind of life, from Aristotle's point of view, does not require, even given his views about the dangers of menial labor, that some persons take up lives of menial labor to provide the necessities for others who live political lives.[19]

I have considered whether the ideal described by Aristotle is necessarily exploitative. I have argued that if citizens determine how the menial labor is to be carried out, they will not involve themselves in the dehumanizing relations of dependence Aristotle found so objectionable. And if the menial labor is distributed among the citizens in ways so as not to absorb much of any one citizen's time, then there is no reason to think that the possible monotony of some menial labor will impede the continuing exercise of the human rational powers.

One point should perhaps be emphasized. Aristotle's citizens enjoy the complete exercise of the human rational powers that participation in ruling provides. Therefore, they want to avoid both the slavishness of a menial life and the slavishness of a Pheidian life. For, as we have seen, Pheidias's life, though involving sophisticated and subtle uses of the human powers, remains seriously limited and incomplete. Just as Aristotle is not crazy to think that a life of routine menial labor is incompatible with his rational ideal, so too he is not crazy to think that a "physical" life of the Pheidian type is also defective and incomplete. But this does not commit Aristotle to the view that physical activity itself is dehumanizing. There is nothing to prevent Aristotle's democratic decision-makers from being artisans and tradespeople, as well as farmers and warriors.

I now consider the second issue I raised above—that is, the issue of whether Aristotle's ideal is masculine, and, if so, whether this is reason to reject it. I take it that the ideal is considered masculine because the life considered most worth living is the life in which the characteristic human powers, considered as rational powers, are fully realized. Since, as I suggested at the outset, reason and rational deliberation have, in the history of Western thought, been associated primarily with men, and since the non-rational (which includes passions, emotions, and feelings, all of which are thought to have some relation to the body) have been associated with women, to recommend a way of life that praises and prizes reason over all else is implicitly at least to denigrate what has traditionally been associated with women. And, historically, to accept a view that prizes and praises reason above all else provides room not only for sexist views but also for racist views—views that denigrate other peoples because they have traditionally been thought more bodily or more physical than white males. Indeed, we have seen this tendency to be true of Aristotle, whose view of slaves and women as less than fully rational enables him to justify their low status in the political community.

I want to consider whether Aristotle's view of the rational, in particular, requires a devaluation of the non-rational side of the human being. This might be true if his view were a simple one, in which reason "rules" in some straightforward way over the passions, emotions, and feelings. But his view is not simple. I shall suggest, instead, that in Aristotle's virtuous person, the proper development of the non-rational side of the person can be seen to constrain and limit the operations of the rational side. In effect, it is as if to say that the rational part of the virtuous person's soul cannot work properly unless it is properly guided by the non-rational part.

Both Plato and Aristotle insist that the non-rational part of the soul (which includes appetites, feelings, emotions, and passions) must be educated—in the case of Plato, before one can begin to think sufficiently abstractly ultimately to see the Form of the Good, and, in the case of Aristotle, before one can learn how to deliberate properly about the contents of the best life (before, that is, one can acquire practical wisdom). For Aristotle, many of the individual virtues involve feeling or responding in the appropriate way. For example, it is a vice to take too much pleasure in eating, drinking, and sexual activity; it is also a vice to take insufficient pleasure in these activities. It is a vice to get too angry, or angry at the wrong times, or angry toward the wrong persons, and so on. But it is also a vice not to get angry or to exhibit anger at all, or not to do so when the situation is appropriate for anger. It is a vice to feel too much fear or not enough, or to feel it on the wrong occasions or toward the wrong persons. Reason, by itself, cannot create these feelings; nor can reason, by itself, destroy them. If reason could create or destroy feelings, then Aristotle would not be faced with the problem of *akrasia* (*EN* VII.1–3). Thus, the first things to note about Aristotle's rational ideal are that it does not involve the suppression of feeling and emotion and passion and that if reason does rule over passion, its rule does not consist either in producing or in destroying passion. Nor does it consist simply in offering some general directives to the non-rational side of the soul, since there are no rules or rational guidelines for determining how much of an emotion or feeling is appropriate in different situations (*EN* ll09b21–24).

More important, however, is the psychological basis for all the different virtues. I have argued elsewhere[20] that they can be viewed as expressions of what Aristotle calls true self-love. The virtuous person is characterized by a love of what is most himself—that is, by a love of the exercise of the human rational powers, where these are the powers of judging, choosing, deciding, and discriminating that I have listed before (*EN* 1168b34–1169a3; cf. 1168a7–9 and 1170bl0ff.). In enjoying the exercise of his rational powers, the true self-lover enjoys rational activity in general rather than a particular kind of rational activity. His life is therefore broadly based; it is not devoted to the pursuit of specialized goals or to the completion of specialized projects. The true self-lover enjoys the intricacies and subtleties of different intellectual endeavors and also the intricacies and subtleties of endeavors not considered intellectual: he enjoys playing, or watching, a good game of baseball or tennis; he delights in telling a story others will appreciate or in finding just the right gift for a special occasion; he enjoys pleasing and benefiting his friends.

In loving what is characteristic of himself, the virtuous person enjoys who he is and what he can do. His self-love is thus a kind of self-esteem and self-confidence. But as my examples of self-expression have indicated, true self-love is to be distinguished from the self-love that we associate with selfishness and that we normally condemn (*EN* IX. 8). Given that the virtuous person enjoys rational activity in a general way, he is able to take pleasure both from the exercise of his own rational powers and from others' exercise of these powers.

The self-love Aristotle admires becomes even more generalized and more stable when a person exercises the human rational powers in political activity where decision-making is shared and evenly distributed. Self-love is more generalized because its source, the exercise of the human rational powers, is now extended to cover comprehensive, higher-level decisions, as well as decisions about activities specific to one's own life. And because the decision-making has been extended in this way, it is flexible and less vulnerable to changes in circumstance and fortune than a more specialized exercise of rational activity would be. Democratic decision makers can adjust to changes in circumstance and can redirect the use of their abilities to meet these changes. Hence, the more stable and continuous their self-esteem will be. But for someone whose decision-making powers have been focused on a particular activity, self-esteem is tied to the success of that particular activity. Hence, this person's self-esteem is precarious and easily upset. This person is like Aristotle's professional soldiers who, though (improperly) confident from past success, turn and run when circumstances are against them (*EN* 1116b15–17).

The enjoyment that a person takes in who he is and in what he does, though its source and basis is the exercise of the rational powers, is not itself an instance of such exercise. Although enjoyment may be produced by rational deliberation, the pleasure taken in rational deliberation, like the enjoyment we take in any other activity, is non-rational. This affects the extent to which my enjoyment can be altered by rational deliberation, even if rational deliberation is what I enjoy and even if that deliberation produces rational desires for what I enjoy. When, for example, I want to play tennis because I enjoy it, I desire to play because I find it pleasant, not because I believe playing tennis is good for my health. In this sense, my desire to play tennis is non-rational. I might also want to play tennis because I think it is good for my health, and I might have reached this conclusion on the basis of deliberation about what conduces to my good overall. The desire to play tennis that arises from such deliberation is therefore rational, and it can be altered by further such deliberation. If I cease to believe that playing tennis is good for my health, I will cease to want to play tennis for that reason. My newly acquired beliefs produce a rational aversion to tennis. But no such deliberations will undermine my general non-rational desire to play tennis. If I somehow come to believe (correctly) that I no longer enjoy playing tennis, my having that belief is an indication that I have already stopped liking tennis. In this case, my beliefs do not produce my non-rational aversion. It comes about in some other way. The same holds for my non-rational enjoyment of rational activity itself, which, on Aristotle's view, accounts for my having self-love.

On the assumption, then, that Aristotle's virtues require self-love and that they can be understood as different ways in which self-love is expressed, being virtuous is importantly a matter of having one's non-rational desires properly structured. Without the appropriate background of non-rational desire, the agent will not perceive correctly the nature of situations calling for practical decision and action and will thus respond in ways that Aristotle describes as non-virtuous rather than virtuous. Aristotle's notoriously vague remarks at *EN* 1144a34–36 are consistent with the idea that the structure of one's non-rational desires crucially affects one's ability to perceive practical situations correctly: "[The highest end and the best good] is apparent only to the good person; for vice perverts us and produces false views about the origins of actions."

There is a second aspect to the role of the non-rational desires in Aristotle's conception of virtue. The enjoyment taken in the expression of the human powers in cooperative democratic activity not only produces a stable self-confidence; it also produces stable feelings of friendship between the parties involved in the decision-making. Feelings of friendship arise from the fact that the democratic activity is self-expressive, that it is beneficial to the parties engaged in it, and that it is itself enjoyable (*Rhet.* 1381a30 and *EN* 1168a7–9). Friendship includes a care and concern that friends have for each other for each other's own sake (*EN* 1156b31), a tendency to rejoice and take pleasure in each other's good fortune, and a tendency to help when friends need assistance (*EN* IX. 4). Feelings of friendship are maintained over time by continuing the activities that originally produced them or the comparable activities that have come to sustain them. Like enjoyment itself, friendly feelings are not produced by beliefs about what is best or about what contributes to my overall good. They thus belong to the non-rational part of the soul.

In the case of democratic decision-making, the relevant feelings of friendship are particularly stable. A combination of factors explains why this is so. First, the feelings of friendship are produced by a form of self-expression that is especially enduring in that it is overarching and generalized. They are not the product of the expression of some contingent features of the self that might disappear in a change of circumstance or fortune. Hence, the friendship is not "coincidental" and easily dissolved (*EN* 1156a14–21). Second, the democratic decision-makers share their most basic values and goals in that they are committed to engaging in cooperative activities that promote and sustain the development and exercise of the human powers (cf. *Pol.* 1280a31–34). Thus, each decision maker can view the deliberations of the others as expressions of his thinking and reasoning self (*EN* 1168b34–1169a3). Deliberators identify with each other's decisions and actions, so that each deliberator's actions become the expression of the other's rational activity. This form of self-expression, now even more generalized, is especially enduring. Citizens in the ideal state are thus tied together by feelings of friendship that are long lasting and strong.

The care, concern, and sympathetic attachment that partly constitute these ties of friendship encourage a healthy dependence among citizens. Citizens are not uninvolved with each other or contemptuous of each other in the way several of Aristotle's vicious types are (*EN* IV. 3). Nor are they overly concerned with others' opinions—that is, concerned in a way that would upset their self-esteem if they were to face criticisms or obstacles. Their concern for each other does not produce a self-destructive dependence; their autonomy does not preclude enduring ties of association. Along with the self-love of virtuous citizens, these ties of friendship will influence what citizens perceive to be central to the type of life they want to maintain. They will not act to jeopardize the activities and relationships they value and enjoy.

In summary, citizens' understanding of what is best to do, their rational deliberations about how to live and act, take place within the limits imposed by educated passions and feelings. They take place within the limits imposed by a stable self-esteem that derives from an enjoyment in rational activity and within the limits imposed by strong ties of friendship that involve care and concern for the other citizens for their own sakes. If this is a rational ideal, it is one in which the proper operation of reason is guided and constrained by feeling and emotion, that is, by the non-rational side of the soul.

FEMINISM AND REASON

I have argued that Aristotle offers a picture of a rational ideal that does not exclude the emotions, passions, and feelings. In particular, the proper operation of reason is limited and constrained by the specific feelings constitutive of true self-love and civic friendship. In describing this ideal, I have not discussed the nature of the actual deliberations virtuous persons will make in specific practical contexts. But it is reasonable to suppose that virtuous persons will recognize the importance of producing and sustaining true self-love and stable ties of civic friendship that are based on enduring features of the self. When citizens come to decide how best to govern their city, these values, one would think, would be paramount in their deliberations. Specific decisions would be made with a commitment to, and appreciation of, the critical role these values play in the lives of every citizen. This does not mean that all civic decisions will be made from an "impartial" perspective, where that is taken to imply that a consideration of the specific circumstances of particular individuals is never appropriate. Nor does it mean that deliberating from such a perspective is never appropriate.

I now want to discuss in more detail the nature of the care and concern I have attributed to Aristotle's virtuous citizens. For it is "care and concern" that have come to be associated with feminist ethics and women's moral experience, where such care includes an interest in preserving relationships and commitments to others. In feminist ethics, an interest in applying impartial rules or comprehensive principles becomes secondary.

Assuming it is true that women's moral experiences focus more on questions of care and on preserving relationships and commitments, ought we to accept these experiences as a general model for our behavior toward others or as a more specific model of our moral behavior? What type of care and concern is appropriate? Are care and concern always to be preferred over more emotionally detached ways of relating to others?[21]

The care and concern that constitutes a virtuous citizen's friendship with other citizens resembles in important ways the care that Aristotle's "complete friends" have for each other. Complete friends, according to Aristotle, are virtuous, know each other well, and spend much of their time together in shared activities (*EN* IX. 10). As a result, it is not possible to have many complete friends, whereas political (or citizen) friendship holds among many. Yet, even though citizen friendship and complete friendship have different characteristics, it is not hard to see a resemblance between them in regard to the care that the friends extend toward each other. For though citizen friends may not know each other to the extent that complete friends do, and though they might not spend much time together, they know each other well enough to know that they share the major aims and values that guide the decisions and practices of their community. Citizen friends perceive each other as Aristotle's complete friends do, that is, as "another oneself" (*EN* 1166a32), meaning that they value and enjoy about each other what they value and enjoy about themselves. They take pleasure, for example, in the exercise of each other's rational powers as they do in their own. In this way they are like each other and take enjoyment in the exercise of the powers they share. Each is, then, a self-lover who takes pleasure in the self-love of the other, since the exercise of self-love in one is like the exercise of self-love in the other. Their ties of friendly feeling are firm and strong and long lasting because they are grounded in the pleasure they take in who the other is as a realized human being.

The care and concern they have for each other comes from the affection that arises from their sharing in each other's rational activity. That is, they share overarching and higher-level interests and goals, and they each participate in the activities associated with these higher-level interests. This does not mean that they share each specific interest and desire.[22] The contents of their individual life-plans might be surprisingly divergent. But each has an individual plan that realizes the human powers in a specific way, and this fact is a source of enjoyment for them. So each takes an interest in the other's interests, rejoices in the other's successes, grieves with the other's losses, and so on.

None lives through the lives of the others or acquires a basis for self-esteem and self-confidence through the activities of the others. Each is independent in the sense that each enjoys the activities in her individual life-plan as well as the higher-level activities her plan shares with the plans of her friends. None is dependent on the praise and admiration of specific individuals for the maintenance of self-love, so each can endure the loss of particular friendships. Aristotle's citizens are likely to be involved in a number of relationships, since their shared general commitments and goals give them a basis for association and affection. Their emotional eggs are not all in one basket, and hence their sense of their own value and importance is not undermined by the loss of specific relationships.

The care they extend to others, then, in times of difficulty and need, is not likely to involve a sacrifice of what they take to be valuable for the sake of someone else. Care does not take the form of altruistic action, where this is thought to require self-denial or a willingness to meet another's needs without consideration for one's own. Thus, among Aristotle's citizens, one would not find relations of unhealthy dependence in which some gain a sense of their own worth only through the assistance they give to others.[23]

But in our contemporary, non-Aristotelian, socio-economic circumstances, women who live with men are often in precisely this position of unhealthy dependence in regard to them. Given the still prevailing ideology which does not consider it deplorable that most employed women have low-paying, dead-end jobs and even that some women choose to remain unemployed, women tend to find themselves in positions of low self-esteem. Even if they are employed, they are usually economically dependent on men.[24] This dependence undermines the realization of their decision-making powers in various ways. Important family decisions, for example, are often left up to the men on whom the women depend. Even women's decision-making authority over matters connected with child care and household maintenance is upset by the extent to which the market has successfully penetrated the household. Many household decisions are now made for women by men through commercials in which men promote one product or another. Women are thought to be good (that is, easily manipulated) consumers, and most commercials are directed toward women, because women often lack the self-esteem necessary to make their own decisions about how to provide the proper physical environment for their families.[25]

These problems apply to the emotional environment as well. In the context of unequal economic power, whatever care and compassion is extended to family members is likely to be distorted and unhealthy. Since family relationships are often the only means through which women obtain a sense of their own worth, preserving these relationships may take place at the cost of encouraging psychologically harmful ways of treating family members. Care within the context of unequal power relations can generate more harm than good.

In such circumstances, where the preservation of a relationship may take priority over the content of the relationship, kindness and emotional support may be offered when other emotional responses might be more appropriate. Women in these circumstances, for example, may tend not to show anger, at least toward those family members with power and control over decision-making. Women may get angry at children, since this anger does not threaten the relationships that sustain women's sense of self-worth. But women in subordinate circumstances who have little self-confidence will be much less likely to feel that they are in a position to judge adult male family members. But a belief that another has acted wrongly or improperly is part of what provokes anger; therefore, to feel angry, one must have at least enough self-esteem to be able to judge another's actions as improper.[26] But judging another in this way is difficult for persons who have survived their oppressive circumstances by encouraging calm relations with those who have power over them. A lack of confidence in their own assessments will make them tend to accept the judgments and perceptions of others as correct, just as Aristotle's inirascible persons do. Kindness in such circumstances would seem only to sustain inequality, to obscure recognition of what is best, and to undermine further the decision-making powers of the person who shows kindness.[27] In these ways, care within the context of unequal power relations can harm both the person who gives it and the person to whom it is given.

These examples suggest that altruistic actions can be damaging when undertaken in circumstances in which the altruistic person lacks self-esteem. By showing kindness and compassion when other responses might be more appropriate, the kind person can act to sustain oppressive and unhealthy ways of relating to others. Through kindness, the kind person can make the acquisition of self-esteem even more difficult. Kindness seems least likely to damage oneself or another, however, when it is offered from a position of healthy independence. But healthy independence is precisely the psychological condition of Aristotle's virtuous person, who has true self-love. Because such a person has the appropriate confidence in who he is, he need not live through the achievements of another. This kind of dependent relationship will not be of interest to him, and he will not feel the need to act in ways to develop and sustain such a relationship. If kindness can be thought of as a concern for another's good for that person's own sake and as a willingness to act to contribute to that good, then Aristotle's virtuous person will act kindly, because this is the attitude he has towards his fellow citizens. Yet Aristotle's virtuous citizen knows that another's good is not equivalent simply to what another wants. He knows that another's good includes the performance of activities that will nurture and sustain the other's self-love. So, Aristotle's virtuous citizen recognizes that showing concern for another's good for the other's own sake may take all sorts of forms, only some of which will look like mere behavioral niceness.

I have been suggesting that if compassion and a concern for relationships constitutes some kind of model or ideal, it is not a simple one according to which we simply act to preserve the relationship or act to help another achieve what he might want. If compassion and concern are directed toward another's good for that person's sake, then for them to be proper objects of an ideal, they must operate against the background of some sound recognition of what another's good consists in. If not, compassion and concern can serve to promote oppressive or destructive relationships. Moreover, if the compassionate person is an ideal, she must be someone whose concern for another is ungrudging and non-instrumental. Aristotle's virtuous person is most likely to offer that kind of concern, since she is secure enough in who she is not to begrudge other's successes and not to rejoice spitefully in other's losses.

Aristotle's ideal has been considered masculine because it deems the best life to be that which fully realizes the rational powers characteristic of human beings. I have argued that Aristotle's emphasis on rational powers should not deter anyone, particularly feminists, from embracing his model. Although Aristotle organizes the best life around the pleasures of rational activity, this does not commit him to a model in which the non-rational is suppressed or even subordinated. As I have argued, the realization of the virtuous person's rational powers are constrained by properly educated non-rational feelings and emotions. Moreover, Aristotle offers a way to explain how reason and emotion (and passion and feeling) can operate together to produce psychologically strong and healthy individuals—individuals who take pleasure from their own lives and from the lives of others, who are caring and concerned but not in ways that are destructive to their own self-esteem, who are independent while retaining strong and enduring ties of friendship and relationship. He offers us a view of compassion and care that is positive and constructive, not oppressive and debilitating.

There are various ways in which reason can be offered as an ideal. I think Aristotle's model of how to organize one's life around the pleasures of rational activity is worthy of emulation by both men and women.[28]

PART III

APPLICATIONS
OF ARISTOTELIAN ETHICS

ARISTOTELIAN VISIONS OF MORAL CHARACTER IN VIRGINIA WOOLF'S MRS. DALLOWAY

Patricia Curd

> Worked at Aristotle all the morning, who remains singularly interesting &
> not at all abstruse, & yet going to the heart of the matter as one feels,
> which somehow puzzles me.[1]

Virginia Woolf maintained that fiction is and ought to be about character. In her May 18, 1924 lecture to the Cambridge Heretics Society, called "Character in Fiction,"[2] she expanded on points she had earlier made in "Mr. Bennett and Mrs. Brown." The lecture declares her interest in exploring and explaining the moral character of human beings, and she notes that this is not a pastime limited to novelists:

> I have said that perhaps I am the only novelist present. But I am quite cer-
> tain that everyone in this room is a judge of character. Indeed it would be
> impossible to live with any success without being a judge of character.
> This gift, or instinct, or faculty—whatever it is, is one that we use begin to
> use (sic) directly we get out of bed in the morning, and go on using more
> or less consciously all day long.[3]

In her own work Woolf is always concerned with character and its evaluation, despite the claim made both in *Mrs. Dalloway* and in *Jacob's Room* that it is difficult to say "of anyone in the world . . . that they were this or were that."[4] In her fictional characters she offers the opportunity to examine and evaluate alternatives, to refine and hone the gift, instinct, or faculty for judging character. This paper explores how an examination of *Mrs. Dalloway* in the light of Aristotelian moral theory can illuminate aspects of Woolf's conception of moral character. I shall focus on characters in *Mrs. Dalloway* against the background of Aristotle's account of moral virtue with its emphasis on practical intelligence, proper emotional states, and moral intuition. In Aristotle the best judge of character is the morally virtuous person, whose own desires and actions are the result of settled dispositions to choose well. This is also the case in Woolf's novel. I begin with a preliminary discussion of Clarissa Dalloway and other characters. Then, after turning briefly to Aristotle's theory, I argue that his conceptions of the nature of the morally good character and of the fundamental place of emotional states in moral virtue help to illuminate Woolf's assessment of character in *Mrs. Dalloway*.[5]

Virginia Woolf read the *Poetics* (in Greek) in 1905[6] and was impressed: "Read the Poetics all the morning—really excellent bit of literary criticism!—laying down so simply & surely the rudiments both of literature & of criticism. I always feel surprised by subtlety in the ancients—but Aristotle said the first and last words on this subject. . . ."[7] While there is no extant evidence that Virginia Woolf herself read the *Ethics*, there was a strong connection with G. E. Moore, and through Moore with Aristotle. Moore began as a classicist, and certainly knew the *Nicomachean Ethics*; moreover, his account of moral evaluation and method in ethics has Aristotelian resonances.[8] Virginia Stephen read Moore's *Principia Ethica*, and even refers to it in her first novel.[9] Leonard Woolf, who, like most of the Cambridge-educated members of Bloomsbury, was heavily influenced by Moore was a reader of Aristotle; he was trained as a classicist, and was familiar with the *Ethics*.[10] It is legitimate to read Virginia Woolf through Aristotle, for there is to be found in Aristotle a theory of character and its development that illuminates Woolf's own views.[11]

I. VIRGINIA WOOLF AND MORAL CHARACTER

The characters of *Mrs. Dalloway* are not perfect illustrations either of virtue or of vice (Woolf is too rich a writer to create characters that are caricatures). But understanding what Woolf says of them, and assessing both how they are deficient and how they succeed, brings us closer to Woolf's own views on character. In *Mrs. Dalloway* Clarissa Dalloway is both the central figure and the moral center of the novel; viewing her through the eyes of others, and being privy to her thoughts about both herself and others, we see Woolf's character evaluation at work.[12] In further examining her through an Aristotelian lens, we can better appreciate both her character and Virginia Woolf's view of virtue.

Clarissa is not without flaw: she is a snob; she is remarkably possessive of her daughter Elizabeth.[13] She "failed Richard in Istanbul," and suffers from envy when Richard is invited to lunch with Lady Bruton and she is not. In Woolf's first novel, *The Voyage Out*, Clarissa and Richard make brief appearances and both have problematic characters. Woolf herself was acutely aware of Clarissa's limitations. In her diary she describes Lytton Strachey's response to *Mrs. Dalloway*:

> He thinks [there is] some discrepancy in Clarissa herself; he thinks she is disagreeable & limited, but that I alternately laugh at her and cover her, very remarkably, with myself. . . . I think there is some truth in it. For I remember the night . . . when I decided to give it up, because I found Clarissa in some way tinselly. Then I invented her memories. But I think some distaste for her persisted. Yet, again, that was true to my feeling for Kitty.[14]

But despite the limitations there is in Clarissa something more:

> And now Clarissa escorted her Prime Minister down the room, prancing, sparkling, with the stateliness of her grey hair. She wore ear-rings, and a silver-green mermaid's dress. Lolloping on the waves and braiding her tresses she seemed, having that gift still, to be, to exist; to sum it all up in the moment as she passed. (264)

(This is Peter Walsh's estimation of Clarissa; but it is consistent with the views of both Richard Dalloway and Sally Seton.[15]) Here is a person of experience and discernment; she can "sum it all up;" moreover, she has Woolf's gift. "Her emotions were all on the surface. Beneath, she was very shrewd—a far better judge of character than Sally, for instance . . . she was honest" (114, 115). In this, she differs in important ways from all the others, and especially from Sir William Bradshaw and Miss Kilman.

Bradshaw, on the face of it, might seem to be a man of perfect virtue; after all he is the one who preaches "proportion"; he is "the ghostly helper, the priest of science" (142). Does he not exemplify and teach the (Aristotelian) doctrine of the mean?

> To his patients he gave three-quarters of an hour; and if in this exacting science which has to do with what, after all, we know nothing about—the nervous system, the human brain—a doctor loses his sense of proportion, as a doctor he fails. Health we must have; and health is a proportion; so

that when a man comes into your room and says he is Christ (a common delusion), and has a message, as they mostly have, and threatens, as they often do, to kill himself, you invoke proportion. . . . Proportion, divine proportion. (149–150)

Bradshaw fails to understand the place of emotion in a complete life. He does not understand the importance of feeling; does not understand the role of choice. "Sir William made England prosper, secluded her lunatics, forbade childbirth, penalised despair . . ." (150). Contrast his clinical view of Septimus Warren Smith with *Mrs. Dalloway*'s:

A thing there was that mattered; a thing wreathed about with chatter, defaced, obscured in her own life, let drop everyday in corruption, lies, chatter. This he had preserved. Death was defiance. . . . But this young man who had killed himself—had he plunged holding his treasure? (280–281)

In her thoughts about the unknown Septimus whose suicide brings death to her party, Clarissa shows far more real understanding of his plight and his action than the great Sir William who sees him for three-quarters of an hour. She alone sees behind the action to imagine and comprehend the motives and emotions that shaped it. Moreover, Clarissa does not like Bradshaw, and her distaste for him is a mark of her discernment of character:

Why did the sight of him, talking to Richard, curl her up? . . . What she felt was, one wouldn't like Sir William to see one unhappy. No, not that man . . . a great doctor, yet to her obscurely evil, without sex or lust, extremely polite to women, but capable of some indescribable outrage— forcing your soul, that was it. (278; 281)

Bradshaw himself does not feel, and fails to give proper importance to the feelings and emotions in himself and in others. He does not see that the whole, complete person must feel certain emotions as a part of happiness; moreover, he does not realize that virtue and living well cannot be dictated by a formula, that the soul cannot be forced. "He swooped; he devoured. He shut people up. It was this combination of decision and humanity that endeared Sir William so greatly to the relations of his victims" (154). His victims include not only his patients, but also his wife. "Fifteen years ago she had gone under;" there had been "the slow sinking, water-logged, of her will into his" (152). Despite his initial attractiveness, Woolf will not count Bradshaw as a person of virtue, for he fails to appreciate that virtue is a matter of emotion as well as of measure and that measure cannot be dictated.[16] Moreover, Bradshaw and Clarissa differ in the ends around which their lives are organized. Clarissa's is what she calls "life": the flourishing of her family, her friends, and herself; Bradshaw seemingly adopts public honor and approbation. He does what he does so that he, and his "victims," will be seen to do the appropriate thing. This underlies Clarissa's thinking of him as a manipulator of souls.

Another forcer of the soul who lives by rules is Miss Kilman. She has many admirable qualities: she lives alone and is trying to make her way in the world. But she, too, has only limited knowledge, not understanding, and she is deeply lacking in self-knowledge. Her own emotions seem closed to her: "Miss Kilman was not going to make herself agreeable. She had always earned her living. Her knowledge of modern history was thorough in the extreme ... It was the flesh she must control. ... At any rate she had got Elizabeth" (190, 194, 195). Clarissa Dalloway partly understands what is wrong with Miss Kilman:

> Miss Kilman would do anything for the Russians, starved herself for the Austrians, but in private inflicted positive torture, so insensitive was she ... she was never in the room five minutes without making you feel her superiority, your inferiority; how poor she was; how rich you were; ... it was not her one hated but the idea of her; ... one of those spectres who stand astride us and suck up half our life blood, dominators and tyrants. (16–17)

> The cruelest things in the world, she [Clarissa] thought, seeing them clumsy, hot, domineering, hypocritical, eavesdropping, jealous, infinitely cruel and unscrupulous, dressed in a Mackintosh coat, on the landing; love and religion. (191)

Miss Kilman does not recognize her anger, spite, and envy for what they are; she masks them with her religious conviction. She longs to humiliate Clarissa Dalloway, to "make her weep; ruin her" (189); but she attributes this to God's will, not her own. "It was to be a religious victory. So she glared; so she glowered" (189). Moreover, she lacks the capacity to imagine others. Her own life seems to her full of troubles, but she never considers that others might be unhappy, have doubts, suffer (195–196). She lacks the "goods of fortune," and her resentment at this lack colors her attitudes to others. The virtue she particularly falls short of is proper pride or magnanimity; she does not have and so cannot act on a correct understanding of her own value. It is resentment at the goods and virtues of others that motivates her actions and shapes her attitudes, particularly towards *Mrs. Dalloway* herself; and as the passages above show, Clarissa is aware both of this failing and of its source. In the course of *Mrs. Dalloway*, Virginia Woolf gives evidence of her views about moral virtue and moral character, but naturally, those beliefs are not presented systematically. But we can find a theoretical basis for many of the moral attitudes exhibited by the characters in *Mrs. Dalloway* in the account of complete moral virtue that Aristotle gives in the *Nicomachean Ethics*.

II. Aristotle and Moral Virtue

In considering Aristotelian and literary accounts of moral virtue, it is appropriate to consider whether the *Poetics* rather than the *Nicomachean Ethics* would provide the better basis for comparison, particularly in the case of Virginia Woolf, who read and appreciated the *Poetics*. Aristotle does, after all, say that tragic poetry should, by means of representation (including representation of character), produce pity and terror in the audience, not only to entertain but also to instruct. For in feeling the emotions, we affect the formation of our own characters.[17] But there are reasons against relying primarily on the *Poetics*. First, Aristotle's focus there is on tragedy and what he says is tailored to that genre. The novel, particularly in the hands of Virginia Woolf, is quite different.[18] According to Aristotle, tragedy deals with universals, but Woolf's novel is concerned with particulars. Aristotle insists that the characters in tragedy must be good, indeed must be better than we are (1454a16–22, 1454b8–10). But the novel explores characters who are often no better than we and who are ambivalent. Second, according to the *Poetics*, in tragedy, human character is secondary to the structure of the happenings in the plot:

> For tragedy is a representation (*mimêsis*) not of human beings but of actions and life (and happiness [eudaimonia] and unhappiness are in actions . . . and [humans] are of a certain sort according to their character, but happy or the opposite according to their actions); therefore they do not act to represent the characters, but they encompass the characters for the sake of the actions. (1450a16–22)

But we cannot understand Aristotle's claims about character in the *Poetics* without first considering his fundamental analysis in the *Ethics*. How are we to know that certain characters are better than we, or that their actions are appropriate as representations of their character without first knowing what character (and especially good character) is?[19] That issue is a concern of the *Nicomachean Ethics*; and thus, it is appropriate to focus attention on that work.

According to Aristotle, the morally virtuous person is the *phronimos,* the person of practical intelligence, who deliberates and chooses well, and whose choices are aimed at achieving happiness. *Eudaimonia* or happiness is, according to Aristotle, "excellent activity of the soul" and of that part of the soul having reason (1098a16–17, 1102a5–6);[20] this excellence is manifested in two ways: in moral and in intellectual virtue. The intellectual excellences include the virtues of wisdom and of practical intelligence; the moral excellences are virtues of character. Put this way, Aristotle's account might lead one to wonder what role moral virtue can play in his schema, for the moral excellences, as having to do with the passions (the "non-rational part of the soul" as Aristotle calls it) would seem irrelevant to an account of happiness that makes it "excellent activity of the part of the soul that has a rational principle." But the non-rational part of the soul itself has two aspects and one—that having to do with the passions rather than nutrition and growth—is such that "it has a rational principle in a way" for it can be persuaded by reason (*EN* I. 13). It is rational "in the sense that one listens to (takes account of) one's family and friends, not as one reckons up a mathematical problem" (1102b31–33). Here at the very beginning of the *Nicomachean Ethics* Aristotle stresses that the emotions and passions have a fundamental role to play in the virtuous and happy life.[21]

In *EN* II. 6 Aristotle offers this account of moral virtue:

> Virtue is a disposition to choose, lying in a mean relative to ourselves and defined by a rule: that rule by which the practically intelligent person would define it. It is a mean between two vices, one of excess and the other of defect; it is a mean, moreover, in that some of these vices are deficient with respect to, and others exceed, what is right both in feelings and actions (*en tê tois pathesi kai en tais praxesi*), while the virtue both finds and chooses the mean. (*EN* II.6 1106b36–1107a6)

There are three claims here that are relevant to a reading of Virginia Woolf's accounts of character, and I shall remark on all three of them. First, both feelings and actions are crucially important in Aristotle's account. Assuming that we can find some criterion of morally correct action, we must see that it is not enough simply to act correctly (as the virtuous person acts, as Aristotle often puts it); we must also have the correct emotional state as well. (It is this criterion for virtue that Bradshaw, Miss Kilman, and Hugh Whitbread all fail to satisfy.) And it is fundamentally important to note that the correct or appropriate emotional state is not one where the emotions are cowed into submission or are "under the control of reason" in the sense that they make no contribution to our moral state, as seems to be the case both in Stoic ethics and in Kant (and as Septimus Smith's doctors, Bradshaw and Holmes, seem to think). The morally virtuous person will *feel* certain things—grief, fear, pleasure, desire, and so on—in addition to acting in certain ways, if he or she is truly virtuous. The importance of the emotional component of virtue makes Aristotle's theory both importantly different from other normative theories and especially relevant to Virginia Woolf's view of character.[22]

Second, there is the doctrine of the mean state of actions, emotions, and passions. It is easily caricatured: "Aristotle says that *x* is too much and *y* is too little; so whatever is halfway between *x* and *y* is fine, and finding that out is just a matter of calculation." But this is incorrect. Aristotle himself says, "the mean relative to ourselves." At a minimum, this must mean that we must take into account more than the mere mathematics of the thing (Aristotle's own example at 1106a33ff. indicates this); and, what is much more likely, it also suggests that the mean between, say, acting with too much or too little fear may differ radically according to who the agent is and what the particular circumstances are.[23] Clearly what Aristotle must have in mind here is that the virtuous action will be the one that is done with neither too much nor too little fear, given the particular circumstances and the particular agent.[24] We ourselves are thus to find the mean of an emotional or passional state.

Finally, Aristotle asserts that the mean "is defined by a rule: that rule by which the practically intelligent person would define it." Now, as stated, it looks as though Aristotle intends that part of being a *phronimos* is knowing such rules, and this might imply that the rules are formulable, knowable, and (perhaps) easy to apply. But this is not the case:

> It is not easy to determine how and with whom and for what grounds and for how long one ought to become angry, or up to what point one acts rightly or is mistaken. . . . It is not easy to render in a rule (*toi logoi*) how much and what sort of deviance is blameworthy. For the decision rests on the particulars and upon perception. (*en gar tois kath' hekasta kan têi aisthêsei hê krisis, EN,* IV. 5 1126a32–b4)

Again it is a matter of "seeing"—the person of practical intelligence who determines the rule is one who perceives correctly, who "has the eye" as Aristotle puts it at 1143b14. At 1142a25–27 he says: "it (*phronêsis*) is concerned with the ultimate particular fact . . . which is the object not of knowledge but of perception."[23] This is moral intuition—perception of a particularly moral sort, for as Aristotle says:

> Now someone might say that all persons aim at the apparent good, but do not have authority over how things appear [to them], but of what sort each character is, that is how the end appears. But [I reply that] if each is somehow responsible for his own character, he himself will also be somehow responsible for the appearances. (*EN* 1114a31–b3)

This passage has special relevance to moral intuition in seeing ends, but it also comes into play here in determining virtues.[26] For Aristotle there is no "neutral eye"; there is only the particular moral eye of each person, determined by character. As a virtuous person, moreover, the *phronimos* is also a good judge of others. In *Mrs. Dalloway*, for instance, Clarissa is clearly such; and her judgments are plainly influenced by the development of her own character. In her youth her assessments were more rigid and conventional (89); as she has matured she has developed a wider moral vision. But this is not to say that a better and a worse, a correct and incorrect cannot be established; nor that such judgments cannot be universalized. Coming to know the better is itself a matter of experience and moral insight:

> We ought to pay attention to the undemonstrated sayings and opinions of experienced and older persons or those of practical wisdom no less than to demonstrations; for because of experience they have an eye [and] they see correctly. (*EN* VI.11 1143b11–14)

Moral intuition (as opposed to demonstration or proof) enters Aristotle's theory in two places: in determining final ends and in determining just what the virtuous act is in a particular case.[27] This latter claim is quite strong, for it includes the determination of what sorts of emotional states are to be valued and how they are to be evaluated, and so what the list of virtues actually is. Aristotle himself offers a fairly traditional list (see Book II of the *Eudemian Ethics*); but we might think it reasonable to add such emotions as love of family or love of country, calling for an account of virtuous familial love as opposed to obsessive possession or hypocritical pretense in the family or fanatical patriotism with regard to one's country. Although Aristotle is committed to reliance on perception and intuition he most certainly does not want to endorse the claim that one view is as good as another or that all we can do is to rely on a kind of sixth sense and agree to differ about moral issues as we do about whether a particular shade is blue or purple.[28] There is a correct account to be given; but its method is not demonstration. Aristotle suggests that his own dialectical argument in the *Nicomachean Ethics*, beginning from the *endoxa* (the views of the many and the wise) is one method. Another is the careful examination and evaluation of character. For Aristotle it is in such character evaluation that we expand and refine our own capacity to judge and come to a better understanding of the principles and standards at work in these evaluations. So the successful Aristotelian moral character is one who has certain emotions and has the capacity to manage those emotional states well; exercises a capacity for moral insight into complex moral situations, correctly perceiving what are and what are not the relevant particulars in each case; and judges character (his or her own and others') well.

III. MORAL CHARACTER IN *MRS. DALLOWAY*

There is a group represented in *Mrs. Dalloway* who might seem to be excellent examples of virtuous character. Aristotle says in Book I of the *Nicomachean Ethics* that he is addressing his remarks to young gentlemen of good family who have been brought up correctly and who are to become political leaders: they are the proper hearers of his lectures on ethics and politics. These are the "perfect gentlemen" of *Mrs. Dalloway*, especially represented by Hugh Whitbread. Hugh serves at Court, writes letters to the *Times*, sends presents, knows his way around. But Virginia Woolf represents him as vacuous, unimaginative, and unthinking: good breeding and good education alone do not make a *phronimos*. Not all hearers of lectures on political theory are able to form their characters in the appropriate way. Hugh observes the forms but lacks understanding. Consider Sally Seton's evaluation of him: "'He's read nothing, thought nothing, felt nothing'. . . . He was a perfect specimen of the public school type, she said" (110). On pages 288–289 we find that Sally's opinion has not changed: "strolling past in his white waistcoat, dim, fat, blind, past everything he looked, except self-esteem and comfort. . . . Hugh's socks were without exception the most beautiful she had ever seen." Aristotle would say that he acts as the virtuous person would act, but not for the reason that the virtuous person does. It is crucial to Aristotle's claims that the political life will include both intellectual and practical intelligence and activity.[29] Woolf's "perfect public school boy" lacks both.

Clarissa Dalloway, on the other hand, is in the process of developing a genuinely good character. Her actions and emotions have become a true part of herself, and are not the result of calculation; she has the capacity to judge character and to manage her emotions in a praiseworthy way. "Anyhow there was no bitterness in her; none of that sense of moral virtue which is so repulsive in good women" (118). Walsh thinks this of the mature Clarissa, in contrast with his view of her as a young woman who is morally repelled by the birth of an illegitimate child: "He could see Clarissa now, turning bright pink; somehow contracting; and saying, 'Oh, I shall never be able to speak to her again!'" (89). Her mature virtue and lack of display of that virtue is in sharp contrast with Miss Kilman who never lets pass an opportunity for such demonstration. It is true that some feelings are missing: she is repeatedly described (both by Peter Walsh and herself) as "cold." Clarissa admits the coldness in herself yet also both sees what she is missing and acknowledges its possibility, particularly in relationships with other women: "She could see what she lacked. It was not beauty; it was not mind. It was something central which permeated; something warm which broke up surfaces and rippled the cold contact of man and woman, or of women together. For that she could dimly perceive.... Only for a moment; but it was enough. It was a sudden revelation." Clarissa's recognition of her failing here may be profitably contrasted with Miss Kilman's failure to recognize her own faults. But in other ways Clarissa Dalloway's emotions are balanced and controlled: she loves her family and her friends; the parties that Peter Walsh despises are an integral part of her feelings for her friends:

> But to go deeper, beneath what people said (and these judgements, how superficial, how fragmentary they are!) in her own mind now, what did it mean to her, this thing she called life? Oh, it was very queer. Here was So-and-so in South Kensington; someone up in Bayswater; and somebody else, say, in Mayfair. And she felt quite continuously a sense of their existence; and she felt what a waste; and she felt what a pity; and she felt if only they could be brought together; so she did it. And it was an offering; to combine, to create; but to whom? An offering for the sake of offering, perhaps. Anyhow it was her gift. (184–185)

As the Aristotelian model helps to explain, her emotions and her actions connect with one another; she feels appropriately; the non-rational emotions are guided by practical reason, the appropriate balance is maintained.

In Septimus Warren Smith there is no such balance. Septimus sees himself condemned because he cannot feel; but the truth is that he feels too much. He is all emotion: emotion breaks over him in waves in the scene in the park (see 104–105); reason, calculation, and deliberation have no role to play here.[30] Septimus, unlike Clarissa, cannot manage his emotions: he congratulates himself on how little he feels when Evans is killed (130), and then "suffers sudden thunderclaps of fear" and panic when he thinks that he cannot feel anything for Evans (131). One might argue that Septimus' response to Evans' death is rational; in the midst of the carnage of the Great War congratulating oneself on still being alive is not, perhaps, an unreasonable thing to do. But from Woolf's and the Aristotelian standpoint, this is mistaken. One naturally does and ought to feel grief and sadness at the death of a treasured friend. Septimus' failure to feel is a failure (as he himself feels it to be), and, for Virginia Woolf, an important mark of the breakdown of his character.[31]

The final tragedy of Septimus' life is not his suicide, but the forcing of his suicide on him by Dr. Holmes, the agent of "proportion." For, in the afternoon, Septimus apparently begins to recover the balance of feeling and thinking (214–224). With Rezia he speaks naturally and quietly of unexceptional things; the ordinary things of life stay ordinary. But into this calm comes Holmes, who clearly understands nothing. Having repeatedly told Septimus that there is nothing wrong with him a good cricket match would not cure, Holmes now forcibly comes as Bradshaw's henchman. "So he was in their power! Holmes and Bradshaw were on him! The brute with red nostrils was snuffing into every secret place! 'Must' it could say!" (223). The only way to defeat them is to destroy himself, an act he undertakes wearily and open-eyed:

> There remained only the window, the large Bloomsbury-lodging house window, the tiresome, the troublesome, and rather melodramatic business of opening the window and throwing himself out. It was their idea of tragedy, not his or Rezia's (for she was with him). Holmes and Bradshaw like that sort of thing. (He sat on the sill.) But he would wait until the last moment. He did not want to die. Life was good. The sun hot. Only human beings—what did they want? Coming down the staircase opposite an old man stopped and stared at him. Holmes was at the door. 'I'll give it you!' he cried, and flung himself vigorously, violently down onto Mrs. Filmer's area railings. (226)

It is Clarissa who is able to understand: "Death was defiance. Death was an attempt to communicate; people feeling the impossibility of reaching the centre which, mystically, evaded them; closeness drew apart; rapture faded, one was alone. There was an embrace in death. . . . She felt somehow very like him—the young man who had killed himself. She felt glad that he had done it; thrown it away" (280–281; 283). From the point of view of both Septimus and Clarissa, Septimus' suicide is not the act of a madman, but a rational choice and an act of courage. Septimus here acts having a proper fear of the doctors, and knowing the alternatives.

It is worth considering a final, enigmatic character in the novel. What are we to make of Richard Dalloway? Some of the characters (particularly Peter Walsh and Sally Seton) are quite dismissive of him. Here is Walsh: "[Richard] was a thorough good sort; a bit limited; a bit thick in the head; yes; but a thorough good sort" (112–113). It is worth noting that Walsh's shallow evaluation of Richard is consistent with his own limited character; his values, too, are those of the "perfect gentleman." But clearly Richard too is a good judge of character (he is enraged with Hugh's treatment of the clerk in the jewelry store [173]); and his life may approach Aristotle's ideal of the political life: he has admirable views about "the detestable social system" (175) and he apparently has political virtue. He clearly loves Clarissa very much (though he can tell her so only by presenting her with a bunch of roses). But Clarissa understands ("But how lovely, she said, taking his flowers [;] she understood; she understood without his speaking" [179]), and she herself sees her own happiness as inextricably linked with Richard (47, 282). We simply are not told enough, but the bits of Richard that we glimpse (particularly from Clarissa's point of view) suggest that he, like Clarissa, has a good character.[32] In seeing Clarissa through Richard's eyes, we come to appreciate further her goodness and her lovableness. The relation between Richard and Clarissa exemplifies the Aristotelian friendship between spouses: "there is virtue in each and they would take delight in this" (*EN* VIII. 12 1162a26–27).[33]

We see the characters in *Mrs. Dalloway* from many points of view, but it is Clarissa Dalloway whose view shapes our own. Her understanding becomes ours, and in examining her accounts of the settled characters of her friends and the people whose lives intersect with hers we refine our own views of moral character. There are no philosophical arguments in *Mrs. Dalloway*; but there are representations of moral character and moral judgment at work. My discussions of Aristotle have concentrated on Aristotle's account of the nature of moral virtue and the proper role of the emotions in the morally virtuous character. These issues have been emphasised because they are concerns that Virginia Woolf shares, and which she treats as a fundamental and important part of human life. Evidence of this can be found in her diary. Recording her discussion with Lytton Strachey about *Mrs. Dalloway* she writes:

Perhaps, he said, you have not yet mastered your method. You should take something wilder & more fantastic, a frame work that admits of anything, like Tristram Shandy. But then I should lose touch with emotions, I said. Yes, he agreed, there must be reality for you to start from. Heaven knows how you're to do it.[34]

According to Virginia Woolf, in her Heretics Society lecture, it is "impossible to live with any success without being a judge of character." In *Mrs. Dalloway* she demonstrates the "gift or instinct" of character evaluation at work. Reading *Mrs. Dalloway* with the assistance of Aristotle provides a setting in which to place and to understand Virginia Woolf's own evaluations of the characters of her novel and of moral character itself.

ARISTOTLE ON *PHILIA*: THE BEGINNING OF A FEMINIST IDEAL OF FRIENDSHIP?

Julie K. Ward

One who is incapable of community or has no need of it . . .
is either a wild beast or a god.

Aristotle, *Politics* 1253 a28–9.

I

While it may seem unlikely to search for the basis of an account of female friendship in Aristotle, hardly a thinker known for his egalitarian views on women, one finds two reasons for reevaluating his theory. First, Aristotle's two major ethical works, the *Nicomachean* and *Eudemian Ethics*, constitute the first sustained philosophical discussion of *philia,* or friendship, in the Western tradition.[1] Second, and more important, feminist criticisms notwithstanding,[2] much of Aristotle's analysis relating to moral and intellectual virtue holds promise for feminist thought.[3] Although his remarks concerning women's status and capabilities in *Politics* I.13 are unremarkably sexist, reflecting conventional Athenian views about women, his *Ethics*, and particularly the account of *philia* they contain, appear fruitful for renewed philosophical consideration by feminists.

A reevaluation of Aristotelian friendship is pressing, too, on the ground that critical appraisal of the topic of friendship among contemporary Anglo-American philosophers has been ever increasing over recent decades.[4] Initially, philosophical focus trained upon the aspects of friendship relevant to moral or political theory, such as its capacity for generating altruistic emotions (Blum, 1980, 43–44, 69–70), for developing relations of trust needed for civic association (Rawls, 1971, 470), and for being generally life–enhancing (Telfer, 1970–1, 238–40). More recently, feminist philosophers have entered the field as well, noting that the philosophical analysis of friendship has been largely mute about friendship as it relates specifically to women. For many feminists, present differences in social and economic status between men and women constitute an impediment to what may be termed "gender-blind" theorizing; consequently, some have begun to investigate the possibility of constructing a theory of female friendship in distinction from the earlier accounts of friendship. For these feminists, the reasons for re-examining friendship have been practical and revisionary, as well as theoretical, insofar as they hold that women as a group have been excluded from certain social goods and institutions. For example, it may be argued that the networks that support friendships among men either do not exist for women or are contradicted by other relationships, primarily the marital relation, such that female friendships become difficult to maintain.[5]

On one line of feminist thought, radical feminists like Rich (1977), Millett (1977), Firestone (1970), Bunch (1981), Dworkin (1983), and Raymond (1986a,1986b) find female subordination to men the primary explanatory factor of women's experience, arguing that female friendships can form part of a system of solidarity among women that challenges the ideology of male supremacy, or patriarchy. Raymond, for example, seeks to establish a basis for female friendship through her discussion of women's association with other women through cultural myths and stories that exist against the background of male-centered institutions that devalue female-female relationships in favor of heterosexual relationships (Raymond, 1986a). While other feminists, specifically Marxist and socialist feminists, have criticized radical feminists for ignoring differences between women in terms of race and class,[6] and so, presumably, would criticize their attempt to provide a theory of female friendship as such, they have not themselves provided a class analysis of friendship among women. Additionally, while radical feminist claims may be more limited in scope than they appear (due to a tendency towards ahistorical theorizing), and so, controverted by social historians who require exact historical evidence of the extent to which female friendship has in fact been marginalized in Western culture,[7] the basic thesis remains unchallenged. One cannot deny that repeated theoretical attempts have been made to cast female-female friendship as adolescent, immature, or homosexual, and thereby to discourage and discount it,[8] even if one finds it difficult to assess precisely the strength of the claim that such friendship has been universally ignored and devalued. Furthermore, cursory observation in contemporary Western cultural representations of female, as opposed to male, friendship reveals a striking difference: while friendship among men is portrayed often and positively, that among women is absent, or worse, is depicted as transitory and instrumental in nature.[9] One might, therefore, concur with radical feminists concerning the need for a practice of female-female friendship, while conceding that since women do not constitute a homogeneous class,[10] a single analysis cannot count as comprehensive.[11]

II

In the delineation of a theory of female friendship, four specific features seem crucial to mention at the outset. First, friendship requires a kind of affection that leads to a mutuality of interests and concerns: it is based in the mutual liking between persons that is expressed in sharing time and activities, with one another. Here one should add, and this brings us to the second feature, that it seems to consist in something like what Claudia Card has called "cherishing"—having special affection for a particular person— rather than simply respecting another person (1990a, 205–6). That is, friendship requires a kind of affection that takes the sentiment beyond that of simply having esteem or regard for another person.[12] Third, it consists in valuing another person for possessing good qualities—qualities that the friend thinks valuable or praiseworthy in themselves. Finally, friendship seems to be the kind of relationship that serves as a natural ground for moral growth.[13] It may be noted that the four forementioned characteristics are of unequal logical status: the first three features distinguish friendship from other psychological states with similar emotional content (say, respect, or some forms of love), while the last holds on account of the other three. Furthermore, it should not be assumed that taken conjointly these exhaustively describe friendship. Similarly, what follows of my discussion of Aristotle's theory should not be understood to be a complete account. Rather, certain characteristics of his theory relevant to the present topic regarding women have been selected.

I propose, then, to turn to Aristotle's two main ethical works, *Nicomachean* and *Eudemian Ethics* (henceforth, *EN* and *EE*) for an understanding of what characteristics Aristotle holds that friendship possesses, and then to evaluate his account in light of what features may be considered relevant to a theory of female friendship. In both accounts of *philia*,[14] Aristotle delineates three kinds of friendship, each different from the other in the goal or aim of the relationship. So, we find that one kind of friendship exists for the sake of pleasure, another kind for the sake of something useful, and a third kind of friendship for the sake of moral virtue itself (cf. *EN* 1155b19–21).[15] More will be said in the following section about the kinds of *philia*, especially the third kind, but we need to focus initially upon three general features of what Aristotle refers to as *philia*. First, he takes it that friendship is a "virtue," or *aretê*, a mode of ethical flourishing naturally expressing itself in actions constitutive of the good human life (cf. *EN* II. 6, 1106a15–24). Second, and related to the first notion, is the idea that friendship is a "disposition," or *hexis*, something which presupposes an emotion but which is not reducible to an emotion. Finally, in terms of its psychological content, *philia* looks similar to a state called *eunoia* which may be seen to consist in having positive regard for another out of respect or admiration. Yet he also takes *philia* to bear close connection to *philêsis*, "affection" or "liking" and this point, as we shall see, distinguishes friendship from *eunoia*, or "well-wishing."

In *EN* VIII. 2, Aristotle initially describes friendship in terms of *eunoia*. He notes that according to common opinion, *eunoia* is described as wishing good things for the other for his own sake (*EN* 1155b31).[16] But while this description looks similar to that of friendship, since *eunoia* may be had without the knowledge of the other person, it is in fact distinct from friendship (*EN* 1155b33, 1166b30–2). For friendship always involves well-wishing recognized by both persons, and also mutual affection—neither of which are required by *eunoia*.[17] So, although at first glance friendship may look like well-wishing, the two are clearly different. This brings us to a third feature of friendship distinguishing it from well-wishing, or *eunoia*, namely, that friendship normally involves *philêsis*, "affection," which Aristotle tells us necessarily connotes intensity and desire (*EN* 1166b32–4). So, well-wishing, or *eunoia*, is differentiated from friendship in virtue of its emotional content. For, *eunoia* is here described as lacking the kind of emotional state that *philêsis* signifies, in the sense that *eunoia* is without the intensity (*diatêsis*) and desire (*orexis*) that *philêsis* possesses. *Philêsis* also requires intimacy, or familiarity (*sunêtheia*), whereas *eunoia* does not (*EN* 1166b34–5). Given what Aristotle uses to differentiate *eunoia*, we can begin to come to an approximation of what he means by it as against *philia*. Both the accounts in *EN* VIII. 2 and *EN* IX. 5 place *eunoia* in the domain of positive feelings that we might consider as a kind of benevolent regard for another—having an attitude of respect, or esteem, for another which is not identical to having the kind of affectionate concern for another that counts as *philêsis*. By emphasizing the distinction between *eunoia* and *philêsis* in terms of the differences of the psychological attitudes involved, Aristotle has secured a distinction between *eunoia*, "well-wishing," and *philia*.

The further part of his argument, that which marks a distinction between *philêsis* and *philia*, is that *philêsis* itself is a *pathos*, or emotion, whereas *philia* is a *hexis*, or dispositional state (*EN* 1157b28–9). For Aristotle, dispositions are not emotions (*EN* 1157b28–31), though they depend upon them; rather, they are states depending upon deliberation and choice (*EN* 1106a2–4). In contrast, emotions are that which move us, but they do not imply will or choice (*prohairêsis*) as dispositions do: Aristotle gives the example of becoming angry or afraid to show that we do not choose to be so affected (1106a2–3). In distinction from *philêsis*, "affection," which is an emotion, Aristotle holds that friendship is a state of character that is the result of deliberation and choice. One of the reasons for which Aristotle is certain that friendship involves choice is that friendship involves "reciprocal affection" (*antiphilêsis*) and this must involve choice (1157b30–31). Here, as in the two other arguments Aristotle gives for identifying friendship as a disposition, the presence of a deliberative element shows friendship to be distinct from a feeling or an emotion which is not something which we can be praised or blamed in having (whereas our vices and virtues are, cf. *EN* 1105b28–1106a2). In this regard, he notes that since friendship consists in wishing the good for others for their own sake, it depends upon a fixed disposition, not upon an emotion alone (*EN* 1157b30–32).[18]

While friendship partly relies upon an emotion, *philêsis*, it is more properly thought of as a purposive state or disposition (*hexis prohairetikê*, cf. *EN* 1106b36–1107a2). Specifically, one may consider friendship to consist in an active disposition involving choice, reciprocal affection, and the disposition to wish for and try to obtain good things for the other. In this last respect, the notion of friendship is suggestive of the characterization Aristotle gives to *philein* ("liking," or "loving") in *Rhetoric* II. 4: "let *philein* be assumed to be the wishing to another whatever we think good, for his own sake, not for our own, and the inclination to do such things to the utmost of our power" (1380b36–1381a2).[19] While Cooper (1980, 302) finds in the *Rhetoric* account of *philein* the crux of what *philia* is about, namely, "doing well by someone for his own sake, out of concern for him (and not, or not merely, out of concern for oneself)," this characterization of *philia* seems inadequate on a couple of counts. First, it obscures friendship's status as a *hexis*, a "disposition" or "state of character." Aristotle defines a *hexis* in *EN* II. 5 in the following way: "By *hexeis* (dispositions) I mean the things in virtue of which we stand well or badly with reference to the emotions, e.g., with reference to anger we stand badly if we feel it too violently or too weakly, and well if we feel it moderately, and similarly with referrence to the other emotions" (Ross 1105b25–28). Thus, considered as a *hexis*, friendship is a state of character, that is, the possession of a certain attitude toward one's emotions. In this respect, friendship is not adequately defined solely in terms of its performative aspect, "doing well for someone." For, friendship depends upon a specific emotional attachment concerning which one makes a certain choice to act; consequently, a full account of the action includes both deliberative and emotional components. This is not to say that *philia* would not naturally express itself in actions and choices with respect to the other person, but rather that the characterization of *philia* in terms of doing good for another glosses the nature of the internal state of the agent.[20]

The excursus into the differentiation of *philein, philia, eunoia,* and *philêsis* shows, first, that while *philia* partly depends upon *philêsis*, or "affection," the former refers to a voluntary and chosen state that is not an emotion. The second point is that although *philia* is a state in which one does good things for another, it is not reducible to a set of beneficent actions. Finally, when Aristotle remarks that to be friends one must have reciprocal and recognized *eunoia*, or well-wishing, for some good (1156a3–5), he does not accurately describe *philia* itself. As we have seen, this statement ignores various aspects of *philia* that emerge later in his discussion about *eunoia* in *EN* IX. 5 (1166b30–1167a21), as well as *EE* VII. 7, (1241a2–14). Summarily, we may say that three features distinguish *philia* from *eunoia*: its performative feature, its occasion, and its affective state. Concerning performance, Aristotle claims that whereas well-wishing, *eunoia*, does not by itself issue in action, friendship does, "for [well-wishers] merely wish good things for the others to whom they wish well, but they do not assist them or take any trouble on their behalf" (*EN* 1167a9–10). In contrast, the friend naturally puts into actions his or her desire for the friend's welfare: "the person wishing well only wishes [the good], but the friend also acts on what he wishes" (*EE* 1241a11–12). Secondly, well-wishing differs from friendship in terms of how it is occasioned: Aristotle claims that *eunoia* may come about suddenly (*ek prospaiou*), as when watching the competitors in a contest (*EN* 1166b34–1167a1, a20–1), whereas friendship does not, although it seems that well-wishing is the beginning (*archê*) of friendship (*EN* 1167a3–4; *EE* 1241a12, a14). Finally, well-wishing involves a kind of high regard for another, perhaps even admiration, as evidenced by the example of competitors who appear beautiful or brave (*EN* 1167a20–21, 1166a35), whereas friendship depends upon a more individualized kind of affection, *philêsis*, that admits of intensity and desire (*EN* 1166b32–34), as was remarked above. This difference in the nature of the emotion involved in friendship—that it consists in a kind of regard for another that is directed specifically to a certain person—also explains Aristotle's remark that what is especially characteristic of friendship, as opposed to well-wishing, is that one desires to share the friend's company (*EN* 1157b17–19, *EE* 1245a18–24).

Consequently, the initial mapping of friendship onto well-wishing in *EN* VIII. 2 stands in need of refinement so as to clarify its emotional component, *philêsis*, as well as its dynamical nature that expresses itself in action (cf. *EN* VIII. 5, 1157b28–33, 1157b5–7, respectively). As we noted earlier, friendship is a purposive state both in the sense that one takes a certain attitude toward one's emotions (cf. *EN* 1105b25, *EE* 1220b19–20), and also in the sense that it naturally expresses itself in activities aimed at the good of the other friend. So, although the disposition (*hexis*) of *philia* is formed out of a feeling (*pathos*) of an affection (viz, *philêsis*), the realization of the disposition is a mode of active choice which implies a synthesis of intellectual and emotional components. The full account of *philia* to emerge from the texts in *EN* VIII and IX, as well as *EE* VII, explains the sense in which friendship is both dispositional and performative in nature.[21]

Thus described, however, we seem to have signified only a generic feature of friendship, one that would fit any of the kinds Aristotle comes to distinguish in *EN* VIII. 3 (1156a6–10) and *EE* VII. 2 (1236a12–17). In both texts, Aristotle argues that since the objects of love or liking can vary, so, too, can the kind of affection one has for the other person in friendship (cf. *EN* 1156a6–7). Thus, while any friendship involves a friendly feeling and is a dispositional state, friendships are individuated by their respective ends: for pleasure, for usefulness, or for virtue (*aretê*). These ends determine to a great extent the nature of the relationship even though each sort consists in wishing good things for the other person. Of the three kinds of friendship, Aristotle holds that one kind fully exemplifies the features that friendship in general possesses, namely virtue, or character, friendship (*EN* 1156b7–10).[22] In fact, Aristotle spends some time in explaining why virtue friendship is to be considered the primary or best kind of friendship (*EN* 1157a30–31, *EE* 1236b27–29).[23] For example, he argues that since pleasure and utility friendships are dependent upon the one friend affording pleasure, or providing something advantageous to the other, they tend to be transitory in nature, ceasing to continue when the person is no longer pleasant or useful (cf. *EN* 1156a19–22). But since virtue friendship is said to obtain between two people who are good in themselves and to exist for the sake of the good, it is not easily shaken (*EN* 1156b11–12, b33–34). In comparison to virtue friendship, Aristotle considers personal friendships based on either pleasure or utility as subordinate kinds because they typically arise out of transitory needs, and consist in liking another solely for being useful or pleasant (*EN* 1156a10–24, 1157b1–5). This idea suggests why these friendships are qualified as "incidental" and "secondary" kinds of friendship.

In contrast, friendships of character, or virtue friendships, are sought for the sake of moral goodness, and so, by Aristotle's reasoning, best exemplify the notion of wishing good for the sake of the other (*EN* 1156b8–10).[24] Since moral excellence is a fairly stable state, according to Aristotle, friendships that are characterized by sharing activities that conduce to moral excellence are bound to be more lasting and permanent than those based upon their mutual usefulness or pleasure (*EN* 1156b11–12, 17–19, 33–34). So, while friendship in general is described as consisting in mutual well-wishing, or *eunoia*, recognized by both persons (*EN* 1156a3–5), only in virtue friendship does one wish for and try to obtain good things for the other person for his or her own sake, rather than for some extrinsic end that one obtains from the friendship (*EN* 1156a10–20, b7–11; *EE* 1237a40–1237b5). Of course, virtue friendship is not only good, but useful and pleasant to each friend and it is so in the fullest sense (*EN* 1156b12–15).[25] So, although Aristotle is not averse to calling friendly ties to others on the basis of pleasure or utility *philia*, he finds the features individuating friendship in general most fully exemplified in the form he calls virtue, or character, friendship.[26]

One might see here a sort of dissipation of the senses of *philia* from the primary to the secondary instances similar to what we see in the case of *eunoia* where Aristotle begins by claiming that to be friends, one must have reciprocated and recognized well-wishing, or *eunoia* (*EN* 1156a3–5). Yet, subsequently he claims that *eunoia* does not arise in friendships based upon pleasure or utility (*EN* 1167a13–14, *EE* 1241a4–5). He does not contradict himself here; rather, he reasons that if I wish good things for another person because that person is pleasant or useful to me, my well-wishing is what we might call self-interested; but since well-wishing seems to involve wishing good things for the other for the other's sake,[27] the secondary friendships do not support well-wishing in this strict sense of that term (cf. *EE* 1241a4–10).[28] In virtue friendships, in contrast, we find the most fully developed expression of the state, including greater permanence, the presence of mutual and recognized *eunoia*, the performance of good acts for the friend, and the desire to spend time and share experiences with the friend (*EN* 1171b26–27, b35–1172a8).

Let us take stock of the points of Aristotle's account of friendship, particularly that of virtue, or character friendship. As noted, Aristotle distinguishes three kinds of friendship in *EN* VIII. 3 and *EE* VII. 2 based upon their respective ends (pleasure, utility, goodness), and then argues that virtue or character friendship is to be considered the highest, or best, kind of friendship. He claims that on the grounds of permanence, the nature of the end of friendship, and of the quality of the affection involved, virtue friendship should be considered the highest expression of friendship. Aristotle contrasts the secondary friendships to the primary kind not on the basis that the primary are not pleasant or useful, but on the ground that they are more fully or completely pleasant or useful than the secondary are.[29] One proof of their difference is borne out, Aristotle thinks, by the fact that secondary friendships tend to be transitory, for the reason that pleasure and utility friendships are dependent upon the friend affording pleasure or providing something advantageous to the other. Hence, when the person is no longer pleasant or useful, the relationship has no further purpose, and ceases to exist (cf. *EN* 1156a19–22). In contrast, since virtue friendship obtains between two people for the sake of virtue, or moral character, and since this tends to be a permanent state, such friendship is characteristically durable. Furthermore, while all three kinds of friendship are described as consisting in mutual affection recognized by both persons, only in virtue friendship does one wish good things for the other person for her own sake, rather than for something one gets out of the friendship (cf. *EN* VIII. 6, 1156b9–10).

However, the distinction between the goal of virtue friendship and those of the other two kinds of friendship is not that between altruistic and egoistic goals, for even virtue friendships clearly have egoistic benefits: they are good, useful, and pleasant to us (*EN* 1156b12–17). In addition, Aristotle holds that our friendly feelings for others seem to follow from our love for ourselves (*EN* 1166a1–2, cf. 1168b1–5), further suggesting an egoistic basis to friendship.[30] So, Aristotle does not distinguish virtue friendship from the secondary kinds in terms of egoism, or self-love; rather, he explains virtue friendship as being the most complete or perfect (*teleia*), for this kind most fully reflects the central features of wishing good things for another, reciprocity, and similarity. Since virtue *philia* has moral goodness as its end, and since the two friends are themselves good, their relationship fully exemplifies the state of "reciprocal rational desire of the good insofar as they are good" (*EN* 1156a8–9). Furthermore, since both persons are good and desire the good for each other, their desire is not incidental to the person (*ou kata sumbebêkos*, *EN* 1156b11). For, in virtue friendship, the thing loved (i.e., moral character) belongs to the one being loved and does not depend upon some relation that the one who loves has to the loved one.[31]

Aristotle claims that only in such cases do we find that the wishing well for others for their own selves is present in the relationship.

We must now try to assess the significance that Aristotle's account of friendship has to a theory of female friendship. I shall argue that Aristotle's theory, in particular his theory of virtue friendship, provides a conceptual framework in which the four central features of friendship mentioned previously are accomodated and explained. If we consider, first, the feature that Card noted about friendship requiring "cherishing" as opposed to merely respecting another, we find the distinction between *philia* and *eunoia* to be relevant. For, Aristotle repeatedly argues that *philia* consists in more than having *eunoia*, i.e., having esteem or high regard for another. As he points out, *philia* consists in having the emotional feeling he calls *philêsis*, "affection" or "loving," which he claims is of a certain intensity, and accompanied by a kind of desire (*EN* 1166b32–34), whereas feeling esteem for another (*eunoia*) lacks these things. Now, the feature of cherishing another is arguably beneficial to any friendship, male or female, but seems to be especially important between female friends. For, it appears true that Western society has traditionally demeaned women (by race, class, religion, etc.), according them secondary status. As a result, we find that for cultural and historical reasons women tend to internalize their secondary status in the form of beliefs about their inferiority (in relation to the men in their race and class). This provides one reason for which female-female friendships are crucial: to assist women in understanding their position and supporting one another.[32] For, as Aristotle points out, the tie of affection found in friendship naturally leads to the desire to spend time together and to share activities. In the case of virtue or character friendship this would mean that the two persons would spend time together doing activities that conduce to their moral and intellectual excellence.

Here one might object that Aristotle's account of friendship, especially that of virtue friendship, would appear to have no application to women for two reasons. First, Aristotle does not concern himself with women's capacity for friendship. Second, insofar as women possess secondary status, it becomes unclear how Aristotle's theory could apply in principle. After all, Aristotle seems to be primarily concerned with demonstrating that the fully virtuous man needs friends. If true, the theory seems restrictive indeed. But, as Cooper (1980, 305) has argued, Aristotle's account should not be interpreted as referring only to perfectly virtuous adult men, even though this case serves a central function. Rather, it may be noted that Aristotle's interest in the friendship of good men is motivated by the desire to counter the claim that the good and happy man[33] needs nothing. His account of male virtue friendship thus answers this paradox (*EN* 1169b3–8). He offers several arguments in *EN* IX. 9 and *EE* VII. 12 disproving the idea that the good and happy man needs nothing, including friends.[34] In any case, the tendency to focus on male virtue friendship does not preclude that relations of friendship, including virtue friendship, can apply to women, and that they may serve to foster the training of good character-states. As will be pointed out, Aristotle alludes to virtue-training through friendship in one passage in *EN* IX. 9, opening the possibility that character friendship can be engaged in by those who are still becoming morally excellent.

An examination of the arguments concerning the good person's need for friends illuminates what function friendship plays in the good life. Here I will not try to comment upon all the arguments in *EN* IX. 9 that he presents; rather, I will mention briefly three that seem to be most relevant to my concerns. The first argument begins with the notion that humans are "political" (*politikon*) and naturally social, and then argues that the "happy" or "flourishing" person must live in society with others, and since friends are preferable to strangers, to live with friends (*EN* 1169b18–22). The second argument begins with the nature of human *eudaimonia*, or "flourishing," arguing that *eudaimonia* is an activity, and the activity of a good man is intrinsically good and pleasant, but since we are better able to observe the good actions of others than our own, we need to have good friends to contemplate good actions that are like our own (*EN* 1169b30–1170a7).[35] Finally, the third argument[36] that is noteworthy for our purposes is one whose central thesis is that since friends are necessary for one's self-knowledge,[37] and if this last is required for a good human life, then the flourishing human life requires having friends as a constituent part (*EN* 1170a13– 1170b19).[38] Each of these arguments rests upon various assumptions (some of which require additional argument) that will be ignored for present purposes. I assume that the arguments themselves convey sufficient plausibility so as to leave aside their technical aspects.

All three arguments depend upon an objective conception of human flourishing which should be useful for women as members of a secondary class to consider. Roughly put, all human beings have similar capacities and needs in virtue of being the kind of animals they are. Consequently, the kinds of activities that go into making a human life a good human life are objective in the sense that they are already specified by virtue of the various capacities human beings happen to possess. So, if it happens that a good human life consists in exercising one's capacities, both ethical and intellectual, for good character, then everyone should be enabled to engage in such activities. The reason that the objective conception of human flourishing is relevant to women is that it provides a theoretical basis for women to have recourse to a similar range of activities as men (allowing for differences such as childbearing), and for the same end, namely, to obtain a flourishing human life. The existence of social or cultural rules and norms preventing human flourishing for women based upon their allegedly inferior or "different" capacities should therefore be viewed with skepticism.[39] By keeping hold of the idea of a human good that promotes flourishing of all humans, women can argue that various restrictive sexist rules and practices should be eliminated since they prevent women from attaining fully human lives.[40]

Returning to the arguments Aristotle gives for having friends, it may be noted that two of these argue for the necessity of friendship on distinct but related grounds. The second argument above claims that friends are necessary for the good human life since one cannot be active by oneself, or as continously as one can if one is in company with others (*EN* 1170a5–8). Aristotle makes the argument on two bases: first, human activities are easier when performed in concert with and in relation to other people (1170a5–6); second, since the activities of the good person are pleasant and since they will be more continuous if practiced with friends, they will also be more pleasant (since more continuous) if practiced with friends (1170a6–8). In contrast, the third argument argues for the necessity of friendship on the grounds of self-knowledge, not on the grounds of the continuity or pleasantness of the activity itself. Now this ground may be considered to be complementary to the previous one insofar as this argument concerns the conditions needed for knowing what one is doing, as opposed to being able to do something. The argument concerning self-knowledge in *EN* IX.9 (perhaps more perspicuous in the version in *EE* VII. 2,1245a26–1245b10), basically consists in the notion that since it is difficult to have knowledge of oneself, and since one's friend is "another self," it is possible to know oneself through having and knowing friends. Even conceding the usual objections about one having a tendency to gloss over the shortcomings and exaggerate the strengths of one's friends (Cooper 1980, 322), the argument is reasonably persuasive. What Aristotle may be thinking about is an ability to engage in a kind of sympathetic knowledge of others through one's identification with others as being significantly like oneself. The reflexive activity here involved also allows one to understand better one's own self as a consequence of the identification with the other. The fact that it is not at all unusual for this to occur when one is sharing activities with friends, those with whom we have chosen to spend time for reasons of similar ideas or shared pursuits, explains the naturalness of Aristotle's suggestion that we can know ourselves through our friends.

There are two senses in which we might be said to know ourselves by observing others. In one sense, we know we are good antecedently and simply have this knowledge confirmed by observing others' good actions. But in another sense, knowing that we are good is partly constituted by what we are observing and that we are observing, so that observing another's good action enables us to know our own goodness.[41] The argument here at issue (*EN* 1170a13–b14) is ambiguous as to which sense Aristotle intends, but *Magna Moralia* 1213a10–26 suggests that persons who are morally good in character need friends to reveal to them that they are morally good. The *MM* passage states " . . . as then when we wish to see our own face we do so by looking in a mirror, in the same way when we wish to know ourselves we can obtain that knowledge by looking at a friend. For the friend is, we assert, a second self" (1213a23–4). Cooper suggests that this passage in *MM* supports the idea suggested in the *EN* argument at hand, namely, that we come to explicit knowledge of who we are by studying our friends' characters (Cooper, 1980, 322) which seems to employ the second sense. On this reading, we would require friends so as to be able to know, in some full, explicit way, that we are good.[42]

In addition to the virtuous person's need for friends, the less than virtuous person also needs friends. In another passage in *EN* IX., Aristotle notes, referring to a saying from Theognis, that a certain kind of training in excellence results from being in company with the good (*EN* 1170a11–13).[43] Although rather brief, I would suggest that Aristotle is here alluding to the idea that friendship can serve as a means of moral training, that is, by having friends who have certain excellences of character, we, too, come to acquire such excellences by observing and imitating them. Aristotle suggests that whether we are already morally developed or are not, we have a need for friends that is intrinsic to the kinds of creatures we are. In either case, Aristotle's arguments are useful to a notion of female friendship: in the first instance, we argue that friendship between two good women is of the best kind, promoting good actions and moral flourishing for both. In the case of women (or girls) who are perhaps not fully morally developed, character friendship—like that between a mentor and a student—can provide the kind of moral training necessary for human development.

The notion of friendship as providing a basis for moral growth has recently been developed by Marilyn Friedman, who argues that friendship can provide a basis for the moral growth of the individuals involved and serve as a source of political change at the level of the community.[44] Friedman, arguing from a pluralistic moral framework, claims that through friends we can gain insight into, and experience of, various moral perspectives distinct from our own that broaden the basis from which we evaluate abstract moral guidelines (1993, 195–202). Although Aristotle would assume that morally good persons possess the same moral framework and in this sense his idea of friendship cannot overlap with the one being proposed by Friedman, her thesis raises two points we might enlarge upon which are consistent with Aristotle's general account. First, we can gain understanding both of others and ourselves through the shared participation in other's experiences[45] that friendship affords, and second, in friendship we find a particular commitment to care about the other.[46] The fact that we do care for the other in friendship may explain our ability to share imaginatively in the experiences of our friends. While this particular kind of attachment is not prominent in Aristotle's account, something like care is suggested when he claims that a central feature of *philein*, "friendly affection," is in giving rather than receiving affection, and points as an example to the way that mothers feel toward their children; so, too, he concludes, *philia* consists more in giving affection (*EN* 1159a27–34).

There are certain basic features to Aristotle's theory that should be preserved in a theory of female friendship. First, the voluntariness of friendships—the idea that they are based on individual choice (not distinguishing here between the voluntary and the chosen as Aristotle does, *EN* 1111b 6–10)—as opposed to being based on kinship relations, for example, has interested feminists. Aristotle finds it characteristic of virtue friendship that it is a relation grounded in mutual choice and mutual excellence. In fact, for Aristotle friendship in general is founded upon choice insofar as one chooses to love someone for some good thing (pleasure, utility, or moral virtue, *EN* 1156a5–10). We need to consider a second Aristotelian feature of our ideal of women's friendship drawn from his acount of character friendship, namely, that the goal of friendship should be what is morally good for the other person (*EN* 1156b6–10). Finally, I would argue that the friendship should be sustained by the performance of good activities together. In these three respects, then, we might say that an ideal of female friendship would resemble the Aristotelian model of virtue friendship.

At this point, I will consider further certain concerns that may be raised in response to my application of Aristotle's theory to women. First, is it not the case that one has to be wholly virtuous (in Aristotle's sense) to have the best kind of friendship, and if so, does this not exclude the possibility that women—as well as most other people—can have such friendships? Although Aristotle sometimes speaks as though virtue friendships are reserved for those who are already morally excellent (and this would restrict the class to a small number of free, adult Greek males), in fact, this cannot be the case. For Aristotle would have to deny then that a young person could have an older person as a virtue friend, and that two good, young persons together could be virtue friends. But Aristotle allows these cases, as he does that a man and woman together can be virtue friends (*EN* 1158b13–19). This fact demonstrates that virtue friendship need not obtain between those who are moral equals. So, good men and women can have the best kind of friendship, but they will be unequal virtue friends because he takes male virtue to be more excellent than female virtue.[47] Additionally, it may be noted that when Aristotle mentions friendships among unequals, he usually stresses that among friends of unequal status or age, the inferior should give more affection to the superior, based on his principle of justice conceived as proportional desert (*EN* VIII. 9, 1159b25 ff.). So, this brings us to a second set of concerns. First, this claim appears to be dissonant with his ideas elsewhere about friendship depending more on giving than on receiving affection, and seeming to consist in the sort of love mothers give to their children (*EN* 1159a27–35). For if it were true that it was more important to friendship to give than to receive affection, then it should not hold true that a person of inferior status ought to give more affection than the person of superior status. Second, the concern is whether, in friendship between a good man and a good woman, Aristotle thinks that the woman must give more affection to the man than the man to the woman because she is of lesser virtue. One passage in *EN* VIII. 11 supports this idea: between a husband and wife, the friendship is the same as in an aristocracy in which each receives what is appropriate but the better one receives more affection (*EN* 1161a22–25).[48] Two comments are in order here. First, since it is the inequality in status between a man and a woman that requires that she give more affection than he, by proposing a friendship between two women, we obviate this consequence that assuming they are of roughly equal moral goodness. Second, Aristotle's point about women's secondary level of virtue does not affect his larger thesis about the nature, function, or need for friendship. Consequently, I do not find Aristotle's thought about the relative value of women as against men to be a problem for a reconsideration of Aristotle's theory of friendship once we have identified it. Discovering the presence of sexist beliefs in his account is only problematic if we wish to import Aristotle's theory whole into present contexts; but this is neither feasible nor necessary.[49]

The present re-evaluation of Aristotle's account has focused upon the aspects of male-male virtue friendship that are suggestive in relation to a theory of friendship between women. What has been shown up to this point is that various features relevant to an ideal of female friendship are present in Aristotle's account of male friendship in *EN* VIII and IX, as well as in *EE* VII. We have seen that, while Aristotle first locates *philia* in relation to what we may call "wishing well," he later modifies his account so as to add two other features. First, he wants to accommodate the relation of *philia* to *philêsis*, "affection," the specific emotional content underlying friendship. Second, he chooses to explain *philia* (like the other virtues) as a disposition which has as its active aspect wishing and choosing the good for another. Aristotle emphasizes here the distinction between *philia* and mere "wishing well" (*eunoia*) which connotes no active aspect, and need not be recognized nor reciprocated. With regard to the *philêsis* feature, this account of friendship recalls Card's notion of love as "cherishing" but extends it in two further directions. First, friendship is not simply an emotion but a disposition, a state of character in which we act upon our emotion, but which is not reducible to an emotion. Furthermore, since it is a state naturally expressing itself in actions, this conception would provide for interaction between women, making it an instrument both of individual development and of wider social action by increasing the ties among women.

The theoretical ground for conceiving of friendship as functioning in the personal and the more extended social domains arises from Aristotle's twin theses concerning human virtues, or excellences, and the social aspect of human beings. As noted above, humans possess certain capacities to function in distinctively human ways, and the virtues are the best expression of such human capacities. Further, since friendship is a moral virtue, it is an activity that is needed for full human development and the good human life, and so, by extension, is something that women should be invited and enabled to attain, in spite of Aristotle's notion of women as morally inferior to men in the nature of their virtues. But friendship, like the other virtues, requires a social setting in the sense that Aristotle thinks human, are fitted for living in complex social organizations. Thus, when Aristotle speaks of humans as "political" animals (*politikon zoon*, *Pol.* 1253a1–3), he means that, generally and normally, human beings need to live in complex social structures, like cities, which aim at certain common goods to which everyone contributes (Cooper, 1993, 305 ff.). The intersocial framework of the *polis* thus serves as the necessary backdrop for various kinds of friendship, according to Aristotle. Although civic friendship, as a distinct kind of friendship,[50] has not been pursued in this paper, Aristotle's postulation of civic friendship as a condition for the political life holds promise for feminist reappraisal insofar as it presents a model of political action and affiliation that is not fundamentally individualistic.[51]

We can, I believe, comprehend the case for a culture of female friendship: first, it conduces to women's development in a significantly different way to be mentored and cared for by other women. What Friedman argues for as fundamental to the moral growth of all persons is especially important for women since women face the task of assessing experience and formulating moral guidelines in a cultural setting which often seems to be "deaf" to women's individual needs and interests. In this regard, friendship, insofar as it is a relationship based upon choice (as opposed to unchosen kinship relations) allows women with similar ideals to become acquainted and support one another,[52] opening up the possibility for action by women with shared conceptions of the good. If friendship among women were to be conceived in the form of an Aristotelian male-male character friendship, it would be constitutive of women's flourishing. Furthermore, it would not merely be incidental to male-female relations, but would be centrally located in their moral and political existence, in the way that *philia* was for the Greek male citizen. Just as virtue or character *philia* represents an institution fostering personal ties and producing social goods for Athenian men, so, too, female character friendship can produce group identity and promote affection among women. In this respect, it could contribute substantially to women's understanding of women as such which is needed not only in the face of social and cultural emphasis on female-male relationships, but in view of women's division from each other by race and class. If we are responsible for our own moral growth, we must learn to respond to the needs of others. Virtue friendship furnishes us with the means and the motivation to do this, for it requires not only that we share affection for one another, but that we actively pursue the good for the other's sake, not intermittently but consistently, as a ground of our flourishing.

PART IV

LOGOS AND DESIRE

DIOTIMA TELLS SOCRATES A STORY: A NARRATIVE ANALYSIS OF PLATO'S *SYMPOSIUM*

Anne-Marie Bowery

INTRODUCTION

Among the many issues facing contemporary feminism, perhaps the most interesting is the postmodern deconstruction of the history of philosophy. Many feminist thinkers address the extent to which writers like Lacan and Derrida break with the *phallogocentrism* of their intellectual heritage.[1] While lauding these powerful poststructuralist linguistic methodologies, many feminists sense that contemporary Continental philosophy preserves the patriarchal hegemony of the tradition[2] If so, this perpetuation is particularly insidious because Postmodernism claims an anarchic freedom from these oppressive modes of thought. Since feminism promotes conceptual, political, and existential liberation, it must seriously grapple with this problem.[3]

By re-examining the history of philosophy in their own terms, feminists attempt to unravel the nuances of this conundrum.[4] Luce Irigaray, among others, seeks "to rewrite the script of western civilization" (Whitford, 1991, 101). Desiring "to undo that founding gesture," feminists occasionally turn to the grand patriarch of Western philosophy, Plato (Whitford, 1991, 101). Some argue that Plato is largely unsympathetic to feminist concerns and any attempt to resuscitate him is misguided.[5] Others recontextualize Platonic texts in a way that uncovers philosophic positions more harmonious to feminism. Feminist interpretations of Plato tend to focus on two particular texts: the *Republic* and the *Symposium*. In the *Republic*, Plato argues, perhaps ironically, that women should train along with men as guardians of the city (*polis*). In the *Symposium*, the enigmatic Diotima appears as Socrates' teacher of Love (*Erôs*). This paper follows the second path, emblazoned by the detailed interpretations of Luce Irigaray and Andrea Nye.[6] My work differs from theirs because it focuses on the narrative structure of Diotima's speech instead of its metaphysical content. This paper examines the narrative aspects of Diotima's speech and analyzes how Socrates and Plato both employ the narrative techniques that she demonstrates in their respective philosophical practices. In doing so, this paper offers a different and often overlooked basis for understanding how Diotima's speech influences Socratic and Platonic philosophy.

Though sympathetic to the aims of feminist philosophy, the inspiration for my methodological approach arises out of a branch of Platonic scholarship, namely, dramatic interpretation. In the past, most scholars ignored the dramatic form of Plato's dialogues and focused on their argumentative content. Since Aristotle, philosophers have extracted metaphysical debates and constructed epistemological arguments from Plato's literary masterpieces. Dramatic interpretation of Plato, on the other hand, emphasizes the significance of the dialogue form of Plato's work and acknowledges that Plato writes about human interaction. After all, the dialogues are replete with conversations, chance encounters, argumentative confrontations, amorous flirtations, raucous parties, and meandering walks beneath the noontime sun. Dramatic interpreters insist that these carefully constructed details are a central component of the dialogues' philosophic nature. Essentially, one cannot understand Plato's philosophy without understanding his drama.[7] Within this methodological school, some interpreters also mention the narrative structure of Plato's dialogues as a part of their dramatic, literary nature.[8] However, close attention to the narrative structure of the dialogues remains a largely untouched field of research.

Since this chapter discusses the narrative structure of Diotima's speech, a brief explanation of narratology, a genre of literary criticism, is appropriate. Briefly stated, narratology studies "the form and functioning of narrative" (Prince, 1982, 4). It acknowledges that "narrative techniques are a means of achieving certain effects" and that we "know what a narrative is in relation to what it does" (Martin, 1986, 152). While close scrutiny of this complex discipline is worthwhile, a fruitful exploration of the narrative aspects of Plato's *Symposium* does not require immersion in the minutiae of narratological scholarship. Plato did not have the benefit of the elaborate theoretical arsenal of contemporary narratology, but he used narrative techniques anyway. So, too, contemporary interpreters can analyze his text without excessive familiarity with the narratological literature.[9]

Additionally, and central to our interests, narrative analysis provides another means for developing many concerns central to feminist philosophy. This kind of analysis provides a structure for philosophical thinking that "engages in an unfolding of local narratives," stories told from a particular politicized perspective, as opposed to more traditional philosophical thinking that seeks to uncover a universal foundation for knowledge and experience (Allen and Young, 1989, 11). Jeffner Allen and Iris Marion Young end their introduction to *The Thinking Muse* asking, "If feminist philosophy thrives neither in the domain of the human universal, nor in a position of marginalization, from where can women's lives [which are told in local narratives] be spoken?" (Allen and Young, 1989, 17). One place feminist philosophy can be spoken is in a narrative like Diotima's that embodies "the fruitfulness of interaction, the fecundity of dialogue" (Nye, 1989, 48). Ideally, narrative analysis can "give voice to that which has been repressed in Plato's texts" (Gatens, 1991, 116). Diotima's narrative philosophy, embraced by both Socrates and Plato, may offer a "vision of women's language opening up the possibility of women's distinct cultural identity" (Whitford, 1991, 5). With this possibility in mind, let us turn to the *Symposium*.

This narrative analysis of the *Symposium* divides into three sections. The first section establishes that Diotima tells two narratives. It also explores why Diotima employs these narratives to promote Socrates' philosophical education. The second section shows that Socrates appropriates Diotima's narrative methodology for his own pedagogical purposes. To teach his fellow symposiasts about *Erôs*, Socrates tells a narrative about himself and Diotima. However, Socrates changes Diotima's narrative methodology. He tells a story about himself where she does not. This self-inclusion emphasizes the pursuit of self-knowledge that is central to Socrates' maieutic philosophy. Socrates' actual practice of philosophy consists in his attempts to lead others toward a philosophical life. In exercising his craft, Socrates uses narrative extensively. By so doing, Socrates reveals the extent to which Diotima influences him.[10]

The third section of the paper maintains that Plato recognizes both the pedagogical power of telling narratives and the limitations of Socrates' particular narrative approach. I shall argue that Socrates' narrative pedagogy, while fostering his own philosophical journey, often hinders the possibility of philosophical growth in others. As a result, Plato employs narrative techniques quite differently than the Socrates he portrays in this dialogue. Unlike Socrates, Plato does not tell narratives about himself. Instead, he creates the complex narrative structure of the *Symposium*. While Plato remains absent from this dialogue, its narrative structure draws the reader into a philosophical world. As a result of this narrative absence, his readers must find philosophical answers for themselves. In many ways, Plato endorses the narrative model that Diotima used when she told a story to Socrates so long ago.

I. DIOTIMA'S NARRATIVES

1. DIOTIMA TELLS SOCRATES A STORY

In order to analyze several qualities of Diotima's, Socrates', and Plato's respective narrative styles that are conducive to the practice of philosophy, a simple definition of narrative is helpful. Robert Scholes and Robert Kellogg offer one: "for writing to be a narrative no more and no less than a teller and a tale are required" (1976, 4). These criteria are not sufficient conditions for a narrative to be a philosophical narrative, but they are necessary conditions. Diotima is the storyteller, and she tells two tales as she interacts with Socrates. The first story recounts the birth of *Erôs*, the God of Love. The second story relates the soul's ascent to the Beautiful itself (*to kalon auton*). When Diotima enters the dramatic setting of the *Symposium*, "we have the presence of a story and a story-teller" (Scholes and Kellogg 1976, 4). We have a narrative.[11] Although this observation may seem obvious, it provides a necessary foundation for my argument. Because so much scholarship devotes itself to the philosophical content of Diotima's speech, it often overlooks her use of narrative. Simply put, what Diotima teaches Socrates often obscures how she teaches him. Therefore, additional analysis demands recognition of her status as a narrator.[12]

To underscore the point that Diotima is a narrator, I will briefly describe each narrative that she tells. In Diotima's first narrative, she tells Socrates about the father and mother of *Erôs* (203b–204b).[13] She narrates "a once upon a time" story about the origin of *Erôs*. The story has a plot. All the gods except Penia are invited to Aphrodite's birthday party. Nonetheless, she comes to the party. Having become drunk on nectar, Poros passes out in Zeus' garden. As a result of these machinations and fortuitous circumstances, Penia seduces Poros and conceives *Erôs*. *Erôs* is born. He exhibits the characteristics of both his mother and father. In telling this narrative, Diotima explains how *Erôs* received his intermediary nature. Though scholars often recognize the importance of the intermediary nature of *Erôs*, they overlook the fact that Diotima conveys this information to us in a narrative.

Similarly, scholars almost universally acknowledge the philosophical importance of the ascent passage (209a10–212a7), but ignore the fact that Diotima narrates the account of the soul's ascent to the Beautiful. However, the account is clearly a narrative. This story has a plot, perhaps the most famous Platonic plot. A person, divinely pregnant in the soul, desires to give birth. Then, one person has intercourse with another beautiful person and gives birth to "beautiful words" (*kaloi logoi*) in the soul (210a8).[14] Then, one perceives that the beauty of the soul is more valuable (*timioteron*) than the beauty of bodies (210b7). Again, one begets *logoi*, this time *logoi* that make the young better (210c1–3). One contemplates more beauty, beauty as it appears in daily pursuits and laws. Then, one sees the beauty of scientific knowledge (*epistêmê*)and gazes upon this vast beauty. Contemplating this great beautiful sea, one begets "many and beautiful *logoi*" (210d5–6). Finally, upon growing strong, one comprehends a certain single knowledge and will suddenly behold a thing that is "wondrously beautiful by nature" (210e3–5). In the presence of the Beautiful, the soul becomes philosophical. Andrea Nye correctly notes that this movement toward the Beautiful "never requires the renunciation of 'lower' forms of engendering, only a widening circle of those with whom we have loving intercourse, and a widening of the benefits of that intercourse" (1989, 48).

Diotima narrates a story about attaining knowledge of the Beautiful itself. That she chooses to narrate this philosophical pursuit of knowledge should not surprise us. Narratives and knowledge exist quite symbiotically. For example, it is no accident that the *Phenomenology of Spirit* is a narrative, just as Proust's attempt to capture lost time in excruciatingly complete detail must also be in narrative form. Postmodern philosophy has furthered awareness of this relationship between knowledge and narrative. Jean-Francois Lyotard speaks of "the preeminence of the narrative form in the formulation of traditional knowledge" (1989, 19). As we learn about the world around us, we construct narratives that structure and order our understanding. For instance, as we learn about the spread of the AIDS virus, we can construct a narrative that tells of its probable origins in the African rainforests and how the paving of the Kinshasa highway which links Zaire with East Africa helped spread the disease more rapidly (Preston, 1994). Furthermore, when transmitting knowledge to others, we frequently do so by means of telling a story. For example, James Watson (1969) relates the excitement of the discovery of the structure DNA in *The Double Helix*. Because she recognizes the ease with which one can convey knowledge by telling narratives, Diotima uses narratives to teach Socrates philosophy.

To narrate the plot-based story, to tell the tale, the narrator must have a certain level of knowledge. The narrator must be able to order events and fit them together coherently. The narrator must be able to distinguish cause from effect, discern reasons, and attribute motivations to human action.

Genevieve Lloyd explains, "The narrator has knowledge. He is able to bestow unity and meaning on the events of a life directly experienced as fragmentation" (1993, 15). In other words, to tell a narrative, the narrator must understand the subject and intend to convey that understanding to the listener. It might appear that one could narrate an account unintentionally while drunk or while dreaming, or that one might narrate an account without possessing the knowledge contained in the narrative, like the rhapsode Ion. In these anomalous cases, however, the subject's intention is other than to illuminate a series of events. If they do so, the result is unintended. Hence, from a philosophical perspective, they can be discounted as potentially philosophical narratives. However, Diotima's story is a narrative of the first sort. Throughout his encounters with Diotima, Socrates portrays her as a wise and thoughtful person. As Socrates begins to recount the philosophical lessons he learned from her, he remarks that she "was wise about such things and many others as well" (201d). In fact, as he narrates his experiences with her, Socrates refers to Diotima's wisdom four times.[15] This characterization is not accidental. Diotima controls the narratives she tells and intentionally conveys them to Socrates with the purpose of furthering his philosophical education.

Furthermore, narratives contain knowledge that the wise narrator has and the unwise listener does not. In this way, the power of narrative knowledge is enormously seductive.[16] The rapturous appeal in being audience to a narrative is not simply, as Peter Brooks would have us believe, "plotting, the dynamic aspect of narrative [that] makes us read forward" (1984, viii). Rather, the appeal lies in the belief that one will come to have the knowledge contained in the narrative. A narrative promises us this knowledge. According to Aristotle, this promise of knowledge seduces us because "to be learning something is the greatest of pleasures not only to the philosopher but also to the rest of humanity, however small their capacity for it" (*Poet.*, 1448b13–15). The seductive power of narrative lies in this enjoyment. As he receives this narrated knowledge from Diotima, Socrates begins to become wise, or at least to love wisdom, the very essence of philosophy.

As a narrator, Diotima exhibits two qualities that both display her own philosophic orientation and potentially evoke the practice of philosophy in her audience. First, she interacts with other people as she narrates. In doing so, she creates a participatory community that fosters philosophical exchange. Second, she exhibits an awareness of the fact that she tells narratives. In doing so, she displays self-consciousness, an integral aspect of Platonic philosophy. Plato's dialogues portray interaction with other people as an essential component of the philosophical life. Philosophical inquiry is a shared, communal activity because the participants must reach a level of agreement in order to philosophize. For example, Socrates speaks to Protrarchus: "come then, we must agree about these things and one thing more" (*Phil.*, 11d). Similarly, in the *Symposium*, Socrates tells Alcibiades: "counseling together, we will do what appears best concerning these things and others" (219b). The potentially philosophic participants then must use this agreement as a foundation for further inquiry. If philosophy occurs, it arises out of this participatory context.

Narrating an account also requires this participatory context. To narrate successfully, the narrator must include the audience—the narratee—in the narrative. The narrator must make the narrative relevant to the narratee. As a result, a successful narrative, like successful philosophizing, reflects an engagement with other people. Telling a narrative necessitates a participatory relationship between the narrator and the audience.[17] Gerald Prince remarks, "a narrator may thus postulate some sort of initial intimacy between himself and his narratee" (1982, 43–44). Wayne Booth explains how this initial intimacy functions: "Though it is most evident when a narrator tells the story of his own adventures, we react to all narrators as persons" (1973, 273). The narrator enters this participatory community, as well. Perhaps reflecting this harmonious philosophical community, Diotima "speaks in a style that is loosely woven but never definitively knotted" (Irigaray, 1989, 39).[18]

Indeed, Diotima's narrative style reflects a high level of participation with her audience.[19] Diotima involves Socrates in several ways. First, she converses with Socrates before she narrates (201e–202e). Diotima does not simply speak at Socrates. Instead, she establishes a cooperative relationship between them. Second, Diotima insists that Socrates participate in their inquiry into the nature of *Erôs*. She elicits his participation by addressing Socrates by name thirteen times and by asking him direct questions throughout their discussion.[20] Third, Diotima includes Socrates by using plural verb forms: "How would it be, let us imagine" and "Let's imagine how it would be if someone were to see the Beautiful itself" (211d10). By using these plural verb forms, Diotima associates herself with Socrates' position and simultaneously raises him to her level. In this way, Diotima establishes a partnership between herself and Socrates. James Phelan notes that such addresses and the narrator's various comments to a generalized 'you' explicitly acknowledge the importance of the narrator's relationship to a narrative audience" (1989, 139). Diotima makes their philosophic partnership explicit when she hypothetically supposes, "If someone were to ask us, 'What is the love of beautiful things, Socrates and Diotima?'"

(204d2–6). As a result of Diotima's inclusive efforts, Socrates becomes an integral part of the narrative she tells. Philosophy could, and in fact does, flourish in this participatory context that Diotima creates by narrating these accounts to Socrates.

While philosophical awakening can arise through an exchange with other people, it is clear that philosophy is also an inward journey. Throughout the dialogues, Plato portrays self-consciousness as a component of philosophical inquiry. In keeping with this idea, Diotima is reflective about the narrative process in which she engages. She frequently comments on the narratives that she tells Socrates.[21] Some examples include: "It's long to narrate, nevertheless I will tell you"; "just as I went through"; and "I will try to teach you" (203b1, 204c6, and 204d1–2). Insofar as Diotima reflects upon how she narrates and upon what she intends to accomplish by narrating these accounts, she demonstrates self-consciousness. This self-consciousness is a precondition for self-knowledge. Self-consciousness is an awareness of one's various activities: eating, speaking, narrating, thinking. Self-knowledge entails an awareness of oneself in terms of a system of beliefs or a theoretical understanding of the nature of the self and its relation to the world. Understood in these terms, Diotima's narrative style does not reveal her self-knowledge. Hence, one might argue that she lacks self-knowledge. However, Stanley Rosen (1973) argues that while Plato thinks self-consciousness is an integral aspect of philosophy, self-knowledge is, in fact, impossible. If his insight is correct, then Diotima exhibits the only kind of self-awareness that is actually attainable.

In fact, Diotima's narrative style serves a higher function: it promotes Socrates' philosophical education. Diotima's narrative style functions as *Erôs* does in the ascent passage. It leads the listener toward philosophical insight. Furthermore, by telling narratives in the manner in which she does, Diotima enables Socrates to move beyond a level of self-absorbed frustration as would happen if she merely used the *elenchos*, a process of argumentative refutation, to produce an *aporia*, a state of intellectual perplexity. Just as Aristophanes hopes that Eryximachus and Pausanias will teach others the true nature of *Erôs* (189d), Diotima instructs Socrates with the same intention. She hopes he will teach others. To what we can imagine as Diotima's delight, he does. Socrates ends his account of Diotima's teachings by reiterating that he is "persuaded by her speech" (212b). Socrates also believes in the pedagogical power of these narratives and "wants to tell others" (212b). In the end, he is not only persuaded by what she says, but also by how she says it.

Narrative analysis can enhance a feminist interpretation of Diotima by showing that in the *Symposium*, Plato produces an account of truth tethered

to the female. Many feminists argue that the patriarchal conception of philosophy, which Plato is typically thought to represent, refuses to allow a
female voice (Lloyd, 1984). For example, Donna Stanton sees philosophy
as "reproduc[ing] the dichotomy between male rationality and female mate-
riality, corporeality, and sexuality" (Stanton, 1989, 167). Irigaray, another
example, is "attempting to show that if you produce an account of truth
which includes, or is derivative of, an imaginary primal in which the role of
the mother is written out, leaving engenderment entirely to the father, then
your whole theory and its consequences will be marked by that forgetting"
(Whitford, 1991, 112).

Here, however, we do not find the patriarchal hegemony that so concerns
Stanton and Irigaray. Rather, in this dialogue, Plato portrays Socrates, his
teacher and by extension himself, as learning from a woman. By focusing
on the fact that Diotima, Socrates, and Plato all tell narratives in order to
promote philosophical education, one sees an undeniable affirmation of the
kind of philosophy practiced by a woman. Even if Irigaray plausibly decon-
structs the content of Diotima's speech, her argument does not diminish the
fact that Plato portrays both himself and Socrates imitating her method. By
focusing on the narrative aspects of Diotima's speech and by tracing out the
subsequent Socratic and Platonic uses of narrative techniques, one begins to
see that Diotima is not excluded from philosophy at all. In this way, this
"thinking muse" is not "forever outside the activity of philosophizing"
(Allen and Young, 1989, 1). Insofar as she persuades Socrates and Plato to
follow her narrative path, Diotima exists at the birthplace of philosophy.

II. Socrates' Narrative

In this section, I will accomplish three things. First, I will establish that
Socrates tells a narrative. Second, I will describe the philosophical qualities
exhibited in Socrates' narrative style. Third, I ask why Socrates chooses to
narrate an account to the symposiasts and suggest that his pedagogical use
of narrative techniques extends far beyond the dramatic context of the
Symposium.

(1) SOCRATES TELLS THE SYMPOSIASTS A STORY

When Socrates reduces Agathon and, by extension, the other symposiasts to *aporia,* he tacitly criticizes their conception of *Erôs.*[22] However,
Socrates does not merely criticize their ideas. He also posits a different way
of conceiving the nature of *Erôs*. More specifically, by reporting Diotima's
speech, Socrates stresses the intermediate and indeterminate nature of *Erôs*

(202a) over and against the fixed definitions of *Erôs* that the symposiasts present in their encomia. However, just as Socrates criticizes the symposiasts for their nonphilosophical conception of *Erôs*, he faults the unphilosophical manner in which the symposiasts speak as well. Just as Socrates delivers a new philosophical conception of *Erôs*, he proposes a new philosophical method of speaking as well.[23] Socrates' words make this proposal clear. He declares, "For I will not give an encomium in this way, as I am not able. However that may be, the truth, if you desire, I am willing to speak according to myself and not against your speeches so that I not be liable for being an object of laughter" (199a–199b2). Though Socrates does not explicitly prescribe the adoption of a narrative style of speech to the symposiasts as a means of becoming philosophical, he does remark that he will speak differently than they did. Indeed, he does not "give an encomium" (199a). Instead, Socrates says he will speak "the truth according to myself and not against your speeches" (199a). With these words, Socrates distinguishes his style of speech from the preceding non-narrative encomia and "bluntly repudiates this method" (Rosen, 1987, 205). He repudiates it by telling a narrative about himself and Diotima.

In Socrates' narrative, we again have the presence of a teller and the presence of a tale. Socrates tells a story about his education in *ta erotika*. In doing so, he creates characters that interact with each other. The first character is a youthful version of himself. The second is Diotima, a priestess from Mantinea. First, Diotima and Socrates converse; Diotima disabuses him of his Agathonistic conception of *Erôs* and offers the conception of *Erôs* as an intermediary between gods and humans (201e–203a). Irigaray notes that Diotima "teaches the renunciation of already established truths" (1989, 33). To illustrate the daimonic nature of *Erôs*, she tells him the story of the birth of *Erôs* (203b–204a). Again, Irigaray notes, Diotima "establishes the intermediary and she never abandons it as a mere way or means" (1989, 32). After this story, they discuss the purpose of *Erôs* and its usefulness for human beings (204d–206b). Diotima then tells Socrates the process that one must go through to ascend to the realm of the Beautiful itself (209a–212a). The tale ends as Socrates proclaims his allegiance with Diotima's conception of *Erôs*. He is persuaded and wants to persuade others (212b). Socrates appropriates Diotima's narrative methodology and affirms the philosophical suitability of it.

(2) THE PHILOSOPHICAL ASPECTS OF SOCRATES' NARRATIVE STYLE

Socrates' narrative illustrates the same three philosophical qualities that Diotima's did: it aims at increasing the listener's knowledge, it produces a participatory community with others, and it promotes self-knowledge in the narratee. The claim that Socrates displays knowledge by narrating this account may seem counterintuitive because Socrates regularly professes his ignorance (*Ap.*, 21b). Apart from aporetic knowledge of his ignorance, knowledge of *ta erotika* is one of the only positive claims that Socrates makes. Early in the *Symposium*, for instance, Socrates asserts, "I claim to know nothing other than erotic things (*ta erotika*)" (177d). Even taking into account Socrates' own erotic exceptions, his contention is clearly ironic. Socrates knows all kinds of things. He knows the exact location of where "Boreas carried off Orithyia from the river" (*Phdr.*, 478b–c). He knows the myth of Er, the story of Theuth and Ammon, and a number of theories about the immortality of the soul. He knows the entire content of the *Republic*, the *Charmides*, *Euthydemus*, and the *Protagoras*. Indeed, Socrates displays knowledge whenever he narrates. His pervasive narratives provide persuasive evidence that Socrates is ironic when he professes to know nothing but his ignorance.

Again like Diotima, Socrates involves his audience in his narrative. Following Diotima's lead, he converses with the symposiasts before narrating his account to them. For example, he banters with Eryximachus (194a) and compliments him (198b). He asks Phaedrus' permission to question Agathon (199b). He refutes Agathon and reduces him to *aporia*. Then, he explains the applicability of his narrative to Agathon directly: "I was saying to her the same things exactly as you were to me just now, Agathon" (201e).[24] When Socrates makes Diotima refer to Aristophanes' speech, he also includes Aristophanes in the narrative (205d–206a1). Essentially, Socrates flatters Eryximachus, Phaedrus, Agathon, and Aristophanes. Socrates makes them believe that their support and agreement are important to him. By paying attention to his audience, Socrates implicitly asks the symposiasts to return the favor. They should pay attention to his narrative.[25] In these ways, Socrates creates a receptive and participatory context for his narrative, a context in which philosophy might occur. Indeed, Socrates' attempts at inclusion seem successful. His audience applauds his narrative and Aristophanes even acknowledges a similarity between his discourse and Socrates' (212c). One danger of this receptive environment is that the narratee may be led to a unphilosophical position such as occurs with sophistic persuasion. However, such an eventuality is possible, according to Plato, only where the possibility of knowledge is denied and when a responsible context in which the student can learn fails to develop (*Gorg.*, 448b). In contrast, the necessary relationship between narrating, knowledge, and its participatory community mitigates against the possibility of sophistry.

(3) SOCRATES' USE OF DIOTIMA'S NARRATIVE STYLE

If Socrates had merely displayed knowledge, included his audience in his narrative, and reflected on his narrative activity, then his narrative style would not differ substantively from Diotima's. However, Socrates adds another dimension to the content of his narrative. Socrates tells a story about himself. That he does so should not surprise us. Socratic philosophy arises out of the Delphic oracle's dictum, "Know thyself." Socrates emphasizes this point to Phaedrus, "I am not yet able to know myself." As a result, "it indeed appears to me laughable, while still being ignorant [of myself] to examine other things" (*Phdr.*, 229e). Therefore, he continues, "I direct my inquiries, as I have just said, rather to myself" (230a). Laszlo Versenyi argues this point precisely. He remarks, "The maieutic method awakened self-awareness, self-reflection, and a self-critical inquiry into the truth it aimed to teach *nothing but* self-awareness, self-reflection, and a critical inquiry into oneself" (1963, 122). For Socrates, philosophy cannot be divorced from the search for self-knowledge. When Charles Griswold speaks of a "metaphysical connection between self-knowledge and knowledge of Ideas," he affirms this interdependence of philosophy and self-knowledge (1986, 3).[26] Telling a narrative intertwines with self-knowledge. One has only to think of Proust's *Remembrance of Things Past* or the auto-biographical books of Augustine's *Confessions* to see a central interplay between self-knowledge and narrative.[27] Gerald Prince even contends that "narratology can help us understand what human beings are" (1982, 164).

Indeed, in contemporary philosophic literature it has become commonplace to acknowledge a connection between self-knowledge and the activity of narrating an account. In fact, a pervasive theme of postmodernism affirms an identity between the self and the activity of telling stories. As one critic claims, "The meaning of a life can be adequately grasped only in a narrative or storylike framework" (Kerby, 1991, 4). Richard Rorty typifies this view, as well (1989). The view here articulated is that the self or subject is the product of language. It is itself a discursive result and not a prelinguistic item. If the self is a narrative construct, surely self-knowledge arises out of an exploration of the narratives that construct it.[28] Because Socrates tells an autobiography, his narrative style manifests a conception of self-knowledge that is more in keeping with Postmodernism than Platonism.

Socrates certainly does not have to tell a narrative about himself. He could simply relate Diotima's speech as a myth (*muthos*), just as he recounts the Theuth and Ammon story for Phaedrus (*Phdr.*, 274c–275b2). However, Socrates chooses to narrate an account about himself as a youth, a youth who receives Diotima's teaching. This self-inclusion shows that Socrates

believes that narrating should be an activity in which a person explains oneself. Socrates narrates how he came to have a philosophical conception of
Erôs. In essence, Socrates narrates how he became the person he is.[29]
Socrates tells "a story of how a life came to be what it was, or [how] a self
became what it was" (Martin, 1986, 75). When Socrates makes himself a
character in his narrative, he portrays narrating as an activity that pursues
the self as its focus of study. By narrating an account of himself, Socrates
obeys the Delphic oracle's command.

Diotima would not so readily associate with this Socratic precursor to
Postmodernism. Though Diotima narrates a story about the origin of *Erôs*
and a story about the soul's erotic ascent to the Beautiful itself, she does not
tell a story about herself. She does not tell her narrative to find out anything
about herself or to demonstrate her self-knowledge for Socrates. Though
she reflects upon the manner in which she narrates, Diotima remains significantly uninvolved with her *logos* because it is not about herself. Diotima's
absence prefigures Plato's own absence from the dialogues. Her absence
from the narrative allows it to function as *Erôs* functions, leading the listener toward the Beautiful itself. Hence, her narrative is equally applicable to
anyone. From a feminist perspective, Diotima's narrative style reflects a liberating universality. Andrea Nye notes that "there is no reason to think that
Diotima's teaching would have been meant only for men. The content of
that teaching clearly refers to both women and men" (1989, 58). The absence of Diotima's particular self in the the content of her narrative symbol-
izes the universality of Diotima's message.

(4) SOCRATES' NARRATIVE PHILOSOPHY

In the *Symposium*, Socrates implicitly posits narrating as a philosophically provocative activity in which the symposiasts should engage. As long
as they remain mired in their non-reflective, non-narrative encomia, they
will never be able to philosophize. Socrates wants the symposiasts to see the
philosophical benefit that narrating an account can offer. Why, though,
would Socrates care if the symposiasts became philosophical? As a partial
answer to this question, I will briefly consider how Socrates describes the
purpose of his interactions with other people. At his trial, Socrates characterizes himself as a "stinging fly rousing, persuading [and] reproving, every
one of you." As this gadfly, he attempts to prod the "big and noble
[Athenian] horse" toward philosophy (*Ap.*, 30e). In the *Theaetetus*, Socrates
characterizes himself as a midwife whose "patients are men [whose] concern is not with the body but with the soul that is in travail of birth" (149c).
Socrates draws out nascent philosophical impulses that might otherwise

remain buried in the souls of his interlocutors. Socrates explains that "the highest point of my art (*technê*) is the power to prove by every test whether the offspring of a young man's thought is a false phantom or instinct with life and truth" (*Thaet.*, 149c). These passages reveal Socrates' belief that he can evoke some type of philosophical reflection in others. In essence, Socrates practices a maieutic art. I maintain that the process of telling a narrative is one of the *technai,* like the *elenchos,* that he employs to lead other people to philosophy. Furthermore, Socrates portrays himself as having learned this narrative *technê* from Diotima.

First, while it is generally acknowledged that Diotima uses the sophistic technique of the *elenchos* to refute Socrates' beliefs, it is not generally noticed that Diotima's narratives are told immediately after she employs the *elenchos.* For example, Diotima begins her conversation with Socrates by refuting his previously held conception of *Erôs* (201e–203b). Immediately after this refutation, Diotima tells her first narrative: "That's a rather long story, but I will tell you anyway." (203b). The *elenchos* resumes (204a–210a). Immediately following this long refutative exchange, she begins to narrate the ascent passage (210a). By juxtaposing Diotima's narratives and the *elenchos* in this way, Plato suggests that they are both pedagogical *technai* that Diotima employs to teach Socrates. Socrates regularly adopts both *technai* in his practice of philosophy.

Second, Socrates learns this narrative *technê* from Diotima. While it is true that Socrates uses narrative techniques in many other places without crediting Diotima, he does explicitly say Diotima is his teacher. He calls her his "teacher about Love" (201e). He re-emphasizes the fact: "All this she taught me" (207a) and underscores the point a third time: "But that's why I came to you, Diotima, as I just said. I knew I needed a teacher" (207c). Finally, Socrates ends his account of Diotima's teachings by reiterating that he is "persuaded by her speech" (212b). Thus, Plato's *Symposium* suggests that Socrates learns the narrative strategy that he incorporates into his philosophical practice from Diotima. The *Symposium* is unique in the Platonic corpus because it shows Socrates learning from someone who teaches him to narrate. By focusing on the narrative lessons he learned from Diotima, we understand Socrates' practice of philosophy in a different way. We come to see that it is profoundly narrative in nature.

III. PLATO'S NARRATIVES

Plato, like the dramatic characters he invents, also recognizes the pedagogical power of telling narratives. However, Plato tells stories quite differently than Socrates does, for he produces the narrative frame of the *Symposium*. After analyzing how this narrative frame structures the *Symposium*, a primary difference between Platonic and Socratic narrative methodologies becomes clear. Plato, unlike Socrates, does not tell narratives about himself. Because Plato chooses to remain anonymous from his narratives, he implicitly endorses Diotima's narrative methodology over and against Socrates' narrative practices.

(1) PLATO TELLS US A STORY

In the *Symposium*, Plato creates a teller and a tale. In fact, he creates many tellers and many tales. In dramatic order of appearance, we encounter Apollodorus, Aristodemus, Socrates, Diotima, and Alcibiades. Plato's first creation, Apollodorus, tells two tales. First, when asked by an unnamed interlocutor to tell the story of Agathon's party, Apollodorus narrates an account of how someone asked him to narrate the same story. The *Symposium* begins with this story: "I believe that I am not unrehearsed in what you are asking me." (172a). Second, Apollodorus tells the tale that Aristodemus narrated for him (174a–223d). Apollodorus recounts that Aristodemus meets Socrates coming from the baths. Socrates invites Aristodemus to a party. They go to Agathon's party. The guests at the party give speeches praising *Erôs*. Socrates narrates a story about Diotima narrating a story about Love and the ascent to the Beautiful. Alcibiades arrives. Aristodemus and Socrates leave the next morning.

Plato then creates the narrator Aristodemus. At some point in the past, Aristodemus told Apollodorus about meeting Socrates along the road and following him to Agathon's house. The story follows. Aristodemus meets Socrates coming from the baths. They converse and Socrates invites him to Agathon's party. They go. They listen to speeches praising *Erôs*. A drunken Alcibiades bursts in, accompanied by flute girls and revelers. The party degenerates into chaos. Aristodemus and Socrates leave together the next morning.[30] Clearly, Plato creates the narrator Socrates. Since Socrates tells the story about learning about *ta erotika* from that wise foreign woman, Plato also creates the narrator Diotima. Alcibiades, Plato's final creation, narrates the story of his famous, though failed, attempt to seduce Socrates (217a–222b).[31]

Yet nowhere in any of these tales told by his narrators does Plato tell a story about himself. Plato is anonymous. As one commentator remarks, "one of the features of the Platonic Dialogues which most immediately strikes the reader is the presence on virtually every page of a character called Socrates and the apparent absence of the author, Plato" (Rowe, 1984, 1).

This reticence on Plato's part has vexed, irritated, confounded, and confused Plato scholars for centuries. Solutions to this problem of anonymity vary widely. Some interpreters assume that Socrates must simply be Plato in disguise (Ryle, 1966; Tredennick, 1969).[32] Other interpreters argue that Plato's absence indicates the presence of his "unwritten beliefs (*agrapha dogmata*)" in which he doubtless lectured in his own name (Ryle, 1966; Taylor, 1960). Those concerned with historical correctness point out that the artistic creator did not sign a work in the way that our romanticized and pre-postmodernized conception of the artist demands. For example, Ludwig Edelstein explains Plato's anonymity by asserting that Plato continues the Pythagorean tradition of writing only in the name of the philosophical master, Socrates (1962). Postmodern interpreters use Plato's dramatic absence as they artfully deconstruct this founding father of idealism (Derrida, 1981). Though Platonic anonymity is accounted for in many ways, few interpreters elaborate upon Plato's narrative anonymity.[33]

This author, who so carefully constructed numerous portraits of other people narrating, who foregrounds the activity of narrating so prominently in the *Symposium*, never depicts himself as a narrator in any of his dialogues.[34] This Platonic absence or anonymity stands in sharp distinction to how Plato portrays Socrates. Socrates constantly tells stories about himself. The significance of Plato's absence cannot be overemphasized. This decision to remain anonymous becomes even more momentous when one acknowledges a literary and historical tradition of narrative appearances with which Plato could have aligned himself. Hesiod, Homer, Herodotus, Thucydides, and Xenophon all create distinct narrative voices for themselves. However, Plato does not appear like Hesiod, the shepherd, in the *Theogony*, narrating how he came to have his narrative ability. Similarly, he does not emerge as the "me" of Homer's *Odyssey*, commanding the muse to sing. He does not speak directly to his audience as Herodotus and Thucydides do in their respective histories. One recent interpreter correctly claims that "the attempt to recapture lost time is marked by Plato (no less than by Proust) as an expression of desire" (Halperin, 1992, 102). However, Plato's narratives are quite different from Proust's. Plato does not create a Marcel; he does not create a narrator with a pervasive and unified narrative voice whose fictional biography strongly resembles the author's historical biography. Even a less anachronistic example, Xenophon's *Memorabilia,* shows us that the anonymous narrative style of Plato's dialogues is distinctive. Xenophon begins his text, "Many times I have wondered" (I, I, 1). Throughout the text, he personifies himself, the author, as a narrator.[35] Plato never says anything like this; nowhere does Plato cast himself as a narrator.

This refusal to cast himself as a narrator is another aspect of Platonic anonymity.

(2) WHY PLATO NARRATES

Socrates transformed philosophy into a narrative practice by placing himself in the center of his narratives. Socrates' personality was too prominent in his practice of philosophy. As a result, people loved Socrates and not philosophy.[36] One of the main ways Socrates demonstrates this extreme self-involvement lies in his pervasive practice of telling narratives. Partially because of Socrates' compelling narratives, his disciples could not separate their love for Socrates and the stories he told from their conception of philosophy. Since they imitated Socrates' narrative self-orientation, they could not divorce their practice of philosophy from self-interested stories about themselves and Socrates. By telling stories about themselves and stories about Socrates, Socrates' disciples obscured the practice of philosophy. Plato's anonymous narrative stance attempts to overcome the seeming inevitability of philosophical discipleship.

Plato chose to be anonymous so that people would not love him. Philosophy is able to triumph over discipleship because Plato's narrative absence distances him from the reader. Helen Bacon believes that "the distance serves to engage the reader," in that we become participants instead of "mere spectators" (1959, 419). Roger Hornsby, on the other hand, senses Plato's intention more accurately. He describes the feeling of "aesthetic distance" that arises out of the *Symposium*'s complex narrative frame. He suggests that this aesthetic distance creates a "dichotomy between our intellectual awareness and our emotional involvement" (1956, 37). Plato's absence as a narrator fosters this dichotomy of distance. It severs emotional self-involvement from philosophical awareness. Since Plato himself does not appear, a reader of his dialogues cannot love Plato in the obsessive way that Socrates' disciples loved him. Instead, a reader moves toward a love of philosophy. Plato wants his readers to become philosophers. While Plato's absence does not preclude the possibility that a reader could love him obsessively, as a child might worship an absent parent or an adolescent girl pines after the boy who never returns her glances, Plato's consistent narrative silence suggests that he is willing to risk this danger.

By refusing to narrate as Socrates did, Plato provides a corrective example to Socrates' overwhelming presence in his practice of philosophy. Plato's absence from the dialogues portrays the necessary absence of the particular self from the highest level of philosophical insight. Just as Diotima remains absent as a character in her narratives in order to further

Socrates' philosophical education, Plato's absence turns the reader away from himself and toward philosophy. The reader should recognize that just as there is no complete account of Plato in the dialogues, so, too, there can be no complete account of the self in philosophy. Plato's refusal to represent himself in his narratives is a *pharmakon*, an antidote for Socrates' self-involved narratives. Plato always escapes, much in the way that Diotima's use of narrative escapes our notice. Circuitously, Plato's method of narrating in the *Symposium* returns to its depicted origin. Many aspects of Plato's narrative style resemble Diotima's. Like Diotima, Plato tells stories of love. Like Diotima, Plato tells stories of beauty. However, he does not tell stories about himself. Neither does Diotima. It is only Socrates and his disciples who indulge.

Diotima herself senses this philosophical lack in Socrates. A reexamination of Diotima's conversation with Socrates details the specific nature of Socrates' philosophical weakness. After Diotima narrates the story of the birth of *Erôs*, Socrates and Diotima converse about the nature of love. Near the end of their conversation, Diotima pauses. She does not know if Socrates will be able to follow the "higher mysteries" (210a). Nonetheless, despite her reservations about Socrates' intellectual capacity, she begins to narrate the ascent passage. One begins by a love of beautiful bodies and moves to a love of one body in which we engender "beautiful words" (*kalous logous*) (210a). Then one sees beauty in the soul and desires to produce "*logoi*" that make the young better (210c). One turns and contemplates a "great sea of beauty" and subsequently produces "many great and beautiful *logoi*" (210d). Up to this point, the creation of *logoi*, of which the creation of narratives is certainly a prime example, intertwines with every stage of the erotic philosophical ascent.

Then, one "sees some single knowledge that is of this beauty" (210d). Apparently, Diotima thinks Socrates will have some difficulty seeing this single knowledge because she interrupts her narrative at this moment to address Socrates directly. She urges him to "try to hold your mind to me as much as you are able" (210e). Having indicated her doubt in Socrates' intellectual capacity for the second time, Diotima continues, "All of a sudden, one observes something wondrous and beautiful by nature." Again, she stops narrating. She calls Socrates by name and explains that it is this wondrous beauty for the sake of which "were all the previous toils" (210e). She assumes that Socrates would not understand this crucial point without being told. This interruption marks the third time that Diotima expresses her reservations about Socrates' intellectual capabilities. She resumes her narrative. Finally, one ascends to that knowledge "which is no other than knowledge of the Beautiful itself" (211c). Again, Diotima acts as if Socrates would not understand the enormity of this situation without clarification. She explains the situation to Socrates: "Dear Socrates, here, if anywhere, is life worth living for man (*anthropos*)" (211d).[37]

Diotima's frequent direct addresses to Socrates are not the only indication of her awareness of Socrates' philosophical limitation. As she concludes, Diotima's language shifts. This shift in language further evidences her lack of faith in Socrates' philosophical abilities. Through most of the ascent passage, she speaks of the ascent as a process that any person might experience. Diotima's narrative of the ascent passage becomes a guide for the perplexed. Examples of the "universal" applicability of the ascent include: "It is necessary to begin as a youth"; "if he is guided"; "if he perceives"; "so that one sees"; "in order that he may believe" (210a4– 211d1). After describing the Beautiful itself, Diotima returns to Socrates. She refers to him as "dear Socrates" (*o phile Socrates*) (211d1). This ironically endearing vocative underscores that she will now address Socrates specifically. Her language changes. Diotima switches to a specific conditional use of language, remarking, "if ever you see," "it seems to you to be," and "if you and many others" (211d3–d6). This shift declaims the necessity for Socrates particularly (as opposed to anyone generally) to recognize the Beautiful itself. Furthermore, this viewing of the Beautiful itself does not occur within a linguistic context. Any mention of beautiful words (*kaloi logoi*) is pointedly absent from the last stages of the ascent (211a–212a). When Diotima emphasizes that the Beautiful itself "partakes of no body nor any discourse (*logos*)" (211a), she makes this point explicit. In fact, this assertion marks her last use of the word. A succinct statement about the nonlinguistic aspect of philosophy occurs in the *Seventh Letter*. Plato remarks, "Of these things [Dionysius' writings about philosophy], I know nothing" (*Epist.* VII, 341b). Plato goes on to say that many others have also written on these philosophical matters, ostensibly the same philosophical matters with which Socrates concerns himself. However, according to Plato, regardless of how they claim to have come to this philosophical knowledge, it is obvious they know nothing about it precisely because they have written something about it. To write about philosophy is to betray a lack of it. Plato, in contrast, ironically proclaims, "there is no writing of mine concerning these things nor will there be" (*Epist.* VII, 341c4–5). Though Plato does not write philosophy, this refusal does not immediately entail the nonlinguistic nature of philosophy. For instance, Plato might speak to his close companions about the nature of philosophy or lecture on the Good. To this possibility, Plato emphatically responds, "For it is in no way spoken of like other studies.

Knowing it comes out of much in the matter itself [knowledge of it] then comes suddenly, like a fire kindled by a leaping spark, it is generated in the soul and maintains itself" (*Epist.* VII, 341c–d).[38]

With its reference to sudden recognition, this passage demands comparison to the nonlinguistic ascent to the Beautiful itself that Diotima describes to Socrates, a stage of the ascent that she believes Socrates cannot make precisely because of his linguistic dependency. By continually alerting Socrates whenever she alludes to the Beautiful itself, Diotima implies that philosophical recognition of *kalon auton* without *kaloi logoi* will pose a difficulty for Socrates since the powerful and beautiful *logoi* seduce Socrates. Diotima does not believe that Socrates can comprehend the Beautiful itself because he cannot comprehend without *logos*. For Socrates, the *logoi* are so beautiful and great that he cannot see the Beautiful itself; he sees only himself. This implicit reference in *Letter* VII to the ascent passage and Diotima's reference to Socrates' inadequacy underscores the difference between Plato and Socrates on the issue of linguistic dependency. A bit later, Plato continues his thoughts about the weakness of *logos*: "On account of this, no one having sense (*nous*) would dare ever to place into it (*logos*) the things having been contemplated by him and especially immovable things" (*Epist.* VII, 343a). [39]

So if Plato speaks as Diotima, Plato's charge against Socrates is that he does not recognize the *aporiai* of *logos* or the weakness (*astheneia*) of *logos*.[40] Just as Diotima chastises the youthful Socrates so mired in *kaloi logoi* that he does not see the Beautiful itself, Plato chastises the older Socrates for depending on his self-oriented narratives as a pedagogical method. By depicting Socrates' practice of philosophy as indelibly narrative-based, Plato portrays Socrates as a person continually immersed in kaloi logoi. This immersion in speech marks Socrates' philosophical limitation. Socrates does not recognize that the limitations of his pedagogical approach arise from his inability to perceive *to kalon auton* without *oi kaloi logoi*. As a result, "as a character in the dialogues, Socrates lives on as a disembodied image whose being consists in pure speech" (West, 1979, 232). Socrates remains inexorably tethered to the narratives he tells. Plato, following Diotima's lead, may reach that beautiful realm.

THERAPEUTIC ARGUMENTS AND STRUCTURES OF DESIRE

Martha Nussbaum

We all know that society influences our thinking and our behavior in many ways. But we frequently imagine that we also inhabit a presocietal realm of "nature," and that our desires and emotions derive from that realm. This way of thinking was very much encouraged by romanticism, but it has older roots; it was alive, indeed, in the ancient Greek world. Greeks liked to talk about erotic passion as something that grows in us "by nature," and to refer to the compulsions of nature in explication of their sexual conduct.[1] The contrast between nature and convention, in the Greek world very much as in our own, was used to mark certain things as unchangeable and off-limits, other things as more superficial and potentially more mutable.[2]

On the other hand, in the ancient Greek world as in our own, there were also challenges to the naturalizing of emotion and desire. Philosophical arguments, some very powerful, began to question the idea that either emotions such as anger and fear or bodily desires such sexual desires and the desire for food were simply innate and biological, unshaped by cultural forces. The paper reprinted here is an attempt to begin mining the ancient arguments for what they might yield for our contemporary debates. As such, it is part of a larger and more detailed historical inquiry,[3] and also of a more detailed philosophical inquiry in which I sort out my own position on the issues raised in the historical texts.[4] Here, then, I shall only make a few observations about distinctions that I think need to be observed and questions that need to be asked.

First, it is important to distinguish explananda of different types, and, in particular, to distinguish appetites from emotions. I believe that these are logically distinct categories, although interrelated in complicated ways. The ancient Greek Stoics seem to me to have done better with these distinctions

than the Epicureans, on whom I focus in this paper. Sexual desire probably involves both appetite and emotion, and one way of looking at
Lucretius' proposal is that it attempts to separate the two components, preserving the first and eliminating the second.

Second, we should observe that positions that have been advanced in the
area of "social construction" differ over two questions: (1) What is the origin
of emotions and desires? (2) Is an emotion such as fear, or anger, or sexual
desire, a single thing, or are there many different forms of human emotion
and desire in different times and places, exhibiting no fixed "essence"? The
answers to the two questions are connected in many complex ways. A person who holds that e.g., fear is genetic in origin is likely to be an "essentialist" on the second question, reasoning that human biology remains relatively
stable across place and time; and yet she may readily concede that behavior expressing fear will in many ways be shaped by culture. The person who
holds that basic emotion categories are socially shaped is likely to recognize
a diversity of forms of emotional organization with no single "essence"—
although, as my paper argues, this may also not be so, since there might turn
out to be some reason why human societies all organize things in a very similar way. Getting clear about these two questions and their interrelations is a
very important part of making progress on the issue.

Third, we should insist that there are several different levels on which
claims of biological or social origin may be made. To focus on sexual love,
my central topic in the article, at least five different areas of our life with
respect to love call forth these competing forms of explanation.

(1) Custom and norms regarding the proper expression of sexual
    love—what acts one chooses, what partners are acceptable.
(2) Norms regarding the nature and morality of sexual conduct and
    emotion themselves—whether, for example, they are understood
    as intrinsically sinful and morally problematic.
(3) Norms regarding what is desirable in a sexual partner: body
    shape, features, dress, and so forth.
(4) The basic sexual categories into which erotic agents are divided,
    categories such as "the heterosexual," "the homosexual."
(5) The membership of particular individuals in one category rather
    than another.

Notice that even a hard-core biological determinist is likely to accept a
large role for social construction in (1), and possibly in (2) and (3). More
controversial will be (4) and (5), where the claim of social construction
bites deeper. On the whole, the Hellenistic philosophers are social con-

structionists with respect to (4). They hold, that is, that our basic emotion categories, categories such as fear, anger, love—and also many subcategories of agent within that—are social artifacts, and may be undone by philosophical teaching. Stoics may even hold this position about gender itself; at any rate, it is clear that they treated gender as a morally irrelevant attribute on par with national origin, and as one that would be minimized in the ideal city, by a scheme of unisex clothing, and by the continual teaching that our real identity is that of rational personhood, which is, it would seem, not gendered.[5] Hellenistic philosophers have little to say about (5), since they have little interest in child development. Presumably they would need to invoke some combination of social and parental conditioning to explain the emotional repertoire that the individual comes to have.

Fourth, we must carefully distinguish between the naturalness of a phenomenon, in the sense of its biological or innate origin, and its goodness. The fact that something is "natural" has often been invoked to show that it is good. But of course it shows no such thing, without further premises about the providential design about nature. Many things, such as diseases, are "natural" and bad; many things are man-made and good. The Greek *nomos-phusis* debate was already well aware of this, but some of our modern arguments have not always taken the point.

Finally, we should carefully distinguish between the question of social construction and the question of mutability. The fact that a phenomenon is biological in origin does not mean we are stuck with it forever. Diseases can sometimes be cured. The fact that a phenomenon is social in origin does not mean we can change it at will or easily. Seneca is aware that eradicating anger in a society, or even in an individual, will require a lifetime of patient continual effort, and that even such effort may prove unsuccessful, given the recalcitrance of habit. On the other hand, recognizing the nature of the phenomenon with which we are dealing does show us how we might alter it if we should want to alter it. So, as the Hellenistic philosophers thought, good philosophical argument on this point can be an agent of human freedom.

—*Martha Nussbaum, August 1995*

I begin with a passage from the ancient Greek Philosopher Epicurus (fourth-third century B.C.E.), who, in his *Letter to Menoeceus*, asked how human beings can be released from certain social and psychological constraints so that they can lead more fruitful human lives. This passage always occasions gasps and embarrassed giggles when I read it to undergraduate audiences; and it is from those giggles that I want to begin this inquiry. The passage goes as follows:

> The truly pleasant life is not produced by an unbroken succession of drinking bouts and revels; not by the enjoyment of boys and women and fish and the other things that a luxurious table presents. It is produced by sober reasoning that seeks out the causes of all pursuit and avoidance and drives out the beliefs that are responsible for our greatest disturbances. (*Letter to Menoeceus* 132)

That is a rather literal translation of the original Greek. I note that the most common translation by a very respectable scholar removes its peculiarities as follows:

> It is not an unbroken succession of drinking bouts and revelry, not sexual love, not the enjoyment of the fish and other delicacies of a luxurious table.... (R. D. Hicks)[6]

This is an important passage for anyone who is interested in studying the relationship between sexual desire and socially taught beliefs. It is important for two reasons. First, because it gives striking and characteristic evidence of some ancient Greek conceptions of desire and its objects that are strikingly different from our contemporary conceptions and cast light on the status of ours by their difference. Second, because it is part of the argument for a powerful philosophical theory concerning the social origins of desire. This theory holds that many forms of human desire and emotion are grounded in and partly constituted by beliefs that are learned in society—beliefs that might be criticized and even altered, if rational people decide that they are false, silly, or in other ways inimical to human flourishing. The two interests we might have in the passage are closely connected, as it turns out. For the information about historical difference that it reveals offers us strong reasons to accept the philosophical thesis it presents: desire is, at least in part, a social construct.

I

I shall deal with the historical point first. And I shall deal with it rather briefly, since there has recently been a good deal of excellent work along these lines, some examples of which appear elsewhere.[7] But since the articles here focus on particular areas of sexual life in the ancient world, it is still worthwhile providing a general overview of the state of the question.

For years, then, indeed for centuries, the discourse of the ancient world concerning sexual desire was treated by scholars, insofar as they treated it at all, as something at once impenetrably alien and disgustingly familiar. Around the borders of the great silence that surrounded the subject of ancient Greek homosexuality, one heard embarrassed whisperings that revealed two beliefs on the part of the whisperers: first, that it was highly peculiar, almost inconceivable, and surely incomprehensible that this oth- erwise sensible and even admirable people should accept with equanimity and even praise forms of conduct that Englishmen found thoroughly dis- gusting; second, that what was being praised in works of Plato and accepted laughingly in comedies of Aristophanes was in fact the very same "thing" that Englishmen were accustomed to forbid and find disgusting. This was why, in fact, it was thought so very bizarre that the otherwise rational Greeks did not conceal and condemn it. The result of this complex attitude—in a civilization that memorized the arguments of the *Phaedrus* even while putting homosexuals to death by hanging—was denial and embarrassed silence: the silence that is sternly enjoined at the moment in the film of E. M. Forester's *Maurice* when the eager young students are told that they may skip over certain passages in the *Phaedrus* in which they take a lively inter- est; the silence that is proudly proclaimed in the major scholarly edition of the works of *Catullus* by C.J. Fordyce, published in 1961 by the Oxford University Press, at the beginning of which we are told that "A few poems which for good reason are rarely read have been omitted." (When one exam- ines the editor's principle of selection one discovers that poems of a "het- erosexual" and scatological nature are unproblematically included.)

The silence was officially broken in 1978, with the publication of Sir Kenneth Dover's important and first-rate book, *Greek Homosexuality*.[8] But Dover, while determined to confront the subject with both tolerance and meticulous scholarship, took over in certain ways a major assumption from previous generations of non-scholarship: namely that there is such a thing as "Greek Homosexuality"—that is, that the phenomenon lived and described by the Greeks was sufficiently similar to modern-day homosex- uality that it made sense to write a continuous history of this "thing," homosexuality, and to talk about the ways in which Greek attitudes to "it" differed from our own. Dover was so determined to bring to light what had been pushed behind the courtliness that it never sufficiently occurred to him to ask whether what had been denied and pushed behind was in fact the same "thing" at all as what was there to be brought to light by historical inquiry—whether, indeed, there was any one "thing" at all corresponding to our conception of homosexuality. Dover is a marvelous scholar; his methodological care, his mastery of evidence from many different areas, and his general intellectual acumen make his book an extremely important one, and one from which the reader can learn an enormous amount about cultural differences as well as about putative continuities. Its specific conclusions are by no means invalidated by the philosophic assumptions that I am questioning. Nonetheless, questions of a fundamental kind remained to be asked, and the unity of the phenomena had to be called into question.

More recent scholarship has asked these necessary questions—inspired by the suggestive work of Foucault in *The History of Sexuality*, but by now pressing beyond Foucault's work in historical detail and precision. The essays in this issue give some examples of ways in which younger scholars have been arguing that the ancient discourse about and also the experience of sexual desire and its objects were very different from our own. I can, therefore, simply summarize the general direction of these findings very briefly.[9]

In order to do this, it will be useful to return to our Epicurus passage.

> The truly pleasant life is not produced by an unbroken succession of drinking bouts and revels; not by the enjoyment of boys and women and fish and the other things that a luxurious table presents.

What is it that makes modern undergraduates uneasy and amused here? What is it that makes our respectable translator feel that he has to translate it oddly, in order to make sense of it? It is not only the presence of males alongside females as objects of desire for the male recipient of Epicurus' letter, and the evident absence of any question as to the naturalness or naturalness of such enjoyment. That is certainly one thing that is striking about the passage; and it is one of the things that Hicks' translation, with its vague expression "sexual love," obscures. But it is surely not the only, or even the primary odd thing. What is odd and amusing above all is the grouping of boys and women together with fish and other delicacies of "the luxurious table"—as if the problem of sexual appetite was just one part of a general problem of bodily appetite and its management. Epicurus' oddly constructed sentence begins with something that we tend to think of as profound, intimate, defining of our selfhood, and morally problematic in a special way, and ends up with the superficial area of gastronomic choice, as if there were no difference of level or moral intensity between the two spheres. If we attempt to reconstruct what produced a sentence like this, a sentence that was supposed to speak vigorously to the experience of Epicurean pupils from many different backgrounds and social classes, we are led to attribute to Epicurus a general conception of appetitive enjoying that includes eating and drinking along with sexual activity, and does not make a very strong distinction between the two spheres.

The two striking features of this passage—its indifference about the gender of the object of desire and its treatment of sexual desire as just one part of a more general moral problem of appetitive self-control—are in fact characteristic not only of Epicurus' thought elsewhere, but also of a great deal of the discourse about desire in the ancient world. The recent scholarship to which I have alluded has convincingly argued that there was for the ancient Greeks no salient distinction corresponding to our own distinction between heterosexuality and homosexuality: no distinction, that is, of persons into two profoundly different kinds on the basis of the gender of the object they most deeply or most characteristically desire.[10] Nor is there, indeed, anything precisely corresponding to our modern concept of a "sexuality"—a deep and relatively stable inner orientation towards objects of a certain gender. There are morally salient distinctions in the sexual sphere, certainly, but they lie elsewhere: distinctions between activity and passivity, between controlling and being controlled, and also between being self-controlling and being un-self-controlled. But the moral assessment of persons with respect to their "sexuality" that is so ubiquitous in the modern world would have seemed to the ancient Greeks peculiar, arbitrary, and unmotivated.

David Halperin has proposed a parallel that will help us to have a vivid sense of this (Halperin, 1990b, 26–27). Imagine, he says, how we would react to a society that divided people into two distinct classes on the basis of their taste, or distaste, for a particular food. To stay close to Epicurus, let us take fish as our example, and let us imagine people divided into the ichthuphages and the non-ichthuphages. Let us, furthermore, imagine these preferences explained by the positing of an "edility"—a deep inner orientation towards foods of a certain sort that is a fundamental determinant of one's entire identity. Let us suppose that the members of the society in question believe that the ichthuphages are somehow problematic, "unnatural," "queer," while the others are normal, "straight," "all right." Let us, finally, imagine that they believe you cannot really know who a person is, deep down, without knowing that. This example seems to show us two things about ourselves. First, it shows us that distinctions that we take to be fundamental, inevitable, and "natural" might, from some other perfectly reasonable point of view, seem just as factitious, arbitrary, and peculiar as these food distinctions, which we ourselves would readily brand as superstitious and odd. Second, it gives us a way of beginning to imagine how social distinctions that are non-necessary and in some cases arbitrary can, nonetheless, form not only conceptions of desire but the very experience of desire, at a rather deep level. For, to take our fish example, wouldn't the member of the society in question have an experience of eating and food choice that is rather different from our own? Wouldn't the social beliefs, learned from youth and deeply internalized, totally transform the simple pleasure of biting into a grilled salmon, and cause many joyful acts to be hedged round with secrecy, guilt, and anger on the part of some agents, by embarrassment, silence, and worse on the part of others? Asking these questions helps us to begin to ask how, and to what extent, our own experience of sexual desire is informed by our own distinctions, distinctions that a study of ancient Greece shows to be non-necessary, non-natural, and perhaps not even terribly reasonable, obvious, or sensible.

These are complicated historical issues. Much more qualification and distinction-making is required if we are to understand fully how far and in what ways ancient Greek views really are different from our own. As I have said, I shall not attempt to present here the more detailed investigation that would be required. But now I want to use these historical observations to approach my second theme, the central issue of this paper. I have said that the Epicurus passage is part of a powerful argument for a philosophical conception of emotion and desire, a conception that holds that these elements of human life are to a great extent formed by socially learned beliefs, beliefs that can be altered if the participants decide that they are false, confused, or in some other way inimical to human flourishing. It is the primary purpose of this paper to investigate this conception as it was developed by ancient Greek philosophers, especially of the Hellenistic period, to ask about its implications for the analysis of sexual desire, and to see what light it may shed on contemporary debates about the "social construction of sexuality."[11]

II

Frequently we speak as if the emotions and desires are timeless ahistorical entities, springing up as parts of an animal level of human nature that is untouched by history and culture. Anger, fear, sexual desire, and many relatives of these are taken in this way to be parts of "human nature," parts that have nothing to do with what we have learned to believe as the result of the way in which we have been brought up. This picture of emotion and desire was dominant in Western intellectual circles for a long time, largely on account of the influence of British empiricism and related psychologies. And although it is now under heavy attack from many sides—

from philosophy, from anthropology, from psychoanalysis, and even from cognitive psychology[12]—it retains a surprising degree of influence in people's thought and talk about themselves.

Epicurus, and with him almost all major philosophers of the ancient Greek world, had a different view about the emotions. This view is that emotions such as fear, grief, anger, pity, and love rest on, and are in part made up out of, beliefs about the way things are in the world, beliefs in which the value-laden distinctions taught in society are prominent. Take, for example, anger. Anger, as Aristotle, Epicureans, and Stoics all argue, is not a mere animal reaction; it involves an attitude towards an object that is based upon certain beliefs. It requires, that is, the belief that one has been wronged, and wronged in a more than trivial way, by the person at whom the anger is directed. If we were to alter those beliefs—either by showing that the alleged wrong did not take place, or that it was really not important, or that it was not in fact caused by the person in question, we would expect the person's anger at that other person to go away. Even if some residual irritated feeling remains, it does not seem appropriate to call it anger unless it has that complex cognitive structure. Obviously, if this general point is correct, then people's experiences of anger will vary, not only in accordance with their view of the facts as to what has happened to them, but also, and more importantly, with their view about what things are damages and what damages have importance. As the Stoics were fond of pointing out, if we could get people to believe that nothing that could even in principle be damaged by another person is of any importance at all, we would have done away with anger completely.[13]

Much the same appears to be true of other major emotions. Fear, it is argued, requires the belief that there are important damages that one may suffer in the future, in a way that one is powerless to prevent.[14] Once again, one can imagine altering those beliefs. In a particular case, one might become convinced that the impending damage is not at all likely to occur, or that if it does occur it will not be a bad thing. Or one might become convinced that a whole class of possible future events usually thought to be damages are not really such. Or finally—as the Stoics urge—one might become convinced that the only truly important things are one's own thoughts and inner activities of willing. And then, if one believes as well that these inner activities are always fully under one's own control—as, again, the Stoics teach—then there will be no room at all for fear. Indeed, one can see that the changes in belief that remove fear would remove grief and pity as well. For a loss that one fears, looking to the future, is an object of grief when it has taken place. And pity is the other-directed relative of these emotions: for it requires the belief that the suffering of another person is of serious magnitude, and also that the damage or loss is not that person's fault. (For if one thought that it was the person's fault, one would blame and reprove, rather than pity.)[15]

In short, the major emotions seem to this entire philosophical tradition to rest upon a complex family of rather controversial evaluative beliefs, beliefs that can be assessed as either rational or irrational (with respect to the manner of their formation, the evidence on which they rest), and also as either true or false (with respect to their content). They can be examined and criticized by rational arguments, and in many cases they can be altered, if agents decide that the relevant beliefs are false. At this point, the various philosophers part company. For Aristotle holds, on the whole, that these emotions are frequently well-founded, and thus have a valuable role to play in the life of a good person. There are, to be sure, many instances of ill-founded anger and fear, many things (for example, money and reputation) that people care about more than they should and whose loss they therefore fear or resent more than they should. But, he holds, human life does contain possibilities for undeserved reversals of fortune, reversals that are truly serious and that provide good reasons for fear, grief, anger, pity—or, if the changes are good ones, for sudden delight and intense gratitude and passionate love.[16] His Hellenistic successors, the Epicureans and Stoics, deny this. Because they hold that the most important things in human life are always within the agent's own control, they also hold that emotions such as fear, grief, pity, and anger are always groundless, involving a belief in the great importance of that which lies beyond one's own control, and are to be extirpated completely from human life. Their radical ethical position—which requires them to deny the outstanding importance of such highly valued goods as the love of children and spouse, affiliation and activity within a political community, even the opportunity to perform virtuous actions—grounds an equally radical position concerning the emotions.

Emotions, then, are social artifacts, formations in the soul that result from the implantation of belief by society. But what can be implanted can also be examined and assessed. This job, these philosophers argue, is the task of philosophy. And notice that the critical scrutiny of philosophy, successfully performed, will change not only people's beliefs about the emotions. It will change the emotional experience itself. The truly convinced Aristotelian will not experience anger over slights to reputation or losses of wealth. The convinced Epicurean or Stoic will experience no fear at all, and will live in a calm and undisturbed condition. Epicureans defined philosophy as "the art that secures the happy life by means of reasonings and arguments."[17] Reasoning does not simply produce intellectual conviction; it changes the life of desire.

This position seems to me to be a powerful one, grounded in an extremely impressive analysis of the emotions in their relation to belief. Nor are the philosophers at all naive when it comes to describing the means by which emotion-grounding beliefs can be altered by philosophical "therapy." The emotion-grounding beliefs have been presented to the pupil almost from birth; they are bound to be deeply lodged in the soul, and difficult to dislodge. A one-shot argument might produce superficial assent; but that is very far, these philosophers know, from real, thoroughgoing inner conviction. "He does not really grant what he professes," says the Roman Epicurean Lucretius of a person who professes various rational convictions while fearing death in his heart (III. 876). And he characterizes the depth and the frequently subconscious nature of the fear-grounding beliefs by calling them "silent voices" that speak to the pupil despite her official protestations, and "hidden goads beneath the heart" that motivate her behavior "without conscious awareness" (III. 55–58, III. 873–78, cf. 1053–75). This means that philosophy, if it is to have the power to change such beliefs, will need to be something much more comprehensive than an avocation or a subject of study. It must suffuse the whole of life, constructing (whether in the existing culture or in an alternative community apart from it) an alternative mode of life, in which the frequent repetition of philosophical arguments and a continual practice of self-scrutiny fill up the pupil's daily life, transforming all other activities. Epicureans were asked to live outside of the city, and Epicurus wrote to a prospective pupil: "Happy youth—take sail, and flee from all culture." And it seems that the Epicurean teacher asked pupils to divulge thoughts and feelings, in order to receive intense philosophical criticism.[18] The Stoic Seneca reports that at the close of every day he reviews the day's activities critically, in an extended process of self-examination and "confessions," while his wife, "long since familiar with this custom of mine," waits patiently for him to come to bed (*On Anger* III.36). And the practice of self-scrutiny is central to all of Stoic therapy. In this way, these radical social critics expect that the philosophical arguments can, as Epicurus puts it, "become powerful" (*Letter to Herodotus* 83), in the soul and life of the pupil, transforming not simply intellectual adherence, but the experience of desire and emotion itself.

So far, I have focused on very general evaluative beliefs that are likely to be shared, in some form, by many, if not all, societies. I have not focused on the ways in which different societies construct the emotion-grounding beliefs differently, and I have not asked to what extent the ancient Greek philosophers recognize the possibility of such cultural differences. The answer here is, I think, a complex one. On the one hand, these thinkers about emotion do appear to believe that, where the major, highly general categories of emotion are concerned, all the societies with which they are concerned teach, in some form, the emotion-grounding beliefs. Death is feared in Greece and in Rome; everywhere in the known world people care about people and things in such a way as to make room for grief, for anger, for passionate joy and desire. On the other hand, when we examine the highly specific enumerations of concrete varieties of these passions, and the proposals for concrete instances of therapeutic treatment we find, I believe, a good deal of interest in cultural specificity. Lucretius assumes that Epicurus is right to suppose that everywhere there are fears and angers that need philosophical therapy. But he devotes a good deal of attention to the specifically Roman forms of these emotions in constructing his therapeutic argument for a Roman interlocutor: to the connection of the fear of death with subservience to priests, to the conventional understanding of aggressiveness and anger as linked with admirable military behavior. Not only the occasions on which these passions manifest themselves but also the peculiar shape and tonality of the experience of passions, the connections these have with other experiences, are seen to have a cultural component. (We shall shortly see this in greater detail when we discuss his account of erotic desire.) Attention to the culture's own categories shapes the lists and definitions of emotions given in the various schools.[19] Thus instead of simply translating all the terms of the Greek lists, the Roman theorists tend, instead, to look at the shape of their own experience. This cultural specificity is an essential part of therapeutic argument since, they argue, therapy is only as effective as is its grasp of the concrete experience of the pupil, including not only the pupil's theoretical beliefs, but also her fantasies, her images, even her dreams. Thus in reality, while holding that most human societies (indeed, all societies short of perfected philosophical societies, real or imagined) contain the major members of this family of diseases, the philosophers believe that, like good doctors, they ought to understand the symptoms that prevail locally and not simply do medicine from the textbook. Emotions are not simply general cultural constructs; they are complex syndromes that vary in subtle ways from place to place, and each culture constructs them somewhat differently, in keeping with its traditions of evaluation.

III

Is sexual desire like this? In the ancient world there were two schools of thought on this issue. One, represented by the Plato of the *Republic* and

Phaedo, held that sexual desire is simply a bodily urge, like hunger and thirst. It is to be classified with these and other bodily appetites, rather than with emotions such as fear, pity, grief, and anger, which are understood to have a complex cognitive structure. The appetites are seen as pushes, forces that in their very nature reach out for a certain characteristic type of object; they do not contain in themselves any conception of a good object, or any beliefs about what is important or fine. For this reason, they are thought to be impervious to rational therapy; if they are to be managed, it will have to be through some form of suppression. Good argument about the reasons for fear can actually remove fear; but argument about the worthlessness of food does nothing to alter the bodily feeling of hunger—and sexual desire is taken to be like this as well.

The other picture also has its origins in Plato—but in the more complex account of erotic desire that Plato gives in the *Phaedrus*. According to this picture, desire still has an animal component; but the complex experience of erotic desire involves all parts of the soul together—including reason. Desire itself conceives of its object as beautiful or valuable, has various beliefs about the object, and is responsive to changes in belief. In this picture, one's experience of sexual desire is in large part a function of one's thoughts and aims, of the ways one has been brought up to see the world, the distinctions one has learned to make.[20]

This picture of sexual desire and erotic love is further developed in Epicurean teaching—above all, in a brilliant section of Lucretius' *De Rerum Natura*. The purpose of this section of Lucretius's argument is to show to what extent and in what ways the experience of erotic love is shaped by social learning, to develop a critique of these social teachings, and to propose both a therapeutic treatment for those enmeshed in bad forms of love and a glimpse of a good or healthy form that will survive the therapeutic treatment. I have analyzed these arguments at length elsewhere:[21] I shall try to provide, rather briefly, an overview of the primary points, as they bear on our overall argument.

Lucretius links his account of desire to a general account of perception. For it is essential to show the variety of ways in which experience and learning can influence the inner life, if one is really going to get a good understanding of sexual experience and its cultural formation. In this general account, he argues that perceptual experience can mislead, unless perceptions are scrutinized and criticized by mind (IV.755 ff., 818–22). One way in which such deformation can occur is through the mutual influence of desire and perception. Desire is aroused by perception; but perception is also shaped by desire, since people see things in a way that is heavily influenced by their expectations and wishes, attending only to what corresponds to those wishes and often ignoring other parts of what is present (779 ff.). The mind, furthermore, has a tendency to extrapolate rapidly from its perceptions, building up a whole picture on the basis of a few signs, instead of attending closely to all the evidence that is actually before it (816–17). Clearly, wishes, habits and expectations will all influence the way in which the mind does this. So, too, he now argues, will our physiological state: for states of need and dissatisfaction lead us to focus on objects that might seem to promise an end to the dissatisfaction (858 ff.).

Lucretius now turns to influence of habit. In waking life, and even in sleep, our habitual pursuits influence what we see (what we attend to, what we construct). Forms of habitual activity—one's professional daily life, the books one regularly reads—contain characteristic structures of pleasure and attention that influence thought even at the unconscious level. Thus, in their dreams, lawyers see themselves pleading cases, generals fighting battles. Lucretius remarks that in his dreams he does philosophy: "I do this, and investigate the nature of things at all times and having found it I write it up in my ancestral language" (962 ff.). Since we observe similar phenomena in animals (who dream of hunting, etc.), we can conclude that this is a natural and not a god-sent process (986 ff.).

These observations, taken together, prepare us to understand how complex the experience of erotic love and its associated perception actually is, and how deeply shaped, in many different ways, by social features that work not just on consciousness, but even on the unconscious life of each of us. Stories, poems, myths, habits, expectations—all these lead us to see the person before us in a certain way, a way that may not be either correct or healthy. And Lucretius' remarks about the power of his poetry to shape thought reminds the reader that the verbal constructions of love with which any reader of love poetry is constantly assailed must have a corresponding power. Reading love poems and hearing love stories produce images and patterns of attention.

Lucretius now turns officially to the topic of erotic love. As we might by now expect, he argues that love, as most people experience it, is bad because it is based on false beliefs. But his account of the false beliefs, and the mechanism of their social transmission, is extremely complex. In his remarkable account of sexual intercourse, one of the most violent and arresting passages in all of Latin poetry, he assails both (conventional) love's beliefs about its aim and its conception of its object, describing the bad consequences of pursuing that aim and having that object.

The person in love—and his constant references to the clichés of love poetry show that he is speaking of a construction of love learned through the culture, and especially through literature—aims, above all, at union or fusion with the object of desire. (Throughout the passage, and in related passages in other books, this aim is contrasted with another aim that is available, and frequently pursued in nature: the aim of mutual pleasure.) But the aim of fusion is both internally incoherent and impossible. Incoherent because (speaking always from the point of view of the male interlocutor and pupil), the natural bodily function culminates in ejaculation into, whereas the wish of love is for taking in from. Nature's structure is at odds with love's design. Impossible, because the person never can be taken in. Even if little bits of flesh could be rubbed off, he says (cf. 1103, 1110)—or, one might add, if one's gender or sexual practices are such that one does take in something physiologically from one's partner—still, the aim of love remains unfulfilled. The aim will be satisfied only by complete possession and incorporation of the other person: and the person is far more than little surface pieces of matter. Lucretius concludes that lovers must necessarily remain frustrated, feeding themselves on perceptions, and on these alone (1095–96). We notice here that the fact that the partner is a separate person with a separate life is no delight to these lovers, but a permanent obstacle to the fulfillment of their deepest wish.

This account of love's aim must be understood in connection with the accompanying diagnosis of love's false beliefs about its object. Why does love want to incorporate or devour this person, and no other? Because this person is seen to be perfect, divine, the only one, the one he has to have. Lucretius repeatedly shows how many poetic clichés of the beloved woman as a goddess, a "Venus," inform male experience. Each natural property is transformed into a mythological perfection. The lover's perception, guided by stories and poetic myths, looks for a Venus in the real woman who is before him. Glimpsing a few signs, he makes up "attributes," the rest (1154), "blind with desire" (1153). Thus he hardly looks at the actual person before him, nor does he accurately notes the aims and goals she has, the real qualities she possesses. The lover's desire for complete possession and incorporation can now be seen as a desire to possess something of the more than human, to devour the divine.

This complex illusion, Lucretius now argues, has many bad consequences, both external to the erotic relationship and within it. The external consequences are familiar from the tradition's arguments against love: waste of strength, and force; loss of control over the rest of one's life; damage to one's fortune; damage to political activity; damage to reputation (1121–32). The internal consequences are more striking. The aim to possess the other, and its inevitable frustration, produce in the lovers a continual sense of frustration and non-fulfillment. Even at the moment of greatest sexual pleasure, "some bitterness rises up to torment them even in the flower of their enjoyment" (1134). This bitter feeling, we see, is caused by the discrepancy between the cultural fantasy and natural reality. To these torments are added the frustrations of jealousy. For love's aim is intolerant of the other person's separate life; and glances, smiles at others, all remind the lover of his incomplete possession. This leads, in turn, to suspicious behavior that is injurious to the other person, and, in general, to a disregard of the other's real existence and separate needs.

Finally, Lucretius argues, such a lover, armed with such aims, and with the overestimation of the loved one that goes with them, will prove unable to tolerate the evidence of the woman's everyday bodily existence. This passage is extremely important for any understanding of his views concerning the cultural construction of love, and its philosophical therapy.

> But let her be as fine of face as she can be, still . . . she does just the same in everything, and we know it, as the ugly, and reeks, herself, poor wretched thing, of foul odors, and her housemaids flee, far from her and giggle in secret. But the tearful lover, turned away from her door, often smothers the threshold with flowers and garlands, and anoints the proud doorposts with marjoram, and plants kisses, poor wretch, on the door. Yet if he were finally let in, and if just one whiff of that smell should meet him as he came in, he would think up some good excuse to go away, and his deep-drawn lament, long planned, would fall silent, and on the spot he would condemn his stupidity, because he sees that he has attributed to her more than it is correct to grant to any mortal. Nor are our Venuses in the dark about this. That's why they are all the more at pains to conceal the backstage side of their lives from those whom they want to keep held fast in love. All for nothing, since you can still drag it all into the light in your mind, and look into the reasons for all this laughing, and, if she has a good mind and is not spiteful, overlook all this in your turn, and yield to human life (*humanis concedere rebus*). (1171, 1174–91)

The passage begins as a piece of satirical unmasking. It asks the lover to look behind love's radiant appearance to see what is really there. It tells him that if he does so he will find that things are not as godlike and glamorous as they seem. We now have a stock scenario from Latin love poetry: the lover standing outside his mistress's door. In front of the door the lover places sweet-smelling flowers on the posts and kisses the door his divine mistress has touched. Inside we find foul odors and knowing giggles.

What is going on here? In my longer analysis (Nussbaum, 1986, ch. 7), I have argued that the most likely explanation of the scene is that the woman is having her period. The man, who has formed the habit of thinking of her as more than mortal (has "attributed" to her more than is right to grant to any mortal) would be expected to react to this ordinary bodily event with disillusionment, disgust, and repudiation. In this way, Lucretius continues, male illusions force the female to live a dishonest life, staging herself as in a theater and concealing the stage machinery. Since this lover has been brought up on myths of Venus, a Venus is what he must see. And so the poor human women ("our Venuses" says Lucretius with irony) must strain to give him what he wants, even if it means concealing themselves.

But it is the ending of the passage that we must now try to understand. We might expect that the reaction of the disappointed lover would be rejection of the woman, and disgusted scorn. But, clearly, that is not where Lucretius' therapeutic argument ends. The argument now takes a sudden and surprising turn, moving the pupil beyond disgust as well, to an attitude altogether new: "If she has a good mind and is not spiteful, overlook all this in your turn, and yield to human life" (*humanis concedere rebus*). What is the nature of the transition to this advice, from the moment of unmasking and disillusionment? And what does the advice itself mean?

What has happened, I think, is that Lucretius, by writing a surprise ending to the lover's story, has forced us to reflect on the oppositions contained within the story. He invites us to recognize that these opposites depend on one another. If there is not illusion, there is no moment of disillusionment. If there is no glamorous on-stage show, there is not backstage that looks, by contrast, mean and poor. If the loved one is not turned into a goddess, there is no surprise and no disgust at her humanity. The really cured state would not be the state of the disgusted lover. It would be a condition beyond both obsession and disgust, in which the lover could see the beloved clearly as a separate and a fully human being, accurately take note of the good properties she actually does possess, and accept both her humanity and his own. The fantasies of love taught through love poetry and in the culture more generally constrain and enclose both men and women, dooming the former to an exhausting alternation between worship and hatred, the other to a frantic effort of concealment and theater, accompanied by an equal hatred of everyday human things.

Lucretius does not repudiate altogether the social element in desire. By itself, social teaching and shaping is neither good nor bad: it all depends on the character of the social teaching involved. Without any social element, he shows us in Book V of the poem, human sexual life would be conducted "in the manner of the beasts" (*more ferarum*), and there would be no room for the experience of desire mingled with tender concern, or for the careful concern with mutual pleasure, that would characterize human society at its best. (In fact, Book IV concludes with an emphatic insistence on the importance of female pleasure, and with an account of a good marriage, based on mutual respect and on the accurate perception of one another's characteristics.) On the other hand, the myths concerning sexuality in his own society seemed to him to be pernicious and constraining, dooming all participants to an alternation between unfulfillable expectation and a disgust with perceived reality. It is his belief that the social teaching lies very deep: it shapes experience itself, not just belief about experience. And it affects what we experience not only in moments of conscious control, but also in our dream-life and fantasy-life, in ways not directly accessible to rational persuasion.

And yet, Lucretius also believes that these illusions can be therapeutically treated by philosophical argument; and that such teaching, repeatedly and skillfully applied, will result in a beneficial transformation of experience, even at the unconscious level. We learn from his poem to be skeptical of the social constructions that shape our thinking; and through its rhetorical and satirical elements we learn to distance ourselves from them, to begin to laugh at them. Longer and fuller experience of studying such arguments, and of looking at life in their light, can be expected, he claims, to form new habits of attention, new patterns of desire.

IV

This Lucretian argument, and the entire ancient debate that I have all too briefly sketched here, seems to me philosophically convincing, and highly relevant to current debates about the "social construction of sexuality." I think that these arguments show that, while sexual desire does have an important biological dimension, the beliefs we are brought up with, the stories we know, the terms and distinctions we use, all shape not only our discourse about desire, but also the experience of desire itself. These beliefs are not always evident to us as pieces of social learning, since they are very habitual, lie very deep, and frequently inform our entire language, in such a way that alternatives are hard to see, and our own current way looks like the only way. But history, anthropology, and philosophy, working together, can make them visible. And one of the most valuable consequences of the new scholarship on Greek homosexuality is that it is doing just that for our understanding of what we now tend to call homosexual desire. By confronting us with the reality of other possibilities, it forces us to confront what is historically made in our own discourse and experience. And once we have confronted some of our deepest beliefs and patterns of perception as contingent, as culturally constructed, we are then in a position to ask the questions that the Stoics and Epicureans asked about those constructions, and to subject them to critical philosophical "therapy" if we find that they are inimical to human flourishing.

As we undertake that project, the arguments I have described here have much assistance and insight to offer. This is so above all because they are good arguments—because the proposals about therapy are anchored to a deep and elaborate philosophical conception (or really, conceptions) of emotion and desire, defended with good arguments against rival conceptions. Thus they will help us link our accounts of sexual desire to our inquires concerning fear and grief and anger, and to pursue the investigations of rival conceptions in all these areas with rigor that is sometimes lacking from the contemporary debate.

There are three areas, in particular, in which I think we can profit from a close study of Lucretius' arguments and their relative. First, in the area of cultural relativism. For, the ancient debate seems to me to show a promising way of striking the balance between what is culturally specific and what is likely to be shared, in one or another form, by all human beings. As Lucretius's reader readily sees, the concrete experience of love that is depicted in the poem is in certain ways peculiarly Roman. Cultural constructions are transmitted not in lofty abstractions, but in concrete ways of putting things—for example in the particular poetic clichés in which lovers think of love. And Lucretius' lover thinks about love in some characteristically and concretely Roman ways, imagining the woman as a Venus—with all the baggage of concrete mythology that entails. He also imagines love with metaphors of battle and combat, and with a number of other concrete images that give the experience a particularly Roman texture. (As the large number of Greek words in this section of the poem attests, this Roman experience, being mediated though literature, is also culturally eclectic, and this fact cannot help affecting the lover's self-perception as well, and affecting the ways in which live is experienced differently by different social classes, with their differing degrees of connection to Greek culture.) Loving is not simply the acceptance of a set of propositions, it is taking on and living out of a whole scenario, or set of stories—and these narratives are in many ways culturally specific.

Nonetheless, as the larger shape of the ancient debate informs us, there is likely to be much overlap among cultures with respect to the emotions and desires. For they are all, as Stoic arguments emphasize, grounded in the recognition that things outside us, things that we do not ourselves control, have great value. This very general belief—which, to be sure, always turns up in some culturally specific form—is the sufficient basis for a whole family of emotions. One cannot wipe out grief, fear, anger, and pity, without getting rid of it completely, in every form. Thus the ancient writers feel justified, while offering particular therapeutic arguments to culturally specified interlocutors, in claiming that some such problem is the problem of every human being, and some such argument is an argument that needs to be heard by every human being. Seneca's *On Anger* is careful to attend to the interlocutor's particular Roman experience of anger, and to focus on examples that depict the family, military obligations, etc., in a concretely Roman way. Still, it is obvious that the work is at the same time addressed to any and every human being; for anyone who has not become convinced by Stoicism or some view like it will have some external attachments that can give cause for anger and resentment. The contemporary debate seems to me to err, by contrast, by taking up positions that are too simple and unsubtle to accommodate the delicate interplay between the shared and the local. Some writers on emotions and desire—many, for example, in psychoanalysis, and cognitive psychology—tend to speak as if anger, love, fear, and sexual desire are cultural universals, neglecting the ways in which different societies set things up rather differently. The anthropological literature, on the other hand, and the part of the philosophical literature influenced by a certain reading of Foucault, speaks very often as if there is no overlap among the different societies with respect to emotional experience, no such thing as a human common ground. The ancient debate will help, I suggest, in clarifying what we shall want to say on this question.

Second, the ancient debate suggests ways in which we might do justice to the importance of both social learning and individual's personal history, when thinking about the formations of emotion and desire. Once again, here the contemporary literature usually focuses on either one or the other—on the individual in psychoanalysis, on general cultural forces in Foucault and in anthropology. The Epicureans and Stoics forcefully argue that good therapeutic argument is searchingly personal, dedicated to a scrutiny of the entirety of the individual pupil's thought and desiring, capable, therefore, of eliciting from the pupil "acknowledgment" or "confession" of deep and sometimes unconscious desires. On the other hand, they do not forget the fact that the unconscious, while deep "inside," is in many respects a social artifact. Lucretius's patient dreams in the language of Roman love-lyric, just as his lawyers dream in the language of the courts. Seneca insists that all Romans need to examine themselves for certain difficulties connected with anger and aggression; and yet his own process of "confession," as he describes it, is searchingly personal, going through all idiosyncrasies of his own daily history and individual responses. The material suggests how much illumination might come out of an intelligent conversation between contemporary psychoanalysis and anthropology, if conducted with the philosophical rigor of these ancient conversations.

Finally, the ancient arguments, with their emphasis on therapy and their interest in radical personal and social change, offer us promising paradigms for ways in which we ourselves might ask society and ourselves to change, if we should discover, through argument, that our own ways of constructing the discourse of desire are at odds with other things we wish and hope for ourselves, with our ideas of what it takes for human beings to flourish. The ancient arguments illustrate that even in an extremely corrupt society one can frequently find a healthy part of the pupil's beliefs to appeal to, find a conception of flourishing that will be agreed to express the wishes of that healthy part, even though it may conflict with many other things that the pupil says and does. Many modern arguments of the "social-construction" kind suggest that there is no place in human life for change. We are the more or less passive constructs of forces larger than we are, and about the most we can do is to realize the nature of the ways of thinking that have bound, bind, and will continue to bind us. This way of thinking is especially common in the area of sexual desire. It is rare to find an anti-racist who believes that racist belief and feelings can never in any way be changed by any process of rational "therapy." And yet it does seem to be the positions of some leading figures in the debate on the "social construction" of sexuality that we will never be able to stop thinking of ourselves under the categories of "sexuality" made for us by nineteenth-century science—even if we decide, by argument, that they are arbitrary, unhelpful, and inimical to human flourishing.

Frequently such social determinisms trace their origin to Nietzsche, who is taken to hold that we can never escape from the categories in which we were raised, although we can perhaps come to see their contingent and arbitrary character. But Nietzsche, who was profoundly influenced by Hellenistic philosophy, who published his first article on a topic in that area, and who repeatedly taught and reflected on Stoic ethics, is, I believe, closely allied with Stoicism and Epicureanism on this point. For he does appear to hold that there is a healthy element in the human being that can flourish if, and only if, certain deep cultural conventions are criticized. The "re-valuation of values" begins by noticing that the values we believed to be necessary and essential are actually contingent and to some extent arbitrary. But once this perception is accepted, things can never be the same: for to admit this much opens the door to a new question: "What do these values do for us? How do they serve or impede life?" And this second phase of re-evaluation, closely modeled on Hellenistic therapies, does not leave things in place. People who accept the fact that god is dead do not live on as before, with just a little more awareness. Or rather, they do that only if they would really rather not have this knowledge and are determined merely to pay it lip-service. Lucretius already spoke eloquently about such people: people who mouth philosophical arguments about death but do not allow the arguments to enter in and to change them. Suppose, on the other hand, one really goes through the therapeutic argument in a thoroughgoing way. Then one will emerge, Nietzsche claims, with a view of oneself as an artist—not one who plays around, does anything she likes, throws all discipline and all history to the winds, but one who exercises an intelligent and disciplined freedom with respect to her own cultural heritage, refusing it the tyranny over her thought and experience that it otherwise would have exercised.

It is this sort of radical criticism of convention, and this sort of human freedom, that I find eloquently portrayed and exemplified in the Hellenistic tradition of writing about emotion and desire. And this is why it was the belief of the Hellenistic philosophers that philosophical education and philosophical argument were the instruments of freedom for the individual, and, for the community, the bases of universal citizenship in a truly rational society.

NOTES

INTRODUCTION

1. See, for example, P. DuBois (1982, 1988), N. Felson-Rubin (1994), N. Rabinowitz (1993a, 1993b), J. Peradotto, J. Sullivan (1984), S. Pomeroy (1975, 1984), M. Skinner (1987), J. Snyder (1988), and F. Zeitlin (1984). See also the groundbreaking works by J. Harrison (1912, 1922).
2. Discussion of the differences between the two kinds of feminist thinking are found in Iris Young (1985, 173).
3. See, for example, C. Whitbeck (1976, 54–80), L. Lange (1983), P. DuBois (1988); a full discussion of this issue appears in Tress (this volume). The "flower pot" view of generation appears to be similar to the one echoed in the (in)famous lines uttered by Aeschylus' Apollo in the tragedy, *The Eumenides*, at ll. 610–12. Apollo finds Orestes innocent of matricide (although he did in fact slay his mother, Clytemnestra) because "the parent is the one who mounts."
4. See, for example, N. Bluestone (1987), C. Freeland (1987, 1994), E. Cole (1994), D. Modrak (1994).
5. After all, the term is used to signify a variety of views relating to women and gender, as indicated by the range of feminist positions from liberal to socialist to difference feminism. See Jaggar (1983, chs. 3–6).
6. A further objection to the project of blaming the source is that often the origin of the sexist notion is some earlier, inchoate idea that existed at the time the thinker composed the theory. If one were consistently to blame the source for the influence, one should have to trace the sexist idea back to its very first source, which is undoubtedly impracticable.
7. See, for example, B. Bar On (1994, xii–xiii), P. Du Bois (1988), J. Peradotto, J. Sullivan (1984, 3), and C. Whitbeck (1976).
8. The argument in fact closely parallels a Utilitarian one that John Stuart Mill offers in *On the Subjection of Women*, where he argues that educating women will double the intellectual resources of the society (Mill 1970, 18).
9. See, for example, Jaggar (1983), Tong (1988), Bordo (1987) on the implicit danger of dualistic metaphysics. Jaggar mentions this in conjunction with the radical feminist conception of patriarchy in which we find, it is claimed, a grounding set of oppositions, such as mind and matter, reason and emotion, male and female, etc., and that

these serve to perpetuate the inequality between women and men (Jaggar 1983, 96–97).

10. Plato introduces the idea about the common possession of women at the beginning of *Republic* V, where Socrates is represented as having to overcome "three waves" of opposition concerning the possibility of the ideal state: the first, that women be philosopher-rulers, and the second, that women and children be held in common (see *Rep.* 451c ff.).

11. Some exceptions to the common Athenian assumption of class and gender inequality are found in certain schools, like the Cynics, possibly the Cyrenaics, and the Sophists. For discussion of some of these schools, see C. De Vogel (1966), D. Dudley (1937), E. Cantarella (1987), A. Malherbe (1977), M. Meunier (1932), and K. Wider (1986).

12. One might point out, in this regard, that Aristotle's notion of the good human life does not presuppose an atomistic notion of the self, such as that which some have argued undergirds Western individualism: see, for example, Jaggar (1983, 28–48), MacPherson (1962, 1–8, 263–77), Young (1987, 56–7).

13. It should be pointed out that what Aristotle considers an equivocal is not the term "good" but that to which the term refers; see Aristotle's *Categories* 1a1–6.

14. For discussion of feminist standpoint theory, see, for example, L. Code (1991), S. Harding (1986) and (1987, 181–90); L. Anthony (1993) provides a criticism of standpoint epistemologies. See also J. Allen and I. Young (1989, 11).

CHAPTER ONE: PLATO'S *REPUBLIC* AND FEMINISM

1. Rousseau (1911, ch. 5) and Schopenhauer (1974) are the most striking examples.

2. (R. Lucas, 1973). The claim that Plato was a feminist is very common in discussions of *Republic* V, and also in recent feminist discussions. (Cf. A. Rosenthal 1973): "The feminism of Plato is exemplary and unparalleled in philosophy or political theory."

3. The term "nuclear family" may be found dislikable, but it is useful in avoiding the suggestion that Plato wants to abolish the family in favor of impersonal institutions of a *1984* type. He stresses that family affection will remain, though spread over a wider class of people (463d–e).

4. And children, though I shall not be considering them in this paper. In modern discussions the question of children's rights is often raised along with that of women's rights, but significantly no one has ever tried to see Plato as a precursor of these ideas.

5. Plato justifies the abolition of the nuclear family solely on grounds of eugenics and of the unity of the state (see below) and there seems no reason why these grounds should not hold even if women were not full Guardians and had a subordinate status; Plato's second proposal is thus in principle independent of his first.

6. Mill in *On the Subjection of Women* deals with this type of argument as an objection to women having political rights. Nowadays the idea that women differ intellectually from men is directed rather against women having serious careers comparable to men's; cf. C. Hutt (1973, ch. 5).

7. As it certainly is Plato's aim. He does not use the patronizing argument that on grounds of "respect for persons" women should have equal pay and status with men even if their contribution is recognized to be inferior.

8. 452a4–5, a10–b3, b8–c2, 453a3–4, 457a6–9, 458d1–2, 466c6–d1, 467a1–2, 468d7–e1.

9. The word is used literally at 459e1, e3, and (possibly) as a metaphor at 451c7–8.

10. It is, however, true that Plato's argument breaks some ground at least, in making it possible to consider women as individuals and not as a class with mixed capacities, at 455e–456a, after the argument just considered, women are compared with other women in various ways, not with men. Hence Plato has removed objections to considering his proposals at all on the ground that women as a class are incompetent.

11. 456c4–9: the question is, are the proposals best, *beltista.* Jowett (1871) translates this and similar phrases by "most beneficial." At 457a3–4 the proposals are "best for the city," *ariston polei.* At 457b1–2 women's nakedness in the gymnasium will be "for the sake of what is best," *tou beltistou heneka,* and people who find it ludicrous will be foolish, because "what is useful *(ophelimon) is* fair and what is harmful *(blaberon) is* ugly," and the proposals are useful as well as possible (c1–2). Cf. 452d3–e2, where the supposed analogy of men exercising naked is justified in terms of benefit.

12. It *is* found even in Firestone (1970, 206–210), though her main argument is not utilitarian. Interestingly, it is not the main argument in the utilitarian Mill, for whom the main objection to sexual inequality is the curtailment of the freedom, and hence the happiness, of women. Mill causes confusion, however, by also including utilitarian arguments.

13. Of course there are other objections to housewifery as an occupation for women, e.g. that it is hard, unpleasant and unpaid, and these may well be more important from the viewpoint of practical reforms, but the charge that it does not satisfy a woman's capacities is the most relevant to discussion of Plato's argument.

14. However, the equal and free association of men and women appears as one of the bad effects of the completely democratic state (563b7–9). This is discussed below.

15. Gosling (1973, ch. 3 "Admiration for Manliness."). As the title suggests, Gosling conducts the discussion wholly in terms of male ideals, and does not remark on any difficulty arising from the fact that half the Guardians will be women.

16. *Laws* 802e declares that pride and courage are characteristic of men (and should be expressed in their music) whereas what is characteristic of women is restraint and modesty. Plato seems to endorse in the *Meno* the idea that the scope of men's and women's virtue is different—that of a man is to manage his own and the city's affairs capably, that of a woman is to be a good and thrifty housewife and to obey her husband (71e, 73a). This makes it hard to see how women can possess the thumoeidic part of the soul necessary for the complete justice of a Guardian. The *Laws* concludes, consistently, that a woman has less potentiality for virtue than a man (781b2–4): Plato says that it is women's weakness and timidity that makes them sly and devious.

17. Cf. *Laws* 917a4–6, where this is clearly brought out.

18. A woman can choose her own husband, if she is an heiress, only in the extremely unlikely situation of there being absolutely no suitable male relative available; and even then her choice is to be in consultation with her guardians.

19. Even so, a limited amount of gymnastic activity and fighting is left open for women in the *Laws;* this shows how little this has to do with real liberation of women.

CHAPTER TWO: WOMEN'S NATURE AND ROLE
IN THE IDEAL *POLIS*: *REPUBLIC* V REVISITED

I wish to thank Justina Gregory, Julius Moravcsik, and Julie Ward for helpful comments on an earlier version of this paper.

1. Doubts have also been expressed, e.g., by Strauss (1964, 116), who characterizes the proposal as "laughable," and Saxonhouse (1976, 196), who maintains that the proposition is infeasible since it "ignores the peculiar natures of [men and women] and thus undermines the perfection of the political society in the *Republic*." According to Taylor (1960, 278), Plato's comments about women in *Rep.* V do not represent his own view, but rather that of Socrates.

2. See, e.g., N. Smith (1983), Vlastos (1989), and J. Smith (1983); cf. Calvert (1975, 243), according to whom "[a]t his most rigorous and philosophical level [Plato] is certainly an advocate of equality for women." It is difficult to pick any one term that specifies adequately the position which Plato defends. For current purposes, I choose "equality," with two important provisos: first, I speak here strictly about the Guardian class, and second, by "equal" in the present context I mean simply that Plato argues that both men and women are capable of performing successfully the highest functions in society; Halliwell (1993, 15) terms the latter "role-equality." With respect to the first proviso, it should be noted that while Plato does not state explicitly how the arguments he offers would apply to non-Guardian women, he supplies all the ingredients necessary for such an extension (cf. Halliwell 1993, 147).

3. By "misogynist" I mean here, roughly, "tending to blame women rather than to praise them"; cf. Fantham et al. (1994), ch. 1 ("Women in Archaic Greece: Talk in Praise and Blame").

4. My focus in this paper is on Plato's position in dialogues up to and including the *Republic*; an exploration of subsequent dialogues would be a topic for another paper.

5. Vlastos (1989, 138). Vlastos' claim is made with reference to a small group of passages from the *Republic*. My account, which takes Vlastos' discussion as its point of departure, confirms via the study of a much larger group of passages his view about the absence of *phusis* and the significance of that absence.

6. *Technê* (pl. *technai*) is often translated "art" or "craft." "Rational purposive discipline" is closer to Plato's meaning in the *Gorgias* and other dialogues which discuss his highly normative conception of this type of activity.

7. See, e.g., *Symp.* 187e4–5, where cookery, dubbed an *empeiria* at *Gorg.* 462d9–11, is identified as a *technê*; with regard to tragic poetry, whose *technê* status is denied at *Gorg.* 502b–d, see *Symp.* 223d5; though *Gorg.* 501e1–7 denies that harp-playing and flute-playing are *technai*, they are affirmed to be such at *Euthyd.* 289c1–4 and *Prot.* 323a8–9, respectively; sophistry, grouped with *empeiriai* at *Gorg.* 463b1–6, is called a *technê* at *Prot.* 316d3–4 and 317c1–2; and prior to its explicit classification as an *empeiria* at *Gorg.* 462b–c, rhetoric is identified repeatedly as a *technê* (at 448c9 it is even characterized as the finest *technê* of all).

8. In the *Ion* it is because rhapsodes and poets do not operate with understanding, and their disciplines lack genuine subject matters, that they are not viewed as practitioners of *technai*. For an emphasis on the understanding requirement, see 534b–d, 535b–d, and 542a. Plato combines discussion of the two conditions at 537d–e, when he says that *technai* are distinguished from one another based on the fact that their

practitioners have *epistêmê* of different subject matters (cf. 538a). He stresses the importance of the subject-matter condition at the dialogue's end, when Socrates says that, far from giving him a display of his *epistêmê* regarding Homer, Ion is unwilling to say precisely "what he is so clever *about*" *(peri hôn deinos ei)* (541e5–6).

9. In my formulation of this requirement I follow Moravcsik (1992, 15).

10. Based on the framework and discussion of the *Gorgias* and on Plato's remarks else-where (e.g., the *Protagoras*), one can develop a similar account of Plato's challenge to the *technê* status of rhetoric and sophistry. Unless otherwise noted, translations of the *Republic* are those of Shorey (Hamilton and Cairns 1963), at times with modifica-tions, and those of other dialogues are my own.

11. Poets' writings had an educational impact in multiple contexts: on the one hand, the works of poets like Homer were introduced in primary schools; on the other hand and more generally, the influence of these poets and their writings pervaded Athenian cul-ture, notably through the presentation of tragedies at the dramatic festivals.

12. My translation.

13. The basic criticisms of poets—for their failure to have a positive impact on people's souls, for their lack of knowledge, and for their occupation with appearance—have received much attention (for an account which comments on them all, see Moravcsik (1982). For a discussion that notes Plato's denial to poetry of the rank of *technê*, con-centrating thereby on its failure to meet what I call the "understanding condition," see Woodruff (1982). My own interest in Plato's treatment of poetry lies in exploring and linking the three criticisms based on their role in Plato's systematic challenge to poet-ry's *technê* status, in showing how that critique goes hand in hand with Plato's depic-tion, also systematic, of philosophy as the *technê par excellence*, and in illustrating how Plato's critique of poetry in the *Republic* is tied to those offered elsewhere, above all in the *Cratylus* (for an account of Plato's critique in the *Cratylus*, see Levin 1995).

14. In addition, Plato notes that passages in the writings of Homer and other poets that promote a fear of death will be expunged, not because they are not pleasing *(hêdea)* to the audience, but because they do not benefit those who are to become Guardians (387b2–5). Lines that describe heroes as indulging too much in food and drink will be deleted; while they do indeed yield pleasure *(hêdonê)* in their hearers, they fail to pro-mote the development of *sôphrosunê* (389e–390a). With regard to the dichotomy between the pleasant and the good insofar as it involves poets, see also 397d and 493c–d.

15. My translation.

16. My translation.

17. The cornerstone of future Guardians' basic education is *mousikê*, which includes poet-ry, stories, and music.

18. For an emphasis on the importance of being able to provide a rational account *(logon didonai)* which exhibits one's understanding, see also 533c and 534b.

19. In the *Republic* Plato considers how *praxeis* which all qualify as *technai* in the nar-row sense may nevertheless differ from one another in significant ways. All *technai* are both teachable and learnable; differences here, to the extent that they exist, are less substantial than in the case of other requirements.

20. Although there is a special relationship between the Good and other ethical Forms, more generally Plato views order and harmony as marks of goodness (for his assign-ment to the Good of far wider than ethical significance, see 508e). The concept of

goodness is thus pertinent to such disciplines as astronomy, which studies the ordered movement of heavenly bodies. Moreover, there is a close connection between the cosmic and human planes insofar as the proper study of disciplines like astronomy helps to create order and harmony within the human soul.

21. Regarding the *Gorgias* cf. Moravcsik (1992, 20, 24).

22. In contrast, as Malcolm (1991, 75) has noted, the Form, i.e., the F itself, "*is* what it is to be F."

23. Cf. his table of contents (xii), which classifies the discussion of women as an appendix to Books II–IV. On Book V as transitional, see also Halliwell (1993, 3–5).

24. For discussion see Levin (1995).

25. Book V does not specify how *technai* such as geometry are to be accommodated in terms of this dichotomy. This stems from the fact that Plato is beginning his detailed exploration of how philosophers differ, cognitively speaking, from everyone else. In his presentation of the Divided Line (509d–511e), Plato claims that *dianoia* is intermediate between *pistis* and *noêsis* (or *epistêmê*, 533e–534a). Like *noêsis* it is directed toward Forms, but its access to those entities is mediated rather than direct. When Plato draws a general contrast between the visible and intelligible realms, which are symbolized by the halves of the Line, he speaks of the bottom two segments collectively as *doxa,* and of the top two as *noêsis* (533e–534a). (While *pistis* is the term used in the *Gorgias* to designate belief in contrast to knowledge [see 454d], in the *Republic doxa* has this role, and *pistis* is used to mark off one portion of the bottom half of the Line.) When Plato speaks precisely, however, a distinction within each half—in particular the upper one—comes to the fore. Hence, in the *Republic*, while no practitioners of activities that the *Gorgias* would classify as *technai* operate with mere belief, those on the *Republic*'s second tier, unlike philosophers, achieve something short of full understanding. With regard to the understanding requirement, the philosopher thus surpasses not only those who practice *empeiriai*, but also all other *technê* practitioners.

26. If one calls to mind here Aristotle's discussion of substantial unity in *Meta.* VII.17, one might say that Book V is like the syllable rather than the heap (1041b11–33).

27. There is common ground between the two approaches in the view that not all women are good, and that in fact there are outstanding examples of female *kakia*. At least in part, the point of contention is whether one is justified in making inferences about women as a *genos* based on the presence of striking defects in one or more individual women. For negative comments about individual women's *phuseis,* see *Med.* 1339–45 and *Or.* 126; for instances in which inferences are made on the aforementioned basis, see *Hec.* 1178–82 and *Hipp.* 966–67 (in the latter case, Theseus speculates that Hippolytus might offer such a generalization in his own defense).

28. There Heracles speaks disdainfully of Deianira as "a woman, a female, quite different in nature *(phusin)* from a man" (my translation). For a similar remark see Soph. *El.* 997. For a criticism by Oedipus of his two sons, which uses *phusis* in likening them to Egyptian men said to act like women, see *O.C.* 337–45; interestingly, Oedipus praises his daughters by likening them to sons, when he states that Antigone and Ismene "have saved me, they are my support, and are not girls, but men, in faithfulness. As for you two, you are no sons of mine!" *(m' eksôizousin, haid' emai trophoi, haid' andres, ou gunaikes, es to sumponein; humeis d' ap' allou kouk emou pephukaton)* *(O.C.* 1367–69, tr. Fitzgerald).

29. Tr. Warner.
30. My translation.
31. For blanket condemnations of women which do not make use of *phusis* or *phuein*, see Hes. *W.D.* 53–105, 373–75; *Th.* 570–602; Soph. fr. 187N^2; Eur. fr. 429N^2; and Eur. *Hipp.* 616–68. As Barrett (1964, 280) notes with reference to the final passage, for Hippolytus "all women are vile"; he distinguishes only between greater and lesser evils. Moreover, at *Andr.* 272–73 it is said that no remedy or vaccine *(pharmakon)* has yet been discovered for the *gunê kakê*, which is such an evil *(kakon)* to humanity (even if line 273, which is bracketed by Diggle, is omitted, one still finds here a negative comment about the *genos* of women).
32. Tr. Fitzgerald.
33. For a different interpretation see Loraux (1978).
34. Tr. Willetts, slightly modified.
35. For a negative generalization about the entire class *(pan genos)* of women made and promptly criticized, see *Hec.* 1178–84. Theseus rejects out of hand any argument that Hippolytus might make according to which "you will tell me that this frantic folly is inborn in a woman's nature *(gunaixi . . . empephuken); man* is different: but I know that young men are no more to be trusted than a woman when love disturbs the youthful blood in them" (*Hipp.* 966–69; tr. Grene). For positive comments about individual women's *phuseis*, see Eur. *I.A.* 1410–11, *Hel.* 1002–3, and *Ion* 239–40; for Electra described as having a nature exceptional for a woman, see *Or.* 1204–6.
36. Plato's relation to the literary tradition is more significant and wideranging than previously thought. Scholars have long recognized that when treating ethical questions in the *Republic*, specifically the matter of character development in Books II–III and X, Plato views the poets as direct and central opponents. In Levin (1995 and 1996) I argue that in his philosophy of language as well—specifically his treatment of etymology in the *Cratylus* and eponymy in the *Phaedo*—Plato relates himself in fundamental ways to the literary tradition; in the latter case, Plato, operating against a literary backdrop, develops a revised version of eponymy that better suits his own philosophical purposes. As elsewhere, in *Rep.* V Plato takes literary *praxis* as his point of departure, and develops a revamped way of treating the issue in question.
37. In the *Republic* Plato makes frequent reference to a "philosophical nature" (see, e.g., 485a10, c12–d1, 489e3–490a3, and 490c8). Someone of this type exhibits the disposition and traits required for the apprehension of *phuseis* or *ousiai* (i.e., Forms), and hence is said to possess a philosophical *phusis*. With regard to this connection between the two uses of *phusis,* one may cite 490a8–b3, where Plato emphasizes that someone is said to have a philosophical nature because he or she possesses a special aptitude and determination to apprehend natures proper; cf. 485a10–b3, where what is distinctive of the philosophical *phusis* is the fact that it is enamored of essences rather than mere appearances. The fact that in both passages Plato uses language of aspiration *(erôs)* calls to mind the *Symposium*'s ascent, which only one with a philosophical nature is able to complete; in using "aspiration" as a translation of *erôs,* I follow Moravcsik (1971).
38. When the topic is human nature, this terminology is used in multiple contexts: 1) with reference to human nature generally (as, e.g., at *Phaed.* 79b10, *Symp.* 206c4, *Prot.* 358d1, and *Rep.* 395b4, 514a2, and 558e2); 2) in reflections on the natures of types or subdivisions of human beings and individual representatives thereof (see, e.g., *Phaed.*

109e6; *Symp.* 219d4; *Gorg.* 463a8, 484a2, c8, 485d4, e7, 486b5, 492a7, *Rep.* 366c7, 370a8, b1, c4, 374b10, e4, 7, 375b10, c8, d7, e11, 376c1, 5, 401c4, 410a3, e1, 6, 411b6, 415c1, 423d3, 430a4, 431c7, 433a6, 434b1, 435b5, 443c5, 453a1, b5, 8, c1, 5, e3, 4, 454b4, 7, 8, d2, 455a2, b5, c1, d8, e1, 7, 456a8, 10, b3, 6, d1, 458c8, 466d3, 473d4, 474c1, 485a5, 10, c1, 486a2, b3, d4, 10, 11, 487a3, 489e4, 490a9, c8, d6, e2, 491a2, 8, b8, d7, e2, 5, 492a1, 494a11, d9, 495a5, b1, 5, d7, 496b3, 6, 497b2, 500a1, 7, 501d4, 502a6, 503b8, 519c9, 526b5, 6, c6, 535a9, b2, c4, 537c6, 538c3, 539d4, 540c7, 547b5, e4, 548e2, 549b2, 550b3, 558b3, 564e6, 572c8, 573c8, 576a6, b7, 579b4, and 597e7); and 3) in comments about aspects of the human *psuchê* (see, e.g., *Rep.* 431a5, 432a8, 439e4, 441a3, 442a6, 444b4, d9, 10, 530c1, 589b4, 606a5, and 7).

39. In using the term "Principle of Specialization" I follow Annas (1981, 73).

40. In addition, *hê anthrôpeia phusis* ("human nature") at *Symp.* 212b3 may refer to reason; on this point see Moravcsik (1971, 294).

41. Here I am in accord with the conclusion of Vlastos (1989, 138) regarding those comments he discusses.

42. Here Plato distinguishes the youth's father, who appeals to the rational aspect of his son's soul, from all other men and women, who appeal to the spirited and appetitive elements.

43. On this point cf. Vlastos (1989, 138), who notes that "there is no reference to women's *phusis* in [431b–c] or any of the [other passages] I have cited from the *Republic*, as there would have been if his point had been that those bad 'womanish' traits were inherent in femaleness as such." In what follows I explore Plato's use of, or failure to use, *phusis* in greater detail, and the results of that inquiry serve to extend the scope of Vlastos' claim, which was based on a group of four passages from the *Republic* (431b–c, 469d, 563b, and 605d–e). Rankin (1964, 98) cites *Rep.* 469d and 579b in support of the claim that Plato believed in the *natural* inferiority of women; in fact, however, neither passage discusses women's *phusis*. For a treatment of women's nature with an emphasis different from my own, see Okin (1979, 51–70).

44. The following remarks take as their point of departure a TLG search for the relevant terms in the *Euthyphro, Apology, Crito, Ion, Hippias Minor, Charmides, Laches, Protagoras, Lysis, Euthydemus, Menexenus, Hippias Major, Meno, Gorgias, Phaedo, Cratylus, Symposium,* and *Republic*. For a recent defense of the view that the *Phaedrus* was written after the *Republic*, and functions as a "companion piece" to the *Parmenides*, see Nehamas and Woodruff (1995); for an endorsement of the sequence *Republic, Parmenides, Theaetetus, Phaedrus*, see Brandwood (1990 and 1992). It is worth noting, however, that an investigation of the *Parmenides, Theaetetus*, and *Phaedrus* provides additional support for the results of the present inquiry. The one passage worth mentioning for its combination of the relevant terms, *Theaet.* 149c1–150a6, occurs in remarks setting the stage for Socrates' discussion of his own brand of midwifery; the topic there is not women's *phusis*, and Plato makes no critical remarks about women.

45. The criterion most often used to determine closeness is spatial proximity, regardless of whether the terms in question fall in the same speech.

46. Tr. Nehamas and Woodruff.

47. It is only at 620c, where Plato notes that the soul of Epeius entered "into the nature of an arts and crafts woman" *(eis technikês gunaikos ... phusin),* that he uses *phusis* in an explicit reference to women. While the reference is direct, Plato's concern there is

not to investigate the nature of women, and the term is not used to offer a pronounce-ment about that nature. For further discussion of this passage, see p. 28.

48. At 579b–c Plato speaks of the tyrant, with the degenerate *phusis* described in what precedes, as "cowering in the recesses of his house like a woman, envying among the other citizens anyone who goes abroad and sees any good thing."

49. Four passages warrant separate discussion. First, at *Symp.* 181b3–c6 Pausanias distin-guishes between two types of *erôs,* and claims that those inspired by that of Heavenly Aphrodite are attracted to males, taking pleasure in "what is by nature *(phusei)* stronger and more intelligent" (tr. Nehamas and Woodruff). This passage has a strong ideological basis, and has as its purpose the justification of a particular *ethos*; that is, it reflects a view about sexual preferences that was widespread in the upper social class-es, and occurs in a speech which itself constitutes an *apologia* for homosexual *erôs.* In addition, the remark, which makes no direct reference to women, might be taken at most to imply a claim about female inferiority under present conditions. Second, at one point in his speech, Aristophanes says that, of the three types of possible relations involving the sexes—male-male, male-female, and female-female—"[p]eople who are split from a male are male-oriented. While they are boys, because they are chips off the male block, they love men and enjoy lying with men and being embraced by men; those are the best of boys and lads, because they are the most manly in their nature *(phusei)*" (191e6–192a2) (tr. Nehamas and Woodruff). At this point in his encomium—which itself consists of a myth—Aristophanes compares, not male and female natures, but superior and inferior male ones; moreover, his remark has the same ideological basis, and reflects the same *ethos,* as that of Pausanias. Third, at *Rep.* 395d1–e3 Plato states that "imitations, if continued from youth far into life, settle down into habits and second nature in the body, the speech, and the thought. . . . We will not then allow our charges, whom we expect to prove good men, being men, to play the parts of women and imitate a woman young or old wrangling with her hus-band, defying heaven, loudly boasting, fortunate in her own conceit, or involved in misfortune and possessed by grief and lamentation—still less a woman who is sick, in love, or in labor." As in the *Symposium*, there is no direct criticism of women's *phu-sis*; Plato simply warns of the danger of imitating women under current conditions, in which the nuclear family—the attachments of whose members are grounded on emo-tion and desire—remains intact, and in which emotional displays are common. Plato's focus here on women's emotional displays is counterbalanced by his concentration elsewhere on the proneness to emotional expressions of human beings more generally. Finally, 431a5–c7 includes a reference to "the mob of motley appetites and pleasures and pains one would find chiefly in children and women and slaves and in the base rabble of those who are free men in name." In what precedes, Plato praises a state in which the naturally better part of the soul controls that which is worse; in the criticism that follows, which in any case does not single out women, Plato does not say that they are by nature precluded from having souls in which the aforementioned relation obtains. In fact, Plato has not yet raised that question; it is precisely the discussion of women in Book V that is devoted to the consideration of this issue. On this passage cf. Vlastos (1989, 138), who emphasizes that Plato is "speaking of women as they are under present, nonideal, conditions"; he is not saying that what is presently observ-able "is there as the permanently fixed, invariant, character of the female of the species, its nature. . . . In the absence of any such indications, the right way to read

[such] passages is as reflections on what Plato thinks women are now, formed and shaped, deformed and misshaped, by the society which has reared them."

50. For the phrase *para to ethos* ("contrary to custom"), see 452a7.

51. In the *Phaedo* the soul is often identified with intellect, while the body is correlated with desire, feeling and emotion, and sense-perception.

52. Here Socrates and Glaucon find ridiculous the idea that whether one is bald or long-haired would matter when the concern is to determine individuals' fitness to perform the various jobs in society.

53. By linking his discussion of the two types of differences so closely, Plato seems to use an implicit argument by analogy to show that one's reproductive role, like the amount of hair one has, is an incidental property (i.e., not determinative of essence).

54. While Plato indicates that there may be variations in the manner in which individuals undertake jobs requiring physical strength due to differences between men and women with respect to this characteristic, he makes clear that women are not to be excluded on this basis from the performance of a particular function in society.

55. For a recent critique of Plato's dualism, which holds it responsible for his view of femaleness as "a curse, the source of evil, chaos and dissolution," see Genova (1994, 42). For an account of the contradiction in Plato's views about women, which focuses on his dualism, see Spelman (1982, 111–19).

56. On the soul as sexless, cf. Wilamowitz (1919, 18 and 1920, 398). For an argument that Plato views the soul itself as gendered, in the sense that there are "manly" and "womanly" types of souls, see Spelman (1988, 30–34). A range of other views of why Plato introduces the proposal about women is found in the literature. According to Annas (1976, 312), for example, "Plato's sole ground for his proposals is their usefulness to the state"; for a critique of this view, see J. Smith (1983, 606). Okin (1977 and 1979) maintains that the abolition of the private family results in the emancipation of women; for objections see Jacobs (1978) and N. Smith (1980).

57. Allen (1975, 136) comments on the issue of recollection, but interprets Plato to hold that "women were an inferior incarnation" and that it is desirable for a woman Guardian to recollect the Forms, though harder "because of her weakness." For interpretations which view the inferiority in question as physical rather than mental or intellectual, see Burns (1984, 137) and J. Smith (1983, 602).

58. Regarding Xanthippe's temper, as reported in Xenophon's *Memorabilia* and *Symposium*, see Walcot (1987, 14–15).

59. Cf. N. Smith (1983, 473), who connects Plato's statement in the *Republic* that women can be lovers of wisdom to the *Symposium*'s presentation of Diotima, "a woman who gives Socrates instruction in the philosophy of love." For a range of other views of the significance of Diotima's presence, see Halperin (1990); Rosen (1987); Wider (1986); Saxonhouse (1984); Allen (1975); Freeman (1988); and Irigaray (1989), with the introduction by Kuykendall (1989) and critical essay by Nye (1989). The *Symposium* does not, as Dickason (1973–1974, 49) maintains, itself *express* the belief that "women and men have the same essential nature and worth"; for a critique of Dickason's use of Aristophanes' speech as direct evidence of Plato's own view, see Osborne (1975). In my view, Hawthorne (1994, 92) goes further than the text warrants in suggesting that Diotima has "the status of one of the earliest women philosophers we can name, a woman with her own developed philosophy and not just simply the woman whose words Socrates reports." More generally, contra Wider (1986, 48), one

cannot infer anything about women's *contemporary* engagement in philosophy from the fact that Socrates' teacher is a woman. There is disagreement among scholars about Diotima's historicity: for assertions of her fictionality, see, e.g., Nehamas and Woodruff (1989, 45, 52) and Nussbaum (1986, 177); for defenses of her historicity, see, e.g., Nye (1989, 46), Wider (1986, 44–48), Taylor (1960, 224), and Hawthorne (1994, 92, 96). Even if Plato took a historical person as his point of departure, the content of the doctrine attributed to Diotima indicates that in all fundamentals she is a Platonic construction; cf. Friedländer (1969, 148), Guthrie (1975, 385), and Dover (1980, 10).

60. As previously noted, a sustained defense of these claims about the *Phaedo* and *Symposium* would be a topic for another paper.

CHAPTER THREE: THE METAPHYSICAL SCIENCE
OF ARISTOTLE'S *GENERATION OF ANIMALS* AND ITS FEMINIST CRITICS

I would like to thank Helen Lang for her helpful comments on earlier drafts of this paper.

1. Eve Browning Cole (1989, 88–89).

2. As evidence of Aristotle's sexism, Mary Mahowald offers, without comment, passages from *Generation of Animals* in Mahowald (1983, 266–72). Caroline Whitbeck speaks of Aristotle's "flower-pot" theory of pregnancy (Whitbeck, 1976, 54–80). Linda Lange holds that Aristotle's sexist views on sex difference are not separable from his general philosophical thought, that they are interwoven with and may, she proposes, be the basis for ideas he develops in his political, metaphysical, and logical writings; see Lange (1983, 1–15). Prudence Allen's thesis (Allen 1985) is that Aristotle systematically devalues women, with long-term effects both for women and for the history of philosophy. Page DuBois offers a similar assessment of Aristotle in her book (Dubois, 1988). Kotzin (1989) lists Aristotle's offensive assertions in the biological and political treatises. Kotzin believes not only that "it is beyond dispute that Aristotle was wrong about women" (21), but also that Aristotle is not entitled to make the claims that he does and that they are inconsistent with other elements of his philosophy.

3. The promotion of fertility goddess worship, for example, by some feminist writers must be regarded at best as an attempt to imaginatively infuse a desiccated modern notion of conception and pregnancy with some meaning.

4. As Peck remarks in the Preface to his translation of *Generation of Animals:* " . . . for in reproduction, as understood by Aristotle, not only the individual is concerned but the cosmos at large: it is a business in which the powers of the universe are concentrated and united" (Peck 1979, v). Translations of *Generation of Animals* in this article are for the most part those of Peck, although occasionally I make modifications.

5. See Horowitz (1976).

6. The demand that male and female contributions be the same in kind follows along the lines of ancient theories such as those of Empedocles and Hippocrates (as will be seen later in this essay), as well as of modern genetic views of reproduction. In both the ancient theories cited and the modern scientific one, strong materialist assumptions are at work. Feminist critics (e.g. Allen) who endorse this criterion of acceptability may, wittingly or not, adopt a materialist framework along with it.

7. Other commentators have responded to the apparent sexism in *GA*. Johannes Morsink (1979, 87–88) sees Aristotle not as a sexist but as a scientist involved in a battle of scientific theory with Hippocrates and his school. Anthony Preus (1970, 4) sees Aristotle making the mistake of linking matter and form exclusively with female and male respectively. Montgomery Furth (1988) sees the source of the sexism in Aristotle's reluctance to divide form.

8. Aristotle explains the distinction between natural generation (*genesis*) and artificial production (*poiêsis*) in *Metaphysics* VII. 7. He distinguishes nature and things natural from art and things humanly produced in *Physics* II.1.

9. Peck (1979, viii).

10. This line of thought is termed "metaphysical" here because in the *Physics* Aristotle declares that the formal cause and its nature is the work of first philosophy, or metaphysics, to determine (192a34–36). In the *Metaphysics* he says that the form is a cause because "the question 'why' is ultimately reduced to the *logos,* and the primary 'why' is cause and principle" (983a28–29). Thus, the formal cause and the ultimate meaning of an entity should be regarded as metaphysical—or should be regarded metaphysically. Joseph Owens (1978, 176–177) cites both of the above passages.

11. See Hans Jonas (1966, 33–34).

12. See also the preliminary justification at 716a11–12. See also 716b10–12, 731b18, 732a1–3; and at 732a12: "Thus things are alive in virtue of having in them a share of the male and the female." We may note that in the *Metaphysics* too, in defining *archê as* a source from which come motion and change, Aristotle adds "as the child comes from the father and mother" (1013a8–9).

13. On this particular sort of structuring of the argumentation in Aristotle, where the thesis is stated first and the remainder of the discussion in a given book secures that thesis, see Helen Lang (1989). Lang demonstrates the teleological structure of argumentation in the *Physics,* where Aristotle posits his thesis at the start, and the discussion that follows in that book supports rather than extends or alters the initial thesis. Also see Joseph Owens' observation, regarding the first sentence of the *Metaphysics,* "All men by nature desire to learn." Owens writes, "This one short sentence, as will be seen . . . contains the whole *motif of* the Aristotelian *Metaphysics*" (Owens 1979, 158, n. 5). On the philosophical importance of Aristotle's form of presentation see also Werner Jaeger (1948 6), and Owens (1979, 72).

14. In the translation of *GA* by Peck in the Loeb edition, *sperma* is routinely translated as "semen." Platt also translates *sperma* as "semen" in the Oxford edition; A. Platt, *Generation of Animals,* in Barnes (1984). Translating *sperma* in this way gives the wrong impression that Aristotle regards only the male discharge as authentically generative, and completely obscures an important question raised in *GA* I : whether the female parent contributes *sperma,* that is, generative fluid, to the process. It can be noted in advance that Aristotle's answer is that the female does contribute *sperma,* although it differs from that of the male parent, that is, it is not semen. Sexism here has its sources, not in Aristotle, but in his nineteenth- and early twentieth-century translators. In my discussion I will simply transliterate *sperma* when it appears in the text, rather than follow Peck's translation of the term.

15. See *Metaphysics* X. 9, where Aristotle states that male and female do not differ substantially. They possess the same human form and their differences are only with respect to matter. Also see *GA* 730b34–35, where he states that male and female "are

identical in species"; and *GA* 741a6: "Granted that the female possesses the same soul [as the male] . . ."

Aristotle's view of female and male difference is not, however, a simple functionalist one. He recognizes the ways in which the generative parts have complex ties to other aspects of an entity's life. The extensiveness of these ties is what leads Aristotle to regard femaleness and maleness as each a "principle," rather than a natural variation on the order of hair or eye color. That is, he notes that in general it is when a principle changes, even in a small way, that numerous other dependent things are affected. He has observed, for example, that castrated animals undergo extensive changes after the generative organ alone has been destroyed. He concludes, based on the frequency of this observation, that femaleness and maleness are on the order of "principles."

16. For an example of the necessary anatomy-better anatomy distinction see 717a16–17.
17. Of interest on the subject of ancient embryological theories is chapter 1 of Joseph Needham (1959) (although Needham is not always a careful reader of Aristotle). Also see Preus (1970, 5–7).
18. See the extended discussion which begins at 721b12.
19. See Preus (1970, 7). Also of interest is the Hippocratic treatise, "The Seed" (Hippocrates 1978); and Needham's comments on Hippocrates' "mechanical approach" to viewing generation in Needham (1959, 33).
20. See Peck, *Generation of Animals,* 372–3, n. *a;* and Preus (1970, 196, n. 6). Needham discusses "Denials of Maternity and Paternity," in Needham, (1959, 43–46).
21. *Eumenides* 610–12; quoted from Needham (1959, 43). (Peck and Preus also cite this passage from *Eumenides.*)
22. Caroline Whitbeck (1976, 55) describing Aristotle's view as "the flower pot theory" of pregnancy, believes that Aristotle holds that "the woman supplies the container and the earth which nourishes the seed but the seed is solely the man's." Page DuBois (1988, 126) writes, "The great scientific work of Aristotle, read and accepted as truth for centuries, takes up the metaphorical system . . . that the female body is a container, like an oven, to be filled up with the semen, which provides soul and form to the material container." Maryanne Cline Horowitz (1976, 186) regards Aristotle's theory as "an extreme position in the process of the masculinization of procreation." She states, "Unlike the medical school of Hippocrates, Aristotle taught that *sperma*, in its narrow sense as the seed from which an embryo grows, is secreted only by males" (192). Prudence Allen says, "Borrowing the use of hot and cold from Empedocles and Hippocrates, Aristotle developed a theory of sex identity that argued that the female provided no seed in generation because she was by nature colder than the male" (Allen 1985, 34).
23. At 728a25, near the close of these considerations, he states, "Hence, plainly it is reasonable to hold that generation takes place from this process: for, as we see, the menstrual fluid is *sperma*, not indeed *sperma* in a pure condition, but needing still to be acted upon." In addition, at 730a35 he says, "The male and female both deposit together what they have to contribute in the female." Preus's careful reading of the text leads him, too, to the conclusion that for Aristotle the menstrual contribution of the female is *spermata:* "Given Aristotle's notion that the 'menstrual fluid' is the female *sperma* of the mammalia . . . " Preus (1970, 8). And also, "The menstrual fluid should be that spermatic contribution which serves as matter for generation" (Preus 1970, 9).

Among Aristotle's feminist critics, the misinterpretation seems to arise from a failure to appreciate the importance of the material cause in Aristotle's metaphysics, and from reading "matter" in a post-seventeenth-century sense. This might be particularly the case in Whitbeck's criticism (1976, 55–57). Horowitz (1976) notices that Aristotle calls both semen and menstrual blood *sperma*, but she does not notice or find it significant that he also calls them both the principles of generation. Her attention is directed exclusively at the higher degree of concoction of the semen, and this leads her to exaggerate the subordination of the material principle in Aristotle's scheme, making that principle almost worthless.

Other commentators on *GA* have read the text in this way as well. John M. Cooper (1990, 57) writes, "The menstrual fluid is also a 'seminal residue' *(spermatikon perittoma),* less concocted and less pure than sperm, and so not capable of generating anything, i.e. not capable of coming alive by itself or making anything else come alive (I. 20.728a18, 26 [sic.]; II. 3.737a27–30; II. 7.746b26–9)." Nothing, for Aristotle, comes alive by itself ("nothing generates itself" 735a14), so this is not a legitimate criterion for determining the spermatic status of menstrual fluid. The capacity "to make something come alive," which as a way of describing generation sounds a bit magical rather than Aristotelian, is a potential that can only be exercised in concert with specialized material which itself has a potential capacity to be formed as a particular kind of creature. See also Cooper's note on symmetry, where he explicitly denies that "there is any kind of interaction between the two factors, in the sense of a joint working together by two independent but proportionately coordinated agents with a view to a common product" (1990, 59, n. 6). What Cooper eloquently denies is very much the same thesis that Aristotle is developing in *GA.*

24. Allen (1985, 33–34, 84–86).

25. For Aristotle, the puzzle appears not so much to be generation out of the union of the same sexes, but independent generation by the female: "Why does not the female accomplish generation all by itself and from itself?" (741a4–5). Note that his first answer to this question depends on what he has already argued: that the fetation will be alive only on acquiring sentient soul, and this is what the male contributes. But, almost recognizing that this answer begs the question, he pursues the puzzle to arrive at a metaphysical explanation, in keeping with the tenor of Book II. His explanation relies on the concept of *telos*: "The female [by herself] is unable to generate offspring and bring it to completion; if it could the existence of the male would have no purpose, and nature does nothing which lacks purpose" (741b3–4).

26. It appears to have been Hippocrates' theory, sometimes termed the "double seed theory, that both male and female contribute semen. Aristotle may have Hippocrates in mind when he argues against the suggestion that both female and male contribute semen to generation; see "The Seed," and Morsink's discussion of *GA* in relation to it (1979, 87–88). Aristotle's argument at 727a26–30 is that no one animal produces two spermatic fluids, and since the female contributes the menstrual fluid, she does not contribute semen *(gonê)* as the male does.

There is a difficulty with the Greek terms which undoubtedly has aided the misunderstanding of Aristotle's intentions. He does not restrict the designation *sperma* to semen, as has been shown, but often enough when referring to semen he simply uses the broader term *sperma.* Sometimes it is plain from the context and his description which of the two *spermata* he has in mind; sometimes he seems to distinguish "generative fluid" from "semen" by use of *sperma* and *gonê*, respectively, but this usage is far from consistent (for example at 729a21–23: "The foregoing discussion will have made it clear that the female, though it does not contribute any semen (*gonê*), yet contributes something, namely, the substance constituting the menstrual fluid"). While the lack of clear and consistent terminology easily can lead to confusion and support the sexism charges against Aristotle, it is plausible that the difficulty he has maintaining a clear distinction in the text by means of the language then available is, on the contrary, evidence of the conceptual advance that he is attempting in regarding both fluids as spermatic.

27. Matter is always "formed," too, to some extent (see Furth 1988, 84–87): matter is that which is capable of further formation, and so it too is linked to the metaphysical dimension). See also Peck's note on prime matter and on matter at its highest degree of formation being equivalent to form (Peck, 1979, 110–11, n. e).

28. At 730b5–6 he offers a preliminary analogy to house building to help explain this at 730b5–6.

29. See also *De Anima* 415a25–26.

30. Aristotle's higher animal types almost always correspond to Darwin's "later" types.

31. Notice again that the material contribution is considered within the topic of the working of *sperma,* indicating once more that Aristotle regards the maternal fluid as generative.

32. For Aristotle's fuller exposition of these concepts, see *Physics* III. 3.

33. See also 735a13: "The cause of this process of formation is not any part of the body."

34. This holds true, of course, for the mother as well. She is in actuality what the offspring is only potentially.

35. Regarding the maternal contribution, he speaks of " . . . the generating parent, who is in actuality what the material out of which the offspring formed is potentially" (734b35). Regarding the paternal contribution he says, "It is clear that *sperma* (in context, "semen") possesses soul, and that it is soul, potentially" (735a9); see also 739b18–19. In *Metaphysics* IX. 7 he says, "We must, however, distinguish when a particular thing exists potentially and when it does not. . ., e.g. is earth potentially a man? No, but rather when it has already become *sperma,* and perhaps not even then" (1048b37–1049a5). In *Parts of Animals* he says, "Moreover, the seed is potentially something, and the relation of potentiality to actuality we know" (641b36). In *De Anima* he says, "So seed *(sperma)* and fruit are potentially bodies [which have the capacity to live]" (412b26).

36. With respect to the mutuality posited in this interpretation, Aristotle, speaking of body and soul, makes the following comment in *De Anima:* "For it is by this association *(koinonian)* that the one acts and the other is acted upon, that the one moves and the other is moved; and no such mutual relation is found in haphazard combinations" (407b18–20). The partnership of matter and form is emphasized, the partnership whereby the one *can* move and the other *can* be moved. Regarding Aristotle's theory of the initiation of movement, as Frederick Woodbridge (1965, 13–14) explains, "Motion strictly is not a transfer of movement from one body to another, but the change from rest to movement or the change from what can happen into an actual happening." There must be contact between the two bodies; but according to Aristotle, movement cannot be grasped as a mechanical collision. Some of Aristotle's commentators seem to assume a mechanical model when considering his explanation of the moving cause in generation—a model characteristic of modern science rather than Aristotle's physics. It is the modern model which involves one body in motion and

one inertly at rest. For Aristotle, on the other hand, matter actively desires form, as he says in *Physics* I. 9; its potentiality is its orientation toward form. Thus, matter is not just the passive recipient of an external, haphazardly arising force. On this subject Helen Lang (1992, 26) writes, commenting on *Physics* I. 9: "Here we reach a key issue: for Aristotle, to be moved does not imply a passive principle. Matter (or potential), which is moved by form (or actuality), is moved precisely because it is never neutral to its mover: matter is aimed at—it runs after—form. Because of the active orientation of the moved towards its mover, no third cause is required to combine matter and form. They go together naturally: form constitutes a thing as natural and matter is aimed at form."

37. Peck offers "underdeveloped" as an alternate translation for *peperomenom:* "underdeveloped," then, relative to the full range that is available to the female. See, too, Aristotle's statement that "the female's contribution ... contains all the parts of the body potentially, though none in actuality; and 'all' includes those parts which distinguish the two sexes" (737a24–25). Compare this with the comment in the Hippocratic treatise, "The Seed": "The children of deformed parents are usually sound. This is because although an animal may be deformed, it still has exactly the same *components* as what is sound" (Hippocrates 1978, 323). This comment can be read in keeping with the interpretation of Aristotle offered here, that is, that Aristotle holds that the female parent has all the anatomical components (male as well as female) potentially, even though she herself does not exhibit them. She is not, therefore, a deformity; it is only the principle that applies analogically. It is possible that the Hippocratic passage influenced Aristotle's statements, but Aristotle does not mention Hippocrates by name in *GA*.

38. Preus (1970, 9, n. 14).

39. At the start of the treatise, just after Aristotle has stated his thesis that the female and male are the *archai* of generation, he makes this remark about cosmology: "This is why in cosmology too they speak of the nature of the Earth as something female and call it 'mother,' while they give to the heaven and the sun and anything else of that kind the title of 'generator' and 'father'" (716a15). Aristotle does not himself subscribe to this mythic way of speaking, but it is suggestive, perhaps, that he thinks of earth and heaven directly after establishing his thesis.

40. In the Greek, Aristotle mentions "the female" before "the male" twice in this passage, although both Peck and Platt render these lines with "the male" first. The adjustment in Peck's translation above is mine. Platt translates the last phrase as follows: "That they exist because it is better and on account of the final cause, takes us back to a principle still further remote" (Platt, *The Generation of Animals,* 1135–36).

41. Peck (1979, 568).

42. As one immediate indication that in Book II Aristotle's interest has expanded beyond that of Book I and the working of generation in the case of particular male and female mates, to the consideration of generation with regard to classes of animals, see his statements at 732a1–2. He explains that since "the better" cannot be brought about in and for each individual creature, "there is always a class of men, of animals, of plants; and since the principle of these is 'the male' and 'the female' ... " That is, Aristotle now takes up male and female as the principles of the classes, not just of the offspring of individual acts of generation.

CHAPTER FOUR: SEXUAL INEQUALITY IN ARISTOTLE'S THEORIES
OF REPRODUCTION AND INHERITANCE

I would like to thank Margaret Atherton, Mary Louise Gill, Richard Kraut, and Julie Ward for their comments on earlier versions of this paper Margaret Atherton for a number of helpful discussions of my ideas, and Julie Ward for her extraordinarily generous and patient editorial support.

1. The issues raised by the second are not otherwise addressed in this paper. On this topic see, for example, Modrak (1994), Mulgan (1994), and N. Smith (1983).

2. For example, Horowitz (1976, 187–88):

> Just as Aristotle's biological sexism influenced many human beings' per-
> ceptions of themselves and their offspring, his political sexism influenced
> their beliefs on the proper distribution of roles in society.... Aristotle's
> "proportionate justice," a justice that is applied not equally between per-
> sons but proportionately according to their worth, judged in practical
> terms by their position in natural and social hierarchies, has given an eth-
> ical justification to the discriminatory policies that still pervade the West.
> By introducing his book on politics with an analysis of the patriarchal
> Greek household, Aristotle legitimized the patriarchy as the proper form
> of government for the family.... [A]n indication of the consistent anti-
> feminism of Aristotle is that while upholders of many sides of the woman
> question have used the Bible to support their case, it was a rare defender
> of woman who managed to use Aristotle to bring credit to the female
> branch of the human race.

3. For example, Morsink (1979, 84), in discussing the accusations of sexism in Aristotle's biology in Horowitz (1976), argues that Aristotle had "good scientific rea-sons" for accepting the "apparently sexist theory ... that the male contributes the all-important form and the female the mere matter of the offspring" and did not accept it for sexist reasons. He then concedes, "In that case, Aristotle's biology, though not now sexist in conception and origin, *was still sexist because of the consequences it has.*" Even Tress (1994, 310) admits that " ... there appears to be a long history of the use of Aristotle's treatise against women," but she believes this is mostly a result of mis-understanding a hard text and misusing it.

4. Although this might seem to be a theory-laden way of dividing up the territory, I do not mean it to be. I use "theory of reproduction" and "theory of inheritance" here as aids for the reader. There is disagreement in the scholarly literature about the extent to which we need see these as part of a single theory or as separate. This topic need not concern us here, but I do not intend by my choice of terminology to be weighing in strongly on the two-theory side of the debate.

5. For a brief discussion of the four *aitiai*, see *Phys.* II. 7 198a14–b10, esp., a22–26.

6. This analysis of sensible substances into two components, form and matter, is often referred to as Aristotle's "hylomorphic" analysis or as "hylomorphism" from the Greek words *hulê* (matter) and *morphê* (shape or form). See *Meta.* 1029a3–6.

7. See, for example Zeitlin (1984, 177–82).

8. G. E. R. Lloyd (1987, 84–87) has documented insertions of value judgments of vari-ous kinds in Aristotle's scientific writing. See also G. E. R. Lloyd (1985, 56) on moral values and science.

9. Morsink (1979, 84–87) argues against the possibility that what he calls "the form-matter hypothesis" ("Aristotle's theory that the male contributes the all-important form and the female the mere matter of the offspring") might be found to be a "value-ridden premise."

10. As a matter of fact, a careful reading of her paper makes clear that Tress herself does not deny these facts, although one can be misled by her antifeminist and antimaterialist rhetoric. In her view, there are inequalities in the male and female roles, but they are seen as determined by Aristotle's metaphysics, not by sexism or views about female inferiority. While I, too, think Aristotle's metaphysical commitments carry the argument some distance here, I do not think they can carry it all the way.

11. Preus (1977) contains a particularly helpful discussion of the alternative theories. Quite recently, Coles (1995) has written a complex and striking paper in which he explores the notion that Aristotle's theory of inheritance shares more affinities with the views associated with the authors of a particular subset of the Hippocratic treatises than is usually thought. Interestingly, Coles also criticizes Aristotle for proceeding as if the only options were his theory and a particular version of an alternative theory.

12. It has become somewhat of a commonplace in feminist criticism of Aristotle to blame the endoxic method which Aristotle takes as the starting point for his theorizing *endoxa* (opinions, both common opinion and the views of other past and present philosophers and scientists) as providing an inviting entranceway through which various prejudices (including sexist ones) might be incorporated and even given pride of place in his political and biological theories. This issue must of necessity be neglected here, but for an important though contested interpretation of the general role of *endoxa* in Aristotle, see T. Irwin (1988). For attempts to consider the issue of Aristotle's endoxic method and its effects from a feminist perspective see Nussbaum (1986, 370–71), Modrak (1994), Freeland (1994, 158–59) and Green (1992, 70–96).

13. In fact, there is a great deal of controversy among Aristotle scholars at the present time about to what extent, if at all, the theories are inconsistent. Furth (1988, 132–41) believes that they are inconsistent and suspects some sexist element in Aristotle's reasoning. A number of others, including Balme (1987 and 1990) and J. Cooper (1988), think that by interpreting "form" in both theories as including not only species-wide essential traits, but also inessential inheritable traits, inconsistency can be avoided. In fact, however, such an interpretation tends to exert pressure on the interpreter to also see the female as contributing form and that in turn leads to further difficulties and apparent inconsistencies. Cooper's paper contains a successful attempt to handle these difficulties, but they are difficult to dispel. Coles (1995) accepts the anti-essentialist reading and decides it leads to unresolvable inconsistencies. Code (1993) and Witt (1985) each argue in somewhat different ways for a consistent reading of the two theories that does not involve giving up essentialism.

14. It is an important feature of Aristotle's theory of inheritance that he thinks a distinct mechanism called slackening, or *lusis,* is operating in those cases in which the offspring inherits a characteristic such as nose shape not from a parent but from a grandparent or some more distant relative. His idea here seems to be that sometimes the motion of the male parent is affected by the material upon which it is operating (analogously, he suggests, to the way a knife may be dulled by what it cuts or the way in which something might be cooled by that which it is heating); in such cases the motions of the grandparent or more distant relative (which are present potentially but

not actually in the semen) "take over" in a way analogous to the second line in a battle. He claims that a similar replacement occurs in the case of the more distant ancestors of the female parent, but it is less clear exactly how this case works.

15. I am talking a lot about physical features, such as sense organs, but of course, in so far as the soul of an animal is identified by Aristotle with its capacities to function in certain ways essential to living the life characteristic of that kind of animal, it is those capacities, rather than the structures, that are essential. Aristotle, however, tells us that the structures are needed in order to exercise the capacities (or most of them—set aside thought about pure form) and that it is just when the structures come to be that the associated capacities come to be also. So the dog needs a nose to smell to perceive in a way central to leading the life of a dog.

16. See Cynthia Freeland's extremely helpful discussion of the role of blood in "Aristotle on Bodies, Matter, and Potentiality" (in Gotthelf and Lennox, 1987).

17. See in this connection Cooper's artifact analogy, similar in various ways to this story (Cooper 1988). I suspect part of the intractability of these texts to interpreters results from it being extremely difficult to incorporate smoothly all the salient features of Aristotle's account into a story using an artificial analogy.

18. Unfortunately, it was not until after writing this paper that I read C. D. Reeve's appendix to his book on Aristotle's ethics (Reeve 1995). It is an important contribution to the debate on matter and form in the embryology, in which Reeve claims that Aristotle's doctrine that the female is a deformed male is crucial to his ability to maintain that the mother contributes only matter and no form to the offspring. See especially pp. 206–9.

19. There are undoubtedly various "sexist" remarks in Aristotle's biological writings, but my special concern here is with his theories, in this case those formulated to explain reproduction and inheritance. What is of particular interest to me as it has been to many who have criticized or defended Aristotle is the relationship between his biological theorizing and the fairly uncontroversial fact that Aristotle seemed to believe, along with many of his male peers, that female animals and humans were inferior to their male counterparts in a variety of ways.

20. See, for example the early examples in Okin (1979, 191–94, 197–200) on Hobbes, Locke, and Rousseau.

21. See Skinner in Tully (1988) and Macpherson (1962, 7–9) for two different perspectives on this issue.

22. Mayr (1982, 634) claims it was quite typical during this period for theorists to believe that the paternal and maternal contributions to inheritance were qualitatively and quantitatively different.

23. I am assuming that much of his analysis would apply to early modern philosophy or nineteenth-century philosophy; Frede uses the understanding we have about those things that affect our own adaption of philosophical positions as evidence for the likelihood of this same pattern occurring in the case of past philosophers.

24. In Bar On (1994). This rich and far-ranging paper includes a careful and convincing analysis of the differences between Aristotle's scientific theory, methodology, and practice and those of later scientists with whom he is often indiscriminately lumped by feminist science criticism.

25. There is, of course, an extensive and complex literature on the more general issues that I am barely touching on here: the appropriate goals and uses of the history of

philosophy and its relationship to philosophy proper; how we should understand and practice charity; and the tensions between attention to historical context and a desire to trace problems, issues, or ideas through history and across historical periods. See, for example, Rosenthal (1989), papers by and in reaction to the work of Skinner in Tully (1988), and papers in Rorty, Schneewind, and Skinner (1984). These contain further references, and a number of recent books and papers have continued this discussion.

26. Matthews stresses that the difficulty would come for Aristotle with any commitment to the agency of parents of only one gender (or sex—Matthews' paper deals specifically with the question of whether femininity and masculinity are parts of human essences for Aristotle and with Aristotle's application of the Norm-Defect Theory to women; it is, of course, used by Aristotle to refer broadly to all animals with sexual differentiation). Aristotle's operative commitment in Matthews' analysis is to what Matthews calls the Doctrine of Paternal Agency, but he points out that either this doctrine or the weaker Doctrine of Single-Gender Agency (not held by Aristotle) would prevent him from postulating two *eidê*, a male and a female, and saying that female offspring get their *eidê* from their mothers and male offspring get theirs from their fathers.

27. For a discussion of Aristotle and New World Slavery, see Hanke (1959).

28. For a compelling discussion of how the work of Susan Bordo (1987) on Descartes can be seen as spawning both these sorts of distortions, see Margaret Atherton (1993).

CHAPTER FIVE: THE STOICS ON WOMEN

I am much indebted to Julie Ward, the editor of this volume, for her many valuable suggestions.

1. Diogenes Laertius, *Lives of the Philosophers* (henceforth, DL) VII.131: *koinas einas tas gynaikas dein para tois sophois, hôste ton entychonta têi entychousêi chrêsthai. Chrêsthai* has a wide range of meanings, from "use" or "treat" to "consort with," "have relations with," including "have sexual relations with." Cf. DL VII.33.

2. Schofield has recently argued in support of this view (1991, 43–46); see also Baldry (1959, 9–10).

3. *SVF* 3.253. *SVF* here refers to the collection of stoic fragments listed under Von Arnim 1964 in the bibliography under "Ancient Sources." Clemens refers to the Christians at *SVF* 3.254; his testimony need not be taken to apply to the Stoics.

4. The fragments of Musonius (written in Greek) have been collected by Hense (1905). Lutz (1947), offers a complete translation of the texts.

5. DL VI. 72: *elege de kai koinas einai dein tas gynaikas, gamon mêdena nomizôn, alla ton peisanta têi peistheisêi syneinai.* According to Philodemus (PHerc 399/155, col. 9; Crönert 1906, 64), there is utter sexual promiscuity: everyone "has intercourse with all men and all women, just as it happens by chance," and "married men have sex with their own female servants." In this section (Crönert 1906, 60–65), Philodemus argues for the influence of Diogenes on the early Stoa; cf. DL VII. 4.

6. Philodemus, PHerc 399/155, col. 9, Crönert 64.

7. I am grateful to Will Deming for first drawing my attention to these texts in his University of Chicago dissertation, which has now been published as *Paul on*

Marriage and Celibacy: The Hellenistic Background of 1 Corinthians 7, Cambridge 1995. Among authors who have given attention to these texts are Gaiser (1974), and Foucault (1984a, 177–92).

8. *On Duties* I. 55–56; cf. Cicero *On Laws* I. 34.
9. Stobaeus *Florilegium*, v. 3, 134 Meineke, 61 Von Arnim.
10. Stobaeus *Florilegium,* v. 3, 7–8 Meineke, 52–53 Von Arnim; and col. 11 of his "Elements of Ethics."
11. Col. 9 of "Elements of Ethics."
12. At the same time, *eunoêtikê* suggests the development of the intellect (*nous*).
13. *SVF* 3.179. Wild animals are also "conciliated" to their offspring "according to their need" (*SVF* 2.724).
14. The continuity between self-love and socialization has been questioned; see Inwood 1983. I agree with the view that children are loved as parts, or extensions, of oneself; see Inwood (1983, 198), and Blundell (1990, 229–30). At the same time, as Blundell has shown, the propagation of children is continuous with the desire to help and preserve humanity in general.
15. The Stoic system of concentric circles came to be adopted into Peripatetic ethics. Antiochus (first century B.C.E.), who mixed Stoic with Peripatetic ideas, took it over (Cicero *On Ends* V. 65 and 67).
16. See Hierocles in Stobaeus *Anthology*, v. 3, 731. Hense, 51 Von Arnim.
17. On "indifferents" and their divisions, see esp. *SVF* 3.136, 163, 164, and 1.244.
18. See *SVF* 3.717, also 1.249, 250. I am much indebted to Malcolm Schofield's discussion of Stoic love throughout his book (1991), and to Martha Nussbaum's analysis in "Eros and the Wise," forthcoming in *Oxford Studies in Ancient Philosophy*.
19. *SVF* 3.397. In Stoic terminology, it is a subdivision of *epithymia*, one of the four main kinds of *pathê*, irrational emotions.
20. Plutarch (*Marriage Precepts*, 140e) uses the same metaphor of wine and water to describe conjugal relations. The metaphor seems to have become commonplace.
21. Hierocles, in Stobaeus *Anthology* v. 3, 732. Hense, 51 Von Arnim.
22. Epictetus *Diatribes* 2.10.3–4.
23. *Consolation to Marcia* 16.1: *par illis, mihi crede, vigor, par ad honesta, libeat, facultas est.* ("They have an equal strength, believe me, an equal capacity for virtuous things, if they please.")
24. Fr. 3 Hense.
25. Musonius mentions the claim, at one point, that men are "stronger in judgment" (fr. 12). But this is a premise in an *ad hominem* argument, and Musonius does not himself accept it.
26. Van Geytenbeck 1963, 64–65 traces the twofold aims, reproduction and partnership in life, to Aristotle. He also rightly points out that Musonius' "demand of complete mutual devotion" differs from Aristotle's more pragmatic conception.
27. Stobaeus *Florilegium*, v. 3, 8–10 Meineke, 54 Von Arnim.
28. Stobaeus *Florilegium*, v. 3, 8 Meineke, 53 Von Arnim.
29. See Pomeroy, 1975, 125–31.
30. They did point out that *anthrôpos* can be feminine in gender; one can speak of *hê anthrôpos*, the female human being (Hülser, 567).
31. See Long and Sedley (1987, v. 1, 401–10).
32. Stobaeus *Florilegium*, v. 3, 7 Meineke, 52 Von Arnim.

33. See further Cicero *On Ends* III.68 and *On Duties* III.63. The topic "should a person marry," and specifically, "should the wise man marry," came to be much treated in rhetoric (as a so-called "thesis," or abstract question, which could be argued on either side, see Spengel v. 2, 50–53, 120, etc.). Other topics included "will the wise person participate in politics?" See Spengel v. 2, 123, etc. These questions were introduced into rhetoric from philosophy rather than the other way around.

34. This conclusion differs from Schofield (1991), esp. 25–26, who holds that the sharing consists in a sexual sharing.

35. Cicero writes that whereas some Stoics allowed Cynic behavior under special circumstances, others prohibited it altogether (*On Ends* III.68). Zeno reportedly said that the wise man will be a Cynic (DL VII. 121). Presumably he meant "under special circumstances." Panaetius is a plausible example of a Stoic who did not allow Cynicizing under any circumstances (cf. Cicero *On Duties* I.128).

36. I disagree, therefore, with Schofield's distinction (1991, 119–27) between the behavior of the wise person in existing society (where he or she will marry) and in utopia (where he or she will not marry).

37. *SVF* 1. 248. The physical appearance as such, I suggest, need not be beautiful. What matters is that an aptitude for the beauty of virtue shines through the physical appearance. Zeno paints a detailed picture of such a young man at *SVF* 1.246, as quoted by Schofield (1991, 115–16).

CHAPTER SIX: ARISTOTELIAN RESOURCES FOR FEMINIST THINKING

My thanks to Emily Hauptmann and Julie Ward for helpful comments on earlier drafts of this essay.

1. For North American object relations theorists, see, for example, Mahler (1968, 1975), Rinsley (1982, 1989), and Masterson (1988). For European object relations theorists, see, for example, Klein (1975), Kernberg (1980), Kohut (1971), and Winnicott (1965). For recent developments in the theory, see Akhtar and Parens (1991).

2. Consider the description of particular examples of awareness as "richly colored rather than monochromatic," "suffused with loving emotion," and morally adequate due to "fullness and richness" in Nussbaum (1987, 152). For another example, consider Noddings's claim that "To care is to act not by fixed rule but by affection and regard" and her claim that the one who cares acts "with special regard for the particular person in a concrete situation." (Noddings, 24). For a general discussion of the importance of awareness of particulars over knowledge of universal rules, see McDowell (1979), Noddings (1984), Nussbaum (1985; 1986, 290–317; 1987), Sherman (1989, 13–55), Salkever (1990, 105–61).

3. See note 2.

4. See McDowell (1979, 343–45), Nussbaum (1985, 74; 1986, 305), and Sherman (1989, 28ff).

5. Consider, for example, Noddings's claim that the language of the ethic of care is "in the realm of ethical feeling" and that those using it do not claim "to present or to seek moral *knowledge*" (1984, 3).

6. Hobbes (ch. 15, 115).

7. Freud (1924, 198).
8. In this essay, I disregard the *Eudemian Ethics* definition (1220b11–13) since it contradicts all the other definitions. Leighton (1984, 138, note 9) suggests Aristotle found his *Eudemian Ethics* definition disadvantageous and so dropped it in the *Rhetoric* and the *Nicomachean Ethics*.
9. Nussbaum and Putnam (1992, 44).
10. They cite *De Sensu* I. 436a8–10 and *Metaphysics* VI. 1 1026a2–3, which include three examples of phrases of the same form, in support of this claim.
11. Presumably they are perceptions not of proper sensibles, but of incidental or common sensibles. See *De Anima* II. 6 418a8–25.
12. Deborah Modrak (1987, 140) makes a similar claim. "An emotion," she says, explaining Aristotle's views, "is a pleasure or pain experienced with respect to a particular type of object under particular circumstances." A longer essay would include consideration of apparent counter-examples. Leighton (1982, 155–56, 170, note 14; 1984, 138) cites hate as one, since Aristotle claims in *Rhetoric* II. 4 (1382a12–13) that hate is not accompanied by pain. However, since in his definition of emotion three chapters earlier (*Rhet.* II. 1 1378a19–22, cited above), Aristotle says that emotions are accompanied by pleasure and pain, the example is not decisive. Having raised the example, Leighton himself (1982, 155–57, 170, note 14) treats it as anomalous rather than decisive and argues that the link between emotion and pleasure or pain is a conceptual one. He also argues there that Aristotle's claim that emotions are accompanied by pleasure and pain is not meant to preclude the idea of a conceptual connection between them.
13. Modrak, too, cites this passage as support for a claim that pleasures and pains are forms of perception according to Aristotle. In explanation of the passage, she says: "To feel pleasures and pains, to experience emotions and desires, is just another way of relating to objects in the world and thus is a form of perception" (141). She does not make the further claim about what the perception is perception of, however, namely, what is good or bad as such.
14. I discuss good as a transcategorial in Achtenberg (1992, 318–23).
15. Fortenbaugh (1975, 12–16) has a different interpretation. He argues not that emotions are types of cognition, but that cognitions are the efficient cause of emotions. His tendency to slide from that claim, for which he argues, into the assertion that emotions are cognitive, for which he does not argue, is instructive, however, as is the fact that he does not discuss the formal cause of emotion.
16. The beautiful is another type of value for Aristotle. Discussion of it would go beyond the limits of this essay, however.
17. For a general discussion of equivocals and of the three types of equivocals, see Owens (1978, 107–35). For an argument that equivocity does not simply reflect the different senses of words, see Irwin (1981). For a previous discussion of mine on the equivocity of the good, see Achtenberg (1992, 320–22).
18. *Categories* 1, 1a1–6.
19. *Nicomachean Ethics* V. 1 1129a26–31. Aristotle's example is not "sharp" but "key" (*kleis*) which is merely ambiguous in Greek and means either "the collar-bone" or "that with which we lock a door." See also *Nicomachean Ethics* I. 6 1096b26–27 where Aristotle speaks of chance equivocals and *Metaphysics* IV. 2 1003a33–34

where he contrasts focal equivocals with mere equivocals (what I am calling merely ambiguous equivocals).

20. *Metaphysics* IV. 2 1003a33–1003b10, VII. 4 1030a34–b3, XI. 3 1060b31–61a3.
21. *Metaphysics* IX. 6 1048a35–b9.
22. *Metaphysics* IV. 2 1003a34–b1, XI. 3 1061a5–7.
23. Irwin (1985, 303), suggests concurrence with the claim that Aristotle's view in this passage is that good is an analogical equivocal. Irwin's suggested argument for the claim is different but complementary to the one I give here and below.
24. See also I. 2 982b4, b10; I. 3 983a31; XI. 1 1059a35.
25. For a confirming interpretation of the first part of this passage, see Apostle (1979, 356, n. 3), "Not everything is definable; and there are principles and attributes of being *qua* being which are indefinable, such as actuality and potentiality."
26. Irwin (1981, 540) makes a similar point. It is the case both that there is a single true description of good and that good is multivocal according to him; for "goods are different because they are ends and ends are different."
27. I make this proposal first in Achtenberg (1988, 28).
28. In order to include not just final but also instrumental ends, a more complete account would put the distinction this way: a *telos* is a constitutive (final end) or enabling (instrumental end) limit. Then the distinction would be between limits that are destructive or harmful on the one hand and limits that are constitutive or enabling on the other. Enabling limits are those that enable what they limit to be, more fully or securely, what it already is. They enable it to flourish. Since instrumental ends are ends because they lead to final ends, and in order to simplify the argument of this essay, I do not here discuss enabling limits.
29. I use the term "development" to mean positive or successful development and "maldevelopment" to mean negative development or deterioration.
30. For a previous discussion of this passage, see Achtenberg (1989, 38).
31. For a previous discussion of the first example, see Achtenberg (1989, 38). For a concurring interpretation of the second example, see Apostle (1981, 113, n. 17). Apostle, too, speaks of "preservation." Where I speak of fulfilling or securing, Apostle speaks of reinforcing, strengthening, or stabilizing.
32. In a book currently in progress, I argue at greater length for the interpretation of the mean that follows.
33. That by "*t'anangkaion*" Aristotle means "the inevitable" is clear from the context.
34. In another context, Burnet gives a similar interpretation of "*dei*" for Aristotle. "The verb *dei* means *agathon esti*" (1900, 302).
35. The statement here is in the negative, but Aristotle's affirmation of the positive can be inferred from the context.
36. See Aristotle *Metaphysics* VIII. 3 1043b25 for another example of this.
37. Rousseau (1986, 146: *Second Discourse*, Part II, paragraph 11). See also Rousseau (1986, 4–5: *First Discourse*, Part I, paragraph 9), where Rousseau identifies government with despotism and claims that the sciences and arts spread "garlands of flowers" over its chains and make men "love their slavery."
38. Hobbes (ch. 13, 98–100).
39. I discuss rational activity as intentional activity in Achtenberg (1989, 42). For a related discussion, see Achtenberg (1992, 330–34).

CHAPTER SEVEN: FEMINISM AND ARISTOTLE'S RATIONAL IDEAL

I am grateful to David Cappall, Jean Hampton, Janet Levin, the editors of C. Witt, and L. Antony, ed. (1994) for helpful comments on earlier versions of this paper.

1. The title also suggests that the organizers thought it appropriate, even in this special context, to refer to the three of us as "girls." I leave aside the problems associated with the use of this term in relation to adult women.

2. For Aristotle's views on women, see *GA* 728a17ff., 732alff., 775al5; *EN* I 1162al9–27; *Pol.* I 1259b28–1260a24, 1277b20. For Kant, see Kant (1960, sec. 3). For Hobbes, see Hobbes (1968, chs. 19–20).

3. For a useful discussion of these issues, see Spelman (1988, especially ch. 5).

4. See Carol Gilligan (1982). In her more recent writings, Gilligan has softened her position, to claim that though women can have the "justice" perspective as well as the "care" perspective men are more likely to have only the "justice" perspective. See Gilligan (1988). For the influence of Gilligan's work on moral theory, see L. Blum, (1988); and E. Kittay and D. Meyers, (1987). For a different approach to these issues, see W. Flanagan and K. Jackson (1987).

5. See, for example, John Rawls' account of the principles of justice as chosen in special circumstances of rational deliberation in Rawls (1971).

6. For a discussion of the role of "particularity" in the moral life, see L. Blum (1991), and the works cited therein.

7. L. Blum (1982).

8. Claudia Card questions whether it is appropriate to associate care and compassion more with women than with men, and offers some helpful criticisms of the care perspective in Card (1988). See also C. Greeno and E. Maccoby (1986) and Gilligan's reply (Gilligan 1986).

9. For considerations in favor of the view that even natural slaves are men and women for Aristotle, see Fortenbaugh (1977, 136).

10. For an enumeration of the various different types of non-citizens in Aristotle's ideal state and for a discussion of their legal status, see Keyt (1986, 23–46).

11. What to make of Aristotle's views in *EN* X.7–8 and how to integrate them into the rest of the *EN* and *Pol.* are not matters I shall discuss here. I shall be concerned only with Aristotle's broadly based view of human good which includes the goods of social, political, and family life *(EN* 1097b8–11), as well as various intellectual goods.

12. It should be clear that Aristotle's implied and stated reservations about manual labor are not dissimilar from some of Marx's criticisms of wage labor under capitalism, in particular from Marx's view that such labor alienates the worker from the activity of production and from his species-being. See Marx (1971–78, Vol. 3, 274–77 and Vol. 6, passim).

13. I discuss the nature of these higher-level decisions in more detail in Homiak (1990).

14. For a helpful discussion of Plato's views on women see J. Annas (1976) and J. Annas (1981, 181–185).

15. Fortenbaugh draws a similar conclusions in Fortenbaugh (1977).

16. I use the translation by Terence Irwin of Aristotle's *Nicomachean Ethics* (Indianapolis: Hackett Publishing, 1985).

17. I follow, in broad outline, the more detailed argument for the same conclusion offered by Irwin (1988, 411–16).
18. As translated by B. Jowett in Barnes (1984).
19. It is not clear that one could provide the same type of argument for Plato. This is in part, I think, because the content of the good life is less well articulated in Plato than in Aristotle and also because, however we are to understand the content of the good life, it does not include democratic decision-making as a good in itself. For the philosopher-rulers, ruling is a burden they would prefer to be without, since they would prefer to be without the responsibilities and activities that take them away from a continual contemplation and love of the Forms. They accept the burdens of ruling only because there is no other way to replicate the beauty they see in the Forms. Although it is best for the state as a whole that they rule, their interest in ruling is purely instrumental. And since menial labor is often monotonous and routine, requiring little use of the rational powers, it would be inefficient for rulers to take it up. It is therefore better left to others.
20. In Homiak (1981, 633–51) , and in Homiak (l985, 93–110).
21. See Card (1988) and Greeno and Maccoby (1986).
22. For a related discussion, see Bishop (1979, 147–54).
23. Cf. Nancy Chodorow's description of healthy dependence in Chodorow (1974).and (1978, pp. 211ff).
24. For current wage differentials between full-time working women and men, see U.S. Department of Labor (1987).
25. See M. Benston (1984, 239–47, esp. 244–45).
26. For further discussion of anger in the context of unequal power relations see E. Spelman (1989) and F. Nietzsche (1967, passim).
27. For more discussion of these and related points, see Blum (1979) and Mill (1970).

CHAPTER EIGHT: ARISTOTELIAN VISIONS OF MORAL CHARACTER IN VIRGINIA WOOLF'S *MRS. DALLOWAY*

1. Diary entry, 24 February 1905, from Woolf (1990).
2. The surviving typescript of this lecture, heavily corrected, is printed as Appendix III (502–17) of Woolf (1988).
3. Woolf (1988, 503).
4. Woolf (1925, 11). All further page references are to this edition. In *Jacob's Room,* Woolf offers the following observations: "It seems that a profound, impartial, and absolutely just opinion of our fellow creatures is utterly unknown" (71). "It is no use trying to sum people up. One must follow hints, not exactly what is said, nor yet entirely what is done" Woolf (1978b, 154).
5. In what follows I shall offer an account of those claims that Aristotle makes that seem to me relevant to a reading of Woolf's text. This is certainly not a full account of Aristotle's moral theory.
6. The confirmation for Virginia Woolf's reading of the *Poetics* is to be found in Woolf (1990). The evidence of the 1905 diary is that Virginia Stephen began reading the *Poetics* on 21 February, and finished on 2 March. The entry for 21 February (240) includes the following: "Then I read a bit of Aristotle, the *Poetics*, which will fit me

for a reviewer! This book, I tried to read at Florence, I remember—& couldn't!"

7. Woolf (1990, 22 February 1905 pp. 240–41). In her letters and diaries Woolf also mentions reading Plato and the tragedians.

8. Regan (1986) and Levy (1981) both discuss Moore's influence on Bloomsbury. For another view of Moore's influence on the novels of Virginia Woolf, see Rosenbaum (1971). Rosenbaum concentates on the issues of epistemology and philosophy of mind rather than on ethics.

9. See Woolf (1968, 32–33: Helen Ambrose, sitting on deck, reads "a sentence about the Reality of Matter or the Nature of Good" in "a black volume of philosophy." (Levy, Moore's biographer, says that the original cover was dark brown.) For evidence of Virginia Stephen's reading of (and reaction to) *Principia Ethica*, see her August 1908 letters to Clive Bell and Saxon Sydney-Turner in Woolf (1977, 342, 347, 352–53).

10. See L. Woolf (1975) for Leonard Woolf's own account of Moore and his influence. On Aristotle, Leonard Woolf writes in a letter to Saxon Sydney-Turner: "I have just finished the *Ethics* & as usual with Aristotle it seems to me an eminently futile work as a whole, but extraordinarily shrewd in isolated observations. Chapter XI of Book VI [on moral judgment and moral intuition] beats me completely, it seems to contradict & to be absolutely irreconcilable with what has gone before in that book & the commentators seem quite fuddled over it." L. Woolf (1989, July 28, 1902, 25).

11. We also know that Virginia Woolf was reading Greek at the time she was writing *Mrs. Dalloway*; she worked on "The Hours" (the working title for *Mrs. Dalloway*) and "Reading" (the working title of *The Common Reader*) during the same period. *The Common Reader* contains her essay "On Not Knowing Greek," and it was for this essay that she was reading Greek authors (or at least intending to) in 1922, 1923, and 1924 (see her reading plans throughout Woolf (1978a) esp. 27 November, 3 December 1922; 11 May, 16 November 1923; 5 April, 3 August 1924). In her first response to Desmond MacCarthy ("Affable Hawk") on the issue of the intellectual status of women (in the *New Statesman* of 9 October 1920) she refers to Plato's and Aristotle's literary appreciation of Sappho; see Woolf (1978a, Appendix III).

12. See Rowe (1978) for an analysis of Clarissa's role as the "mean of place" in *Mrs. Dalloway* and some trenchant comments on both her defects and her virtues.

13. For what Woolf might mean in portraying Clarissa Dalloway as a snob, see "Am I a Snob?" in Woolf (1985). We should also note that Clarissa herself responds to the snob charge: "They thought . . . that she enjoyed imposing herself; liked to have famous people about her; great names; was simply a snob in short. . . . And both were quite wrong. What she liked was simply life" (183); this account is consistent with Woolf's claims about herself in "Am I a Snob?"

14. Woolf (1980, 32). "Kitty" was Katherine Lushington Maxse, on whom Clarissa was modeled.

15. We should also note that Peter Walsh has a mixed view of Clarissa (see 114–19, for instance) that is, on the whole, favorable.

16. Bradshaw apparently believes that the emotions can have no role to play in the best life. In Aristotelian terms, he would perhaps claim that they do not belong to the part of the soul having reason. But as *EN* I.13 shows, Aristotle places great importance on the fact that the part of the soul in which the emotions are to be found "have reason in a way" for they can be obedient to reason.

17. See Halliwell (1986, especially chs. V and VI) and Halliwell (1987) for fuller

accounts of Aristotle's views of character in the *Poetics*. References are to Kassel's OCT edition of the *Poetics*. Throughout, translations from the Greek are my own.

18. A comment from Halliwell seems appropriate here: "it was obvious [to the Romantics] that the *Poetics* could hardly provide any guidance with genres such as subjective lyric, or the novel, for which Aristotle had made no provision" (Halliwell 1986, 22).

19. Despite my claims denying the relevance of the *Poetics'* account of character to my project, it is possible that Aristotle's claims about *katharsis* would carry over to the effect of the novel. A full exploration of the problems associated with *katharsis* is well beyond the scope of this paper. Halliwell (1986) and R. Janko (1987) both offer careful discussions of the problem.

20. References to the *Nicomachean Ethics* (*EN*) are to Bywater's OCT.

21. As I am here concerned with the help Aristotle can give us in understanding Virginia Woolf's view of moral character, I shall not enter into the important debate about the role of contemplation in Aristotle's account of *eudaimonia*. The issues are well set out in Cooper (1987), in Kraut (1989), and Broadie (1991, 383–433).

22. See Cooper (1988a) and also Striker (1988).

23. "But the mean with respect to us is not to be taken so [as an arithmetical proportion]; for it is not the case that if ten *mnai* are too much to eat and two too little, the trainer will prescribe six *mnai*; for this also is perhaps too much or too little for the one receiving it; for Milo it is too little, for the beginner in exercises too much" (1106a36–b4).

24. See *EN* 1126b3–4; the decision rests with the particular facts.

25. This does not mean that the decisions of the *phronimos* are not universalizable; the decision would hold good for anyone in those particular circumstances.

26. See Kraut (1989, 38, note 22).

27. There is also the issue of working out how to perform the correct act; this is the role of the so-called practical syllogism, and it too involves the perception of the *phronimos*.

28. Compare this with G. E. Moore's intuitionism about good. It is clear that a correct answer is possible; moreover it is also clear that people can make mistakes. See Moore (1903).

29. See Kraut (1989, esp. 58–59 and 345–47).

30. "I am now in the thick of the mad scene in Regents Park. I find I write it by clinging as tight to fact as I can, & write perhaps 50 words a morning." Diary entry, 15 October 1923 Woolf (1978a, 272).

31. See especially Cooper (1988a) on this. Septimus is, of course, not to be held morally responsible for his breakdown, but his not feeling grief may well be a sign that something is wrong.

32. The differences between Clarissa and Richard also point up differences between public and private virtues. Aristotle's complete account of virtue, of course, includes both; as he says, he is speaking to young men who are to take their places in the political life of the city.

33. This is a claim made on the basis of fragmentary evidence; little is said of Richard Dalloway, but I think that he is present in Clarissa's thoughts throughout the novel; it is his importance to her (and hers to him) that supports my claims about their friendship. See Cooper (1980) and Annas (1977).

34. Diary entry, 18 June 1925, Woolf (1980, 32).

CHAPTER NINE: ARISTOTLE ON *PHILIA*:
THE BEGINNING OF A FEMINIST IDEAL OF FRIENDSHIP?

I would like to thank Deborah Achtenberg, Richard Kraut, and Ezio Vailati for their comments and objections to earlier versions of this paper.

1. Henceforth, *Nicomachean Ethics* and *Eudemian Ethics* are abbreviated as *EN* and *EE*, respectively. The discussion of *philia* or friendship (see Cooper (1980, 301–3)) in *EN* covers two full books (roughly, one fifth of the total work), that in *EE*, one full book (roughly, one third). On the issue of the differences between these two works, see Kenny (1978, 1992). I am excepting here Plato's *Lysis* as it does not present a developed theory of friendship.

2. See, for example, Spelman (1988, ch. 2), DuBois (1988, ch. 9), Tuana (1994), Senack (1994).

3. See, for example, Homiak, Achtenberg, and Curd (this volume), as well as Freeland (1994).

4. One of the earliest papers entitled "Friendship" by Telfer dates from 1970–71, but the flood of academic papers seems to follow Blum (1980); see Stocker (1981), Slote (1982), Thomas (1987).

5. One scholar notes that in Western society, female friendships occur against a backdrop in which marriage is the focal institution, and romantic love its ideological center; thus, because friendships between women are threatening to the marital relation they are socially discouraged (O'Connor, 1992, 33).

6. See, for example, Hartmann (1976), Young (1981), Lugones and Spelman (1983), Jaggar (1983), and Spelman (1988).

7. See Fantham, et al. (1995). As Abderson and Zinsser (1989) make clear, women in the medieval and Renaissance periods had various means of social interaction with one another through domestic work in large households, artesan guilds, and merchant activities; convents also afforded women the possibility of female friendship.

8. So Raymond (1986a, 173) finds that female friendship has been disadvantaged in two ways: either it is considered to be non-existent by the culture or it is "disabled" by being seen as perverse; one canonical source for which may be found in Freud's analysis of the "unresolved" Oedipal complex in girls which is said to result in homosexual choice, described as immature and abnormal (see Freud, *Female Sexuality*, 1931).

9. In this essay, I shall be speaking about the place of female friendship specifically within Western society, by which I intend to signify the developed, capitalist economies of the West. I acknowledge that certain indigenous cultures in the West, e.g., Native American cultures, may have a wholly different model of female friendship since they possess different conceptions of gender and gender-relations. See, for example, Allen (1986) Lamphere (1974).

10. Here the underlying assumption is that relative to their class and race, women's lives (needs, interests, etc.) are nevertheless accorded less value than are those of men.

11. Consequently, the present account, insofar as it touches upon various features of female friendship, does not pretend to be representative of all female friendships, but illustrative of certain features within the group.

12. On the distinction between feeling respect, or even beneficence, and friendship, see Blum (1980, 43–66).

13. On this feature, see Friedman (1993, ch. 7).
14. That is, in both *EE* VII, and *EN* VIII and IX. Although the two accounts are not identical, in general, I will treat them as consonant, for although there are differences, they do not bear on the characterization of *philia* developed here. See also note 1.
15. Taking the *dia* at *EN* 1156a3–5 as expressing an aim or end of *philia* as opposed to describing *the occasion on which* the friendship came about.
16. The fact that this description is introduced by "they say that" (*phasi*) indicates that the account is an *endoxon* or opinion that may or may not coincide with Aristotle's own description of *eunoia*; in *EN* IX. 5 (1166b30 ff.), *eunoia* is not similarly described. With regard to " . . . for his own sake," I have followed the Greek in using the masculine personal pronoun; where the Greek does not require it, I use the feminine case throughout.
17. Burnet (1900, 354) claims that the three features of *philia* alluded to here emerge from current usage of the term in Aristotle's time. The second feature rules out that one can have *philia* toward an inanimate thing, like wine, suggested by Plato's use of *philoinos* in *Lysis* 212d.
18. Aristotle seems to present a further reason for which *philia* is a *hexis*, namely, that since the object of the friendship is (in one case) the good itself, rather than the apparent good, it must be dependent upon deliberation and not emotion alone (cf. 1157b33–34). See also Burnet (1900, 370).
19. Translation from Cope (1877, 42), in the note to Aristotle's *Rhetoric* II. 4, 1380b36.
20. Second, and briefly, Cooper's account of *philia* (Cooper 1980, 310–14) takes *eunoia* as wishing well for the sake of the other and claims it is present in all three types of *philia*. But this ignores the passage in *EN* IX. 5 where Aristotle denies that *eunoia* exists in the two secondary kinds of friendship (1167a12–14). This in spite of Cooper's ingenious solution to the problem of how *eunoia* can be present in the secondary friendships (i.e., he takes the *dia* construction at 1156a3–5 to be used retrospectively to describe the cause of the *eunoia*, rather than prospectively).
21. In *EN* VIII. 5, Aristotle claims: "As with the virtues, so it is with friendship, the good are so called both in respect of disposition (*hexis*), and in respect of realization" (*energeia*, (1157b5–7), where I read "realization" to refer to the virtues as expressed in action.
22. These lines qualify virtue friendship as "complete" (*teleia*); further, persons who wish each other good in this way are friends in the fullest sense (*malista philoi*). Burnet (1900, 359) argues that here *teleia* is used "in the strict of the word, that the growth is complete, and that the form (*eidos*) of *philia* is realized in it so that none of it is left out (*to teleion = ou mêden hexô*). It is, in fact, "full-grown" *philia*."
23. The claim that virtue friendship is "primary" and "proper" form (*protôs kai kuriôs*, 1157a30–31) stands in contrast with the secondary forms of friendship which bear a resemblance to virtue friendship (*EN* 1157a1). For "primary" and "proper," see also Bonitz (1849) on *Meta.* 1015b11.
24. One might see a distinction between the needs of morally good persons and those who are not such that the latter group of persons are interested in friendship conditional upon their imperfections, or lack of positive moral qualities; see O'Connor (1990, 117–18).
25. In the last part of the argument, *EN* 1156b7–24 (on which compare *EE* 1237a9–30), this friendship is *teleia*, or "complete," in the sense that it includes the features of the

secondary kinds—it is both pleasant and useful as well as conducing to *aretê*, or virtue. Cf. Burnet (1900, 360).

26. I will not here discuss the precise nature of the relation between the primary and secondary kinds of friendship—whether the stated relation in *EN* VIII. 3 of a "similarity" between them (1156b20) amounts to the same thing as the claim in *EE* VII. 2 about a focal relationship (1236a17–21); see Fortenbaugh (1975); Walker (1979); J. Ward (1995).

27. It may be noted that Burnet (1900, 355) holds that the notion that *eunoia* involves wishing well for the other's sake is "merely a popular belief" or *endoxon* which does not itself enter into the definition of *philia* (note to *EN* 1155b31).

28. This argument is found only in *EE*, not *EN* (which contains only the denial that *eunoia* obtains in the secondary kinds), and while the text of *EE* appears to contain a lacuna, I believe that the sense of the text is fairly clear. It would have been preferable for Aristotle to have suggested that *eunoia* does not obtain in the same sense in the various kinds of *philia*, rather than claiming it is not present in the secondary kinds of *philia*.

29. The relation of the secondary kinds to the primary kind, however, is not one of degrees: the primary kind is not "more" friendship than the other two in the strict sense; rather, the secondary kinds of friendship are related to the primary kind by a "resemblance" (*kath' homoiotêta*, *EN* 1156b20).

30. It must be said that Aristotle distinguishes between two kinds of "self-love" (*philautia*), one of which is blameworthy, the other denotes the state of exercising the virtues, and so, is praiseworthy (*EN* IX. 8, 1168b15–30). Richard Kraut (1989, 131–39) disputes the egoistic interpretation of Aristotle's account; he argues that self-love is simply the paradigm case of the features he identifies as present in the various instances of friendship (cf. *EN* IX. 4, 1166a2–10).

31. This is so because in the case of virtue friendships the thing loved is a *per se*, or essential, property of the person loved, not merely an accidental, relational property that obtains between me and other person, such as being pleasant or useful (cf. *EN* 1156b8–11).

32. Here Kraut (in correspondence) has objected that the affiliation of two persons both of whom feel oppressed does not necessarily benefit either one, and that perhaps a friendship with someone else, say, a man, who does not feel oppressed is preferable, and more beneficial. To this, I reply that if women as such are oppressed, though in varying degrees (by race, class, etc.), it would not assist a woman's understanding of her situation to befriend a privileged man, but it would a woman. However, I do not suppose here that women's friendship is itself sufficient to end their oppression; rather, it is a "helping" condition towards female emancipation.

33. The term *eudaimonia* is standardly translated as "happiness" and so the adjective *eudaimon* as "happy," but these are not adequate in themselves as they may suggest passive, transitory states (as when a child has eaten a bowl of pasta). Instead, the term should be thought of as signifying a secure state consisting of activities toward human excellence, thus "flourishing."

34. The two works do not coincide in these arguments; in general, I propose to follow those in *EN* IX. 9.

35. This argument is more complex than I have indicated here; for more analysis see Burnet (1900), Stewart (1892), Ross (1963), Joachim (1962, 258).

36. In their notes to *EN* 1170a13 ff., Ross (1925) claims that the argument about self-knowledge and friendship consists in a set of eleven syllogisms, Burnet (1900) similarly claims that the argument consists in three main syllogisms, the first of which is supported by two prosyllogisms. See also Joachim (1962, 259–61), Gauthier and Jolif (1959, 756–62).

37. In spite of the frequent references to "self-conscious" activities in the argument in *EN* IX. 9 (using forms of *aisthanesthai*), Cooper (1980, 320) seems to be right in maintaining that the point of this argument is not self-consciousness but self-knowledge; the version in *EE* VII. 2 has: "Therefore, to perceive a friend must be in a way to perceive oneself and to know oneself" (Ross 1963, *EE* 1245a35–37).

38. On a related version of the argument, see Aristotle's *Magna Moralia* 1213a10–26; for a complete analysis of the two versions, see Cooper (1980, 318–324). Cooper does not, however, deal with the version of this argument as it appears in *EE* VII. 2 (1245a26–b9).

39. Here I intend to imply my disagreement not only with some versions of cultural feminism but of multiculturalism which do not observe basic egalitarian principles between men and women. It should be noted that Aristotle was one of the many thinkers who held that free women did not possess the same capacities, moral or intellectual, as free men did. The precise nature and degree of this difference, however, is debatable; see Cole (1994), Fortenbaugh (1977), Modrak (1994), Spelman (1988, 37–56), Smith (1983).

40. In recent papers, Nussbaum has argued that the Aristotelian conception of human flourishing can be applied to the modern social context: see Nussbaum (1992a, 1993).

41. I do not see another way of plausibly construing Aristotle's earlier explicit argument that we need friends so as to contemplate the goodness that we possess (through the virtuous actions of our friends) at *EN* 1169b28–1170a4. Kraut objects against Cooper's interpretation that the good person already knows he is good, and so does not need friends to confirm this knowledge, but only has friends because observing goodness in one's friends is easier. But Aristotle claims that "we are *better able* to contemplate our neighbors than ourselves (*theorein de mallon tous pelas dunametha e heautous*) and their actions than ours" (1169b33–34), which suggests to me that it enables us to learn something we could not otherwise learn. This seems also Joachim's point when he notes that the value of our good actions is not obvious to us while acting since "we are absorbed in the doing and not divided into spectator and agent" (Joachim 1962, 258).

42. Here the transition might be from the dispositional knowledge that one is good to a state like the actual exercise of a faculty, a second actuality stage of knowing one is good; see *De Anima* II. 5, 417a21–b16.

43. Gauthier and Jolif (1959, 755) note here that the lines recall Xenophon, *Memorabilia* I, II, 20, concerning fathers training their sons to virtue by having them socialize with the good; the textual reference to the poet Theognis is said to be to the notion that good or noble people learn from the good (verse 35–36).

44. See Friedman (1993, chs. 7 and 9).

45. Admitedly, as Kraut noted to me, the remedial, educative direction is not the one that Aristotle is primarily concerned with in his account of *philia*; however, Nussbaum (1986, and 1990, 54–105) finds various parts of Aristotle's ethical theory to be

focused upon the use of moral imagination in the discernment of virtuous actions and habits. And just as it takes experience and practical reason to become courageous or just, so, too, it would require practice to learn about friendship.

46. This point relates, of course, to the voluminous literature on ethics of care: see, for example, Gilligan (1982); Noddings (1984); Kittay and Meyers (1987); Cole and Coultrap-McQuinn (1992).

47. See Cooper (1980, 307) for further discussion of these issues.

48. I am supplying "affection" (*philêsis*) here because the term "good" (*agathon*) appears to be an interpolation, and does not make strict sense. See Rackham (1975, 494), note on *EN* 1161a24.

49. In the same way that his political theory may be considered in abstraction from his claims about slavery, so, too, his theory of virtue friendship may be separated from his claims about gender inequality.

50. Interpretations of civic or political friendship vary: Barker (1945, xlvii) claims it is similar to familial affection, and the association within the *polis* is similiar to that of a band of intimates; Irwin (1988, ch. 18) disputes this reading as does Yack (1993, ch. 1).

51. For a discussion of the extent to which Aristotle's notion of political community implies unity, as opposed to diversity, see Yack (1993, chs.1–2). Yack himself argues for an individualist interpretation of Aristotle's notion of political community.

52. See, for example, Card (1990, 290–99).

CHAPTER TEN: DIOTIMA TELLS SOCRATES A STORY: A NARRATIVE ANALYSIS OF PLATO'S *SYMPOSIUM*

1. *Phallogocentrism* refers to an ongoing textual interplay between language, or *logos*, and traditional metaphysical inquiry that creates and perpetuates sexual inequality by privileging the phallus over the feminine as the prime manifestation of true being.

2. Martha J. Reineke questions "Irigaray's own ability to displace and overturn phallogocentric discourse through *l'ecriture feminine* [because of] Jacques Lacan, whose veiled presence in Irigaray's writing threatens to distort and to co-opt her aims" (Reineke 1987, 67).

3. *The Thinking Muse* (Allen and Young, 1989) is an interesting collection of essays clustered around this dilemma.

4. For example, Margaret Whitford describes Luce Irigaray's work as "steeped in the history of philosophy from the pre-Socratics to the post-structuralists" (Whitford 1991, 10).

5. See Annas (1976) and Bluestone (1987).

6. Monique Schneider remarks, "I think that it could be very useful if psychoanalysts went further into the text of Plato, and specifically into Diotima's speech" (Schneider 1991, 30).

7. Some dramatic interpreters include Paul Friedländer, Leo Strauss, Jacob Klein, Stanley Rosen, Mitchell Miller, Drew Hyland, David Lachterman, David Roochnik, and Charles Griswold. See any of these writers for a detailed explanation of their methodological approach. For example, in his book, *Self-Knowledge in Plato's*

Phaedrus, Charles Griswold lists the numerous proponents of this interpretive stance and summarizes some critical objections to it. Ultimately, he claims that, "in general, this approach to interpreting Plato is now widely accepted" (Griswold 1986, 8n).

8. See Rosen (1987, 1–39).

9. Genevieve Lloyd's bibliographical essay in *Being and Time* provides a good survey of the narrative literature (176–82). See also Martin (1986).

10. I do not intend to imply that the conversation between Diotima and Socrates actually took place. Its conceptual existence does not depend on its historical existence.

11. When I use narrative as a noun, I am referring to the plot-based account that the teller tells. The narrator refers to the one telling the tale. The narratee is the intended audience of the narrative. Narrative style refers to how the narrator comports him or herself with respect to the narrative and the narratee. Narrative structure refers to the placement narratives that occur in a larger speech or text. Narrative aspects of a text include the narratives within it, the narrative styles of the narrators within the text, the intended narratee, and the narrative structure of the text itself.

12. Curiously, the scholarly literature overlooks this fact. For example, Halperin calls her "the personage who stands at the end of the hall of narrative mirrors that constitutes Apollodorus' tale of Plato's *Symposium*" (1992, 123). This comment implies that Diotima's speech is different from the narratives that precede it.

13. Unless otherwise noted, all translations from the *Symposium* are my own.

14. The Greek word *logos* has many referents: a word, a saying or statement, or an argument, or a discourse, or broadly, speech, language, reason, or rational account. To avoid difficulties of translation, I have transliterated the word into English.

15. 201d, 206b, 208b, 208c (in the manner of a perfect sophist).

16. Eric S. Rabkin asserts, "It is the subliminal-suspense that engages us with the fictional world, and it is subliminal-suspense to which we most immediately react" (1973, 69).

17. An examination of reader-response theory best captures the importance of participation in narrative. See Steven Mailloux (1982).

18. The participatory context in which philosophy occurs could also symbolize the participation of soul *(psychê)* with the forms *(ideai)*.

19. In contrast, examine the encomia of Phaedrus, Pausanias, Eryximachus, and Agathon. Their encomia neither provide nor require the participatory context that is necessary to philosophize.

20. These references to Socrates occur at 202b10, 202d13, 204b10 *(philê)*, 204d1, 204d4, 204e2, 205a10, 206c2, 207a6, 208c1, 209e5, 210e5, 211d1 *(philê)*. Some of these direct questions occur at 205a3, 205b2, 206a4, 207a6, 207b10, 207c4.

21. These references to her own activity occur at 202c4, 202c6, 203b1 204c1–2, 204c3, 204c6, 204d1–2, 205e1, 205e5, 206b7, 206c1, 207c10, 208c2–3, 209b4, 209c2, 210a2, 210a3, 210a3.

22. Many others have noted that Socrates' definition of Erôs is radically different from the preceding speeches. See Rosen (1987), Anton (1974), Dorter (1969), Dover (1966).

23. Just as the dialogue can be read as a series of definitions of Erôs progressing to Socrates' philosophical speech about the daimonic nature of Erôs, the dialogue can also be read as a philosophical development from non-narrative speech to narrative speech. (See Frosolono 1993).

24. See also 199c, 201d, and 201d.

25. Rosen (1983) argues that this agreement is a test for discipleship.

26. Griswold (1986) offers a compelling account of the importance of self-knowledge in Platonic philosophy.
27. Genevieve Lloyd (1993) explores the relationship between selves and narrators in philosophy and literature. See also Genette (1980), Ricoeur (1981).
28. See Bowery (1995) for a similar articulation of this point.
29. If this remark seems to oversimplify Socrates' essence, see Anton (1974).
30. Because Apollodorus decides to tell the story "just as that one told it to me," the reader often believes that Aristodemus is the actual narrator of the *Symposium*.
31. In the *Symposium* alone, Plato creates six characters who are narrators: the five listed above and Aristophanes. It is important to note that Aristophanes tells a narrative. While the secondary literature often notes that Aristophanes responds to a perceived similarity between Diotima's speech and his own (212c), few commentators have noted their formal, i.e., narrative, similarity.
32. Gilbert Ryle (1966), for example, believes that Socrates is Plato, as does Hugh Tredennick, who alleges that "Plato undoubtedly felt that he was little more than Socrates' mouthpiece" (1969, 13).
33. In *A Rhetoric of Fiction* (1973), Wayne Booth discusses some implications of authorial silence.
34. In the present formulation of this argument, I do not discuss the *Letters* in which a character named Plato enters Plato's narrative. Plato does mention himself by name three times in the dialogues (*Ap.* 34a, 38a; *Phaed.* 59b). However, these appearances can be read as part of Plato's criticism of Socrates (Frosolono 1993, 194–206).
35. To list just a few examples: "I will first say that I once heard him conversing about the *daimonion* with Aristodemus" (I, IV, 2); "it appears wondrous to me"(I, II, 1); "to me he seemed to be more worthy of honor than death by the state" (I, II, 62).
36. The development of a cult of personality of Socrates has not gone unnoticed in the secondary literature. See Halperin (1992), Nussbaum (1986), and Rosen (1983). However, to my knowledge no one other than myself has linked this discipleship specifically to Socrates' pervasive use of self-oriented narrative.
37. However, the *anthropos* who reaches this realm should not be viewed as a fixed, unitary subject. Rather, if one were to attribute a theory of personal identity to Diotima, as Andrea Nye does, one would see that "Diotima's theory of personal identity [is] based on the realization that the self is not unitary but constantly in a process of renewal and destruction" (1989, 47).
38. This final stage would, of course, transcend any narrative account, as well.
39. The claim that Socrates is tethered to *kaloi logoi* and therefore unable to perceive *to kalon auton* will meet with a certain level of incredulity. Unfortunately, a full proof of this argument lies well beyond the scope of this particular *logos*, but it would involve a careful examination of the narratives that Socrates and his disciples tell, a consideration of Socrates' use of myth to provide an account of issues about which one cannot give a *logos*, the dramatic contexts in which his numerous conversations about the forms occur, and a reconsideration of the enigmatic appearances of his *to daimonion saemion*.
40. Recall that in the *Phaedo*, Phaedo remarks, "Plato, though, I believe, was ill" (59b). Plato absents himself from this narrative situation. The word Plato uses for his own illness is *asthenês*. In addition to referring to illness, meanings of *asthenês* include being without strength, weak, or feeble. Plato uses the same word in the *Seventh*

Letter to refer to "the weakness of *logos*" (*Epist. VII*, 343a). Read symbolically, it is not the immediacy of Socrates' death that weakens Plato, but more specifically Socrates' dependence on *logos* that makes Plato ill. It is from *logos* that Plato, and philosophy, are absent.

CHAPTER ELEVEN: THERAPEUTIC ARGUMENTS AND STRUCTURES OF DESIRE

1. See Kenneth Dover (1989, 61 ff.). Especially interesting is a passage from Xenophon's *Hiero*, in which the poet Simonides and the morally worthy Hiero both refer to Hiero's passion for a young man as a constraint deriving from nature—using the category "natural," for an inclination that our own society has frequently judged "contrary to nature."
2. See Winkler (1990a).
3. Nussbaum (1994, 1994a and 1995).
4. Nussbaum (1997, 1996).
5. See Schofield (1991).
6. Compare Cyril Bailey: " . . . not continuous drinkings and revellings, nor the satisfaction of lusts, nor the enjoyment of fish and other luxuries of the wealthy table."
7. For general treatments of the subject see Dover (1978), Foucault (1984), Halperin (1990a, 1990b) Winkler (1990a, 1990b) and Konstan (1990).
8. The work is especially valuable for its judicious treatment of evidence of many different kinds, including oratory, comedy, and vase-painting.
9. See Foucault (1984) and Halperin (1990a).
10. See especially Foucault (1984) and Halperin (1990a).
11. This is the theme of Nussbaum (1994).
12. For a variety of examples of this, see Rorty (1980), Lutz (1988), Harré (1986), Klein (1975), de Sousa (1987).
13. On anger in Aristotle, see *EN* IV.5 1378a31ff. See also Nussbaum (1994, 359–401).
14. See Aristotle, *Rhet.* 1382a21 ff. *Poet.* 1453a4–5: see Nussbaum (1986, 378–95).
15. See Aristotle *Rhet.* 1385b13 ff. *Poet.* 1453a3: and Nussbaum (1986, 378–95).
16. See Nussbaum *(*1986, chs. 11–12).
17. For references and discussion, see Nussbaum (1986a).
18. For these and other references, see Nussbaum (1986a).
19. For the standard definitions, see Von Arnim (1964: 3: 391–420).
20. See Nussbaum (1986, ch. 7), and also Price (1989).
21. What follows is a brief summary of the reading of Lucretius presented in Nussbaum (1994, 140–92).

REFERENCES

The standard edition of the Greek texts of Plato is listed under J. Burnet, and a standard English translation under E. Hamilton and H. Cairns. The standard Greek edition of Aristotle's works prepared by I. Bekker in 1831 has largely been replaced by the texts of the Oxford Classical Text series (OCT) edited by W. D. Ross, and by the Loeb Classical Library series. Authors follow the practice of citing the page, column, and line given by the standard Greek texts.

I. ANCIENT SOURCES

Allen, Thomas W., ed. 1917–1919. *Homer, Opera. Volumes 3–4. Odyssey.* Oxford: Clarendon Press.

Apostle, Hippocrates G. 1979. *Aristotle's Metaphysics.* Grinnell, Iowa: Peripatetic Press.

Apostle, Hippocrates G. 1981. *Aristotle's On the Soul.* Grinnell, Iowa: Peripatetic Press.

Aristotle. 1954. *The Rhetoric & the Poetics.* Tr. W. Rhys Roberts and Ingram Bywater. New York: Modern Library.

Bailey, C., ed. and tr. 1975. *Epicurus: The Extant Remains.* Hildesheim: Olms.

Barnes, Jonathan, ed. 1984. *The Complete Works of Aristotle: The Revised Oxford Translation.* Princeton N.J.: Princeton University Press.

Barrett, W. S., ed. 1964. *Euripides, Hippolytos.* Oxford: Clarendon Press.

Bloom, Allan, tr. 1991. *The "Republic" of Plato.* 2nd edition. New York: Basic Books.

Bonitz, Hermann. 1849. *Aristotelis Metaphysica.* Vol. 2. Reprinted 1960. Hildesheim: Olms.

Burnet, John. 1900. *The Ethics of Aristotle.* London: Methuen & Co.

Burnet, John, ed. 1900–1903. *Plato, Opera.* Volumes 1–4. Oxford: Clarendon Press.

Bywater, I. 1894. *Aristotelis Ethica Nicomachea.* Oxford: Oxford University Press.

Cicero. 1931. *On Ends.* In *De Finibus Bonorum et Malorum.* Tr. H. Rackham. Loeb Classical Library. Cambridge, MA. and London: Harvard University Press.

Cicero. 1968. *On Duties.* In *De Officiis.* Tr. W. Miller. Loeb Classical Library. Cambridge, MA and London: Harvard University Press.

Cope, E. M. 1877. *The Rhetoric of Aristotle with a Commentary*. Cambridge: Cambridge University Press.

Cornford, Francis Macdonald, tr. 1941. *Plato, Republic*. London: Oxford University Press.

Crönert, W. 1906. *Kolotes und Menedemos*. Leipzig: E. Avenarius.

Demosthenes. 1939. *Demosthenes*. Vol. 6. Tr. A. T. Murray. Loeb Classical Library. Cambridge, MA and London: Harvard University Press.

Diggle, J., ed. 1986–1989. *Euripides, Fabulae. Volumes 1–2*. Oxford: Clarendon Press.

Diogenes, Laertius. 1931. *Lives of the Philosophers*. Tr. R. D. Hicks. 2 Vol. Loeb Classical Library. Cambridge, MA and London: Harvard University Press.

Dover, Kenneth, ed. 1980. *Plato. Symposium*. Cambridge and New York: Cambridge University Press.

Epictetus. 1925. *Diatribes*. In *The Discourses* as reported by Arrian. Tr. W. A. Oldfather, 2 Vols. Loeb Classical Edition. Cambridge, MA: Harvard University Press.

Fitzgerald, Robert, tr. 1954. *Sophocles, Oedipus at Colonus*. In *The Complete Greek Tragedies*, eds. David Grene and Richmond Lattimore, Sophocles, volume 1. Chicago: University of Chicago Press.

Fitzgerald, Robert, tr. 1963. *Homer, Odyssey*. Garden City, New York: Anchor Books.

Gauthier, R. A., and J. Y. Jolif. 1958. *L'Ethique a Nicomaque: Introduction, Traduction et Commentaire*. Louvain: Publications Universitaires de Louvain.

Grene, David, tr. 1955. *Euripides, Hippolytus*. In *The Complete Greek Tragedies*, eds. David Grene and Richmond Lattimore, *Euripides*, volume 1. Chicago: University of Chicago Press.

Grube, G. M. A., tr. 1974. *Plato, Republic*. Indianapolis: Hackett Publishing Company.

Halliwell, S. 1987. *The Poetics of Aristotle: Translation and Commentary*. Chapel Hill: University of North Carolina Press.

Halliwell, S., tr. 1993. *Plato, Republic 5*. Warminster, England: Aris and Phillips.

Hamilton, Edith, and Huntington Cairns, eds. 1963. *The Collected Dialogues of Plato*. Princeton: Princeton University Press.

Hense, O., ed. 1905. *Musonii Rufi Reliquiae*. Leipzig: Teubner.

Herodotus. 1982. *Histories*. Tr. A. D. Godley. Cambridge: Cambridge University Press.

Hesiod. 1985. *Theogony*. Tr. Richmond Lattimore. Ann Arbor: University of Michigan Press.

Hett, W. S., tr. 1975. *Aristotle: On the Soul, Parva Naturalia, On Breath*. v. 8. Loeb Classical Library. Cambridge, MA and London: Harvard University Press.

Hippocrates. 1978. *The Seed*. In *Hippocratic Writings*, ed. G.E.R. Lloyd, 317–23. New York: Penguin Books.

Homer. 1961. *Iliad*. Tr. Richmond Lattimore. Chicago: University of Chicago Press.

Homer. 1975. *Odyssey*. Tr. Richmond Lattimore. Chicago: University of Chicago
Press.

Irwin, Terence. 1985. *Aristotle: Nicomachean Ethics*. Indianapolis: Hackett
Publishing Company.

Jaeger, W., ed. 1957. *Aristotelis Metaphysica*. Oxford: Oxford University Press.

Janko, R., tr. 1987. *Aristotle: Poetics*. Indianapolis: Hackett Publishing Company.

Joachim. H. H. 1962. *Aristotle: The Nicomachean Ethics*. Oxford: Clarendon Press.

Jowett, B. 1871. *The Dialogues of Plato*. Vols. 1–5. London: Oxford University
Press.

Lloyd-Jones, H., and N. G. Wilson, ed. 1990. *Sophocles, Fabulae*. Oxford:
Clarendon Press.

Long, A. A., and D. Sedley. 1987. *The Hellenistic Philosophers*. 2 vols.
Cambridge: Cambridge University Press.

Minio-Paluello, L. 1986. *Aristotelis Categoriae et Liber de Interpretatione*. Oxford:
Oxford University Press.

Monro, David B., and Thomas W. Allen, eds. 1920. *Homer, Opera*. Vol. 2. *Iliad,
Books 13–24*. Oxford: Clarendon Press.

Murray, Gilbert, ed. 1913. *Euripides, Fabulae*. Volume 3. Oxford: Clarendon
Press.

Nauck, August, ed. 1889. *Tragicorum Graecorum Fragmenta*. Second edition.
Leipzig: Teubner.

Nehamas, Alexander, and Paul Woodruff, trs. 1989. *Plato, Symposium*.
Indianapolis: Hackett Publishing Company.

Nehamas, Alexander, and Paul Woodruff, trs. 1995. *Plato, Phaedrus*. Indianapolis:
Hackett Publishing Company.

Peck, A. L., tr. 1979. *Aristotle: Generation of Animals*. v. 13. Loeb Classical
Library. Cambridge, MA and London: Harvard University Press.

Plato. 1961. *Collected Dialogues*. Ed. E. Hamilton and H. Cairns. Princeton:
Princeton University Press.

Plato. 1976. *The Platonic Epistles*. Tr. J. C. Harward. Cambridge: Cambridge
University Press.

Plato. 1980. *Symposium*. Ed. K. Dover. Cambridge: Cambridge University Press.

Plutarch. 1927. *Marriage Precepts*. In *Moralia*, v. 2. Tr. F. C. Babbitt. Loeb
Classical Library. Cambridge, MA and London: Harvard University Press.

Rackham, H., tr. 1935. *Aristotle: The Athenian Constitution, the Eudemian Ethics,
on Virtues and Vices*. Cambridge: Harvard University Press.

Rackham, H., tr. 1975. *Aristotle: The Nicomachean Ethics*. Loeb Classical Library.
Cambridge, MA and London: Harvard University Press.

Ross, W. D., ed. 1925. *Ethica Nicomachea*. v. IX. *The Works of Aristotle*. Oxford:
Clarendon Press.

Ross, W. D., tr. 1963. *The Eudemian Ethics of Aristotle*. London: Oxford
University Press.

Ross, W. D., tr. 1963. *The Nicomachean Ethics of Aristotle*. London: Oxford
University Press.

Ross, W. D. 1980. Aristotle: *The Nicomachean Ethics.* Oxford: Oxford University Press.

Seneca. 1970. *Epistles.* In *Ad Lucilium Epistulae* Morales. Tr. R. M. Gummere. 3 vols. Loeb Classical Library. Cambridge, MA and London: Harvard University Press.

Smith, J. A., and W. D. Ross, eds. 1910–52. *The Works of Aristotle Translated into English.* Oxford: Oxford University Press.

Solmsen, Friedrich, ed. 1983. *Hesiod, Theogonia; Opera et Dies; Scutum.* R. Merkelbach and M. L. West, eds. Fragemnta Selecta. Oxford: Oxford University Press.

Spengel, L., ed. 1853–56. *Rhetores Graeci.* 3 Vols. Leipzig: Teubner.

Stewart, J. A. 1892. *Notes on the Nicomachean Ethics of Aristotle.* 2 vols. Oxford: Clarendon Press.

Stobaeus. 1856. *Florilegium.* Ed. A. Meineke, vol. 3. Leipzig: Teubner.

Stobaeus. 1884. *Anthologium.* Ed. O. Hense, vol. 3. Berlin: Weidmann.

Thucydides. 1972. *The Peloponnesian War.* Tr. Rex Warner. London: Penguin Books.

Tredennick, H., tr. 1969. *The Last Days of Socrates.* London: Penguin Books.

Von Arnim, J., ed. 1906. *Hierokles, Ethische Elementarlehre.* Berlin: Weidmann.

Von Arnim, J., ed. 1964. *Stoicorum Veterum Fragmenta.* 4 Vols. Stuttgart: Teubner.

Warner, Rex, tr. 1955. *Euripides, Medea.* In *The Complete Greek Tragedies,* ed. David Grene and Richmond Lattimore, Euripides, volume 1. Chicago: University of Chicago Press.

Willetts, Ronald Frederick, tr. 1958. *Euripides, Ion.* In *The Complete Greek Tragedies,* ed. David Grene and Richmond Lattimore, Euripides, volume 3. Chicago: University of Chicago Press.

Xenophon. 1968. *Memorabilia.* Tr. O. J. Todd. Cambridge, MA and London: W. Heineman.

II. CONTEMPORARY TEXTS

Abderson, Bonnie, and Judith Zinsser. 1989. *A History of Their Own: Women in Europe from Pre-History to the Present.* New York: Harper & Row.

Achtenberg, Deborah. 1988. "Human Being, Beast and God: The Place of Human Happiness According to Aristotle and Some Twentieth Century Philosophers." *St. John's Review* 38, 2: 21–47. Reprinted in *The Crossroads of Norm and Nature: Essays on Aristotle's "Ethics" and "Metaphysics."* Ed. May Sim. Rowman and Littlefield Press, 1995.

Achtenberg, Deborah. 1989. "The Role of the Ergon Argument in Aristotle's Nicomachean Ethics." *Ancient Philosophy* 9, 1: 37–47. Reprinted in *Essays in Ancient Greek Philosophy IV: Aristotle's Ethics.* Ed. John P. Anton and Anthony Preus. State University of New York Press: Albany. 1991.

Achtenberg, Deborah. 1992. "On the Metaphysical Presuppositions of Aristotle's Nicomachean Ethics." *Journal of Value Inquiry* 26: 317–40.

Akhtar, Salman, and Henri Parens, eds. 1991. *Beyond the Symbiotic Orbit: Advances in Separation-Theory. Essays in Honor of Selma Kramer, M.D.* Hillsdale, New Jersey: The Analytic Press.

al-Hibri, Azizah, and Margaret A. Simons, eds. 1985. *Hypatia Reborn: Essays in Feminist Philosophy.* Bloomington: Indiana University Press.

Allen, Christine Garside. 1975. "Plato on Women." *Feminist Studies* 2: 131–38.

Allen, Jeffner, and Iris M. Young, eds. 1989. *The Thinking Muse: Feminism and Modern French Philosophy.* Bloomington: Indiana University Press.

Allen, Paula Gunn. 1986. *The Sacred Hoop: Recovering the Feminine in American Indian Traditions.* Boston: Beacon Press.

Allen, Prudence. 1985. *The Concept of Woman: the Aristotelian Revolution 750 B.C.–1250 A.D.* Montreal: Eden Press.

Annas, Julia. 1976. "Plato's Republic and Feminism." *Philosophy* 51: 307–21.

Annas, Julia. 1977. "Plato and Aristotle on Friendship and Altruism." *Mind* 86: 532–44

Annas, Julia. 1981. *An Introduction to Plato's "Republic."* Oxford: Clarendon Press.

Anthony, Louise. 1993. "Quine as Feminist: The Radical Import of Naturalized Epistemology." In *A Mind of One's Own: Feminist Essays on Reason and Objectivity,* ed. Anthony and Witt, 185–225. Boulder: Westview Press.

Anthony, Louise, and Charlotte Witt, eds. 1993. *A Mind of One's Own: Feminist Essays on Reason and Objectivity.* Boulder: Westview Press.

Anton, John P., and George L. Kustas, eds. 1971. *Essays in Ancient Greek Philosophy.* Albany: State University of New York Press.

Anton, John P. 1974. "The Secret of Plato's *Symposium.*" *Southern Journal of Philosophy* 12: 277–93.

Archer, L., S. Fischler, and M. Wyke, eds. 1994. *Women in Ancient Societies.* London: Routledge.

Atherton, Margaret. 1993. "Cartesian Reason and Gendered Reason." In *A Mind of One's Own: Feminist Essays on Reason and Objectivity,* ed. Anthony and Witt, 19–34. Boulder: Westview Press.

Atherton, Margaret. 1993a. "Doing the History of Philosophy as a Feminist." *American Philosophical Association Newsletter on Feminism and Philosophy.* Ed. L. Antony and D. Meyers.

Bacon, Helen. 1959. "Socrates Crowned." *Virginia Quarterly Review* 35: 415–30.

Baldry, H. C. 1959. "Zeno's Ideal State." *Journal of Hellenic Studies* 79: 3–15.

Balme, David. 1987. "Aristotle's Biology Was Not Essentialist." In *Philosophical Issues in Aristotle's Biology,* ed. Gotthelf and Lennox, 291–312. Cambridge: Cambridge University Press.

Balme, David. 1990. "*Anthropos Anthropon Genna*: Human is Generated by Human." In *The Human Embryo,* ed. G. R. Dunstan, 20–31. Exeter: University of Exeter Press.

Bar On, Bat-Ami, ed. 1994. *Engendering Origins: Critical Feminist Readings in Plato and Aristotle.* Albany: State University of New York Press.

Benhabib, Seyla, and Drucilla Cornell, eds. 1987. *Feminism As Critique.* Minneapolis: University of Minnesota Press.

Benston, Margaret. 1984. "The Political Economy of Women's Liberation." In *Feminist Frameworks,* 2nd ed., eds. A. Jaggar and P. Rothenberg, 239–47. New York: McGraw Hill.

Bishop, Sharon, and M. Weinzweig, eds. 1979. *Philosophy and Women.* Belmont, California: Wadsworth.

Bishop, Sharon. 1979. "Love and Dependency." In *Philosophy and Women,* ed. S. Bishop and M. Weinzweig, 147–54. Belmont, California: Wadsworth.

Blaxall, M., and Reagan, B. eds. 1976. *Women and the Workplace.* Chicago: University of Chicago Press.

Bluestone, Natalie Harris. 1987. *Women and the Ideal Society: Plato's Republic and Modern Myths of Gender.* Amherst: University of Massachusetts Press.

Blum, Lawrence et al. 1979. "Altruism and Women's Oppression." In *Philosophy and Women,* ed. S. Bishop and Weinzig, 190–200. Belmont, California: Wadsworth.

Blum, Lawrence. 1980. *Friendship, Altruism, and Morality.* London: Routledge, Kegan and Paul.

Blum, Lawrence. 1982. "Kant's and Hegel's Moral Rationalism: A Feminist Perspective." *Canadian Journal of Philosophy* 12: 296–97.

Blum, Lawrence. 1988. "Gilligan and Kohlberg: Implications for Moral Theory." *Ethics* 98, 3: 472–91.

Blum, Lawrence. 1991. "Moral Perception and Particularity." *Ethics* 101: 101–726.

Blundell, M. W. 1990. "Parental Nature and Stoic Oikeiôsis." *Ancient Philosophy* 10: 221–42.

Booth, Wayne. 1973. *A Rhetoric of Fiction.* Chicago: University of Chicago Press.

Bordo, Susan. 1986. "The Cartesian Masculinization of Thought." *Signs* 11, 3: 439–56.

Bordo, Susan. 1987. *The Flight to Objectivity: Essays in Cartesianism and Culture.* Albany: State University of New York Press.

Bowery, Anne-Marie. 1995. "Plato Visits Postmodernity." *Southwest Philosophy Review,* vol. 11. 135–42.

Brandwood, Leonard. 1990. *The Chronology of Plato's Dialogues.* Cambridge: Cambridge University Press.

Brandwood, Leonard. 1992. "Stylometry and Chronology." In *The Cambridge Companion to Plato,* ed. Richard Kraut, 90–120. Cambridge: Cambridge University Press.

Broadie, Sarah. 1991. *Ethics with Aristotle.* New York and Oxford: Oxford University Press.

Brooks, P. 1984. *Reading for the Plot: Design and Intention in Narrative.* New York: A.A. Knopf.

Bunch, Charlotte. 1981. "Not for Lesbians Only." In *Building Feminist Theory,* ed. C. Bunch, A. Flax, A. Freeman, N. Hartsock, M. Manther, 67–73. New York: Longman Press.

Burns, Steven. 1984. "Women in Bloom." *Dialogue* 23: 135–40.

Calvert, Brian. 1975. "Plato and Equality of Women." *Phoenix* 29: 231–43.

Cantarella, Eva. 1987. *Pandora's Daughters.* Tr. E. Fant. Baltimore: Johns Hopkins University Press.

Card, Claudia. 1988. "Women's Voices and Ethical Ideals: Must We Mean What We Say?" *Ethics* 99, 1: 125–36.

Card, Claudia. 1990a. "Gender and Moral Luck." In *Identity, Character, and Morality,* ed. O. Flanagan and A. Rorty, 119–218. Cambridge, MA: MIT Press.

Card, Claudia. 1990b. "Lesbian Attitudes and The Second Sex." In *Hypatia Reborn,* ed. M. Simons and A. al-Hibri, 290–99. Bloomington: Indiana University Press.

Chodorow, Nancy. 1974. "Family Structure and Feminine Personality." In *Women, Culture, and Society,* ed. Rosaldo and Lamphere, 43–66. Stanford: Stanford University Press.

Chodorow, Nancy. 1978. *The Reproduction of Mothering: Psychoanalysis and the Sociology of Gender.* Berkeley: University of California Press.

Chodorow, Nancy. 1989. *Feminism and Psychoanalytic Theory.* New Haven: Yale University Press.

Code, Alan. 1993. *Essentialism and the Life Sciences in Aristotle.* Unpublished manuscript.

Code, Lorraine. 1991. *What Can She Know? Feminist Theory and the Construction of Knowledge.* Ithaca: Cornell University Press.

Cole, Eve Browning. 1989. "Review of Sowing the Body," by Page Dubois. *American Philosophical Association Newsletter on Philosophy and Feminism* 89: 88–89.

Cole, Eve, and Susan Coultrapp-MacQuin, eds. 1992. *Explorations in Feminist Ethics: Theory and Practice.* Bloomington: Indiana University Press.

Cole, Eve. 1994. "Women, Slaves and "Love of Toil" in Aristotle's Moral

Philosophy." In *Engendering Origins: Critical Feminist Readings in Plato and Aristotle,* ed. Bar On, 127–44. Albany: State University of New York Press.

Coles, Andrew. 1995. "Biomedical Models of Reproduction in the Fifth Century and Aristotle's Generation of Animals." *Phronesis* 40, 1: 48–88.

Cooper, John. 1980. "Aristotle on Friendship." In *Essays on Aristotle's Ethics,* ed. A. O. Rorty, 301–40. Berkeley: University of California Press.

Cooper, John. 1987. "Contemplation and Happiness: A Reconsideration." *Synthese* 72: 187–216.

Cooper, John. 1988. "Metaphysics in Aristotle's Embryology." *Cambridge Philological Society Proceedings* 214 (new series 34): 14–41. Reprinted in *Biologie, logique et metaphysique chez Aristotle,* ed. Devereux and Pellegrin, 55–84. 1990. Paris: Editions du CNRS.

Cooper, John. 1988a. "Some Remarks on Aristotle's Moral Psychology." Spindel Conference on Aristotle's Ethics, Memphis State University. In *The Southern Journal of Philosophy Supplementary Volume* 27: 25–42.

Cooper, John. 1990. "Metaphysics in Aristotle's Biology." In *Biologie, logique et metaphysique chez Aristote,* ed. Daniel Devereux and Pierre Pellegrin: 55–84. Paris: Centre National de la Recherche Scientifique.

Cooper, John. 1993. "Political Animals and Civic Friendship." In *Friendship: A Philosophical Reader,* ed. N. K. Badhwar, 303–26. Ithaca: Cornell University Press.

De Sousa, Ronald. 1987. *The Rationality of Emotion.* Cambridge, MA: MIT Press.

De Vogel, Cornelia. 1966. *Pythagoras and Early Pythagoreanism.* Assen: Van Gorcum.

Deming, W. 1995. *Paul on Marriage and Celibacy: the Hellenistic Background of 1 Corinthians 7.* Cambridge: Cambridge University Press.

Derrida, Jacques. 1981. *Dissemination.* Tr. Barbara Johnson. Chicago: University of Chicago Press.

Devereux, D., and P. Pellegrin, eds. 1990. *Biologie, logique et metaphysique chez Aristote.* Paris: Centre National de la Recherche Scientifique.

Dickason, Anne. 1973–1974. "Anatomy and Destiny: The Role of Biology in Plato's View of Women." *Philosophical Forum* 5: 45–53.

Dorter, Kenneth. 1969. "The Significance of the Speeches in Plato's Symposium." *Philosophy and Rhetoric* 2: 215–34.

Dover, K. J. 1966. "Aristophanes' Speech in Plato's Symposium." *The Journal of Hellenic Studies* 86: 41–50.

Dover, K. J. 1978 and 1989. *Greek Homosexuality.* Cambridge, MA: Harvard University Press.

DuBois, Page. 1982. *Centaurs and Amazons: Women and the Pre-History of the Great Chain of Being.* Ann Arbor: University of Michigan Press.

DuBois, Page. 1988. *Sowing the Body: Psychoanalysis and Ancient Representations of Women.* Chicago: University of Chicago Press.

Dudley, D. 1937. *A History of Cynicism.* London: Methuen.

Duncan, Roger. 1977. "Plato's *Symposium*: The Cloven Eros." *Southern Journal of Philosophy* 15: 277–90.

Dworkin, Andrea. 1983. *Right-Wing Women: The Politics of Domesticated Females*. London: The Women's Press.

Edelstein, Ludwig. 1962. "Platonic Anonymity." *American Journal of Philology* 83: 1–22.

Fantham, Elaine, Helene Peet Foley, Natalie Boymel Kampen, Sarah B. Pomeroy, and H. Alan Shapiro, eds. 1994. *Women in the Classical World: Image and Text*. New York: Oxford University Press.

Felson-Rubin, Nancy. 1994. *Regarding Penelope: From Character to Poetics*. Princeton: Princeton University Press.

Ferrari, G. R. F. 1989. "Plato and Poetry." In *The Cambridge History of Literary Criticism. Volume 1: Classical Criticism,* ed. George A. Kennedy, 92–148. Cambridge: Cambridge University Press.

Firestone, Shulamith. 1970. *The Dialectic of Sex*. New York: Morrow.

Flanagan, Owen, and Jackson, Kathyrn. 1987. "Justice, Care and Gender: The Kohlberg-Gilligan Debate Revisited." *Ethics* 97, 3: 622–37.

Fortenbaugh, W. W. 1975. *Aristotle on Emotion: A Contribution to Philosophical Psychology, Rhetoric, Poetics, Politics and Ethics*. New York: Harper and Row.

Fortenbaugh, W. W. 1977. "Aristotle on Slaves and Women." In *Articles on Aristotle* vol. 2, eds. J. Barnes, M. Schofield, R. Sorabji, 135–39. New York: St. Martin's Press.

Fortenbaugh, W. W., ed. 1983. *On Stoic and Peripatetic Ethics: The Works of Arius Didymus*. New Brunswick, N.J.: Transaction Books.

Foucault, Michel. 1984a. *Le souci de soi*. Paris: Gallimard.

Foucault, Michel. 1984b. *L'Usage des plaisirs*. Paris: Gallimard.

Frede, Michael. 1987. *Essays in Ancient Philosophy*. Minneapolis: University of Minnesota Press.

Freeland, Cynthia. 1987. "Aristotle on Bodies, Matter, and Potentiality." In *Philosophical Issues in Aristotle's Biology,* ed. Gotthelf and Lennox, 392–407. Cambridge: Cambridge University Press.

Freeland, Cynthia. 1994. "Nourishing Speculation: A Feminist Reading of Aristotelian Science." In *Engendering Origins: Critical Feminist Readings in Plato and Aristotle,* ed. Bar On, 145–88. Albany: State University of New York Press.

Freeman, Barbara. 1988. "(Re)writing Patriarchal Texts: The Symposium." In *Postmodernism and Continental Philosophy,* ed. Hugh J. Silverman and Donn Welton, 165–77. Albany: State University of New York Press.

Freud, Sigmund. 1924. "The Economic Problem of Masochism." Reprinted in *General Psychological Theory,* ed. Philip Rieff, 1963, 190–201. New York: Collier Books.

Freud, Sigmund. 1931. "Female Sexuality." In *Complete Psychological Works of Sigmund Freud,* vol. 22, 112–35. London: Hogarth, 1961.

Freud, Sigmund. 1963. *General Psychological Theory*. Ed. Philip Rieff. New York: Collier Books.

Friedländer, Paul. 1969. *Plato: An Introduction*. Tr. by Hans Meyerhoff. Second edition. Princeton: Princeton University Press.

Friedman, Marilyn. 1993. *What Are Friends For?* Ithaca: Cornell University Press.

Frosolono, Anne-Marie. 1993. *Narrating Plato's "Symposium": A Critique of Socratic Discipleship.* Diss. The Pennsylvania State University.

Furth, Montgomery. 1988. *Substance, Form and Psyche: An Aristotelian Metaphysics.* New York: Cambridge University Press.

Gaiser, Konrad. 1974. *Für und wider die Ehe: Antike Stimmen zu Einer Offenen Frage.* Munich: Heimeran

Gallagher, Donald. 1974. "In Praise of Pausanias: Dialectic in the Second Speech of Plato's *Symposium*." *Kinesis* 6 : 40–55.

Gatens, Moira. 1991. *Feminism and Philosophy. Perspectives on Difference and Equality.* Bloomington: Indiana University Press.

Genette, Gerard. 1980. *Narrative Discourse.* Tr. Jane E. Lewin. Ithaca: Cornell University Press.

Genova, Judith. 1994. "Feminist Dialectics: Plato and Dualism." In *Engendering Origins: Critical Feminist Readings in Plato and Aristotle,* ed. Bar On, 41–52. Albany: State University of New York Press.

Gill, C. 1979. "Plato's Atlantis Story and the Birth of Fiction." *Philosophy and Literature* 3: 64–78.

Gilligan, Carol. 1982. *In a Different Voice: Psychological Theory and Women's Development.* Cambridge, MA: Harvard University Press.

Gilligan, Carol. 1986. "Reply to Greeno and Macoby." *Signs* 2: 324–33.

Gilligan, Carol. 1988. "Adolescent Development Reconsidered." In *Mapping the Moral Domain,* ed. C. Gilligan, J. V. Ward, J. Maclean Taylor, 3–20. Cambridge, MA: Harvard University Press.

Gosling, J. C. B. 1973. *Plato.* London: Routledge and Kegan Paul.

Gotthelf, Alan. 1985. *Aristotle on Nature and Living Things.* Pittsburgh: University of Pittsburgh Press.

Gotthelf, Alan, and J. G. Lennox, eds. 1987. *Philosophical Issues in Aristotle's Biology.* Cambridge: Cambridge University Press.

Green, Judith. 1992. "Aristotle on Necessary Verticality, Body-Heat, and Gendered Proper Places in the Polis: A Feminist Critique." *Hypatia* 7: 70–96.

Greeno, Catherine, and Eleanor Macoby. 1986. "How Different is the Different Voice?" *Signs* 2: 310–16.

Griswold, Charles. 1986. *Self-Knowledge in Plato's "Phaedrus."* New Haven: Yale University Press.

Guthrie, W. K. C. 1975. *A History of Greek Philosophy.* Vol. 4. Cambridge: Cambridge University Press.

Halperin, David. 1990a. *One Hundred Years of Homosexuality and Other Essays on Greek Love.* New York: Routledge.

Halperin, David. 1990b. "The Democratic Body." *Differences* 2: 1–29.

Halperin, David M. 1990c. "Why is Diotima a Woman?" In *One Hundred Years of Homosexuality and Other Essays on Greek Love,* ed. Halperin, 113–51. New York: Routledge.

Halperin, David. 1992. "Plato and the Erotics of Narrativity." In *Oxford Studies in Ancient Philosophy,* ed. Julia Annas, 93–129. Oxford: Oxford University Press.

Hanke, Lewis. 1959. *Aristotle and the American Indians.* Bloomington: Indiana University Press.

Harding, Sandra, and Merrill Hintikka, eds. 1983. *Discovering Reality: Feminist Perspectives in Metaphysics, Epistemology, Methodology and Philosophy of Science.* Dordrecht: Reidel.

Harding, Sandra. 1986. *The Science Question in Feminism.* Ithaca: Cornell University Press.

Harding, Sandra. 1987. *Feminism and Methodology: Social Science Issues,* Bloomington: Indiana University Press.

Harré, Rom, ed. 1986. *The Social Construction of Emotions.* Oxford: Blackwell.

Harrison, Jane. 1912. *Prolegomena to the Study of Greek Religion and Themis.* Cambridge: Cambridge University Press.

Harrison, Jane. 1922. *Epilegomena.* Cambridge: Cambridge University Press.

Hartsock, Nancy. 1983. "The Feminist Standpoint: Developing the Grounds for a Specifically Feminist Historical Materialism." In *Discovering Reality: Feminist Perspectives in Metaphysics, Epistemology, Methodology and Philosophy of Science, ed. Harding and Hintikka,* 283–94. Dordrecht: Reidel.

Hartman, Heidi. 1976. "Capitalism, Patriarchy, and Job Segregation by Sex." In *Women and the Workplace,* ed. M. Blaxall and B. Reagan, 137–69. Chicago: University of Chicago Press.

Hawthorne, Susan. 1994. "Diotima Speaks Through the Body." In *Engendering Origins: Critical Feminist Readings in Plato and Aristotle,* ed. Bar On, 83–96. Albany: State University of New York Press.

Hernadi, Paul. 1972. "Dual Perspective: Free Indirect Discourse and Related Technique." *Comparative Literature* 24: 32–43.

Hobbes, Thomas. 1962. *Leviathan, or the Matter, Form and Power of a Commonwealth, Ecclesiastical and Civil.* Ed. Michael Oakeshott. New York: Collier Books.

Homiak, Marcia. 1981. "Virtue and Self-Love in Aristotle's Ethics." *Canadian Journal of Philosophy* 11, 4: 633–51.

Homiak, Marcia. 1985. "The Pleasure of Virtue in Aristotle's Moral Theory." *Pacific Philosophical Quarterly* 66, 1–2: 93–110.

Homiak, Marcia. 1990. "Politics as Soul Making: Aristotle on Becoming Good." *Philosophia* 20, 1–2: 167–93.

Hornsby, Roger. 1956. "Significant Action in Plato's Symposium." *Classical Journal* 52: 37–40.

Horowitz, Maryanne Cline. 1976. "Aristotle and Woman." *Journal of the History of Biology* 9: 183–213.

Howland, Jacob. 1990. "Socrates and Alcibiades: Eros, Piety, and Politics." *Interpretation* 18: 63–90.

Huby, Pamela. 1972. *Plato and Modern Morality.* London: Macmillan.

Hülser, Karlheinz. 1979. *Die Grammatik der Stuiker.* Wiesbaden: Viewig.

Hutt, Corinne. 1973. *Males and Females.* Harmondsworth: Penguin.

Hyland, D. 1981. *The Virtue of Philosophy. An Interpretation on Plato's Charmides.* Athens: Ohio University Press.

Inwood, B. 1983. "Comments on Professor Görgemanns' Paper: The Two Forms of Oikeiôsis in Arius and the Stoa." In *On Stoic and Peripatetic Ethics: The Works of Arius Didymus,* ed. Fortenbaugh, 190–201. New Brunswick, N.J.: Transaction Books.

Inwood, B. 1985. *Ethics and Human Action in Early Stoicism.* Oxford: Clarendon Press.

Irigaray, Luce. 1989. "Sorcerer Love: A Reading of Plato's Symposium, Diotima's Speech." *Hypatia* 3: 32–44.

Irwin, Terence 1981. "Homonymy in Aristotle." *The Review of Metaphysics* 34, 3: 523–44.

Irwin, Terence. 1988. *Aristotle's First Principles.* Oxford: Clarendon Press.

Jacobs, William. 1978. "Plato on Female Emancipation and the Traditional Family." *Apeiron* 12: 29–31.

Jaggar, Alison. 1983. *Feminist Politics and Human Nature.* Totowa, N.J.: Rowman & Allanheld.

Jaggar, Alison, and Paula Rothenberg, eds. 1984. *Feminist Frameworks.* New York: McGraw Hill.

Jonas, Hans. 1966. *The Phenomenon of Life.* New York: Dell Publishing Co.

Kant, I. 1960. *Observations on the Feeling of the Beautiful and Sublime.* Tr. John Goldthwait. Berkeley: University of California Press.

Kennedy, George A., ed. 1989. *The Cambridge History of Literary Criticism. Volume 1: Classical Criticism.* Cambridge: Cambridge University Press.

Kenny, Anthony. 1978. *The Aristotelian Ethics: A Study of the Relationship Between the Eudemian and Nicomachean Ethics of Aristotle.* Oxford: Clarendon Press.

Kenny, Anthony. 1992. *Aristotle on the Perfect Life.* Oxford: Clarendon Press.

Kerby, A. 1991. *Narrative and the Self.* Bloomington: Indiana University Press.

Kernberg, Otto. 1980. *Internal World and External Reality.* Northvale, N.J.: Jason Aronson Press.

Keyt, Donald. 1986. "Distributive Justice in Aristotle's *Ethics* and *Politics.*" *Topoi* 4: 23–46.

Kittay, Eva, and Diana Meyers, eds. 1987. *Women and Moral Theory.* Totowa, N.J.: Rowman & Littlefield.

Klein, Jacob. 1965. *A Commentary on Plato's "Meno."* Chapel Hill: University of North Carolina Press.

Klein, Jacob. 1977. *Plato's Trilogy: Theaetetus, the Sophist, and the Statesman.* Chicago: Chicago University Press.

Klein, Melanie. 1975. *Love, Guilt, and Reparation and Other Works 1921–1945.* London: Hogarth.

Klein, Melanie. 1975a. *Envy and Gratitude and Other Works 1946–1963.* London: Hogarth.

Kohut, Heinz. 1971. *The Analysis of the Self: A Systematic Approach to the Psychoanalytic Treatment of Narcissistic Personality Disorders.* Madison: International Universities Press.

Konstan, David. 1990. "Love in the Greek Novel." *Differences* 2: 186–204.

Kosman, A. 1976. "Platonic Love." In *Facets of Plato's Philosophy*, ed. W. Werkmeister, 53–69. Phronesis. Suppl. vol. 2. Assen: Van Gorcum.

Kotzin, Rhonda, 1989. "Aristotle's Views on Women." In *American Philosophical Association Newsletter on Philosophy and Feminism* 88: 21–25.

Kraut, Richard. 1989. *Aristotle on the Human Good.* Princeton: Princeton University Press.

Kuykendall, Eleanor H. 1989. "Introduction to Sorcerer Love, by Luce Irigaray." *Hypatia* 3: 28–31.

Lamphere, Louise. 1974. "Strategies, Co-operation, and Conflict among Women in Domestic Groups." In *Woman, Culture and Society,* ed. Rosaldo and Lamphere, 97–112. Stanford: Stanford University Press.

Lang, Helen. 1992. *Aristotle's Physics and Its Medieval Varieties.* Albany: State University of New York Press.

Lange, Lynda. 1983. "Woman is Not a Rational Animal: On Aristotle's Biology of Reproduction." In *Discovering Reality: Feminist Perspectives in Metaphysics, Epistemology, Methodology and Philosophy of Science,* ed. Harding and Hintikka, 1–15. Dordrecht: Reidel.

Latcherman, D. 1990. "Preface to Four Essays on Plato's Republic." *The St. John's Review* 34: v–ix.

Leighton, Stephen, R. 1982. "Aristotle and the Emotions." *Phronesis* 27, 2: 144–174.

Leighton, Stephen R. 1984. "*Eudemian Ethics* 1220b11–13." *Classical Quarterly* 34: 135–38.

Levin, Susan B. 1995. "What's in a Name?: A Reconsideration of the Cratylus' Historical Sources and Topics." *Ancient Philosophy* 15: 91–115.

Levin, Susan B. 1996. *Platonic Eponymy and the Literary Tradition.* Forthcoming in *Phoenix*.

Levy, P. 1981. *G. E. Moore and the Cambridge Apostles.* Oxford: Oxford University Press.

Liddell, H. G., and R. Scott. 1986. *An Intermediate Greek-English Lexicon.* Oxford: Clarendon Press.

Lloyd, G. E. R. 1966. *Polarity and Analogy.* Cambridge: Cambridge University Press.

Lloyd, G. E. R. 1985. *Science and Morality in Greco-Roman Antiquity.* Cambridge: Cambridge University Press.

Lloyd, G. E. R. 1987. "Empirical research in Aristotle's biology." In *Philosophical Issues in Aristotle's Biology,* ed. Gotthelf and Lennox, 53–64. Cambridge: Cambridge University Press.

Lloyd, G. E. R. 1990. "Aristotle's Zoology and His Metaphysics: The Status Quaestionis." In *Biologie, logique et metaphysique chez Aristotle,* ed. Devereux and Pellegrin, 7–35. Paris: Editions du CNRS.

Lloyd, G. E. R. 1993. *Being and Time: Selves and Narrators in Philosophy and Literature.* London and New York.

Lloyd, Genevieve. 1984. *The Man of Reason: "Male" and "Female" in Western Philosophy.* Minneapolis: University of Minneota Press.

Lloyd-Jones, Hugh, ed. and tr. 1975. *Females of the Species: Semonides on Women.* London: Duckworth.

Loraux, Nicole. 1978. "Sur la race des femmes et quelques-unes de ses tribus." *Arethusa* 11: 43–87.

Lovibond, Sabina. 1994. "An Ancient Theory of Gender: Plato and the Pythagorean Table." In *Women in Ancient Societies,* ed. Archer, Fischler and Wyke, 88–101. London: Routledge.

Lucas, J. R. 1973. "Because You Are a Woman." *Philosophy* 48: 161–71.

Lugones, Maria, and Elizabeth Spelman. 1983. *Have We Got a Theory For You! Feminist Theory, Cultural Imperialism, and the Demand for "the Woman's Voice."* Women's *Studies International Forum* 6: 573–81.

Lutz, C. 1947. "Musonius Rufus, 'The Roman Socrates,'" *Yale Classical Studies* 10: 3–147.

Lutz, Catherine. 1988. *Unnatural Emotions.* Chicago: University of Chicago Press.

Lyotard, Jean-Francois. 1989. *The Postmodern Condition: A Report on Knowledge.* Tr. Geoff Bennington and Brian Massumi. Minnneapolis: University of Minnesota Press.

MacIntyre, Alisdair. 1984. *After Virtue.* Second Edition. Notre Dame: University of Notre Dame Press.

Maclean, Ian. 1980. *The Renaissance Notion of Woman.* Cambridge: Cambridge University Press.

Macpherson, C. B. 1962. *The Political Theory of Possessive Individualism.* Oxford: Oxford University Press.

Mahler, Margaret. 1968. *On Human Symbiosis and the Vicissitudes of Human Individuation: Infantile Psychosis.* Madison: International University.

Mahler, Margaret, Fred Pine, Anni Bergman. 1975. *The Psychological Birth of the Human Infant: Symbiosis and Individuation.* London: Maresfield Library.

Mahowald, Mary. 1983. *The Philosophy of Woman.* Indianapolis: Hackett Publishing Company.

Maillioux. S. 1982. *Interpretive Conventions.* Ithaca: Cornell University Press.

Malcolm, John. 1991. *Plato on the Self-Predication of Forms: Early and Middle Dialogues.* Oxford: Oxford University Press.

Malherbe, A. J. 1977. *Cynic Epistles.* Missoula: University of Montana Press.

Manning, Rita. 1992. *Speaking from the Heart: A Feminist Perspective on Ethics.* Lanham, Md.: Rowman & Littlefield.

Marrou, Henri-Irénée. 1982. *A History of Education in Antiquity.* Tr. by George Lamb. Madison: University of Wisconsin Press.

Martin, Wallace. 1986. *Recent Theories of Narrative.* Ithaca: Cornell University Press.

Marx, Karl. 1971–1978. *Economic and Philosophic Manuscripts of 1844.* In *Collected Works,* Vol. 3, Karl Marx and Friedrich Engels, 229–346. New York: International Publishers.

Marx, Karl. 1971–1978. *Communist Manifesto.* In *Collected Works,* Vol. 6, Karl
   Marx and Friedrich Engels, 477–519. New York: International Publishers.

Masterson, James F. 1988. *The Search for the Real Self: Unmasking the Personality
   Disorders of Our Age.* New York: Free Press.

Matthews, G. B. 1986. "Gender and Essence in Aristotle." *Australasian Journal of
   Philosophy* 64 (supplement): 16–25.

Mayr, Ernst. 1982. *The Growth of Biological Thought.* Cambridge MA: Harvard
   University Press.

McDowell, John. 1979. "Virtue and Reason." *The Monist* 62: 331–50.

Meunier, Mario. 1932. *Femmes pythagoricienne: fragments et lettres.* Vol. 1. Paris:
   G. Tredaniel.

Mill, J. S. 1970. *On the Subjection of Women.* Cambridge, MA: MIT Press.

Miller, Mitchell. 1980. *The Philosopher in Plato's "Statesman."* The Hague: Nijhoff.

Miller, Mitchell. 1991. *Plato's Parmenides.* University Park: Pennsylvania
   University Press.

Millett, Kate. 1977. *Sexual Politics.* London: Virago Press.

Modrak, Deborah. 1987. *Aristotle: The Power of Perception.* Chicago: University
   of Chicago Press.

Modrak, Deborah. 1994. "Aristotle: Women, deliberation, and nature." In *Engendering Origins: Critical Feminist Readings in Plato and Aristotle,* ed. Bar On,
   207–22. Albany: State University of New York Press.

Moore, G. E. 1903. *Principia Ethica.* Cambridge: Cambridge University Press.

Moravcsik, Julius. 1971. "Reason and Eros in the 'Ascent'-Passage of the
   Symposium." In *Essays in Ancient Greek Philosophy,* ed. John P. Anton and
   George L. Kustas, 285–302. Albany: State University of New York Press.

Moravcsik, Julius, and Philip Temko, eds. 1982. *Plato on Beauty, Wisdom, and the
   Arts.* Totowa, N.J.: Rowman and Allanheld.

Moravcsik, Julius. 1982. "Noetic Aspiration and Artistic Inspiration." In *Plato on
   Beauty, Wisdom, and the Arts,* ed. Julius Moravcsik and Philip Temko, 29–46.
   Totowa, N.J.: Rowman and Allanheld.

Moravcsik, Julius. 1992. *Plato and Platonism: Plato's Conception of Appearance
   and Reality in Ontology, Epistemology, and Ethics, and Its Modern Echoes.*
   Oxford: Blackwell.

Morsink, Johannes. 1979. "Was Aristotle's Biology Sexist?" *Journal of the History
   of Biology* 12, 1: 83–112.

Mulgan, R. 1994. "Aristotle and the Political Role of Women." *History of Political
   Thought* 15, 2: 179–202.

Needham, Joseph, 1959. *A History of Embryology.* New York: Abelard-Schuman.

Neumann, Harry. 1965. "Diotima's Concept of Love." *American Journal of
   Philology* 86: 33–59.

Nietzsche, Friedrich. 1967. *On the Genealogy of Morals.* Tr. W. Kaufman and R. J.
   Hollingdale, New York: Vintage.

Noddings, Nel. 1984. *Caring: A Feminine Approach to Ethics and Moral
   Education.* Berkeley: University of California Press.

Nussbaum, Martha. 1985. *The Discernment of Perception: An Aristotelian Conception of Private and Public Rationality.* Reprinted and revised in Nussbaum 1990, 54–105.

Nussbaum, Martha C. 1986. *The Fragility of Goodness: Luck and Ethics in Greek Tragedy and Philosophy.* Cambridge: Cambridge University Press.

Nussbaum, Martha. 1986a. *Therapeutic Arguments: Epicurus and Aristotle.* In *The Norms of Nature: Studies on Hellenistic Ethics,* ed. M. Schofield and G. Striker, 31–74. Cambridge: Cambridge University Press.

Nussbaum, Martha 1987. *"Finely Aware and Richly Responsible": Literature and the Moral Imagination.* Reprinted in Nussbaum 1990, 148–67.

Nussbaum, Martha 1990. *Love's Knowledge: Essays on Philosophy and Literature.* Oxford: Oxford University Press.

Nussbaum, Martha, and Hilary Putnam. 1992. "Changing Aristotle's Mind." In *Essays on Aristotle's 'De Anima,'* ed. Nussbaum and Rorty, 27–56. Oxford: Oxford University Press.

Nussbaum, Martha. 1992a. "Human Functioning and Social Justice." *Political Theory* 20: 202–46.

Nussbaum, Martha, and Amartya Sen. 1993. *The Quality of Life.* Oxford: Oxford University Press.

Nussbaum, Martha. 1993a. "Non-Relative Virtues: An Aristotelian Approach." In *The Quality of Life,* ed. Martha Nussbaum and Amartya Sen, 242–69. Oxford: Oxford University Press.

Nussbaum, Martha 1994. *Therapy of Desire.* Princeton: Princeton University Press.

Nussbaum, Martha. 1994a. "Platonic Love and Colorado Law: The Relevance of Ancient Greek Norms to Modern Secular Controversies." *Virginia Law Review* 80: 1515–1651.

Nussbaum, Martha. 1995. "Eros and the Wise: the Stoic Response to the Cultural Dilemma." *Oxford Studies in Ancient Philosophy.* Forthcoming.

Nussbaum, Martha. 1996. "Constructing Love, Desire and Care." In *Laws and Nature: Shaping Sex, Preference and Family,* ed. D. Eastaland and M. Nussbaum. New York: Oxford University Press. Forthcoming.

Nussbaum, Martha. 1997. *Upheavals of Thought: A Theory of the Emotions.* Cambridge: Cambridge University Press.

Nye, Andrea. 1989. "The Hidden Host: Irigaray and Diotima at Plato's Symposium." *Hypatia* 3: 45–61.

O'Connor, David. 1990. "Two Ideals of Friendship." *History of Philosophy Quarterly* 7, 2: 109–22.

O'Connor, Pat. 1992. *Friendships Between Women.* London: The Guilford Press.

Okin, Susan Moller. 1977. "Philosopher Queens and Private Wives: Plato on Women and the Family." *Philosophy and Public Affairs* 6: 345–69.

Okin, Susan Moller. 1979. *Women in Western Political Thought.* Princeton: Princeton University Press.

Osborne, Martha Lee. 1975. "Plato's Unchanging View of Women: A Denial That Anatomy Spells Destiny." *Philosophical Forum* 6: 447–52.

Owens, Joseph. 1978. *The Doctrine of Being in the Aristotelian Metaphysics.*
    Toronto: Pontifical Institute of Mediaeval Studies.
Peradotto, J., and J. P. Sullivan, eds. 1984. *Women in the Ancient World: The
    Arethusa Papers.* Albany: State University of New York Press.
Phelan, James. 1989. *Reading People, Reading Plots.* Chicago: University of
    Chicago Press.
Plochmann, G. 1963. "Hiccups and Hangovers in the *Symposium.*" *Bucknell Review*
    11: 1–18.
Pomeroy, Sarah. 1975. *Goddesses, Whores, Wives, and Slaves: Women in Classical
    Antiquity.* New York: Schocken Books.
Pomeroy, Sarah. 1984. *Women in Hellenistic Egypt: From Alexander to Cleopatra.*
    New York: Schocken Books.
Preston, Richard. 1994. *The Hot-Zone.* New York: Anchor Books.
Preus, Anthony. 1970. "Science and Philosophy in Aristotle's *Generation of
    Animals.*" *Journal of the History of Biology* 3, 1: 1–52.
Preus, Anthony. 1977. "Galen's Criticism of Aristotle's Conception Theory."
    Journal of the History of Biology 10, 1: 65–85.
Price, Anthony. 1989. *Love and Friendship in Plato and Aristotle.* Oxford:
    Clarendon Press.
Prince, Gerald. 1982. *Narratology: The Form and Functioning of Narrative.* Berlin:
    Mouton Publishers.
Rabinowitz, Nancy. 1993a. *Anxiety Veiled: Euripedes and the Traffic in Women.*
    Ithaca: Cornell University Press.
Rabinowitz, Nancy. 1993b. *Feminist Theory and the Classics.* New York and
    London: Routledge.
Rabkin, E. 1973. *Narrative Suspense: "When Slim Turned Sideways."* Ann Arbor:
    University of Michigan Press.
Rankin, H. D. 1964. *Plato and the Individual.* New York: Barnes and Noble.
Rawls, John. 1971. *A Theory of Justice.* Cambridge, MA: Harvard University Press.
Raymond, Janice. 1986a. *A Passion for Friends.* London: The Women's Press.
Raymond, Janice. 1986b. "Female Friendship: Contra Chodorow and Dinnerstein."
    Hypatia 1, 2: 37–48.
Reeve, C. D. C. 1992. *Practices of Reason: Aristotle's "Nicomachean Ethics."*
    Oxford: Clarendon Press.
Regan, T. 1986. *Bloomsbury's Prophet: G. E. Moore and the Development of His
    Moral Philosophy.* Philadelphia: Temple University Press.
Reineke, Martha J. 1987. "Lacan, Merleau-Ponty & Irigaray. Reflections on a
    Specular Drama." *Auslegung* 14: 67–85.
Rich, Adrienne. 1977. *Of Woman Born: Motherhood as Experience and Institution.*
    New York: Norton.
Ricoeur, Paul. 1981. *Time and Narrative.* Vol 1. Tr. K. McLaughlin and D.
    Pellauer. Chicago: University of Chicago Press.
Rinsley, Donald B. 1982. *Borderline and Other Self Disorders.* New York: Jason
    Aronson, Inc.

Rinsley, Donald B. 1989. *Developmental Pathogenesis and Treatment of Borderline and Narcissistic Personalities.* Northvale, New Jersey: Jason Aronson, Inc.

Roochnik, David. 1987. "The Erotics of Philosophical Discourse." *History of Philosophy Quarterly* 4: 117–29.

Rorty, Amelie, ed. 1980. *Explaining Emotions.* Berkeley: University of California Press.

Rorty, R. 1989. *Contingency, Irony, and Solidarity.* Cambridge: Cambridge University Press.

Rorty, R., J. B. Schneewind, and Q. Skinner, eds. 1984. *Philosophy in History.* Cambridge: Cambridge University Press.

Rosaldo, M. Z., and L. Lamphere. 1974. *Women, Culture and Society.* Stanford: Stanford University Press.

Rosen, Stanley. 1973. "Sophrosyne and Selbstbeweusstein." *Review of Metaphysics* 26: 617–42.

Rosen, Stanley. 1983. *Plato's "Sophist": The Drama of The Original and the Image.* New Haven: Yale University Press.

Rosen, Stanley. 1987. *Plato's "Symposium."* Second edition. New Haven: Yale University Press.

Rosen, Stanley. 1988. *The Quarrel between Philosophy and Poetry: Studies in Ancient Thought.* New York: Routledge.

Rosenbaum, S. P. 1971. "The Philosophical Realism of Virginia Woolf." In *English Literature and British Philosophy,* ed. S. P. Rosenbaum, 316–56. Chicago: University of Chicago Press.

Rosenthal, A. 1973. "Feminism Without Contradictions." *Monist* 57: 28–42.

Rosenthal, David M. 1989. "Philosophy and its History." In *The Institution of Philosophy,* ed. A. Cohen and M. Dascal, 141–76. Lasalle, Illinois: Open Court.

Rousseau, Jean-Jacques. 1911. *Emile.* London: J. M. Dent and Sons.

Rousseau, Jean-Jacques. 1986. *The First and Second Discourses Together with the Replies to Critics and Essay on the Origin of Languages.* Ed. and tr. Victor Gourevitch. New York: Harper and Row.

Rowe, C. J. 1984. *Plato.* New York: St. Martin's Press.

Rowe, M. M. 1978. "Balancing Two Worlds: Setting and Characterization in *Mrs. Dalloway.*" *Virginia Woolf Quarterly* 2: 268–75.

Ryle, G. 1966. *Plato's Progress.* Cambridge: Cambridge University Press.

Salkever, Stephen G. 1990. *Finding the Mean: Theory and Practice in Aristotelian Political Philosophy.* Princeton: Princeton University Press.

Saxonhouse, Arlene W. 1976. "The Philosopher and the Female in the Political Thought of Plato." *Political Theory* 4: 195–212.

Saxonhouse, Arlene W. 1984. "Eros and the Female in Greek Political Thought: An Interpretation of Plato's Symposium." *Political Theory* 12: 5–27.

Schneider, Monique. 1991. *Interview in French Philosophers in Conversation.* Ed. Raoul Morteley, 22–44. London and New York: Routledge.

Schofield, M. 1991. *The Stoic Idea of the City.* Cambridge: Cambridge University Press.

Scholes, Robert, and Robert Kellogg. 1976. *The Nature of Narrative.* London: Oxford University Press.

Schopenhauer, Arthur. 1974. "On Women." In *Parerga and Paralipomena: Short Philosophical Essays,* tr. E.F.J Payne, 2: 614–33. Oxford: Clarendon Press.

Senack, Christine. 1994. "Aristotle on the Woman's Soul." In *Engendering Origins: Critical Feminist Readings in Plato and Aristotle,* ed. Bar On, 223–36. Albany: State University of New York Press.

Senter, Nell W. 1977. "Plato on Women." *Southwest Philosophical Studies* 2: 4–13.

Sharples, R. W. 1985. "Species, Form, and Inheritance." In *Aristotle on Nature and Living Things,* ed. A. Gotthelf, 117–28. Pittsburgh: University of Pittsburgh Press.

Sherman, Nancy. 1989. *The Fabric of Character: Aristotle's Theory of Virtue.* Oxford: Oxford University Press.

Silverman, Hugh J., and Donn Welton, eds. 1988. *Postmodernism and Continental Philosophy.* Albany: State University of New York Press.

Silverstein, Olga, and Beth Rashbaum. 1994. *The Courage to Raise Good Men.* New York: Viking Press.

Sissa, Guilia. 1990. *Greek Virginity.* Cambridge, MA: Harvard University Press.

Skinner, Marilyn, ed. 1987. "Rescuing Creusa: New Methodological Approaches to Women in Antiquity." *Special Issue of Helios* 13, 2.

Skinner, Quentin. 1969. *Meaning and Understanding in the History of Ideas, History and Theory* 8: 3–53. Reprinted in *Meaning and Context: Quentin Skinner and His Critics,* ed. Tully: 1988: 29–67. Princeton: Princeton University Press.

Skinner, Quentin. 1976. "Motives, Intensions and the Interpretation of Texts." In *On Literary Intention,* ed., D. N. de Molina, 210–21. Edinburgh: Edinburgh University Press. Reprinted in *Meaning and Context: Quentin Skinner and His Critics,* ed. Tully 1988: 68–78. Princeton: Princeton University Press.

Slote, Michael. 1982. "Morality Not a System of Imperatives." *American Philosophical Quarterly* 19: 331–40.

Smith, J. 1985. "Plato's Myths as Likely Accounts Worthy of Belief." *Apeiron* 19: 24–42.

Smith, Jane Farrell. 1983. "Plato, Irony and Equality." *Women's Studies International Forum* 6: 597–607.

Smith, Nicholas. 1980. "The Logic of Plato's Feminism." *Journal of Social Philosophy* 11: 5–11.

Smith, Nicholas. 1983. "Plato and Aristotle on the Nature of Women." *Journal of the History of Philosophy* 21: 467–78.

Smyth, Herbert Weir. 1920. *Greek Grammar.* Cambridge, MA: Harvard University Press.

Snyder, Jane. 1988. *The Women and the Lyre: Women Writers in Classical Greece and Rome.* Carbondale: South Illinois University Press.

Spelman, Elizabeth V. 1982. "Woman as Body: Ancient and Contemporary Views." *Feminist Studies* 8: 109–31.

Spelman, Elizabeth V. 1983. "Aristotle and the Politicization of the Soul." In

Discovering Reality, ed. Sandra Harding and Merrill Hintikaa, 17–30. Dordrecht: Reidel.

Spelman, Elizabeth V. 1988. *Inessential Woman: Problems of Exclusion in Feminist Thought.* Boston: Beacon Press.

Spelman, Elizabeth V. 1989. "Anger and Insubordination." In *Women, Knowledge and Reality,* ed. A. Garry and M. Pearsall, 263–73. Boston: Unwin Hyman.

Stanton, Donna C. 1989. "Difference on Trial: A Critique of the Maternal Metaphor in Cixuus, Irigaray, and Kristeva." In *The Thinking Muse: Feminism and Modern French Philosophy.* Jeffner Allen and Iris M. Young, eds., 156–79. Bloomington: Indiana University Press.

Stocker, Michael. 1981. "Values and Purposes: The Limits of Teleology and the Ends of Friendship." *Journal of Philosophy* 78: 453–66.

Strauss, Leo. 1983. *Studies in Platonic Political Philosophy.* Chicago: University of Chicago Press.

Strauss, Leo. 1964. *The City and Man.* Chicago: Rand McNally.

Striker, Gisela. 1988. "Response to Cooper." 1988 Spindel Conference on Aristotle's Ethics, Memphis State University. In *The Southern Journal of Philosophy Supplementary Volume* 27: 43–47.

Taylor, A. E. 1960. *Plato: The Man and His Work.* Seventh edition. London: Methuen.

Telfer, Elizabeth. 1970–1971. *Friendship. Proceedings of the Aristotelian Society* v. 71: 223–41.

Thomas, Lawrence. 1987. "Friendship." *Synthese* 72: 217–36.

Thompson, Audrey. 1989. "Friendship and Moral Character: Feminist Implications for Moral Education." *Philosophy of Education Proceedings* 45: 61–75.

Tomasi, J. 1990. "Plato's *Statesman* Story: The Birth of Fiction Reconceived." *Philosophy and Literature* 14: 348–58.

Tong, Rosemarie. 1988. *Feminist Theory: A Comprehensive Introduction.* Boulder: Westview Press.

Tress, D. M. 1992. "The Metaphysical Science of Aristotle's Generation of Animals and Its Feminist Critics." *Review of Metaphysics* 46: 309–41. Reprinted in this volume.

Tress, D. M. 1994. "Relations in Plato's *Timaeus.*" *Journal of Neoplatonic Studies* 3: 93–139.

Tress, D. M. 1995. "Liabilities of the Feminist Use of Narrative: A Study of Sara Ruddick's Story in Maernal Thinking." *Public Affairs Quarterly.* Forthcoming.

Tress, D. M. Forthcoming. "Classical and Modern Roots of Contemporary Environmentalism." In *Ancient Philosophy and the Roots of Environmentalism,* ed. Thomas M. Robinson and Laura Westra. Austin: University of Texas Press.

Tuana, Nancy. 1994. "Aristotle and the Politics of Reproduction." In *Engendering Origins: Critical Feminist Readings in Plato and Aristotle,* ed. Bar-On, 189–206. Albany: State University of New York Press.

Tully, James, ed. 1988. *Meaning and Context: Quentin Skinner and His Critics.* Princeton: Princeton University Press.

U.S. Department of Labor. 1987. *Employment and Earnings: July 1987.* Washington D.C.: Government Printing Office.

Van Geytenbeek, A. C. 1963. *Musonius Rufus and Greek Diatribe.* Assen: Van Gorcum.

Versenyi, L. 1963. *Socratic Humanism.* New Haven: Yale University Press.

Vlastos, Gregory. 1989. "Was Plato a Feminist?" *Times Literary Supplement,* March 17: 276, 288–89. Cited from *Studies in Greek Philosophy,* ed. Daniel W. Graham, 1995. Volume 2: *Socrates, Plato, and Their Tradition,* 133–43. Princeton: Princeton University Press.

Walcot, Peter. 1987. *Plato's Mother and Other Terrible Women.* Greece and Rome 34: 12–31.

Walker, A. D. M. 1979. "Aristotle's Account of Friendship in the *Nicomachean Ethics.*" *Phronesis* 24: 180–96.

Ward, Julie. 1995. "Focal Reference in Aristotle's Account of *Philia*: *Eudemian Ethics* VII 2." *Apeiron* 28: 183–205.

Watson, James. 1969. *The Double Helix.* New York: New American Library.

West, Thomas. 1979. *Plato's Apology of Socrates. An Interpretation with a New Translation.* Ithaca: Cornell University Press.

Whitbeck, Caroline. 1976. "Theories of Sex Difference." In *Women and Philosophy,* ed. Carol C. Gould and Marx W. Wartofsky, 54–80. New York: G.P. Putnam's Sons.

Whitford, Margaret. 1991. *Luce Irigaray. "Philosophy in the Feminine."* London and New York: Routledge.

Wider, Kathleen. 1986. "Women Philosophers in the Ancient World: Donning the Mantle." *Hypatia* 1: 21–62.

Wilamowitz-Moellendorff, Ulrich von. 1919. *Der griechische und der platonische Staatsgedanke.* Berlin: Weidmannsche Buchhandlung.

Wilamowitz-Moellendorff, Ulrich von. 1920. *Platon.* Volume I: *Leben und Werke.* Second Edition. Berlin: Weidmannsche Buchhandlung.

Winkler, John J. 1990a. *The Constraints of Desire: The Anthropology of Sex and Gender in Ancient Greece.* New York: Routledge.

Winkler, John J. 1990b. "*Phallos Politikos*: Representing the Body Politic in Athens." *Differences* 2: 29–46.

Winnicott, D. W. 1965. *The Family and Individual Development.* London: Tavistock Publications.

Witt, Charlotte. 1985. "Form, Reproduction, and Inherited Characteristics in Aristotle's *Generation of Animals.*" *Phronesis* 30, 1: 46–57.

Woodbridge, Frederick, 1965. *Aristotle's Vision of Nature.* New York: Dell Publishing.

Woodruff, Paul. 1982. "What Could Go Wrong with Inspiration?: Why Plato's Poets Fail." In *Plato on Beauty, Wisdom, and the Arts,* ed. Julius Moravcsik and Philip Temko, 137–50. Totowa, New Jersey: Rowman and Allanheld.

Woolf, L. 1975. *The Autobiography of Leonard Woolf, Vol. II: Sowing.* New York: Harcourt Brace Jovanovich.

Woolf, L. 1989. *Letters of Leonard Woolf.* Ed. F. Spotts. New York: Harcourt Brace Jovanovich.

Woolf, V. 1925. *Mrs. Dalloway.* New York: Harcourt Brace Jovanovich.

Woolf, V. 1968. *The Voyage Out.* New York: Harcourt Brace Jovanovich.

Woolf, V. 1977. *The Letters of Virginia Woolf. Vol. I.* Ed. Nigel Nicholson. New York: Harcourt Brace Jovanovich.

Woolf, V. 1978a. *The Diary of Virginia Woolf, Vol. Two.* Ed. A. O. Bell and A. McNellie. New York: Harcourt Brace Jovanovich.

Woolf, V. 1978b. *Jacob's Room.* New York: Harcourt Brace Jovanovich.

Woolf, V. 1980. *The Diary of Virginia Woolf, Vol. Three.* Ed. A. O. Bell and A. McNellie New York.

Woolf, V. 1985. *Moments of Being.* 2nd ed. Ed. J. Schulkind. New York: Harcourt Brace Jovanovich.

Woolf, V. 1988. *The Essays of Virginia Woolf, Vol. Three.* Ed. A. McNellie. New York: Harcourt Brace Jovanovich.

Woolf, V. 1990. *A Passionate Apprentice: The Early Journals, 1897–1909.* Ed. M. A. Leaska. New York: Harcourt Brace Jovanovich.

Yack, Bernard. 1993. *The Problems of a Political Animal: Comunity, Justice, and Conflict in Aristotelian Political Thought.* Berkeley: University of California Press.

Young, Iris. 1981. "Beyond the Unhappy Marriage: A Critique of the Dual Systems Theory." In *Women and Revolution,* ed. L. Sargent, 43–69. London: Pluto Press.

Young, Iris. 1985. "Humanism, Gynocentrism, and Feminist Politics." *Women's Studies International Forum* 8, 3: 173–83.

Young, Iris. 1987. "Impartiality and the Civic Public: Some Implications of Feminist Critique of Moral and Political Theory." In *Feminism as Critique,* ed. Seyla Benhabib and Drucilla Cornell, 56–74. Minneapolis: University of Minnesota Press.

Zeitlin, Froma I. 1984. "The Dynamics of Misogyny: Myth and Mythmaking in the Oresteia." In *Women in the Ancient World: The Arethusa Papers,* ed. Peradotto and Sullivan, 159–94. Albany: State University of New York Press.

CONTRIBUTORS

Deborah Achtenberg is associate professor and philosophy department chair at the University of Nevada, Reno. She specializes in ancient philosophy and ethics and is involved in curricular reform at her university, where she chairs the core-reform committee. Her publications include various papers on Aristotle's ethics.

Julia Annas is professor of philosophy at University of Arizona, Tucson. Her various books include works on Aristotle's *Metaphysics* (Books XIII and XIV), Plato's *Republic* and *Statesman*, ancient skepticism, and Hellenistic ethics and philosophy of mind.

Elizabeth Asmis is professor of classics at the University of Chicago. She has published numerous works in ancient philosophy and classics, including a book on Epicurus' scientific method, as well as various papers on Anaximander, Plato, Epicurus, Lucretius, and the Stoics. She is also currently the editor of *Classical Philology*.

Anne-Marie Bowery is assistant professor of philosophy at Baylor University where she specializes in Greek philosophy, the history of philosophy, and philosophy and literature. She has published articles on Plato and Augustine and is working on a book on narration in Plato's *Charmides* and *Symposium*.

Kathleen C. Cook is assistant professor of philosophy at Ohio State University where she teaches ancient philosophy, medical ethics, and social and political philosophy. Her research centers on Aristotle's metaphysics, science, and psychology. She also has interests in the history of moral and political thought about women and the history of women philosophers. Her published papers are on quantities and Aristotle's *Physics*. She is currently at work on a set of papers dealing with artifacts in Aristotle.

Patricia Curd is associate professor of philosophy at Purdue University. She has published numerous papers on Plato's *Parmenides* and the Pre-Socratics and has recently edited an anthology on readings in ancient philosophy from Thales to Aristotle (with Marc Cohen and C. D. C. Reeve).

Marcia Homiak is professor of philosophy at Occidental College, where she teaches courses in philosophy, women's studies, and ancient history. She is currently working on a book on Aristotle's moral theory entitled *Virtue and the Limits of Reason.*

Susan B. Levin is assistant professor of philosophy at Smith College. Her special areas of interest in ancient philosophy include metaphysics, epistemology, philosophy of mind, and philosophy of language. She is also concerned with the intersection of Greek philosophy and literature, as reflected in her papers on literary etymology in Plato's *Cratylus*, and eponomy in *Phaedo*. She is presently examining Plato's critique of the poets in *Cratylus* and *Republic.*

Martha Nussbaum is professor of law and ethics at the University of Chicago. She is the author of many books on ancient philosophy which reflect her interest in the intersections in philosophy, literature, and moral psychology, including *The Fragility of Goodness* (1986), *Love's Knowledge* (1990), and *The Therapy of Desire* (1994). She also has co-edited a number of books, including *The Quality of Life* (1993), *Essays on Aristotle's De Anima* (1993), and *Women, Culture, and Development* (1995). Her forthcoming books include *Upheavals of Thought: A Theory of the Emotions* (1997).

Daryl McGowen Tress is assistant professor of philosophy at Fordham University. She has published papers on ancient philosophy and on feminist theory, including papers on Plato's *Timaeus*, on ancient sources of environmentalism, and on issues in feminism.

Julie K. Ward is associate professor of philosophy at Loyola University, Chicago. She has published papers on Aristotle's *De Anima* and *Ethics,* Pythagorean women and Simone de Beauvoir. Her research interests include Aristotle's doctrine of focal sense, ancient theories of friendship, and feminist ethics.

INDEX OF PASSAGES

—C—

Cicero

—X—

Xenophon

GENERAL INDEX

Date Due